T0339532

Promoting Black Women's Mental Health

Promoting Black Women's Mental Health celebrates the strengths and complexities of Black women in American life. Many misunderstand and mischaracterize Black women and underappreciate their important contributions to families, communities, and the nation. In this book, a team of Black women mental health practitioners and scholars discuss a range of conditions that impact Black women's self-concepts and mental health. Drawing on a study of Black women across the United States, authors explore the social determinants of Black women's mental health and wellness and Black women's girlhood experiences. The book also explores Black women's stereotypes, their traumas, how they shift in relationships, and images that affect their racial and gender identity development. The book draws on scholarly and popular sources to present Black women's strength and challenges. Authors include commentary, case examples, reflection questions, and resources to improve practitioners' capacities to help Black women clients to recover, heal, and thrive.

DONNA BAPTISTE, EdD, LCP, LCPC, LMFT, is Chair and Clinical Professor of the graduate program in Counseling at The Family Institute at Northwestern University, USA. Dr. Baptiste maintains a clinical practice with people of all backgrounds, including Black women and couples. She also has background in research – studying, writing, and conducting trainings on culturally informed practices related to various aspects of Black family life.

ADIA GOODEN, PhD, received her BA in Psychology from Stanford University, USA, and her PhD in Clinical Psychology from DePaul University, USA. She is now a licensed clinical psychologist whose work focuses on Black women and self-worth. She has provided therapy to many Black female clients and conducted continuing education trainings on cultural competence and working with Black women in therapy.

Promoting Black Women's Mental Health

What Practitioners Should Know and Do

Donna Baptiste

The Family Institute, Northwestern University

Adia Gooden

Unconditionally Worthy Co.

CAMBRIDGE
UNIVERSITY PRESS

Shaftesbury Road, Cambridge CB2 8EA, United Kingdom

One Liberty Plaza, 20th Floor, New York, NY 10006, USA

477 Williamstown Road, Port Melbourne, VIC 3207, Australia

314–321, 3rd Floor, Plot 3, Splendor Forum, Jasola District Centre, New Delhi – 110025, India

103 Penang Road, #05–06/07, Visioncrest Commercial, Singapore 238467

Cambridge University Press is part of Cambridge University Press & Assessment, a department of the University of Cambridge.

We share the University's mission to contribute to society through the pursuit of education, learning and research at the highest international levels of excellence.

www.cambridge.org
Information on this title: www.cambridge.org/9781108842938

DOI: 10.1017/9781108913447

First published 2023

A catalogue record for this publication is available from the British Library.

Library of Congress Cataloging-in-Publication Data
Names: Baptiste, Donna, 1959– author. | Gooden, Adia, 1985– author.
Title: Promoting black women's mental health : what practitioners should know and do / Donna Baptiste (Northwestern University), Adia Gooden (LLC).
Description: Cambridge, United Kingdom ; New York, NY : Cambridge University Press, 2023. | Includes bibliographical references and index.
Identifiers: LCCN 2022039645 (print) | LCCN 2022039646 (ebook) | ISBN 9781108842938 (hardback) | ISBN 9781108823098 (paperback) | ISBN 9781108913447 (epub)
Subjects: LCSH: African American women–Mental health. | African American women–Mental health services. | African American women–Psychology.
Classification: LCC RC451.4.M58 B37 2023 (print) | LCC RC451.4.M58 (ebook) | DDC 362.2089/96073–dc23/eng/20220923
LC record available at https://lccn.loc.gov/2022039645
LC ebook record available at https://lccn.loc.gov/2022039646

ISBN 978-1-108-84293-8 Hardback
ISBN 978-1-108-82309-8 Paperback

Contents

Figures

Tables

Contributors

Kimlin Tam Ashing, PhD, is a professor and founding director of the Center of Community Alliance for Research & Education (CCARE) at City of Hope. She received her PhD in Clinical Psychology from the University of Colorado Boulder. As an advocate-scientist, she is advancing population health science and practice. She is a population, behavioral scientist working to develop and implement evidence-based and culturally, clinically, and community-responsive health improvement interventions.

Sule F. Baptiste, BS, MS, earned a bachelor of science degree in Physics from the University of Michigan and a master of science degree in Biostatistics and Epidemiology from Northwestern University. Baptiste is a data science specialist at a US-based health organization.

Taheera Blount, PhD, LCMHC, is an assistant professor of counselor education at North Carolina Central University. She earned her PhD in Counseling and Counselor Education from North Carolina State University. She was the recipient of the 2015 National Board for Certified Counselors Minority Fellowship from the Substance Abuse and Mental Health Services Administration for her research interest related to the use of spirituality in overcoming substance use–related disorders. In 2017, Blount was selected as an Emerging Leader for the Association for Spiritual, Ethical, and Religious Values in Counseling. Her research interests include the following: the use of spirituality, and religion, to assist African American women with overcoming mental health and substance use–related challenges, and career and college readiness among urban youth.

Susan Branco, PhD, LPC (VA), LCPC (MD), is a transracial and transnational adoptee from Colombia, South America. She is an advocate for increased adoption-related research and training within counselor education and is passionate about improving mental health outcomes for transracially adopted persons. Currently, Branco practices counseling with Spanish-speaking and immigrant populations. Her research interests include transracial adoption and mental health, Colombian adoption policy, and clinical training and supervision practices for BIPOC counselors.

Kesha Burch, PhD, LCPC, is Assistant Program Director at the master's program in counseling at the Family Institute at Northwestern University. Burch leads the clinical training activities for the on-the-ground counseling program and has developed a group supervision curriculum that emphasizes counselor self-awareness and self-reflection. Burch's research and scholarship address the intersection of culture and mental health with a specific focus on the preparation of mental health professionals to serve racially, ethnically, and culturally diverse clients.

Yolande Cooke, MSW, has over 20 years of experience as a school social worker. She previously worked at Planned Parenthood, leading a community and youth development program for pregnant teens and teen parents. Before this work, Cooke was a middle school social studies teacher in Trinidad and Tobago, where she obtained a BA in Sociology from the University of the West Indies, St. Augustine. She holds an MA in Counseling from Virginia Tech, Blacksburg, and attained an MSW from the University of Illinois at Urbana-Champaign. In all of her career positions, she has worked closely with the families of both her students and her clients, and she was the first community social worker to begin a Grandmothers' Support Group for the Subsequent Pregnancy Prevention Program in the state of Illinois.

Tonya Davis, PhD, LCPC, is a licensed clinical professional counselor in the state of Illinois, as well as a clinical training director and core faculty at a private university. Davis received her PhD in Counselor Education and Supervision and her master of science degree in Clinical Mental Health, both from CACREP-accredited programs. Her research and scholarship interests include unconscious/implicit and racial bias, clinical supervisory relationships, familial resilience, crisis and trauma, familial systems, and social justice.

Chisina Kapungu, PhD, is a clinical psychologist, community-based researcher, and program developer, with almost two decades of expertise in adolescent health, sexual and reproductive health, and HIV/AIDS. Kapungu currently serves as Director of Learning and Organizational Strengthening at WomenStrong International, where she provides technical guidance and capacity-strengthening for women-led organizations globally focused on girls' education and empowerment, women's health, and prevention of violence against women and girls. Kapungu has managed maternal and child health projects internationally, and she has also worked as a health policy consultant to the US congress.

Dorcas Matowe, PhD, LMFT, is a clinical lecturer at the Family Institute at Northwestern University and an adjunct professor at Nova Southeastern University's Abraham S. Fischler College of Education and School of Criminal Justice. For over 20 years she has worked and volunteered in mental health and social services with multicultural populations, particularly those from marginalized communities. As a two-time recipient of the Substance Abuse and Mental Health Services Administration/AAMFT Minority Fellowship Award, her research focuses on the prevalence of racial and ethnic health disparities in the United States, highlighting marriage and family therapists' knowledge and perceptions of this issue.

Uchechi A. Mitchell, PhD, is an assistant professor at the University of Illinois Chicago's School of Public Health in the Division of Community Health Sciences. After graduating from Harvard College in 2005 with a degree in Biochemical Sciences, Mitchell obtained her master of science degree in Public Health and her PhD from the University of California Los Angeles. Her research focuses on racial and ethnic health disparities and factors that influence the health and aging experiences of older people of color, in particular. Her research has been funded by national organizations such as the National Institute on Aging (NIA) and the National Institute on Minority Health and Health Disparities (NIMHD).

Candice Norcott, PhD, is a licensed clinical psychologist, national consultant, and public speaker. Norcott is a graduate of Brown University and the University of Connecticut and completed her pre- and post-doctoral work in the Department of Psychiatry at Yale University. Dr. Norcott works as an assistant professor and co-director of the OBGYN Mental Health Program at the University of Chicago. Throughout her career, she has been committed to trauma-informed and gender-responsive services for girls and women, minority advancement in psychology, and cultural responsiveness in the health field.

Kumer Shorter-Gooden, PhD, from 2012 to 2016, served as the first Chief Diversity Officer and Associate Vice President at the University of Maryland, College Park. Formerly, she served as Associate Provost for International-Multicultural Initiatives at Alliant International University, as Professor at the California School of Professional Psychology, as Director of the student counseling center at the Claremont Colleges, and as an administrator in two Chicago community mental health centers. She is a licensed psychologist and the coauthor of *Shifting: The Double Lives of Black Women in America*, a winner of the 2004 American Book Awards. Shorter-Gooden is a thought leader with respect to equity, diversity, inclusion, and justice.

Fangzhou Yu-Lewis, PhD, LCPC, is a bilingual clinician, counselor, educator, scholar, and first-generation immigrant. She serves as the core faculty in the Counseling department at Northwestern University. Yu-Lewis also works as a clinical supervisor and staff therapist at the Family Institute at Northwestern University.

Introduction
Black Women Rising

We are Black women. We know the awesomeness of Black women, and we are proud to provide mental health support to Black women. We want colleagues in our profession to care about Black women's mental health and wellness. And we want Black women to care for themselves. These are our reasons for writing this book.

Black women in the United States are saying, "This is our time." This sentiment is powerful, restless, and exciting, and we feel it too. Black women's voices are rising in multiple spheres of life, including politics, law, business, community organizing, health care, media, the arts, and so much more. Black women are formal and informal leaders, outspoken and influential in every one of these fields and numerous more. They are tackling historical and contemporary oppressions that have remained unchanged in their industries for too long. The phenomenon of Black women's rising influence is not just happening in the United States. It is worldwide (Wingfield, 2019).

As Black women, we feel the same urgency that is coursing through the United States and diaspora to address the status quo, and our voices are also rising. We aim to influence our field, mental health care, in which we have proudly served our clients and have spent most of our professional lives. Our first call is for Black people to consider professional mental health support in holistic health and wellness plans. Specifically, we invite Black women to use psychotherapy to understand themselves, thrive, and engage in self-care as they give deeply to their families, communities, and countries. Our second call is for mental health care systems and practitioners to view Black female clients as a crucial population with unique strengths, resilience, and challenges. Black women's mental health needs deeply connect to their personal, social, ecological, and historical experiences. Black women want their personhood, their Blackness, and their womanhood as well as other identities to be respected and celebrated. Psychotherapy for Black women should frame their capacities and vulnerabilities in the context of historical, sociocultural, familial, and developmental circumstances. This type of psychotherapy for Black women is not yet a reality.

The primary audience for this book is licensed mental health practitioners of all backgrounds who work with Black female clients. These professionals include counselors, social workers, psychologists, intimate relationship and family therapists, psychiatrists and psychiatric nurses; hereafter we call them counselors, therapists, or clinicians. We also invite instructors, students, and trainees in mental health fields to consider our ideas. Lay and religious counselors, health care providers, researchers, elementary and high school educators and scholars working with Black women may be interested in our framework and approaches. We also hope that Black women, as lay readers, may be interested in our ideas to advocate for what they need in mental health care.

I.1   Introducing Ourselves

Our ideas and strategies for working with Black female clients rest on several knowledge bases. First is our lived experiences as Black women in the United States and as clients of therapy ourselves. Second is our education and training as mental health practitioners and our clinical practices that include Black clients and other people of color. Third, we draw on experiences as clinical educators and supervisors in several graduate degree programs in mental health fields. In our professional roles, we support hundreds of Black and non-Black therapists-in-training to be multiculturally competent in mental health practice. Fourth, we have peer relationships with therapists of all backgrounds, with whom we have rich and meaningful cultural dialogues. Finally, we led a workshop series in the Chicago area titled Psychotherapy with Black Women, which is a foundation of this book.

The first author, Donna Baptiste, holds licenses in professional counseling, clinical psychology, and marriage and family therapy. She has been in practice for 25 years. Donna identifies as a cisgender, heterosexual Black–Caribbean American woman who is a first-generation immigrant from Trinidad and Tobago. Donna grew up in a blue-collar household with a mother who was a homemaker and a father who worked as a low-level administrator in the petroleum industry. Both parents did not complete high school, but Donna recalls them as deeply engaged in educating her and her siblings. Donna's love of mental health counseling may have come from her mother, who acted as a lay counselor to many in their family, community, and church.

Early and recent experiences have shaped Donna's understanding of racial-ethnic and gender identities. In Trinidad, she grew up in a household and community where traditional patriarchal values and male privilege were juxtaposed with feminist influence. Donna was familiar with the more muted racial conflict between Black political elites and South Asian Indians who held economic and wealth privilege. In addition, Donna recalls the experience of immigrating to the United States and facing Black-White racism, including a powerful awareness of being Black and female for the first time. By the birth of her first child, Donna became sharply aware of the gendered racism embedded in her experience as a divorced Black woman raising a Black son in a predominantly White town. Donna's stint as associate director of a center for women and gender while at the University of Illinois at Chicago and her work as a Black female educational leader and therapist has dramatically increased her appreciation for the complex dynamics Black women face in the United States.

The second author, Adia Gooden, is a licensed clinical psychologist and has been in practice for 15 years. Adia grew up in Pasadena, California, with married parents. Adia's father is Black and from Jamaica. Though he grew up poor, his father (Adia's grandfather) attended seminary in Canada. Her father came to the United States for college and went on to receive his PhD in clinical psychology. Adia's mother, also a clinical psychologist, is African American and was born and raised in Washington, DC. Her parents (Adia's grandparents) were educators and attended college and graduate school. Having two parents who are Black clinical psychologists helped set the context for Adia's career and the privilege she has experienced in her life.

Adia comes to this work with a deep belief in the power of therapy and the importance of psychology that was seeded for her as she witnessed her parents' careers. Adia acknowledges the privilege of growing up in an upper-middle-class family where pursuing higher education was the norm, with financial resources and social capital available for these pursuits. Adia has also experienced the challenges of navigating racism and sexism in predominantly White institutions. Adia has advocated for diversity, equity, and inclusion in academic institutions and workplaces throughout her life. Her training as a community psychologist also influences her lens in working with Black women. She considers the context that Black women operate in and acknowledges the influence of community-level factors for clients. Together, Adia's personal and professional experiences shape her approach to working with Black women. Her focus is on holding diverging experiences together, acknowledging both the challenges and the opportunities Black female clients face. Adia believes in potential and possibilities and works to empower clients to fully actualize and live the lives they most desire.

I.2   "Black" as Our Preferred Term for Racial Identity

In the United States, women who identify as Black may describe themselves as African American, Black, or some other descriptor that amplifies their ethnic heritage (e.g., Nigerian American). We have done the same in various contexts. In this book, we use the term *Black*, racially, to describe women whose ancestors were forced into the United States during the transatlantic slave trade. *Black* also refers racially to immigrant women or those whose parents immigrated from regions or countries in the African diaspora. The term *Black women*, in our writing, includes women claiming Black heritage and other heritage that intersects with race. Here we are thinking of Black Latinas who proudly acknowledge their national origin. We are aware that some multiracial women with "Black" heritage may not self-identify as Black but others may ascribe to them this racial category. We also hope the themes of this book resonate with such women.

Black women are diverse and embrace many unique and complex ethnicities. For example, Adia is Black and was born in the United States to parents of Jamaican and African American heritage. Donna is Black and a first-generation immigrant from Trinidad and Tobago, and a naturalized citizen of the United States. We encourage therapists to ask their Black female clients how they self-identify in terms of race and ethnicity. For example, some Black women may prefer the term *African American*, while others do not. Other Black women may amplify their biracial or multiracial heritage. Although this book may also apply to our multiracial (with Black heritage) sisters, we also firmly support their right to claim and live out the racial identities that feel most meaningful to them.

The ancestors of most Black women in the United States were part of the chattel slave trade (Hine & Thompson, 1999). However, some Black women's ancestors did not experience US slavery, and therapists should be aware of this difference. We believe that, directly and indirectly, all Black women in the United States experience oppressions connected to slavery. Further, privileged ideologies and hegemony affect Black people in countries where chattel slavery never existed. Worldwide, imperialism, colonialism, and apartheid structures, like slavery, create racial domination systems that affect Black people (Hine & Thompson, 1999). Although we focus on Black women in the United States, this reality leads us to hope that our ideas and strategies might prove helpful for Black women in other regions and countries.

I.3   Range of Black Women's Experiences and Identities

Black women as a group share many similarities based on race and gender, identity and expression. Black women are also not a monolith, and they may have as many differences as they have similarities. For example, women may share race and gender identities but have life experiences based on other social identities, such as social class, religion, age, or disability status. Women may also have personal, educational, and familial differences that determine their life experiences. Here we recognize the work of our colleagues (e.g., Crenshaw, 2017; Settles, 2006; Settles & Buchanan, 2014) who have highlighted and empirically examined intersectional frameworks that better explain

Black women in the United States. We support an intersectional lens in viewing Black women as they navigate being a Black person, Black, woman, Black woman, and more. We have tried to avoid overgeneralizations ("all Black women") as well as stereotyping. We have also tried, as much as possible, to discuss intragroup differences among Black women on selected topics. In discussing Black women's experiences, a point we make repeatedly is that the controlling images and stereotypes generated by dominant culture all shape the reality of Black women's everyday lives.

The book focuses on the experiences of cisgender Black women, who may identify as straight, queer, lesbian, gay, bisexual, pansexual, and other identities. We acknowledge the unique circumstances of Black transgender women, who are marginalized at higher rates than cisgender Black women. Black trans women and their therapists may also find this work of value, with the caveat that there are critical differences in the experiences of cisgender and transgender Black women. At the end of this chapter we have recommended two books about Black trans women.

I.4 Black Women Are Not Broken

Here we highlight an essential tension we wrestled with in describing Black women's experiences. Tamara Winfrey-Harris' book *The Sisters Are Alright: Changing the Broken Narrative of Black Women in America* (2015) captures one of our tensions in writing this book: the predominance of negative story lines about Black women's lives. We talked exhaustively about presenting Black women and our Black female clients' stories with the goal of expanding beyond one-dimensional story lines. These story lines are that Black women are broken or troubled, need fixing, or are inadequate because the weight of history has not been on their side. We do not believe that Black women are broken or troubled or in need of pity, and in fact, we believe the contrary.

Black women's contributions to American life are unsung. Their joy, resilience, and hardiness in the face of tremendous life burdens is a beautiful story line. Throughout the book, we capture the inspiring stories of Black women whose lives are vibrant. We show how these women's work contributes highly to understanding Black women's realities. We remind therapists that their Black female clients do not need pitying, rescuing, or fixing. In Winfrey-Harris' (2015) epilogue, she states this well: "Black women are not seeking special treatment.... We are hoping for relief from twisted images of ourselves .... If society will not give us this – if our communities will not demand this for us ... Black women will still be alright" (p. 119; final ellipsis in original).

Indeed, protective factors buffer Black women against the stress that can destroy their health and mental health. For example, solid self-esteem buffers Black women against stress (Hamilton-Mason et al., 2009). Positive racial-identity and socialization help black women to stay grounded in a world that negatively defines them (Thomas et al., 2011). Black women also tend to be religious and spiritual, which helps them articulate a clear meaning and purpose for their lives rooted in religious and spiritual values. Having a sense of purpose in life activates healthy coping in response to stress (Boyd-Franklin, 2010). Black women also draw on community connections and many build solid family relationships, friendship groups, and sister circles. These outlets can be joyful and fun for Black women and serve as buffers against stress. But there are other sides to Black women's lives.

Despite these buffers in self and community, we believe that in some periods of life, or for some during most of their life course, Black women are *not alright*. Black women struggle profoundly with circumstances that affect their internal world and how they function externally. Many of these women are our clients in therapy. Black women's lives have a duality that Mary-Frances Winters (2020), author of *Black Fatigue: How Racism Erodes the Mind, Body, and Spirit* , captures well. In a media interview about this work (Owens, 2021), Winters noted:

Black women from different walks of life and the stories we share ... carry the same threads. They are messages of pride and power often juxtaposed with deep ... self-doubt and helplessness ... stories of faith, strength, resilience, and hope, along with stories of neglect, abuse, and violence. They are stories of passion and "magic" against a backdrop of labels like angry and less innocent. Black women have amassed a treasure trove of wisdom from living with our identities but too often, our voices are silenced, ignored, or denied. We too are fatigued. (para. 17)

We do not believe that Black women are victims with little or no control over their lives. Neither do we think that Black women are psychologically unaffected by their experiences. We adopt a "both/and" view of Black women's experiences and encourage therapists to do the same, making room for the complexities and contractions in Black women's lives. A metaphor in Walt Whitman's poem *Song of Myself* explains these contractions. Whitman asks: "Do I contradict myself? Well then, I contradict myself; I am large, I contain multitudes" (Miller, 1964). Black women's lives contain multitudes of precious, uplifting and yet contradict-ory experiences that therapists, especially those not Black, might not understand. Our goal is to provide therapists with information and strategies to view Black women's experiences from multiple angles and support them well through tailored and culturally informed treatments.

I.5   The Awesomeness of Black Women

Black women have always been influencing, contributing to, organizing, and reshaping the cultural life of the United States, but with an invisibility that is as shocking as it is unjust. More recently, Black women's leadership and influence are becoming more visible, and we celebrate this phenomenon. In discussing the awesomeness of Black women, we are not just referring to political leaders or celebrities who have large stages. Ordinary Black women also display personality traits, agency, authority, moral influence, power, and status in the face of need. Black women labor for their families, partners, children, grandchildren, extended family, and others. Black women also work in outreach, such as through religious ministries and volunteerism. Black women lead movements nationally, regionally, and locally to improve public education, provide economic assistance to poor families, and promote health initiatives. In many of these efforts, no one picks Black women to lead. Instead, they see a need; they organize, act, and grow in leadership as their movements grow (Davis & Chaney, 2013).

Black women's influence in organized collective actions and movements is made invisible. A powerful example is in the civil rights movement of the 1960s. Dr. Martin Luther King Jr. and Jesse Jackson are household names. But few know of women like Jo Ann Robinson, Ella Baker, and Fannie Lou Hamer (Collier-Thomas & Franklyn, 2001). Today, we celebrate how social media platforms like Twitter and Facebook are advancing Black women's contributions far more than Black women were recognized in the past. To illustrate, three Black queer women founded the Black Lives Matter movement to eradicate police brutality and white nationalism, similar conditions that also existed in the 1960s and 1970s. We know Alicia Garza, Opal Tometi, and Patrisse Cullors as Black Lives Matter founders because of modern technologies and communication. We can celebrate the awesomeness of these women. Tarana Burke, also a Black woman, started the hashtag #MeToo. This movement draws attention to sexual victimization and benefits all people. We also know Burke's name because of Twitter. Our point is that Black women's ordinary and everyday awesomeness has long been present. Social media strategies have pulled the invisible cloak off, and Black women's everyday contributions in significant twenty-first-century movements are on display.

I.6   Black Mental Health Needs

In the past few years, a perfect storm of conditions in the United States has negatively affected the mental health of Black people, who may be experiencing compounded trauma. Cultural scholars are documenting these experiences, and we are seeing the same conditions with our Black female clients. Indeed, the loss, stress, and anxiety of the COVID-19 pandemic are felt worldwide, with vulnerable groups bearing the brunt of failure and disease in many nations. In the United States, Black people's vulnerability to COVID-19 and how they have been uniquely affected by this virus are startling. Yet the pandemic's impact in driving increased disease and mortality among Black people is not surprising, given the decades of Black people's health disparities in the United States (Gaines, 2020).

In tandem with COVID-19, the social and political restlessness gripping the nation have uniquely affected Black people. A mental health assessment of 2.5 million US citizens from January to September 2020 offers a sobering snapshot (Reinert & Gionfriddo, 2020). The report notes that although rates of anxiety and depression and suicide are increasing for all races, Black and African Americans, as well as Native Americans, had the highest average percentage increase in depression and anxiety over time. In *Black Fatigue: How Racism Erodes the Mind, Body, and Spirit*, Winters (2020) describes how the history of White supremacy and racism has led to integrational Black fatigue, which is now at an all-time high. Winters shows that in every aspect of life in the United States, racism may be killing Black people through its impact on their physiology and psychology. Winters' book sounds an alarm on the pervasiveness of exhaustion Black people are experiencing and we hear these same themes in our Black female clients. On a personal level, in our practices Black women are saying, "It's too much," or "I can't deal with one more thing," and herein is the danger we reference. If conditions in the United States maintain the current trajectory, the toll on Black women's health and well-being could be catastrophic.

I.7   Black Women's Mental Health

In an article for Prevention.com titled "Black Women Are Facing an Overwhelming Mental Health Crisis," Floyd (2020) chronicles the mental health status of Black women as a group in the United States. In May 2021, an NBC news report (Gaines, 2021) noted that Black psychotherapists are seeing a significant spike in therapy demand and are busier than ever. One therapist indicated, "From March of last year [2020] until now has been my most lucrative year … it's wonderful, but it's not wonderful" (para. 7). Overwhelmingly, therapy requests are from Black women, who are far more likely than Black men to seek professional mental health support (Lindsey & Marcell, 2012). This dynamic also explains a proliferation of websites, blogs, podcasts, and social media activities focused on Black women's mental health.

Black women intending to become clients may desire to work with practitioners of the same race. When Blacks reach out for therapy, they usually want a Black therapist who they believe understands their experiences. However, such requests are hard to fulfill, given the low numbers of Black mental health clinicians. In 2019, only about 3%–4% of psychologists in the US mental health workforce were Black (American Psychological Association, 2018). Black women are highly likely to be in mental health treatment with non-Black therapists (Harrell, 2017). This reality makes culturally responsive therapy vital.

Black women seeking psychotherapy have concerns about finding clinicians who understand them and their mental health needs. These concerns are valid. Therapists treating Black female clients may not appreciate how race and gender intersecting with other identities drive conditions that marginalize their Black female clients. Additionally, practitioners may lack knowledge and awareness of historical, socioeconomic, and cultural forces that impede Black women's equality, advancement, and wellness (Ashley, 2014; Whaley, 2001). Themes of being underappreciated and misinterpreted are common in popular literature and media narratives on Black women and their mental health. However, practitioners frequently overlook these issues in clinical settings (Whaley, 2001).

Traditional psychotherapy systems can be unwelcoming to Black female clients, at times not even returning their phone calls (Shin et al., 2016). When Black women engage in treatment, therapists may mislabel their mental and emotional symptoms (Spates, 2012). A classic scenario is one in which Black women appear to be functioning normally, even in the face of trauma. Therapists might focus on Black women as "strong" and overlook the detrimental impacts of mental and emotional weathering. Relatedly, some therapists may adopt a lens of deficit and damage in viewing Black women's lives, which drives them to want to save or rescue as therapeutic pursuits (Winfrey-Harris, 2015). These dynamics impact the quality of the alliances therapists forge with Black female clients, cause Black women to terminate treatment prematurely, and direct the interventions designed to help (Nelson, 2006). Black women who feel misunderstood and disconnected from their therapists may have reduced confidence in the usefulness of therapy. In this book, we recommend ideas and strategies in an approach that might increase Black women's interest in using psychotherapy as a resource.

I.8   Our Approach to Addressing Black Women's Mental Health

Our approach and strategies include several themes in working with Black female clients. First, from birth to death, Black women's lives are dramatically affected by an interplay of physical, environmental, and cultural factors that determine their health and wellness. For decades, psychological theories and scholarship have ignored Black women's reality. Eurocentric ideas shape current mental health theories and methods. These ideas prioritize the individual dimensions of clients' lives. However, therapists treating Black women must consider how intrapsychic and structural dynamics interplay define their experiences (Brown & Keith, 2003; Thomas, 2004).

Second, many therapists view Black women through a lens of damage and deficit, which is an aspect of their invisibility in the psychological and counseling literature. Earlier in this chapter, we discussed that Black women have a multiplicity of experiences through which their tenacity, agency, and talents shine. Such experiences can also leave Black women scarred, wounded, and vulnerable. Therapists must reject a one-dimensional view of Black women only as broken and suffering, or extraordinarily strong in the face of adversity (Thomas, 2004; Winfrey-Harris, 2015). We make this point repeatedly in the ensuing chapters.

Third, a powerful aspect in Black women's lives is their experience of gendered racism. Black women experience intersecting and multiplied oppressions based on being *Black* simultaneously with being *female*. Black sociologist and feminist scholar Patricia Hill Collins offers a valuable framework to understand the unique and multiplied oppression of Black women through an intersectional understanding of their lives (Collins, 2000). As discussed further in Chapter 2, Black women encounter everyday experiences of gendered racism that shape how they live and move in the world. Approaches to treating Black women that do not integrate the interlocking nature of their identities and experiences are likely to fall short (Thomas, 2004).

Fourth, Black women must be viewed in the contexts of their unique experiences and not compared to the general Black population, White women, or Black men. Indeed, Black women share many common characteristics with other social and cultural groups yet occupy unique substrata of American society. Black women's complex history explains their motivations, attitudes, cognitions, emotions, and behaviors. Black women's belief systems, values, and attitudes are linked to the distant and present history of race, class, gender, and oppression (Crenshaw, 2017; Settles, 2006; Thomas, 2004). Therapists, especially those who are non-Black, represent privilege systems that have oppressed Black women. Black women seeking therapy from a non-Black clinician may feel guarded and hypervigilant about racial and cultural fit. Symbolically, to Black women, non-Black therapists may represent privileged systems of bias and oppression. Therapists must enter the experience of working with Black women with deep cultural self-awareness and a willingness to offer women positive alternatives to the images that drive their anxieties.

We invite therapists of all backgrounds to consider our ideas and strategies. This invitation includes Black female therapists, like us, who share race and gender identity characteristics with Black female clients. A warm alliance with clients of the same race and gender identity can offer early assets toward a strong partnership. Yet, some of our greatest mistakes have been taking racial and gender similarities for granted. Race and gender similarities only go so far with clients. This lesson became clear to us early in our practices when tensions with our Black female clients arose based on our personality or value differences.

The ideas and strategies in the book might be daunting for non-Black therapists. Non-Black, male, and other gender therapists may worry that they can create a minefield of mistakes that might ruin a relationship with Black female clients. In our experience, while such fears are understandable, they do not have to occur in a therapy relationship with a Black female client. Black female clients may desire a Black therapist but also understand they may not get one. They are open to working with therapists of other racial/ethnic and gender backgrounds because they live and work in majority settings, where they interact daily with people of many backgrounds. We will discuss how therapists can draw on these experiences to build therapy relationships. In the initial phase of therapy, however, specific irritants can roil Black women's treatment experience, and we name some of them so that therapists can be aware of these considerations and approach them in an effective manner.

I.9   The Structure of the Book

This book has four parts, which group together chapters on related themes. In Part I: Black Women in Context, we discuss several predominant contexts that shape Black women's health and mental health experiences, drawing on historical, social, cultural, economic, and political histories. Black women's narratives are highly likely to contain themes reflected in this section.

In Chapter 1, "A Study of Black Women and Psychotherapy," is a foundation for our ideas, we report findings from a mixed-method study of the psychotherapy viewpoints and experiences of Black women. This research involved more than 200 Black women from across the United States who responded to our survey on psychotherapy. This chapter lays an empirical foundation for our work on improving the therapy experiences of Black women. In both the study and the chapter, we collaborate with two colleagues: Dorcas Matowe, PhD, LMFT, a mental health practitioner with significant experience in Black women's mental health, who helped design the study, and Sule F. Baptiste, MS, an experienced data scientist who assisted with data analysis.

In Chapter 2, "Social Determinants of Health and Mental Health for Black Women," we draw on public health and psychological research and scholarship to provide an overview of the historical, social, political, and economic experiences that impact the mental health and wellness of Black women in America. This chapter was coauthored with Uchechi Mitchell, PhD, MSPH, a tenured professor in the field of public health at the University of Illinois Chicago.

Chapter 3, "Black Girlhood: Developmental Experiences of Black Women," examines themes in Black women's childhood experiences. Our coauthor is Chisina Kapungu, PhD, a clinical psychologist with deep expertise in positive youth development domestically and internationally. We discuss the importance of sex and gender identity development and other dynamics that affect Black girls' self-concepts. We explore themes that surface when Black women's girlhood experiences are the primary reasons for seeking therapy.

Chapter 4, "Stereotypes of Black Women: Clinical Implications," reviews historical and contemporary stereotypes of US Black women. Histories of race, gender, and social class drive these stereotypes. We explore the mental health impacts of Black women's internalizing of stereotypes.

The final chapter of the first part, Chapter 5, "Black Women and Trauma," describes Black women's traumatic experiences, some of which may be unique. Candice Norcott, PhD, our chapter coauthor, is a licensed clinical psychologist, assistant professor of psychiatry and behavioral neuroscience at The University of Chicago, and expert in trauma in Black adults and youth.

In Part II: Therapy Contexts, we explore two foundational building blocks of effective therapy that therapists must master to work with Black women: building cultural self-awareness and establishing an effective therapy alliance.

This part begins with Chapter 6, "Therapists' Cultural Self-Awareness," which guides therapists to examine their social and cultural identities and their power and privilege as an essential part of becoming culturally competent therapists. Our chapter coauthor is Kesha Burch, PhD, LCPC, a faculty member at The Family Institute at Northwestern University, licensed professional counselor, and specialist in multiculturally informed clinical practice.

In Chapter 7, "Building Strong and Effective Alliances with Black Women," we review some challenges therapists can face in building therapeutic relationships with Black women. We discuss strategies to gain Black women's trust and send messages of acceptance, cultural humility, and curiosity to clients.

In Part III: Core Themes in Black Women's Stress and Distress, we address several areas of life that can cause Black women to feel unusually stressed or distressed: living within the Strong Black Woman persona, psychological shifting, caregiving, romantic and intimate relationships, and appearance bias.

Chapter 8, "Strong Black Woman Persona: Mental Health Impacts," discusses the everyday experience of Black women's penchant to be overcommitted and overburdened in caring for the needs of others. We discuss the historical, societal, and cultural forces that cause women to internalize Strong Black Woman identities.

In Chapter 9, "Shifting in Black Women: Clinical Implications," we discuss the concept of shifting and how Black women may shift in the context of their workplaces and their intimate and familial relationships. This chapter is coauthored with Kumea Shorter-Gooden, PhD, a licensed clinical psychologist who is also a diversity, equity, and inclusion consultant and the coauthor of *Shifting: The Double Lives of Black Women in America*.

Chapter 10, "Black Women's Mothering and Caregiving," explores Black women as parental and family caregivers and caregiving as a source of joy and yet burden in Black women's lives. We partner with Yolande Cooke, a licensed clinical social worker who has extensive experience in school and community mental health practice with Black families.

In Chapter 11, "Black Women's Romantic and Intimate Relationships," we explore Black women's romantic and intimate relationships in both heterosexual and queer unions. We discuss the strengths of Black women's romantic unions and examine conditions that create stress and distress for Black women in marriage, cohabitation, and sexual and dating relationships.

In Chapter 12, "Appearance Prejudice and Discrimination Against Black Women," we discuss Black women's substantive experiences of discrimination based on their appearance. Our coauthor is Tonya Davis, PhD, LCPC, core faculty member and licensed professional counselor at The Family Institute at Northwestern University, who has expertise in appearance-based discrimination against Black women.

The next part of the book moves the focus to healing and recovery. In Part IV: Helping Black Women to Recover and Thrive, we emphasize several areas in which therapists can help advance Black women's wellness. These areas include inner healing or repair of Black women's self-image and an emphasis on Black women's spirituality.

In Chapter 13, "Improving Black Women's Physical Health and Wellness," we discuss Black women's disproportionate experience of chronic diseases, morbidity, and mortality. We coauthored this chapter with Kimlin Tam Ashing, PhD, a clinical psychologist, professor, and founding director of the Center of Community Alliance for Research & Education at City of Hope, a National Cancer Institute comprehensive cancer center. Research has connected Black women's health conditions to their experiences of aging and weathering.

In Chapter 14, "Black Women's Inner Healing and Resources for Thriving," we explore areas in which Black women can experience inner healing. We coauthored this chapter with Fangzhou Yu-Lewis, PhD, LCPC, a licensed counselor and core faculty member of the counseling program at The Family Institute at Northwestern University. We share strategies to guide Black female clients to heal their relationships with themselves and to create an inner world infused with self-compassion, unconditional self-worth, and self-validation.

In Chapter 15, "Black Women's Spiritual and Religious Coping," we discuss the role of religion and spirituality in Black women's lives and mental health. Our coauthor is Taheera Blount, PhD, NCC, HS-BCP, LCMHC, a professional counselor, assistant professor at North Carolina Central University, and specialist in Black women's religiosity and spirituality.

In the concluding chapter, "How Psychotherapy Helps Black Women," we emphasize how therapy can be a resource for Black women in their mental health and wellness goals, including personal growth and resilience, recovery, and reinvigoration. Our coauthor is Susan Branco, PhD, LPC (VA), LCPC-S

(MD), NCC, ACS, faculty member at The Family Institute at Northwestern University, a Latina therapist with extensive experience working with Black women on their mental health needs, and an expert on transracial adoption dynamics.

I.10   How to Use This Book

The mental health marketplace in the United States is poised for a massive influx of new clients seeking mental health support. Black women will number highly among those choosing psychotherapy as a resource. We encourage our colleagues of all backgrounds and therapy modalities to be ready to serve Black women well. In this work we offer several ideas, borne out of our experiences working with Black female clients, that we hope our readers will find helpful.

The book can be read chronologically, or readers may focus on a chapter or two of interest. We encourage all readers to review Part 1, which explains the social, cultural, and structural conditions that intermingle with and drive Black women's mental and emotional health and wellness. Therapists already in practice should pay close attention to Chapter 1, which outlines our study of what Black women say they want in psychotherapy. They should also read Chapters 6 and 7 to learn about the importance of cultural awareness and building alliances with Black female clients. School- and college-based educators practitioners may be interested in Chapter 3 to understand the developmental experiences of Black girls and Chapter 10 for insight on Black women's parenting and family contexts. Clinicians who work with families and couples might find Chapters 10 and 11 useful to understand how Black women navigate family and couple dynamics. Those focused on survivors of trauma and sexual violence may find the ideas in Chapters 2 and 5 useful to understand unique dimensions of Black women's trauma experiences and how such experiences might affect overall health. Pastoral and clergy counselors may be interested in Chapter 15, on Black women's spiritual and religious identities and coping. Our concluding chapter is one that therapists might provide to Black female clients, before or after the first session, to showcase the potential value of therapy, begin a discussion of what Black women may need in the therapy experience, and to invite radical openness and transparency in the relationship with regard to cultural opportunities and fit.

I.11   A Collaborative Effort

In the academy and publishing, resistance to collaborative scholarship is a traditional and seductive posture that can be at odds with feminist and culturally responsive values. We originally considered authoring the publication just as a dyad. Yet we also wondered how other voices could add to our work, especially professionals of similar race and gender as the population we write about and professionals who are deeply familiar with the content and strategies covered in the book. We are proud to collaborate in chapter coauthorship with other mental health practitioners, researchers, and educators, many of them Black women and men, who added tremendously to our work. We have benefited especially from having other women of color who are mental health practitioners integrated into this work. Our colleagues are individuals of diverse ethnic identities who identify racially as Black, Biracial, Chinese, and Latina.

Our research assistants, all of whom are therapists-in-training working with clients, also collaborated in the work. Three of our research assistants are Black women (Sydney McClure, Jaunai Parsons-Moore, J'mi Worthen); one is a Biracial woman with Black ancestry (Lyrra Isanberg), one is a White woman (Katerine Gow); another is a White man (Grover Hollway) and one is a South Asian woman (Ayla Mian). The multiracial makeup of our collaborators and their enthusiasm for our ideas have dramatically energized our work. We owe all these colleagues a debt of gratitude and celebrate their voices in this book.

Therapist Reflection Questions

1. We contend that Black women's voices and influence are rising. How do you see this in your setting – locally, regionally, and nationally?
2. We mention the idea of "intersectionality of identities" in understanding Black women in the United States. How might this concept apply to you?
3. What is your understanding of the term *gendered racism* as applied to Black women? What do you notice Black women experiencing intersectional oppression in their lives?
4. What do you think and feel about Black people's mental health fatigue from racial oppression?
5. In your relationship Black people or your work with Black clients what stories have they shared about the fatigue of racism or other oppressions?
6. Which chapter or chapters in the book invoke your curiosity? Which ones speak to issues you experience in your work with Black clients?

Databases for Finding Therapists

National Queer & Trans Therapists of Color Network. (n.d.). https://nqttcn.com/en/
Therapy for Black Girls. (n.d.). https://therapyforblackgirls.com

Books

hooks, b. (1994). *Sisters of the yam: Black women and self-recovery*. South End Press.

Mock, J. (2014). *Redefining realness: My path to womanhood, identity, love & so much more*. Simon and Schuster.

Snorton, C. R. (2017). *Black on both sides: A racial history of trans identity*. University of Minnesota Press.

Winfrey-Harris, T. (2015). *The sisters are alright: Changing the broken narrative of Black women in America*. Berrett-Koehler Publishers.

(2021). *Dear black girl: Letters from your sisters on stepping into your power*. Berrett-Koehler Publishers.

Winters, M. F. (2020). *Black fatigue: How racism erodes the mind, body, and spirit*. Berrett-Koehler Publishers.

TV Series

Rae, I., Penny, P., Matsoukas, M., Rotenberg, M., Becky, D., Berry, J., & Aniobi, A. (Executive Producers). (2016–present). *Insecure* [TV series]. Issa Rae Productions; A Penny for Your Thoughts Entertainment; 3 Arts Entertainment.

Media Resources

Barbour, S. (2020, September 23). These virtual mental health resources for black women can make all the difference: Black lives matter, and so does black mental health. *Cosmopolitan*. https://www.cosmopolitan.com/health-fitness/a32731463/mental-health-resources-for-black-women/

Barnes, Z. (2020, June 2). 44 mental health resources for black people trying to survive this country. *Self*. https://www.self.com/story/black-mental-health-resources

References

American Psychological Association. (2018). *Demographics of the U.S. psychology workforce: Findings from the 2007–16 American community survey*. Author.

Ashley, W. (2014). The angry Black woman: The impact of pejorative stereotypes on psychotherapy with Black women. *Social Work in Public Health, 29*(1), 27–34.

Boyd-Franklin, N. (2010). Incorporating spirituality and religion into the treatment of African American clients. *The Counseling Psychologist, 38*(7), 976–1000.

Brown, D. R., & Keith, V. M. (Eds.) (2003) *In and out of our right minds: The mental health of African American women*. Columbia University Press.

Collier-Thomas, B., & Franklin, V. P. (2001). *Sisters in the struggle: African American women in the civil rights-black power movement*. New York University Press.

Collins, P. H. (2000). *Black feminist thought: Knowledge, consciousness, and the politics of empowerment* (rev. 10th anniversary ed.). Routledge.

Crenshaw, K. W. (2017). *On intersectionality: Essential writings*. The New Press.

Davis, D. J., & Chaney, C. (2013). *Black women in leadership: their historical and contemporary contributions*. Peter Lang.

Floyd, L. (2020, November 6). Black women are facing an overwhelming mental health crisis. *Prevention.* https://www.prevention.com/health/mental-health/a33686468/black-women-mental-health-crisis/

Gaines, P. (2020, June 29). *Black Americans experience deadly stress as pandemic and violent-racism collide.* NBC News. https://www.nbcnews.com/news/nbcblk/black-americans-experience-deadly-stress-pandemic-violent-racism-collide-experts-n1231448

(2021, May 27). *Black people are in a mental health crisis. Their therapists are busier than ever.* NBC News. https://www.nbcnews.com/news/nbcblk/black-people-are-mental-health-crisis-therapists-are-busier-ever-rcna1045

Hamilton-Mason, J., Hall, J. C., & Everett, J. E. (2009). And some of us are braver: Stress and coping among African American women. *Journal of Human Behavior in the Social Environment, 19*(5), 463–482.

Harrell, S. N. (2017). *A phenomenological exploration of mental health help-seeking as experienced by African American women.* [Unpublished doctoral dissertation]. Alliant International University.

Hine, D. C., & Thompson, K. (1999). *A shining thread of hope: The history of Black women in America.* Broadway.

Lindsey, M. A., & Marcell, A.V. (2012). "We're going through a lot of struggles that people don't even know about." The need to understand African American males' help-seeking for mental health on multiple levels. *American Journal of Men's Health, 6*(5), 354–364.

Miller, J. E. (1964). *Walt Whitman's "Song of myself": Origin, growth, meaning.* Dodd, Mead and Co.

Nelson, C.A. (2006). Of eggshells and thin-skulls: A consideration of racism-related mental illness impacting Black women. *International Journal of Law and Psychiatry, 29*(2), 112–136.

Owens, D. (2021, May 19). *Microaggressions and straight-up racism are exhausting Black people.* NBC News. https://www.nbcnews.com/news/nbcblk/microaggressions-straight-racism-are-exhausting-black-people-rcna914

Reinert, M., & Gionfriddo, P. (2020, August 26). *New data from MHA screening shows differences in anxiety, depression and suicidal ideation across race and ethnicity.* Mental Health America. https://mhanational.org/blog/new-data-mha-screening-shows-differences-anxiety-depression-and-suicidal-ideation-across-race

Settles, I. H. (2006). Use of an intersectional framework to understand Black women's racial and gender identities. *Sex Roles, 54*(9), 589–601.

Settles, I. H., & Buchanan, N. T. (2014). Multiple groups, multiple identities, and intersectionality. In V. Benet-Martínez & Y.-Y. Hong (Eds.), *The Oxford handbook of multicultural identity* (pp. 160–180). Oxford University Press.

Shin, R. Q., Smith, L. C., Welch, J. C., & Ezeofor, I. (2016). Is Allison more likely than Lakisha to receive a callback from counseling professionals? A racism audit study. *The Counseling Psychologist, 44*(8), 1187–1211.

Spates, K. (2012). The missing link: The exclusion of Black women in psychological research and the implications for Black women's mental health. *SAGE Open, 2*(3), 1–8.

Thomas, A. J., Hacker, J. D., & Hoxha, D. (2011). Gendered racial identity of Black young women. *Sex Roles, 64*(7), 530–542.

Thomas, V. G. (2004). The psychology of Black women: Studying women's lives in context. *Journal of Black Psychology, 30*(3), 286–306.

Whaley, A. L. (2001). Cultural mistrust and mental health services for African Americans: A review and meta-analysis. *The Counseling Psychologist, 29*(4), 513–531.

Winfrey-Harris, T. (2015). *The sisters are alright: Changing the broken narrative of Black women in America.* Berrett-Koehler.

Wingfield, A. H. (2019). "Reclaiming our time": Black women, resistance, and rising inequality: SWS presidential lecture. *Gender & Society, 33*(3), 345–362.

Winters, M. F. (2020). *Black fatigue: How racism erodes the mind, body and spirit.* Berrett-Koehler Publishers.

Part I

Black Women in Context

1   A Study of Black Women and Psychotherapy

with Dorcas Matowe and Sule F. Baptiste*

In the Introduction we detailed how our lived experiences – as Black women, as therapy clients, as clinical mental health practitioners and educators, and as workshop leaders advocating for multicultural competence in the mental health profession – have vastly enriched our approach to this book. We have counseled Black women of different ages and stages in life spanning more than two decades. We have also mentored, educated, and trained others seeking to become mental health practitioners. The rationale, assumptions, and themes that guide our work have been shaped by the views of hundreds of Black women we have encountered in our work. *Yet we want more.* We want to include the voices and direct feedback of Black women, who should play a vital role in determining the nature and quality of mental health services they receive. To accomplish this goal in the book, we collated Black women's viewpoints and recommendations via a research study, that was completed before we wrote one line of this text.

In this chapter we provide a brief summary of the study goals and methods with a more detailed write-up in the Appendix. We also provide a detailed overview of the main study with other results integrated into specific chapters.

1.1   Study Aims

The Black Women and Psychotherapy study was an exploratory and cross-sectional examination of Black women's thoughts and opinions on professional therapy services. The study aims were (a) to understand Black women's perspectives on professional psychotherapy services, (b) to understand Black women's experiences in professional psychotherapy services, and (c) to collate Black women's recommendations for mental health practitioners who work

* D. Baptiste, D. Matowe, S. F. Baptiste, & A. Gooden. (2023). A study of Black women and psychotherapy. In D. Baptiste & A. Gooden, *Promoting Black women's mental health: What practitioners should know and do.* Cambridge University Press.

with Black female clients. We gathered Black women's opinions to validate the topics and strategies we recommend in this publication. We also wanted to offer therapists some concrete, empirically informed recommendations on working with Black female clients. We conducted the study in the traditions of survey research using quantitative procedures and descriptive statistics to summarize overall participant ideas. We also used qualitative procedures and techniques to elicit and report Black women's recommendations for therapists. Northwestern University's Institutional Review Board approved the research. See the Appendix for more details on the research framework.

1.2   The Sample

We targeted a sample of 100 Black women across a geographic and demographic spectrum. We were pleasantly surprised to have 100 participants complete the surveys within a week of launching; however, early data showed a lack of diversity on critical demographics (e.g., age, education, income, US region). We wanted a highly diverse sample, so we conducted further outreach in communities such as churches, local social agencies, and sororities to attract more Black women from the South and those of lower education and income levels. We also asked colleagues residing in the South and working with low-income Black women to distribute our recruitment details to their networks. The final sample of 227 Black women who completed the survey were more diverse, yet there was still limited participation of one demographic of interest, low-income Black women, with less formal education. See Appendix for inclusion criteria, recruitment, and informed consent procedures.

1.3   The Survey

We distributed the anonymous Qualtrics survey to Black women who had never been clients in therapy as well as those in therapy currently or in the past. The survey included five sections: (a) an introduction to the study; (b) informed consent information; (c) personal and demographic questions; (d) questions about therapy among both clients and those who were never clients; and (d) four open-ended questions asking about the helpfulness and unhelpfulness of therapy, why Black women avoid therapy, and Black women's recommendations for therapists working with Black female clients. The final survey ran from July to September 2020. The survey is available on request from the authors. See the Appendix for how the Qualtrics survey was developed and presented and for data analytic strategies.

1.4   Study Findings

1.4.1   Participant Characteristics

A total of 293 individuals began the study, 227 of them met our criteria, and we analyzed their data. Sixty-six individuals completed the requirements to be included and started the research but ended early, and we did not analyze their data. Table 1.1 lists the demographics of the 227 participants remaining in the sample. Most participants (96%) identified as Black. Eight individuals identified as multiracial (including Black). Among the participants, 99% identified as female, with one individual identifying as nonbinary, and 96% identified as non-Hispanic Latino.

We were pleased to get a sample of predominantly Black women from all over the United States who met our study criteria. Black women from the South, Midwest, and Northwest were well represented; the western part of the United States was less well represented. There was nothing remarkable about the sample's age distribution, marital and partner status, the fact that half had children, and the fact that most (69%) reported being very religious/spiritual. One limitation is the lack of diversity in income and education of the Black women in the study. The Black women in our sample are primarily well-educated, cisgender women with relatively high household incomes. Most of our participants (85%) were college educated with at least a bachelor's degree, and more than 50% had graduate degrees. Less than 10% reported an associate degree or less formal education. Roughly 55% of the sample had annual household incomes of $81,000 and above. We value the perspectives of well-educated Black women with above-average household incomes. However, we also really wanted to include Black women who had less education and fewer financial resources. We were disappointed to have so few in the sample, as we had hoped to better understand the opinions and experiences of a less privileged group of women, such as those with less formal education and household income.

Nevertheless, the fact that Black women who had therapy were overrepresented in our sample has significant benefits. The overrepresentation of Black women who have been in therapy provides us with responses based on real, lived experiences of therapy. These data proved to be immensely useful. A more representative sample may have given important opinions on a number of prospective therapy benefits, yet offered us fewer insights into the lived experiences of clients in therapy because many participants would not have had real-life experiences on which to draw.

Table 1.1 *Sample characteristics*

Characteristic	Frequency	Percentage
Age		
20–29	33	14.5
30–39	68	30.0
40–49	54	23.8
50–59	32	14.1
60–69	26	11.5
70 and over	14	6.2
Relationship Status		
Single	112	49.3
Married	68	30.0
Widowed	7	3.1
Divorced	27	11.9
Separated	5	2.2
Other	6	2.6
Total	225	99.1
Have Children		
No	113	49.8
Yes	113	49.8
Education		
High school	6	2.6
Trade school	4	1.8
Associate's degree	7	3.1
Bachelor's degree	49	21.6
Master's degree	83	36.6
Doctoral degree	66	29.1
Other	12	5.3
Total	227	100.0
Annual Household Income		
<9K	5	2.2
10K–30K	25	11.0
31K–50K	30	13.2
51K–80K	40	17.6
81K–110K	48	21.1
111K–140K	25	11.0
141K–170K	15	6.6
171K and over	38	16.7
Region of United States		
Northeast	64	28.2
Midwest	82	36.1
West	20	8.8
South	61	26.9

1.4.2   Views on Finding and Using Therapy

A substantive majority of respondents (N = 192, 84.6%) had therapy, a much smaller number (N = 28, 12%) had never thought of having therapy, and even fewer (N = 7, 3%) tried to get therapy and then changed their minds. Of the 192 who had therapy, 70% were clients for three years or less. As for the number of therapists, 61% worked with one or two therapists, and around 8% had worked with three or more. Responses on the ease of finding a therapist were mixed: 41% found it difficult or very difficult to find a therapist, while 41% found it easy to very easy. In terms of how participants found their therapists, sources were personal referrals (49%), an internet site (30%), insurance (28%), a physician's recommendation (13%), a job referral (10%), an advertisement (5%), or a business card (1%).

Around 85% of our sample had professional therapy, which was likely associated with their income and educational status. Most of the participants were college educated, and more than half had graduate degrees. More than half also had annual household incomes of $81,000 or more. These Black women also likely had stable jobs. The findings in these dynamics did not surprise us. Black women who are well educated and have high income are also more likely than people with low income to have insurance coverage around which they can seek mental health services.

1.4.3   Therapist Preferences

Of those who had been in therapy, we asked, "What did you look for in a therapist?" Table 1.2 includes all qualities endorsed. The top five preferences were therapists who had experience with people of color (67%), took insurance (59%), have cultural knowledge (55%), had the educational background (master's degree or PhD) and professional license to practice (51%), and were of the same sex or gender as the respondent (50%). The least preferred qualities were spiritual or religious emphases (26%) and therapist age (18%).

We asked participants to indicate their comfort level working with both *Black* and *non-Black* therapists (Table 1.2). Among our sample, 38% would be comfortable or extremely comfortable working with a non-Black therapist, 17% would be neutral, and 44% would be somewhat uncomfortable to very uncomfortable working with a non-Black therapist. Alternatively, 91% of our sample of Black women would feel comfortable with a Black therapist.

The predominance of finding a therapist through a personal referral aligns with our experience in practice. Our Black clients and other people of color

Table 1.2 *Black women's comfort working with Black and non-Black therapists*

	Non-Black Therapist	Percentage	Black Therapist	Percentage
Extremely uncomfortable	35	15.4	2	0.9
Somewhat uncomfortable	64	28.2	3	1.3
Neutral	39	17.2	13	5.7
Somewhat comfortable	68	30.0	54	23.8
Extremely comfortable	20	8.8	154	67.8

who seek our services tell us that they have looked long and hard to find a Black therapist. About 41% of our sample found it difficult or very difficult to find a therapist. It may be that Black women are waiting to find a Black therapist, and there are pros and cons to this strategy. The likelihood of finding a Black therapist is low because there are relatively few in the field, less than 5% nationally (Hamp et al., 2016; Lin et al., 2018). Waiting to find a Black therapist means that women may struggle with mental and emotional health conditions for quite a while without being seen. This idea underscores our invitation to Black women in various chapters of the book, to expand their therapy options to consider non-Black therapists. *The limited availability of Black therapists to work with Black women also increases our interest in supporting non-Black therapists to work competently with this population.*

Notably, while Black women might look first for a Black therapist, more than half would be neutral to very comfortable working with a non-Black therapist. Personal referrals can go both ways. People will refer a therapist of any race or ethnicity with whom they have had good experiences and whom they trust. The rise of internet-based sources for seeking therapy should increase therapists' interest in listing their business on sites like Therapy for Black Girls or Psychology Today. We recommend that therapists of any background design a culturally attuned profile on internet sites that signals their cultural proficiency and interest in working with people of color. In these profiles therapists should also indicate themes that may resonate with Black women.

1.4.4   Life Satisfaction and Mental and Emotional State

We asked two questions to assess our participants' subjective sense of navigating life, given that we collected data during the COVID-19 pandemic and quarantine. The first question was "How satisfied are you with your life over-all?" In response, 72% reported being somewhat to extremely satisfied. This finding confirms other studies that, in general, Black women are apt to feel satisfied with their lives despite the difficulties they may experience (Winfrey-Harris, 2015). Another question was "What is your current mental and emo-tional state?" Over 70% of Black women in the sample described their mental and emotional state as neutral to poor. A Pearson chi-square test showed a statistically significant relationship between annual household income and current mental and emotional state. A little over half (53%) of participants who reported a good mental and emotional state had higher household incomes of $81,000–$110,000 (28%), closely followed by those with incomes of $51,000–$80,000 (25%). There is a positive connection between mental and emotional status and economic status. Still, we view these findings with some caution given the small number of low-income women in our sample.

The finding of neutral to poor mental and emotional state among most of our study sample of Black women is disheartening but not surprising. Indeed, COVID-19 and quarantine conditions have taken a toll on people's mental and emotional health worldwide, and many people, including Black women, are feeling these effects. A pandemic of mental health vulnerability is quietly unfolding alongside the virus, occurring on the racial and ethnic spectrum. People of color seem to be uniquely affected in significant ways. Compounded with COVID-19 conditions, Black people are experiencing the mental health impacts of police killings of Black people, the mass riots around antiracism, and the rise in White nationalism (Floyd, 2020; Gaines, 2020). Media reports indicate that Black therapists see a dramatic increase in help-seeking from Black people (Gaines, 2021). We expect this trend to continue for some time. Black women are in desperate need of therapy. We believe they would be willing to try any therapist who welcomes them and shows interest in working with them through the contexts of their lives.

Chapters 6 and 7 discuss how therapists can be ready to showcase familiar-ity with people of color and cultural knowledge to build alliances and a welcoming environment for Black women.

1.4.5   Reasons for Feeling Stressed

We asked participants why Black women might feel distressed. Women were allowed to endorse any of the listed conditions that applied. Table 1.3 lists the endorsements of multiple conditions. The top conditions endorsed by participants were being a Black woman in America (78%), experiencing stress (65%), childhood and adolescent experiences (61%), work pressure (61%), and self-care (61%). Notably, almost all stressors from the list provided to participants were endorsed.

Table 1.3 *Reasons Black women might feel distressed*

Reasons	N	Percentage of endorsement
Being a Black woman in America	176	78
Stress	148	67
Experiences in childhood and adolescence	139	64
Self-care	138	65
Work pressure	138	61
Microaggressions	126	58
People asking too much from me	117	51
Feeling burdened	111	50
Feeling unhappy	110	48
Managing physical health	100	44
Feeling stereotyped	99	43
Self-love	91	41
Financial problems	91	36
Family life	89	39
Physical appearance	87	36
Discrimination	86	38
Worries about children	85	37
Couple life or marriage	83	39
Dating/finding a partner	79	33
Needing more recreation	66	27
Friendships	58	24
Spiritual matters	36	17

1.4.6   Reasons for Seeking Therapy

Table 1.4 lists participants' endorsement of reasons they sought therapy among all that apply. The top reasons were stress (64%), a mental health symptom such as depression (63%), self-care (48%), couple or dating problems (38%), or family issues (34%). The least endorsed reasons were spiritual and religious concerns (7%).

The top list of stressors affecting Black women in the study and the top reasons for seeking therapy match our experiences in practice. Black women are apt to begin therapy with relatively straightforward narratives, but right below their initial story lines are other layers of information related to the stressful conditions of their lives based on gendered racial dynamics. This is captured in the sentiment that some of their difficulties relate to being a Black woman in America. Among several endorsed circumstances and stressors are those this book addresses. Several chapters touch on the primary stressor, which is being a Black woman in America. This stressor relates to women's experience of gendered racism and other oppressions based on their social identities. Along with these experiences come microaggressions and

Table 1.4 *Reasons Black women seek therapy*

Reasons	Frequency	Percentage of endorsement
Stress	122	64
Mental health symptom such as depression, anxiety	121	63
Self-care	92	48
Couple or dating problems	72	38
Family issues/matters	66	34
Work issues	54	28
Grief and loss	51	27
Trauma	47	24
Separation/divorce	30	16
Important decisions	30	16
Abuse	27	14
Parenting/caregiving concerns	19	13
Discrimination	15	8
Friendship problems	14	7
Spiritual or religious concerns	7	7

Table 1.5 *Reasons for ending therapy*

Reasons		Frequency	Percentage
Didn't like therapist/therapy	55	55	31.8
Treatment ended naturally	44	44	25.4
Had nothing to do with therapist/therapy	41	41	23.7
Some other reason	29	29	16.8
Can't recall why	4	4	2.3

experiences of discrimination in multiple contexts. Women's family contexts are also among the reasons for stress or therapy seeking. They include coupling or dating, family life, parenting, or caregiving. Black women's girlhood or childhood and adolescent experiences are also endorsed.

1.4.7   Reasons for Ending Therapy

We asked participants why they ended therapy. Around 32% terminated because they did not like their therapists. We found these results surprising and encouraging because in our experience, when clients do not feel that therapy or a therapist is helpful, they drop out. Our data suggest that nearly two thirds of clients in our sample terminated therapy for reasons that had nothing to do with the therapists or the therapy ended naturally or for other reasons.

1.5   Qualitative Findings in Open-Ended Questions

1.5.1   What Questions Were Asked

Our survey included four open-ended questions. All participants were asked two questions: "Why might some Black women avoid therapy?" and "What are your recommendations for therapists who work with Black women as clients?" Two questions went only to those who had therapy: "Overall in therapy, what has been helpful to you?" and "Overall, in therapy, what has not been helpful to you?" We were pleased to receive 792 unique statements in response to the four questions, with participants writing several lines of text. We consider this one of the richest data sources in our study.

To analyze themes in Black women's statements, we worked with a qualitative data consultant[1] and three research assistants (RAs) to assist with coding and thematic analyses of these data. Our RA coders were 3 graduate students in their 20s studying to be mental health practitioners. The three RAs identify as Black, Black and biracial, and White, and all three identify as women. We followed strategies recommended by Braun and Clarke (2012) to discern commonalities, nuances, and meanings in participant comments. Our goal was to elicit specific and overarching themes in Black women's perspectives. Coding procedures are detailed in the Appendix.

Following our RAs' initial coding of responses, we reviewed the coding, examined themes across the 792 unique statements, and identified core themes, subthemes, and interconnections among the themes. This process exposed the subtleties in participant views that revealed how the meaning of some of participants' sentiments shifted depending on the context. For example, the theme of *time* was a barrier to seeking therapy and related to lack of *time* to visit a therapist because of various responsibilities. However, under the question of recommendations for therapists, *time* was related to wanting longer sessions with the therapist to discuss serious issues. Next, we asked questions of the data: *How do the women talk about their experiences related to the four questions? What assumptions do women make in the interpretation? What kind of worldviews emerged through their narrative account?* Following this thematic analysis, we evaluated all statements for meta-themes present among all four questions. In the following discussion, all *italicized word*s are verbatim from our study participants.

---

[1] Brendaly Drayton PhD, taught qualitative research courses at the University of Memphis and Penn State University. She is co-editor of two adult educational journals and is currently a scholar-in-residence at Penn State University.

1.5.2   Views on Why Some Black Women Avoid Therapy

We analyzed 220 unique statements from participants and found two core themes related to Black women's avoidance of therapy. The first was that Black women might avoid therapy out of *fear of violating sociocultural norms*. Subthemes were that Black women might fear *stigma*, might *violate a strong Black woman image* or *family trust*, and might violate their *religious faith or values*. For example, one participant noted reasons that Black women might avoid therapy:

> Because of the stigma of therapy. Often, and especially for Black women who grew up as Christians, we're told that we just need to pray our struggles away, that a deepening of faith will reduce our troubles; so, it can be hard to reach out when the people (usually women) around you characterize all issues as a result of a lack of sufficient faith.

Overwhelmingly, Black women used the term *stigma* to express this fear of violating norms in the larger society, the Black community, and the church. Women's fears seemed connected to being a Black female. Fears also seem related to being perceived as *crazy, weak, lacking in faith,* and not *handling business* or keeping business *private*. Women described not wanting to be stereotyped, judged, ridiculed, shamed, or in a position that would negatively impact their employment or in child custody matters.

The second core theme of why Black women might avoid therapy was *lack of access to some resources*. Subthemes around a lack of access to resources were *finances or cost, time, information,* and *how to find a good therapist. Finances or cost* was the most referenced factor. Women noted the cost of therapy in general and connected cost to lack of insurance or limited insurance and high out-of-pocket expenses:

> Therapy has a notorious reputation for being expensive and I don't know that the profession does a good job at explaining how therapy can be made affordable for financially strapped people.

The second most referenced subtheme related to a lack of access to resources was lack of *time*. This was expressed as a lack of time to attend therapy due to professional and family responsibilities. The subtheme of finding *a good therapist* seemed to relate to the *daunting task* of finding a therapist to trust. For participants, it appeared that they lack knowledge of how to find the right therapist.

> Though I spend most of my time in the Midwest, I'm originally from the South, where it can be difficult to find therapists (especially Black women) outside of a handful of major southern cities.

Women in the study referenced *connecting* or *identifying with someone*. Therapists that understand their *experiences and culture* seemed to be viewed as the right match.

Not finding a therapist they can identify with. Feeling weak. Having time and other resources to direct to self-care. Unable to focus on therapy because of other overwhelming day to day issues with surviving in America as a woman of color.

Some participants noted the difficulty of integrating therapy into their everyday lives:

Because having to open boxes that you have had to emotionally lock to survive can be difficult. . . . Who puts you back together when you are all alone in the evening after you have [bared] your soul that afternoon.

Other participants talked about how the idea of seeking therapy seemed to contradict how they had been raised:

I think some black women avoid therapy because we feel like we don't need it. Black women are raised to be strong, fierce, brave, and solid. We are taught to fight through whatever we go through alone. That is what we have always seen.

1.5.3   Views on What Has Been Unhelpful in Therapy

We identified several core themes in Black women's comments about what was unhelpful in therapy. Core themes were *lack of cultural competency in therapists, consequences, unsupportive interactions in therapy, challenges in the process, lack of rapport, lack of structure, unprofessionalism, time,* and *cost. Lack of cultural competencies* was in the context of therapists not having the same cultural background as participants. This seemed to make Black women perceive that therapists might be unfamiliar with the issues and experiences of Black people in the United States. One participant stated:

My current counselor is a White woman and she doesn't broach topics of race or discrimination . . . she will talk about it if I bring it up but she won't introduce it and we don't really go into a lot of depth about it.

Black women participants commented on the therapist's *unwillingness to go in depth* on cultural issues and the inability to navigate or integrate a religious perspective. Other contexts were *having to teach therapists* on topics such as *intergenerational trauma.* Examples of the *consequences* of unhelpful therapy were making clients feel *minimized* or *dismissed.*

Lack of supportive interactions included the therapist not listening, talking too much, or focusing on matters unrelated to the client's goals. Other examples included the therapist having a posture as though *listening to gossip* and being focused on diagnosis instead of listening. The challenges in the process on the client's side were *difficulty being open* or *vulnerable, talking about painful things,* and *baring your soul.*

It can force you to confront things all at once sometimes, and that can be overwhelming. You can get the sense that maybe you need to address big questions or "issues" about yourself right now when without therapy, you would have continued being *fine*, or just dealt with those issues in your own time. Overall this is probably a positive thing but it can cause stress in the moment. Additionally, sometimes it can feel like every little thing about how you think needs to be explored or broken down and sometimes, you just don't want to bother – you sometimes can have a natural inclination to leave certain things as is but when in therapy, you can mention something in passing that you don't feel like exploring but then you sometimes have to, and that can be difficult or frustrating. Similar to my last point, however, I assume that these types of discomfort are overall positive in the long run.

Related to therapist's qualities, dislikes included unhelpful interventions such as *homework*.

Sometimes it can feel like every little thing about how you think needs to be explored or broken down and sometimes, you just don't want to bother – you sometimes can have a natural inclination to leave certain things as is but when in therapy, you can mention something in passing that you don't feel like exploring but then you sometimes have to, and that can be difficult or frustrating. Similar to my last point, however, I assume that these types of discomfort are overall positive in the long run.

The therapist's emphasis on matters that are not helpful to Black women was also mentioned.

In the past I had a counselor who was a Black woman but I didn't think she was attentive enough and she was a bit pushy – kind of telling me what she thought I needed and how the session would go . . . none of that was helpful for me.

Challenges in the process related to how much *time* must pass to *go deep* and feelings of *insecurity*. *Lack of professionalism* included therapists falling *asleep*. Other respondents felt the therapist was *overworked* and *needed money*. Other examples were therapists *talking about their own problems, rescheduling, being late*, or engaging in distracting behaviors like *chewing gum or playing with her hair*. Another mention was the therapist seeming in *awe* of clients' lives versus providing help.

In the question of unhelpfulness of therapy, comments about *time* related to participants feeling rushed through the process, the *time* it takes to open up to the therapist, the number of sessions, the therapist's inflexibility regarding scheduling, the search process to find a therapist, and feeling like therapy was unproductive or a waste of time. The context of *cost* seems to relate to therapy being *way too expensive*, therapy not being successfully covered by insurance, or the therapist *not taking my insurance*. Costs and time of therapy are discussed later in this chapter as one of the meta-themes cutting across numerous responses.

1.5.4 *Views on What Has Been Helpful in Therapy*

The first core theme in the helpfulness of therapy was related to having a *safe space*. Subthemes were being able to express feelings, confidentiality, being honest, a space for healing, a trusting environment, and a space to vent *without opinions or reactions*. Participants appreciated:

Having a therapist who listens, validates my experiences, nonjudgmental, and also helps me discover insight and practical ways of dealing with issues.

They also appreciated:

Developing a sense of self-worth, because I was given a safe space to share my concerns, doubts, and uncertainty. In that space my concerns were validated, and that validation allowed me to begin recognizing my needs. Once I recognized my needs, I was able to begin communicating them and doing things that affirmed my worthiness.

A second core theme in the helpfulness of therapy was *positive outcomes* with subthemes of tangible *benefits* such as healing, coping, insight, guidance on managing mental health, and self-care. This sentiment unfolded in the context of actionable advice, self-care strategies, and improved quality of life.

As someone who doesn't generally share thoughts and feelings with anyone, I've appreciated having a safe, confidential space in which to just say things out loud without having to censor myself. I've also learned some really great ways to help manage some of my mental health issues, which has made life much less of a struggle. I also appreciate having a different perspective on happenings in my life.

The third core theme in therapy helpfulness was that the therapist had *cultural and gender competence*. Contexts were knowing *African American culture* and having a therapist who *looked like us*. This theme also seemed related to incorporating spirituality and feeling that therapists understood Black women.

1.5.5　What Are Recommendations for Therapists Who Work with Black Women?

Recommendations for therapists include two core themes. The first was *cultural competency*. Cultural competency subthemes that emerged are learning about Black women or Black people, researching, asking questions, being aware of bias, and speaking honestly. Cultural competency seemed strongly connected to Black women's comfort in sessions and perception of the therapist's ability to help them. Learning about Black women's dual identities (race and gender) and experiences in the United States and their culture were the contexts in which sentiments appeared. Some women do not want to "explain culture" to the therapist.

One of the reasons I sought the therapist that I have is because I knew that there was a good chance that I would not have explain some of my experiences, both personal and professional, because there would likely be commonalities due to my therapist's demographics. Where those commonalities don't exist, I think it's incumbent upon the therapist to do the extra work to ensure that they understand the unique burdens we face.

Another participant echoed the need for cultural understanding:

If a therapist is working with Black women, they really need a deep understanding of the double burdens that come with being both Black and a woman in a nation that is notoriously hostile to both of those demographics. For non-Black and non-women therapists, I think this understanding has to come from extensive, and regular, self-education.

The second core theme among recommendations related to *fostering supportive interactions* in therapy. Subthemes were *listening, affirming, patience, empathy, not judging, building rapport, trust*, and *treating me as an individual*. Supportive interactions focus on how Black women wanted to be treated. The most referenced subtheme carried the connotation of *listening*. Listening appeared in the context of being heard and in several individual statements. Regarding recommendations for therapists, listening was important in the context of the larger society and their communities. Black women express not always being heard.

I think all therapists should really be careful about diminishing the perspectives and experiences of Black women. In general, the world tends to dismiss our pain and viewpoints, so we don't need the people who are meant to help us falling into that cycle.

Listening was described in terms of what is said but also not said by the therapist. Affirming their experiences, being empathetic, and understanding Black women's lived experiences also seem connected to listening. *Safe space* and *being genuine* also seemed to be reflective of listening.

I think recognizing that Black women already have a lot on their plate and just being open to listening and being affirming in the process is invaluable. I don't know that solutions should be pushed at the start, maybe it's just important to have space for Black women to release.

Patience!!!! It will take time to uncover multiple layers of issues that impact us because historically we have been conditioned to 'get over it' and that attitude frames how we view our own incidents as well as how we choose to recall them.

1.5.6   Meta-Themes across All Responses

We analyzed participant statements to all four questions for meta-themes: overarching themes represented powerfully, frequently, and richly throughout respondents' statements. We identified four meta-themes that seem to affect Black women's experience of psychotherapy:

1. *Cultural competence in therapists.* This was a core and nonnegotiable feature of therapy for Black women that affected their capacity to trust and respond to therapy and therapists in several domains.

2. *Cultural comfort in therapy.* This theme is related to how Black women felt in therapy and with therapists. If women were comfortable that they were safe, seen, and understood culturally, they were more apt to trust the process and lean into the therapists' ideas and suggestions.

3. *Listening.* This theme described a type of encounter led by therapists in which Black women felt validated, heard, understood, and accepted. These encounters increased women's appreciation for the therapist and helped them to use therapy well. On the flip side, if therapists did not display *listening*, Black women seemed less apt to find therapy useful.

4. *Time and cost of therapy.* Multiple, intertwined meanings were attached to the cost of doing therapy. Costs were financial, cultural, social, personal, and the like. Cost often had the connotation of a price or penalty for doing therapy or having it not be successful. Related to cost was a sense that therapy was time consuming, and respondents noted alternative costs, such as just leaving things alone. References to time were not just in terms of minutes and hours but also opportunities lost and how negative experiences with one therapist may prevent a positive outlook on therapy itself. Our data suggest that the most consequential cost of therapy for Black women seems to be giving up on therapy altogether.

1.6   How Findings Relate to Ideas in the Book

Our study provides a snapshot of the viewpoints of Black women in our sample at the time of data collection. We cannot draw direct causal inferences, and we could not follow up with participants because of the anonymous nature of the survey. Nonetheless, these data, which nearly 800 individual statements by Black women, provided a wealth of insight into women's perspectives on therapy, both from their own experiences and their perceptions of Black women's experiences overall. Many themes in the data confirm the importance of the *topics* (see chapter titles) that we have included in this book. We should also know that while many topics we have selected are richly represented in the extant literature, there are some topics for which there are scant data as to the everyday experiences of Black women. This represents an opportunity for scholarly inquiry.

> See titles and descriptions of each chapter in the Introduction.

In summing up the findings of the qualitative data, we note first, that while Black women may feel more comfortable with Black therapists, therapist *race and gender alone* are insufficient to gain women's trust, and therapists must be willing to attend to cultural features of alliance building. Attention to Black women's cultural comfort in therapy includes creating a safe space for them, showcasing interest and curiosity in Black women as a unique cultural group, showcasing cultural knowledge, and having information on the issues that affect Black women uniquely. Second, the study identified recurring themes connected to Black women's core mental health conditions. In chapters of this book we have offered some information on why and how these themes might show up in Black women's narratives. Recurring themes include the Strong Black Woman persona, shifting, family life, trauma, spirituality, mothering, and caregiving among others. Finally, the findings of our study endorse a need to build therapy relationships with Black women that are culturally competent. In several chapters of the book we will return to this theme and offer specific culturally competent strategies to gain Black women's trust. The overall aim is to help therapists work with women's needs in the contexts of their historical, social, and cultural experiences.

We provide more details on therapists cultural self-awareness in Chapter 6 and strategies for therapist alliance-building with Black women in Chapter 7.

1.7   How the Study Impacts Our Practices

We learned a lot from our study that will alter aspects of our practice as therapists, and we hope therapists who read this work will find the same to be true for them. For example, Donna was especially struck by the fact that Black women are willing to give therapy a try despite not having their preferred option of a Black therapist. When Donna cannot accept a referral of a Black woman reaching out to her for therapy, she tends to refer the woman to another Black therapist in deference to the woman's request. This has often delayed Black women's ability to be in therapy simply because no Black therapists were available. Results of the study suggest an opportunity to encourage Black women to stick with their search for therapy and to consider culturally competent non-Black therapists among their options. Donna will incorporate such advice in making referrals.

Adia was struck by the number of issues Black women endorsed as contributing to their everyday stress. Adia views these stressors as related to Black women's wellness overall, including physical health. She is considering outreach strategies to provide Black women additional therapy options as well as psychoeducation (e.g., targeted workshops on managing racism stress or group-based therapy services). Essential to this idea will be outreach efforts targeting women in community settings (e.g., churches).

Our three RAs also offered their views on the impacts of the study on them as therapists in training. We provide their comments here to honor their work and show how the themes identified in the study can influence the approach of developing therapists.

Sydney McClure, a Black female therapist in training, addresses the importance of clients' safety in therapy:

What stands out for me that makes therapy helpful is having a "safe space." While some study participants did not feel the need to elaborate on this quality, the qualities of a safe therapeutic space came through in other answers. The safety of therapy came from being a judgment-free zone. The therapist, especially if you are not Black, has to be trustworthy. However, many Black women might be slow to trust, especially. A safe space also means feeling connected with the therapist, feeling seen, feeling heard while not being interrupted or talked over. A safe space is one in which Black women can show vulnerability and be validated. Black women are asking therapists to not rush them, to consider all of their identities, to make time for them, to give them grace, to give them respect, to give them space, to provide them with tools, to listen, to see them, to hear them. Black women want therapists to show them the care and respect and empathy and care that almost every other space in our world does not grant Black women. Overall, I hope that when therapists read these results of this survey, they will feel it necessary to take action.

Katie Gow, a White female therapist in training, reflects on the deep importance of clients feeling understood and the need for therapists to reflect on their own position and reactions:

Engaging with these data has stirred up a variety of thoughts and feelings in me. The most troubling notion standing out to me relates to Black women's fears, expectations, and experiences of being misunderstood. One woman writes that Black women may avoid therapy due to "feeling unheard and thinking a therapist's office would be more of the same." Another notes that avoidance may result from "not having their daily lived experiences understood or even explored by the therapist." It would be a disappointing environment where, implicitly or explicitly, a therapist communicates that a Black woman's life and experiences are not valued or worth seeing.

As I have thought about my privilege (as a White therapist) and consider what might get in the way of my ability (and perhaps others) to truly see and hear Black women, I think about a willingness to sit in discomfort. My privilege allows me to disengage from the reality of oppression when it feels like too much. I will need to consciously recognize when I feel an inclination to distance myself out of discomfort or feeling overwhelmed, to let myself feel what it means to live in Black women's world. I hope not to minimize or fix or avoid the full experience in any way. This will require continuous work around recognizing the racism within me and my "white saviorism" and any tendency to protect myself and my comfort at Black women's expense. I am incredibly grateful that this work is being done to serve them.

Finally, Lyrra Isanberg, a biracial therapist in training, shares concern and frustration in addition to hope for the future of the mental health profession:

As a biracial therapist-in-training (with Black ancestry) my initial response was worry. When I seek therapy for myself, are these experiences of discrimination, stereotyping, and microaggressions going to happen to me, too? It is difficult to understand that therapists with whom we do not share similar lived experiences can cause harm because of their ignorance. In some ways, I was greatly disappointed in this field after reading participants responses. However, I hope that reading about what Black women want such as listening, humility, and curiosity will be heard by present and future mental health workers who pick up this book. These responses renewed my understanding of the importance of taking proper heed to the need to correctly serve Black female clients.

Therapist Reflection Questions

1. How would you respond to the survey questions mentioned in this chapter?
2. What was new or surprising to you about the study findings? How might you change your clinical practice as a result?
3. As a therapist working with Black women what resonated with you? How might you use the ideas in this chapter to improve your practice with Black women?
4. As a student training to become a therapist, what aspects of this chapter did you find helpful? What will you want to know more about work related to Black women?
5. As a client in therapy, how do the ideas in this chapter help you to advocate for what you want?

References

Braun, V., & Clarke, V. (2012). *Thematic analysis.* In H. Cooper, P. M. Camic, D. L. Long, A. T. Panter, D. Rindskopf, & K. J. Sher (Eds.), *APA handbook of research methods in psychology: Vol. 2. Research designs: Quantitative, qualitative, neuropsychological, and biological* (pp. 57–71). American Psychological Association.

Brendaly Drayton PhD, taught qualitative research courses at the University of Memphis and Penn State University. She is co-editor of two adult educational journals and is currently a scholar-in-residence at Penn State University.

Floyd, L. (2020, November 6). Black women are facing an overwhelming mental health crisis. *Prevention.* https://www.prevention.com/health/mental-health/a33686468/black-women-mental-health-crisis/

Gaines, P. (2020, June 29). *Black Americans experience deadly stress as pandemic and violent-racism collide.* NBC News. https://www.nbcnews.com/news/nbcblk/black-americans-experience-deadly-stress-pandemic-violent-racism-collide-experts-n1231448

Gaines, P. (2021, May 27). *Black people are in a mental health crisis. Their therapists are busier than ever.* NBC News. https://www.nbcnews.com/news/nbcblk/black-people-are-mental-health-crisis-therapists-are-busier-ever-rcna1045

Hamp, A., Stamm, K., Lin, L., & Christidis, P. (2016). *2015 survey of psychology health service providers.* American Psychological Association. https://www.apa .org/workforce/publications/15-health-service-providers/index.aspx

Lin, L., Stamm, K., & Christidis, P. (2018, February). How diverse is the psychology workforce? *Monitor on Psychology, 49*(2). http://www.apa.org/monitor/2018/02/ datapoint

Winfrey-Harris, T. (2015). *The sisters are alright: Changing the broken narrative of Black women in America.* Berrett-Koehler.

2   Social Determinants of Health and Mental Health for Black Women

with Uchechi A. Mitchell[*]

On April 27, 2020, Rana Zoe Mungin, a 30-year-old Black woman, passed away due to complications from COVID-19. When Rana sought treatment to address her symptoms, she was denied care at almost every turn. She went to the hospital two times complaining of symptoms related to COVID-19 and was not tested. On her second trip to the hospital, an ambulance worker disregarded her trouble breathing, and believed she was having a panic attack. When Rana finally received treatment, it was too late. Rana's sister, Mia Mungin, shared this Facebook post about the care her sister was receiving: "Racism and health disparities . . . still continues at this day and age. The zip code in which we live in still predetermines the type of care we receive" (Brito, 2020).

Rana graduated from Wellesley and earned her master's degree from the University of Massachusetts. She was a middle school teacher who lived and worked in Brooklyn, New York. Despite Rana's academic achievement and the fact that her sister was a nurse, she did not receive lifesaving care. As Rana's sister stated in her Facebook post, the fact that Rana did not receive competent care was likely related to the fact that she was a Black woman living in a Black community, and this scenario happens in many other places in the United States. Rana's story reflects the intersections of the social determinants of health for Black women, in which conditions such as obesity increase the risk for severe illness from COVID-19 (Centers for Disease Control and Prevention, 2020). Along with health conditions, Black women also experience discrimination in health care, which results in their being denied lifesaving care.

The COVID-19 pandemic and the killings of unarmed Black people in 2020 have uniquely affected the health and mental health of Black women. The pandemic has increased psychological distress and depressive symptoms for most Americans (Ettman et al., 2020). But Black Americans are at greater risk for poor mental health (Meadows-Fernandez, 2020; Purtle, 2020) due to the combined stress of financial insecurity resulting from furloughs and layoffs and

---

[*] U. A. Mitchell & A. Gooden (2023). Social determinants of health and mental health for Black women. In D. Baptiste & A. Gooden, *Promoting Black women's mental health: What practitioners should know and do.* Cambridge University Press.

the grief of losing loved ones to COVID-19. Additionally, for Black women, the burden may be even heavier because they are often the primary caregivers within their households (Navaie-Waliser et al., 2002). These pandemic-related exposures have been coupled with an increase in exposure to racial trauma, stemming from the deaths of George Floyd, Breonna Taylor, and others at the hands of the police. The mental toll of these experiences has deeply affected the entire Black community (Byfield & Intarasuwan, 2020; Dastagir, 2020; Fowers & Wan, 2020). Black women have been on the front lines of the Black Lives Matter movement since its inception. While engaging in social activism can be healing and empowering, it can also lead to stress and exhaustion.

In this chapter, we review the social determinants of health (SDOH) model as a guide to understanding the interconnected systemic and individual-level factors that influence the health and mental health of Black women. It is essential for therapists working with Black women to understand the social, historical, and political factors that influence their health and mental health to adequately contextualize the experiences and concerns of Black women seeking therapy. Understanding the diverse contexts of Black women's lives will increase therapists' ability to provide them with culturally sensitive services. This knowledge will also support therapists and other professionals who work within health, mental health, and governmental systems in being effective advocates for Black women to receive equitable care.

2.1   Health Disparities for Black Women

The daily and lifetime stress Black women experience as they navigate life adds up and results in chronic health issues. Dr. Arline Geronimus, a behavioral scientist at the University of Michigan, coined the term "weathering" to describe the rapid declines in health and increased risk of mortality that Black people experience, when compared with White people, due to racial discrimination, racialized traumas, and social exclusion. Geronimus' research shows that the health of Black women resembled that of White women who were at least 7.5 years older (Geronimus et al., 2010). This difference in health is largely due to higher levels of perceived stress among Black women and their greater exposure to poverty. Dr. Amani Allen's research has similarly found greater declines in health among Black women due to chronic stress exposure but has also shown that in some instances, higher levels of education may slow the rate of biological decline because of the social and financial resources that women with more years of education can access (Allen et al., 2019). While Black women often look younger than their chronological age, this research demonstrates that despite this outward appearance, many Black women are aging at higher rates than White women as they navigate the daily stress of discrimination and trauma.

Weathering is a primary driver of the health disparities Black women experience. Health disparities are differences in the health outcomes and illnesses that Black women experience when compared with women of other racial groups. Health disparities are also seen in the care Black women receive or do not receive.

One of the most heartbreaking manifestations of health disparities for Black women is related to Black maternal and infant mortality (Martin & Montagne, 2017; Villarosa, 2018). Although most pregnancy-related deaths are preventable, Black women are three to five times more likely to die due to pregnancy-related complications (Centers for Disease Control and Prevention, 2019). The infant mortality rate for Black women is more than two times higher than the rate for White women (U.S. Department of Health and Human Services, 2021). The high rates of Black maternal mortality are connected to weathering, higher rates of hypertension and other chronic health issues, and inadequate care.

> Health disparities are discussed further in Chapter 13 on Black women's health and wellness.

Once Black babies and mothers make it past the high-risk postnatal period and enter adolescence and adulthood, their lives are still at risk (Fishman, 2020). Black mothers are more likely to lose their children to police brutality (Meadows-Fernandez, 2020) than mothers from other racial groups. Black people are up to two times more likely to be killed by police use of force than White people (Edwards et al., 2019). Not only are Black women more likely to experience violence at the hands of police, but they also carry the weight of grief when one of their loved ones is killed by police (Rodriguez, 2016). Black women's experiences with motherhood are at the intersection of health and mental health, highlighting the increased stress and emotional toll that Black women navigate and the devastating consequences of the stress and discrimination they experience in health systems. We encourage therapists to be mindful of both the risks Black women face during the process of pregnancy and the fears they carry for the safety and well-being of their children. These fears weigh heavily for Black mothers and go beyond normative parental anxieties about a child's life and future.

> The challenging experiences of Black mothers are discussed further in Chapter 10 on caregiving.

2.2   Mental Health Disparities for Black Women

Although Black–White disparities in physical health are well studied, less is known about mental health disparities. For Black people, mental health disparities show up in both the use of mental health care and the outcomes of psychological treatments. For example, in 2018, around 16% of Black people, close to 4.8 million people, had a mental illness (Substance Abuse and Mental Health Services Administration, 2019). Of those with a mental illness, 22.4% had a serious mental illness, 6.1% had a major depressive episode in the past year, and 4.1% had serious suicidal thoughts. Even with these comparatively high rates of mental illness, only 8.7% of Black people with a mental illness received mental health services, compared with 18.6% of White people with a mental illness. Overall, Black people are less likely than White people to receive outpatient care (4.5% vs. 8.5%) or psychotropic prescriptions (6.4% vs. 15.4%). However, Black people are more likely than White people to receive inpatient treatment (1.5% vs. 0.9%). The discrepancies between inpatient and outpatient care may be due to the overpathologizing of Black people (Snowden, 2003). Stigma around mental illness and lack of access to care may cause Black people not to receive mental health care until they are in crisis and need intensive treatment. While Black women are more likely to utilize mental health services than Black men, fewer Black women use mental health services than White women. For example, in 2018, 32.2% of Black women with any mental health illness used mental health services, compared with 51.7% of White women (Substance Abuse and Mental Health Services Administration, 2015). Similarly, 61.3% of Black women with serious mental illness utilized mental health services, compared with 73.4% of White women. It is essential for therapists to understand these disparities to recognize the importance of supporting Black women who are seeking mental health care treatment. Further, therapists are encouraged to do their part in increasing the accessibility of the services they provide for Black women.

To truly understand the differences in mental health and mental health service utilization between Black women and other groups, we need to consider the social determinants of health and mental health. The next section of this chapter describes the social determinants of health and provides examples of how these determinants influence the experiences of Black women. Understanding the SDOH model will enable therapists to put the challenges their Black female clients navigate into context. In the United States, there is a tendency to "blame the victim" and look at people who are living in poverty, have health challenges, and struggle with mental illness as the problem. The individualistic culture of the United States can inhibit empathy for Black female clients who are navigating oppressive systems that are not designed to support them. The SDOH model highlights these systems and structures, supporting the need for therapists to respond with empathy and compassion. Further, therapists can share this information with their Black female clients to help them cultivate compassion for themselves.

2.3   Social Determinants of Health and Mental Health

The World Health Organization defines social determinants of health as "the conditions in which people are born, grow, work, live, and age, and the wider set of forces and systems shaping the conditions of daily life. These forces and systems include economic policies and systems, development agendas, social norms, social policies and political systems" (World Health Organization, n.d., para. 1). This definition highlights the ways in which forces outside of a Black woman's control might directly influence her health and access to health care. This reality occurs because Black women face inequalities in distribution of money, social and political power, and other resources that are important for good health. These inequities result in Black women experiencing more chronic health issues, higher rates of maternal mortality, and limited access to high-quality health care. These disparities are not incidental; they are unjust because they could be prevented by policy changes. This existence of systems that contribute to disparities does not take away from the fact that Black women have personal agency. Our point here is to highlight that Black women have more obstacles to contend with than people from many other groups.

The social determinants of health can be grouped into a broad set of intermediary, structural, and contextual factors that influence each other and the health of individuals (see Figure 2.1). Although this model is typically used to understand disparities in physical health outcomes, it can also be used to understand disparities in mental health and mental health care use between Black women and other groups. We begin by focusing on the individual – Black women specifically – and the factors that most directly influence their health (i.e., intermediary factors) and then move to broader structural and contextual factors that influence the availability of and access to resources that help a person maintain optimal health. The case presented in this chapter integrates tangible examples to highlight how the factors at each level of the SDOH model might affect a Black woman's life.

2.3.1   Intermediary Factors

Intermediary factors are factors that directly affect the health of an individual. These factors include a person's biology, psychosocial factors, behaviors, and neighborhood conditions, all of which work together to influence mental and physical health.

ADAPTED MODEL OF THE SOCIAL DETERMINANTS OF HEALTH AND MENTAL HEALTH

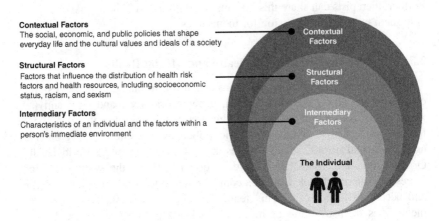

Contextual Factors
The social, economic, and public policies that shape
everyday life and the cultural values and ideals of a society

Structural Factors
Factors that influence the distribution of health risk
factors and health resources, including socioeconomic
status, racism, and sexism

Intermediary Factors
Characteristics of an individual and the factors within a
person's immediate environment

Figure 2.1 Adapted model of the social determinants of health and mental health

2.3.1.1 Biology When referring to biology as a determinant of health, we include genetic risk factors, sex-linked diseases, and the natural aging process. Breast cancer is an example of a health risk that is influenced by lifestyle, environmental, and genetic factors. A Black woman who has breast cancer is likely to have another family member who also had breast cancer, which highlights the genetic connection to breast cancer occurrence. The prevalence of the *BRCA1* and *BRCA2* gene mutations, which have been linked to breast cancer, is highest in the United States (Armstrong et al., 2019). Specifically, people with Ashkenazi Jewish ancestry, Hispanic people, and Black people are most likely to have these mutations and be at greater risk for breast cancer compared with people of other races and ethnicities (John et al., 2007). All three of these groups have experienced high levels of historical trauma, which likely contributes to the gene mutation. This points to the need to look at the social, political, and economic environments as determinants of health that may interact with genetic risk factors to influence disease risk (i.e., epigenetic risk factors). The interaction between biology and social and political factors is also evident in other health issues, including depression.

Case Example

Brenda is a 45-year-old, African American, lesbian, cisgender woman. She is currently in a relationship with a long-term partner. Brenda has a family history of depressive symptoms; her mother had depression that was undiagnosed and

(*cont.*)

untreated. Brenda's mother also experienced traumatic stress when she was pregnant with Brenda, which likely raised her cortisol levels during pregnancy and affected Brenda in the womb. The genetic predisposition along with the stressors Brenda experienced while growing up in a disadvantaged neighborhood contributed to her developing depression.

2.3.1.2 Psychosocial Factors These factors stem from the interaction of social conditions with psychological factors, including an individual's thoughts and emotions. The external circumstances and stressors a Black woman experiences, how she makes sense of those experiences, and how she copes with them all fall under the umbrella of psychosocial factors. Psychosocial stressors and how a Black woman copes with these stressors have long-term effects on the body (i.e., weathering). Adverse childhood experiences and traumas have lasting effects on the physical and mental health of children, with consequences that are felt well into adulthood and old age (Ogle et al., 2013). Experiences of racial and gender-based discrimination are chronic stressors that Black women face throughout their lives. The impact of this stress is real and affects how the body functions. For example, a Black woman who deals with high levels of gendered racism might be more likely to have high blood pressure and inflammation (Slopen et al., 2012). All these physiological changes also lead to an increased risk of death, disease, disorder, and disability.

Brenda grew up witnessing her mother's depressive symptoms and blamed herself. Brenda felt like she was the reason her mother was irritable, tired, and sad. As a result of this developmental experience, Brenda developed a tendency to be harsh and overly critical of herself. On top of this, Brenda grew up in a low-income Black neighborhood that had high levels of community violence. The violence she witnessed while growing up furthered Brenda's feelings of depression and despair. Brenda did not witness healthy coping strategies and did not develop healthy ways to cope with the stress she experienced and the violence she witnessed. Further, Brenda struggled with her sexuality growing up and wondered if there was something wrong with her attraction to women until she found a supportive Black queer community in her late 20s. Brenda felt she had to keep her sexuality a secret in her Black community and never felt fully accepted while she was in the closet.

2.3.1.3 Behaviors Whether a person engages in health-promoting or health-damaging behaviors is also a key determinant of health. For example, we know the benefits of physical activity and nutritious eating habits and the adverse effects of cigarette smoking and binge drinking. While Black women do not engage in as much physical activity as White women, they are less likely to smoke (Dubowitz et al., 2011). This study also showed that Black women were least likely to engage in binge drinking when compared with other race and gender groups. Black women can use their agency in areas like these to improve their health and well-being, and they can support their health by not engaging in risky behaviors. Although people have the ability to choose which behaviors they engage in, this choice is often considered a "constrained choice" because the behaviors a person can engage in are influenced by their neighborhood conditions, another intermediary factor in the SDOH model.

Supporting Black women in taking care of their physical health is discussed extensively in Chapter 13.

When Brenda feels depressed, she has a hard time prioritizing herself; she feels guilty and thinks engaging in self-care is selfish because she doesn't believe her struggles are as serious as what other women in her life have faced. She witnessed the challenges that her mother, aunts, and grandmother faced and saw how they embodied the Strong Black Woman persona, always giving to other people and often neglecting their own health and mental health. Brenda also feels reluctant to seek out mental health care because she saw her mother persevere through depression without formal support from mental health providers, whom she and her family generally mistrust and are skeptical of.

2.3.1.4 Neighborhood Conditions The physical and social conditions that people live and work in are important determinants of health and mental health. If a Black woman lives in an unsafe home (e.g., with structural issues or mold), in an underresourced neighborhood characterized by community violence, and does not have access to healthy fresh food, these things all contribute to her experience of stress. For example, air pollution in a person's neighborhood, the presence of lead in housing materials and water sources, and housing conditions like the presence of mold and overcrowding are all significant risk factors for cardiovascular disease and other chronic conditions (Cosselman et al., 2015). A neighborhood's physical environment, including the presence of sidewalks, parks, and other physical amenities; its social and economic resources; and its levels of crime, graffiti, and other indicators of social disorder have increasingly gained attention as determinants of health because they influence a person's ability to engage in healthful behaviors (Wang et al., 2017), which ultimately affects their health. High crime rates and a lack of green space or affordable and effective indoor options for physical activity can encourage a more sedentary lifestyle; moreover, limited access to grocers that provide affordable healthy food options can lead to increased consumption of fast food (Richardson et al., 2011). Black women are more likely than White women to live in neighborhoods characterized by high levels of crime and disorder; fewer municipal, social, and economic resources; and more limited access to high-quality health care (Massey & Denton, 1993). These characteristics of the neighborhoods in which they live have been linked to adverse reproductive outcomes and may help explain the higher rates of low birthweight and preterm births among Black women (Culhane & Elo, 2005). The combination of these neighborhood exposures with systematic differences in the availability and quality of health care within a neighborhood further puts the health of Black women at risk.

> Brenda grew up in an underresourced neighborhood and witnessed community violence while she was growing up. This contributed to her experience of stress and depression and fueled her desire to go to college and leave that environment. As an adult, Brenda lives in a predominantly Black neighborhood that is middle class but underresourced, Brenda does not have easy access to a gym, and her neighborhood is classified as both a food desert (no grocery stores within 0.5 miles) and a food swamp (an overabundance of fast food restaurants and convenience stores) where healthy, fresh food is not easily accessible. This combination makes it difficult for Brenda to work out regularly and access healthy food. Brenda has struggled with her weight for years, which is likely due to a combination of the stress she has experienced, the difficult experiences she had with her mother growing up (Davis et al., 2005), the limited access to and engagement in physical exercise, and the lack of healthy food options close to her home (Ghosh-Dastidar et al., 2014).

2.3.1.5 Access to Care Where people live can also influence their access to health care and the nature of the health care services they receive. Health care centers often provide programs and services to the public that are designed to prevent diseases or delay their onset while also providing treatment and disease management for common conditions. For this reason, the availability of affordable and high-quality health care centers, including those that offer mental health care services, is important for maintaining physical and mental health and is therefore considered a social determinant of health.

Health care access is tied to the type of health insurance coverage a person has, if any. In 2011, more than half of the uninsured US population were people of color; among those under age 65, 32% of Latinx adults, 27% of American Indian adults, and 21% of Black adults were uninsured, compared with 13% of White adults (Kaiser Family Foundation, 2013). Social insurance programs such as Medicaid and Medicare have been designed to provide health insurance to the poor and elderly and predominantly benefit people of color. The implementation of the Affordable Care Act (ACA) in 2014 expanded health insurance coverage to individuals who previously were not covered by private insurance or through Medicare and Medicaid. In the initial years of its implementation, this expansion in coverage reduced racial and ethnic disparities in health care access, especially for Black people (Chen et al., 2016).

Although greater health insurance coverage improves access to care by making it more affordable, the types of health care services provided and the quality of care received are not always equitable. For example, mental health care services are commonly not covered, vary across neighborhoods in terms of availability, and are not often integrated with primary care services (VanderWielen et al., 2015). This lack of access to integrated behavioral health care has likely contributed to America's ever-growing mental health care crisis (National Council for Behavioral Health, 2018). Further, people of color are less likely to use mental health care services despite having more co-occurring mental health and substance use disorders (Hatzenbuehler et al., 2008). In addition, the quality of the primary and mental health care people receive is not consistent across race, ethnicity, gender, age, and geographic location. People of color are less likely to be satisfied with the care they receive and more likely to feel mistreated within the health care setting (Saha et al. 2003). Moreover, Black people are less likely than White people to receive adequate treatment for pain management, advanced cardiovascular diseases, renal disorders, and other health conditions despite their access to health insurance and the necessary health providers (Smedley et al., 2003). The combination of these deficiencies in our health care system put Black people at an increased risk of poor health and death regardless of the initiative they take to educate and advocate for themselves.

Brenda's feelings of stress and isolation peaked during her sophomore year of college, and she finally went to her university's counseling center for support after she burst out crying in her advisor's office one day. Brenda saw a therapist for a couple of sessions; the therapist was White and remarked at how strong Brenda was during each of their sessions. The therapist then told Brenda that she would benefit from more ongoing therapy and referred her to a different therapist in the community for long-term treatment. Brenda left feeling rejected and embarrassed that she sought help in the first place. Moreover, she didn't tell the therapist at the counseling center that she could not afford the insurance co-pay for a community-based therapist and as a result never followed up with this referral.

As an adult, Brenda reluctantly decided to seek therapy again, at the encouragement of her partner. She found it challenging to find a therapist who would take her insurance and was in a location she could access easily. Brenda also wanted to see a therapist who was a Black woman and would understand her experience as a Black woman. But many of the Black female therapists she called were overworked and not accepting new clients. Brenda finally found a therapist that she felt comfortable with after calling 10 therapists who did not have availability or did not return her calls. The therapist's office was located downtown close to her job because so few therapists were located near her neighborhood.

2.3.2 Structural Factors

Naming and describing the intermediary social determinants of health helps us understand how an individual's health is influenced by forces beyond their control. However, structural factors influence the distribution of the intermediary determinants discussed previously. In other words, they influence who is exposed to certain risk factors and what resources they have for coping with these risk factors. The next level of the SDOH model focuses on these structural factors. Specifically, we discuss the effects of socioeconomic status, racism, and sexism on health disparities.

2.3.2.1 Socioeconomic Status A person's social standing, or rank, is measured by their education, income, and occupation. These indicators of socioeconomic status are associated with varying levels of social and political power and prestige within society. Subsequently, they influence the distribution of the intermediary factors, access to health-promoting resources, and opportunities for social and economic advancement. Research on the relationship between socioeconomic status and health has consistently found that higher socioeconomic status is associated with better health, compared with lower socioeconomic status. However, this general trend does not always hold, especially when race and ethnicity are considered. For example, despite having higher levels of education, which should lead to greater access to social and economic resources, including health care, higher infant mortality rates can be found among college-educated Black women than less educated White women (Williams, 2002).

In other words, the typical health benefit gained from more years of education or higher income does not benefit Black women as much as it benefits White women. The diminished returns of higher socioeconomic status for the health of Black people are evident in several health outcomes, including self-rated physical and mental health and risk factors for cardiovascular diseases, specifically obesity and diabetes (Bell et al., 2018, 2020). Although some argue that these seemingly paradoxical findings demonstrate "inherent" differences in health between Black and White people such that higher incomes, education, and wealth cannot overcome their "innate" health disadvantage, the more accurate explanation lies in the complexity of racism and its manifestations.

> Despite her humble beginnings and limited resources, Brenda was always bright and worked hard in school, which helped her get accepted to a large, out-of-state university with a full scholarship. She became the first person in her family to attend college but experienced a significant culture shock when she arrived at this prestigious university and had to adjust to the culture of its predominantly White student body. Brenda struggled with imposter syndrome throughout her time in college. She felt she did not deserve to be at the university; she felt different from her White classmates, and even in the Black community she could feel cultural differences due to her family's working-class background, because most of the other Black students were middle class and often from immigrant families. Further, while many of her classmates did not have to work, Brenda had two part-time jobs to pay for rent, food, and books, and this left her with little extra time to socialize and have fun in college. Brenda experienced additional stress due to being from a low-income background at a college where most students came from upper-middle-class or wealthy families.

2.3.2.2 Impact of Racism Historical and contemporary forms of racism have shaped the health of marginalized communities of color. Racism is a "system of structuring opportunities and assigning value based on phenotype (e.g., race) that unfairly disadvantages some individuals and communities, unfairly advantages other individuals and communities, and undermines realization of the full potential of the whole society through the waste of human resources" (Jones, 2002, p. 10). Racism operates at multiple levels of society – intrapersonal, interpersonal, and institutional – and can be covert or overt in its manifestation. Experiences of racial discrimination and prejudice are interpersonal forms of racism that negatively impact the life experiences, behaviors, and mental health of the Black community. For example, racial discrimination is associated with insomnia (Bethea et al., 2020) and a higher lifetime incidence of depression (Hudson et al., 2016) and psychological distress among

Blacks. Moreover, Black people who experience racial discrimination during adolescence are more likely to have poor mental health in adulthood (Assari et al., 2017). In addition to the negative health outcomes related to actually experiencing discrimination, the process of anticipating, worrying about, and maintaining heightened vigilance toward discrimination is also associated with adverse health outcomes (Himmelstein et al., 2015). For Black women, in particular, chronic worry about racial discrimination – whether faced by themselves or by a child or loved one – is associated with stress (Sawyer et al., 2012) and an increased risk of preterm birth (Braveman et al., 2017).

Although interpersonal experiences of racial discrimination negatively impact the health of Black women, institutional or structural racism is another determinant of poor mental health that influences the ways in which Black women are treated within our social, economic, and political institutions, including their places of employment and the health care system. For example, experiences of racial discrimination within the health care setting are a primary reason that Black women underutilize health and mental health care services (Burgess et al., 2008). In the workplace, Black women describe experiencing social isolation and exclusion, barriers to being hired or promoted within their workplaces, and a lack of mentorship, coupled with the need to speak up against or counter negative stereotypes about their race (Hall et al., 2012). The culmination of these stressful experiences and their accumulation over a lifetime takes a negative toll on the mental well-being of the Black community in general. Black women, however, have the added burden of dealing with sexism (e.g., gendered racism) within these spaces.

Despite the stressors she faced, Brenda graduated from college on time and got a job in sales at a well-regarded corporation in her hometown, earning more than anyone in her family ever had. At her job, Brenda experienced gendered racial microaggressions in addition to structural racism and sexism. Brenda was never given accounts that would produce big sales and was instead only given accounts for small minority-owned businesses. While Brenda was excited to support these small businesses, she could see that only working with these companies would limit her pathway to getting promoted and receiving the large bonuses that her White male colleagues often enjoyed. In meetings, Brenda was frequently assumed to be the executive assistant and asked to take notes and get everyone coffee. When she would speak up about new sales initiatives, she often felt as though she had to be the representative for all Black people and carried this weight during team meetings. Brenda was frequently ignored or talked over by her male colleagues. One of Brenda's White male colleagues even made sexual advances, saying he had always wanted to know what it would be like to have sex with a Black woman. Brenda didn't talk to HR about this sexual harassment, fearing that she wouldn't be believed and that instead she would be punished for filing the complaint.

2.3.2.3 Intersection of Racism and Sexism The race and sex of Black women cannot be considered separately when trying to understand their lived experiences (Crenshaw, 1990). Their experiences within social, political, and economic settings are both gendered and racialized. To be gendered is to have experiences shaped by one's gender; to be racialized is to have those same experiences shaped by one's race. Black women to varying degrees experience the "double disadvantage" of being Black and being female. The phenomenon of gendered racism was first articulated by Philomena Essed (1991) to describe the interconnected experience of racism and sexism for Black women (Thomas et al., 2008). An example of gendered racism is the limited attention given to the murders of unarmed Black women at the hands of police, compared with the murders of unarmed Black men. Although the death of Breonna Taylor occurred two months before the death of George Floyd, her murder did not spark the same level of global outrage, despite Black women experiencing the highest rates of homicide in general (Young & McMahon, 2020).

Black women also experience gendered racism when they are hypersexualized in the media, which has negative ramifications for the physical and mental health and safety of Black girls. This hypersexualization causes Black women and girls to navigate the tension of being hypervisible and receiving unwanted attention while also being invisible when seeking care. Gendered racism also leads to justification of the abuses Black women and girls face and a disregard of their victimization by the criminal justice system.

> We discuss consequences of gendered racism further in Chapter 5 on Black women and trauma.

> Brenda experiences gendered racism related to her sexuality as a lesbian in particular. When she finally came out to her family, their response was to think of it as a phase that she would get over, and they did not take her seriously. Brenda also felt excluded by the Black community when she was in college because her sexuality was not affirmed, and many of her Black male classmates tried to make advances despite the fact that she told them she was only interested in women. Brenda adopted a hardened interpersonal style and a more masculine style of dressing to defend against the hypersexualization that she experienced as a Black woman. All of this was exhausting for Brenda, and she felt like there were not many spaces where she could be her full self.

2.3.3   Contextual Factors

The structural and intermediary determinants of health are all shaped by social, economic, and political contexts. In other words, where a person is born, lives, works, worships, plays, and ages are all influenced by how our government operates, the laws and policies it enacts, and the cultural norms and values of our society. They generate and maintain social hierarchies based on race, gender, and other social identities, dictating who has access to resources and opportunities and who does not; in essence, they create the backdrop of American daily life.

As mentioned previously, the enactment of the ACA in 2014 is one example of how upstream policies have downstream effects on mental health. The ACA not only reduced racial/ethnic disparities in health insurance coverage generally (Buchmueller et al., 2016); it also improved access to no-cost mental health preventative services and prescription drugs by requiring all employer-based insurance plans to cover mental health services at the same level as medical services and by barring the use of preexisting mental health conditions as a reason for denying or limiting mental health care coverage (Baumgartner et al., 2020). The ACA has benefited Black women directly by leading to an increase in health care coverage, reducing cost-related delays in care, and providing greater access to a regular source of care (e.g., a primary care provider, clinic, or health center; Simmons et al., 2016). From a mental health standpoint, the ACA also increased treatment for mental health conditions and decreased unmet mental health needs (Fry & Sommers, 2018).

It is easy to see how health care policies such as the ACA impact the mental health of Black women. Policies related to labor, housing, social, and the economy are also important. For example, the Earned Income Tax Credit (EITC) reduces the amount of taxes that low- to moderate-income workers pay while also providing a tax credit to subsidize or supplement their income (Hotz, 2003). The EITC has been shown to improve the mental health of women with children, including reducing the number of days with poor mental health (Evans & Garthwaite, 2014) and the incidence of poor birth outcomes among pregnant women, including the risk of having a low-birthweight baby (Hoynes et al., 2015). Black women are more likely than White women to receive the EITC (Marr & Huang, 2019), which means their physical and mental health are more likely to benefit from it.

Other factors, including land use policies (e.g., zoning), housing affordability and eviction practices, and the availability of neighborhood amenities and community resources, also affect the health of communities of color and influence health inequities (Wilson et al., 2008). The root of these inequities, however, and the role of social and economic policies in creating and maintaining health inequities are intricately tied to the cultural norms, beliefs, and values of the United States. Do we value health equity and believe that health is a human right, or do we see health as a commodity afforded to the few? Do we view and treat all people as equally deserving of the needed resources and opportunities for social and economic advancement, or do we distribute these resources and opportunities according to preconceived notions of what race, gender, and/or sexual orientation is more valuable than others? The answer to these questions is evident in how the country is governed and the policies that are put into place.

Racism and sexism have shaped our social, economic, and political contexts in ways that systematically marginalize Black women and disproportionately affect their mental health. From policies and practices that led to segregated neighborhoods, hospitals, and schooling to policies that minimized the political voice and representation of women generally and Black women specifically, racism and sexism have been the primary structural drivers of health inequities and influence all the other contextual, structural, and intermediary determinants discussed in this chapter. As a result, any initiative aimed at improving the mental health of Black women and their access to mental health care must be rooted in antiracist and antisexist practices that place the needs and voices of Black women at the center.

Brenda remembers how her mother saved up in an attempt to get them out of their neighborhood as the violence got worse over the years of Brenda's childhood. Brenda's mother eventually saved enough and told Brenda they could finally move to a better neighborhood. But it never happened; every time Brenda's mother applied for a mortgage for a home in a nicer neighborhood she was denied. She was navigating redlining and ended up with a bad, high-interest mortgage for a home in an all-Black neighborhood that was not much better than the one they left. When Brenda's mom was laid off from her auto manufacturing job, she lost the home due to the bad mortgage she had been given.

2.3.4   Case Summary

The example of Brenda's life is intended to illustrate how the individual, intermediary, and structural social determinants of health could play out in the life of one Black woman. This case shows the systems, structures, and individual risk factors Black women must navigate and how they succeed in some areas and experience challenges in others. We provided this case example focusing on Brenda's background to help therapists understand the experiences of their Black female clients in context. In the following chapters, the case examples will illustrate specific strategies and approaches that therapists can consider when working with Black women clients.

2.4 Using the SDOH Approach in Therapy with Black Women

Therapists working with Black female clients should keep the social determinants of health and mental health in mind as they listen to their clients' narratives. Key to this framework is understanding how Black woman's lifestyles and choices are impacted by their social and cultural standing. First, we encourage therapists to acknowledge the intersection of personal and structural conditions in the United States that work together to shape the quality of Black women's lives. This includes acknowledging the pervasiveness of systemic oppression for Black people. In addition, therapists should avoid viewing Black women as broken or in need of pity. Rather, therapists should celebrate ways in which Black women transcend everyday limitations to create opportunities for themselves and their families. For example, despite growing up in a poor neighborhood and with little family income to afford college, Brenda earned a college degree. A college degree increased her job opportunities, and Brenda used it to advance her career. Second, therapists should help their Black female clients name and acknowledge the impact of social and political issues on their own lives. Helping women name the impact of factors outside of their control can foster self-compassion to mitigate the blaming attitudes Black women encounter in health and medical systems. Black women's self-compassion can also jump-start their desire to make lifestyle changes to fight for health and wellness. Helping Black women make such connections can release them from cycles of self-shame and self-doubt, increasing a sense of agency to change the things they can change. Third, therapists should help Black women cast aside the narrative that they are solely to blame for their health and mental health conditions. In doing so, therapists can help their Black female clients connect the dots between their personal challenges and societal factors. Finally, therapists can be cheerleaders and encouragers as women try to overcome their historical, cultural, and social limitations to increase their wellness. The therapist's posture of encouragement, support, and motivation can be a corrective to the shame, blame, and pity that Black women experience in multiple settings.

Brenda's therapist helped her understand that she grew up in a food desert. Brenda was not aware of this concept and never fully understood how childhood and adolescent choices around food may have affected her adult eating habits. Brenda also never grasped that her family's economic standing and neighborhood resources offered fewer opportunities for the types of recreational pursuits that were available to youths growing up in well-resourced neighborhoods. Brenda's

---

therapist helped her understand the connection between adverse childhood experiences and her body's stress response. Additionally, the therapist helped Brenda recognize how the stress triggers driven by experiences of gendered racism in her workplace could be related to overeating and weight gain. Once Brenda saw these connections, she was open to working with the therapist to expand her coping strategies to avoid overeating. The therapist encouraged Brenda to join a group fitness challenge at work with other women, taking advantage of a company-sponsored event to increase her health literacy. This support of Brenda's acquisition of health information on stress and obesity through psychoeducation acknowledged the intersection of physical and mental health.

2.5   Why Understanding Social Determinants of Health Matters in Therapy

For many non-Black people, reading about the social, political, and historical factors that influence the lives of Black women and hearing the fictional – but true-to-life – story of Brenda's lived experiences can be surprising and overwhelming, and this may also be true for some Black readers. History education in the United States does not adequately cover the systems and structures of oppression in this society. Further, US society prides itself on individualism and typically blames poor people and Black and Latinx people for the difficult circumstances they experience. It is not uncommon for non-Black therapists to feel overwhelmed by the numerous challenges that Black women experience in navigating their daily lives. While this overwhelming feeling may stem from empathy for Black women, it often renders the therapist ineffective in empowering Black women to make sense of their experiences and move forward in their lives with agency.

Given that this information may be new, and it may have challenged some of your worldviews and beliefs, we encourage you to reflect on the questions at the end of the chapter and attend to your cognitive, emotional, and physical responses to this chapter. The reflection questions may evoke feelings of resistance or guilt, and we encourage you to sit with those feelings and allow them to be there and to guide your understanding of yourself and your life experiences. Additionally, throughout the rest of this book we will share specific recommendations of strategies clinicians can use as they support Black women who are navigating the many stressors and systemic forces highlighted in this chapter.

In Chapter 6, which is focused on the cultural self of the therapist, you will be guided to deeply explore the life experiences that have shaped you as a person and influence the therapy you provide to Black women.

Therapist Reflection Questions

1. How do you feel when you read about the systemic oppression that Black women experience?
2. What are your reactions to the idea that Black women may be aging faster biologically than non-Black women?
3. What are your thoughts on the mainstream American narratives that Black people are to blame for the poverty, health challenges, and other issues that they experience?
4. How can understanding the social determinants of health for Black women inform your work with Black women in therapy?
5. How can you utilize the SDOH model to support your exploration of the lived experiences of your Black female clients?
6. How can you help dismantle systemic barriers for Black women related to sexism and racism? Examples might include increasing accessibility of the services you offer by accepting insurance or having a sliding scale and ensuring that you use inclusive language and images in your registration forms and marketing materials.

Resources for Therapists

The following resources are intended to help therapists further understand the social, historical, and political experiences that impact Black women's health and mental health.

Organizations

Black Women's Health Imperative. (n.d.). https://bwhi.org/
Fertility for Colored Girls. (n.d.). https://www.fertilityforcoloredgirls.org/

Books

Evans, S. Y., Bell, K., & Burton, N. K. (2017). *Black women's mental health: Balancing strength & vulnerability.* SUNY Press.
Perry, A. M. (2020). *Know your price: Valuing Black lives and property in America's Black cities.* Brookings Institution Press.
Singh, A. A. (2019). *The racial healing handbook: Practical activities to help you challenge privilege, confront systemic racism, & engage in collective healing.* New Harbinger Publications.
Wilkerson, I. (2020). *Caste: The origins of our discontents.* Random House.
Zeigler, I. B. (2021). *Nobody knows the trouble I've seen: The emotional lives of black women now your price: Valuing Black lives and property in America's Black cities.* Harper Collins Publishers.

Articles

Coates, T. N. (2015). The case for reparations. In S. Holt (Ed.), *The Best American Magazine Writing 2015* (pp. 1–50). Columbia University Press.

References

Allen, A. M., Thomas, M. D., Michaels, E. K., Reeves, A. N., Okoye, U., Price, M. M., Hasson, R. E., Syme, S. L., & Chae, D. H. (2019). Racial discrimination, educational attainment, and biological dysregulation among midlife African American women. *Psychoneuroendocrinology, 99*, 225–235.

Armstrong, N., Ryder, S., Forbes, C., Ross, J., & Quek, R. G. (2019). A systematic review of the international prevalence of BRCA mutation in breast cancer. *Clinical Epidemiology, 11*, 543–561.

Assari, S., Moazen-Zadeh, E., Caldwell, C. H., & Zimmerman, M. A. (2017). Racial discrimination during adolescence predicts mental health deterioration in adulthood: Gender differences among Blacks. *Frontiers in Public Health, 5*, 104.

Baumgartner, J. C., Aboulafia, G. N., & McIntosh, A. (2020, April 3). *The ACA at 10: How has it impacted mental health care?* The Commonwealth Fund. https://www.commonwealthfund.org/blog/2020/aca-10-how-has-it-impacted-mental-health-care

Bell, C. N., Sacks, T. K., Tobin, C. S. T., & Thorpe, R. J., Jr. (2020). Racial non-equivalence of socioeconomic status and self-rated health among African Americans and Whites. *SSM-Population Health, 10*, 100561.

Bell, C. N., Thorpe, R. J., Jr., Bowie, J. V., & LaVeist, T. A. (2018). Race disparities in cardiovascular disease risk factors within socioeconomic status strata. *Annals of Epidemiology, 28*(3), 147–152.

Bethea, T. N., Zhou, E. S., Schernhammer, E. S., Castro-Webb, N., Cozier, Y. C., & Rosenberg, L. (2020). Perceived racial discrimination and risk of insomnia among middle-aged and elderly Black women. *Sleep, 43*(1), zsz208.

Braveman, P., Heck, K., Egerter, S., Dominguez, T. P., Rinki, C., Marchi, K. S., & Curtis, M. (2017). Worry about racial discrimination: A missing piece of the puzzle of Black-White disparities in preterm birth? *PLoS ONE, 12*(10), e0186151.

Brito, C. (2020, April 29). *Beloved New York City teacher dies from coronavirus after family claims she was denied testing twice.* CBS News. https://www.cbsnews.com/news/rana-zoe-mungin-brooklyn-teacher-coronavirus-dies-denied-testing

Buchmueller, T. C., Levinson, Z. M., Levy, H. G., & Wolfe, B. L. (2016). Effect of the Affordable Care Act on racial and ethnic disparities in health insurance coverage. *American Journal of Public Health, 106*(8), 1416–1421.

Burgess, D. J., Ding, Y., Hargreaves, M., Van Ryn, M., & Phelan, S. (2008). The association between perceived discrimination and underutilization of needed medical and mental health care in a multi-ethnic community sample. *Journal of Health Care for the Poor and Underserved, 19*(3), 894–911.

Byfield, E. & Intarasuwan, K. (2020, June 4). *Along with COVID, racial trauma takes extra mental toll on African Americans.* NBC New York. https://www.nbcnewyork.com/news/local/along-with-covid-racial-trauma-takes-extra-mental-toll-on-african-americans/2442886/

Centers for Disease Control and Prevention. (2019, September 5). *Racial and ethnic disparities continue in pregnancy-related deaths* [Press release]. https://www.cdc.gov/media/releases/2019/p0905-racial-ethnic-disparities-pregnancy-deaths.html

Centers for Disease Control and Prevention. (2020). *Obesity, race/ethnicity and COVID-19.* https://www.cdc.gov/obesity/data/obesity-and-covid-19.html

Chen, J., Vargas-Bustamante, A., Mortensen, K., & Ortega, A. N. (2016). Racial and ethnic disparities in health care access and utilization under the Affordable Care Act. *Medical Care, 54*(2), 140–146.

Cosselman, K. E., Navas-Acien, A., & Kaufman, J. D. (2015). Environmental factors in cardiovascular disease. *Nature Reviews Cardiology, 12*(11), 627–642.

Crenshaw, K. (1990). Mapping the margins: Intersectionality, identity politics, and violence against women of color. *Stanford Law Review, 43*, 1241–1299.

Culhane, J. F., & Elo, I. T. (2005). Neighborhood context and reproductive health. *American Journal of Obstetrics and Gynecology, 192*(5), S22–S29.

Dastagir, A. E. (2020, June 21). "A culmination of crises": America is in turmoil, and a mental health crisis looms next. *USA Today.* https://www.usatoday.com/story/news/health/2020/06/20/covid-racism-recession-mental-health-impacts-may-long-lasting/3211464001/

Davis, E. M., Rovi, S., & Johnson, M. S. (2005). Mental health, family function and obesity in African-American women. *Journal of the National Medical Association, 97*(4), 478–482.

Dubowitz, T., Heron, M., Basurto-Davila, R., Bird, C. E., Lurie, N., & Escarce, J. J. (2011). Racial/ethnic differences in US health behaviors: A decomposition analysis. *American Journal of Health Behavior, 35*(3), 290–304.

Edwards, F., Lee, H., & Esposito, M. (2019). Risk of being killed by police use of force in the United States by age, race–ethnicity, and sex. *Proceedings of the National Academy of Sciences, 116*(34), 16793–16798.

Essed, P. (1991). *Understanding everyday racism: An interdisciplinary theory: Vol. 2.* Sage.

Ettman, C. K., Abdalla, S. M., Cohen, G. H., Sampson, L., Vivier, P. M., & Galea, S. (2020). Prevalence of depression symptoms in US adults before and during the COVID-19 pandemic. *JAMA Network Open, 3*(9), e2019686–e201968616798.

Evans, W. N., & Garthwaite, C. L. (2014). Giving mom a break: The impact of higher EITC payments on maternal health. *American Economic Journal: Economic Policy, 6*(2), 258–290.

Fishman, S. (2020). An extended evaluation of the weathering hypothesis for birthweight. *Demographic Research, 43*, 929–968.

Fowers, A., & Wan, W. (2020, June 12). Depression and anxiety spike after George Floyd's death. *The Washington Post.* https://www.washingtonpost.com/health/2020/06/12/mental-health-george-floyd-census

Fry, C. E., & Sommers, B. D. (2018). Effect of Medicaid expansion on health insurance coverage and access to care among adults with depression. *Psychiatric Services, 69*(11), 1146–1152.

Geronimus, A. T., Hicken, M. T., Pearson, J. A., Seashols, S. J., Brown, K. L., & Cruz, T. D. (2010). Do US Black women experience stress-related accelerated biological aging?: A novel theory and first population-based test of Black-White differences in telomere length. *Human Nature, 21*(1), 19–38.

Ghosh-Dastidar, B., Cohen, D., Hunter, G., Zenk, S. N., Huang, C., Beckman, R., & Dubowitz, T. (2014). Distance to store, food prices, and obesity in urban food deserts. *American Journal of Preventive Medicine, 47*(5), 587–595.

Hall, J. C., Everett, J. E., & Hamilton-Mason, J. (2012). Black women talk about workplace stress and how they cope. *Journal of Black Studies, 43*(2), 207–226.

Hatzenbuehler, M. L., Keyes, K. M., Narrow, W. E., Grant, B. F., & Hasin, D. S. (2008). Racial/ethnic disparities in service utilization for individuals with co-occurring mental health and substance use disorders in the general population. *The Journal of Clinical Psychiatry, 69*(7), 1112–1121.

Himmelstein, M. S., Young, D. M., Sanchez, D. T., & Jackson, J. S. (2015). Vigilance in the discrimination-stress model for Black Americans. *Psychology & Health, 30* (3), 253–267.

Hotz, V. J. (2003). The earned income tax credit. In R. A. Moffit (Ed.) *Means-tested transfer programs in the United States* (pp. 141–198). University of Chicago Press.

Hoynes, H., Miller, D., & Simon, D. (2015). Income, the earned income tax credit, and infant health. *American Economic Journal: Economic Policy, 7*(1), 172–211.

Hudson, D. L., Neighbors, H. W., Geronimus, A. T., & Jackson, J. S. (2016). Racial discrimination, John Henryism, and depression among African Americans. *Journal of Black Psychology, 42*(3), 221–243.

John, E. M., Miron, A., Gong, G., Phipps, A. I., Felberg, A., Li, F. P., West, D. W., & Whittemore, A. S. (2007). Prevalence of pathogenic BRCA1 mutation carriers in 5 US racial/ethnic groups. *JAMA, 298*(24), 2869–2876.

Jones, C. P. (2002). *Confronting institutionalized racism.* Phylon.

Kaiser Family Foundation. (2013, March 13). *Health coverage by race and ethnicity: The potential impact of the Affordable Care Act* (Issue brief). https://www.kff.org/racial-equity-and-health-policy/issue-brief/health-coverage-by-race-and-ethnicity-the-potential-impact-of-the-affordable-care-act

Marr, C., & Huang, Y. (2019, September 9). *Women of color especially benefit from working family tax credit.* Center on Budget and Policy Priorities. https://www.cbpp.org/research/federal-tax/women-of-color-especially-benefit-from-working-family-tax-credits

Martin, N. & Montagne, R. (2017, December 7). *Black mothers keep dying after giving birth. Shalon Irving's story explains why.* NPR. https://www.npr.org/2017/12/07/568948782/black-mothers-keep-dying-after-giving-birth-shalon-irvings-story-explains-why

Massey, D., & Denton, N. A. (1993). *American apartheid: Segregation and the making of the underclass.* Harvard University Press.

Meadows-Fernandez, A. R. (2020, May 28). *The unbearable grief of Black mothers.* Vox. https://www.vox.com/platform/amp/first-person/2020/5/28/21272380/black-mothers-grief-sadness-covid-19?__twitter_impression=true

National Council for Behavioral Health. (2018, October 10). *America's mental health, 2018.* https://www.cohenveteransnetwork.org/wp-content/uploads/2018/10/Research-Summary-10-10-2018.pdf

Navaie-Waliser, M., Spriggs, A., & Feldman, P. H. (2002). Informal caregiving: differential experiences by gender. *Medical Care, 40*(12), 1249–1259.

Ogle, C. M., Rubin, D. C., & Siegler, I. C. (2013). The impact of the developmental timing of trauma exposure on PTSD symptoms and psychosocial functioning among older adults. *Developmental Psychology, 49*(11), 2191–2200.

Purtle, J. (2020). COVID-19 and mental health equity in the United States. *Social Psychiatry and Psychiatric Epidemiology, 55*(8), 969–971.

Richardson, A. S., Boone-Heinonen, J., Popkin, B. M., & Gordon-Larsen, P. (2011). Neighborhood fast food restaurants and fast food consumption: A national study. *BMC Public Health, 11*(1), 543.

Rodriguez, C. (2016). Mothering while Black: Feminist thought on maternal loss, mourning and agency in the African diaspora. *Transforming Anthropology, 24*(1), 61–69.

Saha, S., Arbelaez, J. J., & Cooper, L. A. (2003). Patient–physician relationships and racial disparities in the quality of health care. *American Journal of Public Health, 93*(10), 1713–1719.

Sawyer, P. J., Major, B., Casad, B. J., Townsend, S. S., & Mendes, W. B. (2012). Discrimination and the stress response: Psychological and physiological consequences of anticipating prejudice in interethnic interactions. *American Journal of Public Health, 102*(5), 1020–1026.

Simmons, A., Taylor, J., Finegold, K., Yabroff, R., Gee, E., & Chappel, A. (2016, June 14). *The Affordable Care Act: Promoting better health for women.* U.S. Department of Health and Human Services. https://aspe.hhs.gov/system/files/pdf/205066/ACAWomenHealthIssueBrief.pdf

Slopen, N., Koenen, K. C., & Kubzansky, L. D. (2012). Childhood adversity and immune and inflammatory biomarkers associated with cardiovascular risk in youth: A systematic review. *Brain, Behavior, and Immunity, 26*(2), 239–250.

Smedley, B. D., Stith, A. Y., Nelson, A. R., & Institute of Medicine. (2003). *Unequal treatment: Confronting racial and ethnic disparities in health care.* National Academy Press.

Snowden, L. R. (2003). Bias in mental health assessment and intervention: Theory and evidence. *American Journal of Public Health, 93*(2), 239–243.

Substance Abuse and Mental Health Services Administration. (2015). *Racial/ethnic differences in mental health service use among adults* (HHS Publication No. SMA-15-4906). https://www.samhsa.gov/data/sites/default/files/MHServicesUseAmongAdults/MHServicesUseAmongAdults.pdf

Substance Abuse and Mental Health Services Administration. (2019). *Results from the 2018 national survey on drug use and health: Detailed tables.* https://www.samhsa.gov/data/report/2018-nsduh-detailed-tables

Thomas, A. J., Witherspoon, K. M., & Speight, S. L. (2008). Gendered racism, psychological distress, and coping styles of African American women. *Cultural Diversity and Ethnic Minority Psychology, 14*(4), 307–314. https://doi.org/10.1037/1099-9809.14.4.307

U.S. Department of Health and Human Services, Office of Minority Health. (2021, July 8). *Infant mortality and African Americans.* https://minorityhealth.hhs.gov/omh/browse.aspx?lvl=4&lvlid=23

VanderWielen, L. M., Gilchrist, E. C., Nowels, M. A., Petterson, S. M., Rust, G., & Miller, B. F. (2015). Not near enough: Racial and ethnic disparities in access to nearby behavioral health care and primary care. *Journal of Health Care for the Poor and Underserved, 26*(3), 1032–1047.

Villarosa, L. (2018, April 11). Why America's Black mothers and babies are in a life-or-death crisis. *The New York Times.* https://www.nytimes.com/2018/04/11/ magazine/black-mothers-babies-death-maternal-mortality.html

Wang, X., Auchincloss, A. H., Barber, S., Mayne, S. L., Griswold, M. E., Sims, M., & Roux, A. V. D. (2017). Neighborhood social environment as risk factors to health behavior among African Americans: The Jackson heart study. *Health & Place, 45,* 199–207.

Williams, D. R. (2002). Racial/ethnic variations in women's health: the social embeddedness of health. *American Journal of Public Health, 92*(4), 588–597.

Wilson, S., Hutson, M., & Mujahid, M. (2008). How planning and zoning contribute to inequitable development, neighborhood health, and environmental injustice. *Environmental Justice, 1*(4), 211–216.

World Health Organization. (n.d.). *Social determinants of health.* Retrieved October 10, 2022, from https://www.who.int/health-topics/social-determinants-of-health#tab= tab_1

Young, R., & McMahon, S. (2020, June 16). *#SayHerName puts spotlight on Black women killed by police.* WBUR. https://www.wbur.org/hereandnow/2020/06/16/ black-women-deaths-protests

3   Black Girlhood: Developmental Experiences of Black Women

with Chisina Kapungu[*]

> Growing up as a black girl, I was always told I have to work twice as hard because of my skin tone.
>
> Zoe Sinclair Watkins (2016)

The opening quotation is from a poignant poem by author and blogger Zoe Sinclair Watkins. Watkins (2016) describes her experiences growing up as a Black girl. Watkins captures what many Black women say about their childhood and adolescence. In Watkins's picture of black girlhood, she describes conditions that threatened her understanding of herself. However, Watkins also describes buffers and resources such as family and role models who encouraged her aspirations. This poem caught our attention because it mirrors what Black women tell us in therapy about the social, emotional, and behavioral experiences in their developing years. In our Psychotherapy and Black Women study, 64% of our sample of 227 Black women endorsed childhood and adolescent experiences as stressors. Therefore, emotional memories of Black girlhood might trouble Black women even in their adult lives.

We use the term *girlhood* to refer to the childhood and adolescent years of Black women. Historically, Black girlhood has been understudied, and recent research reveals the complexities of this life period (Buckley & Carter, 2005; Butler-Barnes et al., 2017a, 2017b). Some Black women recall girlhood as pleasant, humorous, and fun, not particularly jarring. These could have been some of their best years. For other Black women, their girlhoods were scarred by shaming experiences, leaving wounds in their bodies and souls. For another group of Black women, girlhood involved adverse childhood events. These are the storylines we hear in therapy, and many Black women have experienced more than one. Our Black female clients tell us these stories primarily because their girlhood experiences trouble their present-day lives. Black women might also worry about the girlhood experiences of Black girls they are raising or

[*] C. Kapungu, D. Baptiste, & Gooden, A. (2023). Black girlhood: Developmental experiences of Black women. In D. Baptiste & A. Gooden, *Promoting Black women's mental health: What practitioners should know and do*. Cambridge University Press.

influencing. Therapists serving Black women should be prepared to address the impacts of Black women's early developmental experiences through a past, present, and future lens.

This chapter highlights themes that therapists might encounter in Black women's stories about their girlhood. We examine the experience of racial and gender socialization and gendered racial identity on Black girls' self-concepts and psychological functioning (Brown et al., 2017; Hughes et al., 2006). We also discuss Black girls' self-images based on societal views, especially in media. We explore the ripple effects of the adultification of Black girls, who many see as less innocent and more adultlike than girls of other racial and ethnic groups. We also discuss Black girls' sexual development and vulnerabilities. Finally, we comment on LGBTQ girls, who may be severely misunderstood and marginalized by gender, race, and class, in addition to other minority identities.

An intersectional lens is critical to exploring identity development of Black girls and Black women. For example, although we use the descriptor "*racial*" identity, a more apt term may be *racial-ethnic* identity, that is, experiences in which race and ethnicity are inextricably combined. For simplicity, we maintain the term *race* and *racial* in this chapter's discussions acknowledging that race alone does not explain the marginalizing experiences faced by Black people in the United States.

Our emphasis in this chapter is on adult Black women who attend therapy to address residual stress and trauma from childhood and adolescence. However, this information can also help therapists who work with Black girls as their clients. We recommend a Positive Youth Development framework for working with Black girls, which emphasizes prevention and resilience. Promoting the strengths of Black girls through supportive contexts and providing opportunities for socioemotional development can help facilitate positive outcomes (Lerner et al., 2005). Black girls thrive when they have supportive adults in their lives, when they are connected to their schools and communities, and when they feel empowered to leverage their voices for social change (Search Institute, 2018). Throughout the discussion, we highlight the role of protective and preventive factors that positively shape Black girls into psychologically competent Black women. We start with racial and gender socialization of Black girls, which are core to their self-concepts and identities as women.

3.1   Black Girls: Racial and Gender Socialization

> Growing up as a black girl, I was able to see the First Black President along with his African American wife and two gorgeous daughters come into the oval office. (Watkins, 2016)

Like adults, Black youth face racial stressors and hassles that marginalize them and decrease their social standing (Butler-Barnes et al., 2019). Parents and caregivers (hereafter parents) have the unique challenge of raising Black youth of all genders to understand themselves racially (Brown et al., 2017). Along with racial socialization, gender socialization also matters significantly to Black girls. We offer a brief synopsis of these socialization strategies to emphasize their importance to Black girls' mental health and wellness.

Over 200 studies, including almost 100,000 Black youth of all genders, make it clear that experiences of discrimination and oppression relate directly to the quality of Black youth self-concepts, identities, mental health risk, school achievement, and successes in adulthood (Benner et al., 2018). This reality makes Black parents eager to diminish the impacts of marginalization and oppression in their children's lives. Parents yearn to prepare youth for a country and communities suffused with anti-Black racism and White racial privilege. Peters (1985) defines racial socialization as a parent's responsibility to raise children to understand themselves as members of the Black race, and this kind of socialization prepares youth for the positive and negative connotations of being Black.

Black parents promote racial socialization in their youth by emphasizing Black cultural heritage and traditions and cultural pride. Parents can also help children understand racial hostility, White privilege, and discrimination (Brown et al., 2017; Stevenson et al., 2002; Umaña-Taylor & Hill, 2020). Black parents can directly influence their youngsters' beliefs, attitudes, and behavior through a race-positive posture and their admiration for Black icons (Yasui, 2015). Race positivity in parents and caregivers helps Black youth to think well of themselves and supports development of a positive racial identity in adulthood (Peck et al., 2014).

Family socioeconomic status (SES) may moderate parents' capacity to provide adequate racial socialization for Black youth. Research indicates that lower-SES Black parents report fewer racial socialization efforts than higher-SES Black families (Peck et al., 2014). Overall, through racial socialization, Black parents balance affirming the Black identities of their children while preparing them to navigate direct and subtle anti-Black values.

For Black girls and women, race and gender combine to increase oppression, as explained in earlier chapters. Thus, Black girls need gendered racial socialization as distinct from just racial socialization alone. Gendered racial socialization addresses the experience of being Black *and* female, identities that cannot be disentangled (Brown et al., 2017; Jones & Day, 2018). Parental socialization of girls can at times omit race or gender, and Black girls need both (Stokes et al., 2020). For example, Black mothers might prepare their sons to cope with racial discrimination by emphasizing racial profiling and discrimination in law enforcement and the legal system. Those same mothers might emphasize self-esteem, relationship skills, and independence for Black girls. Parents might also emphasize social advocacy and influence in their daughter's lives (Smith-Bynum et al., 2016). Research suggests that being Black and female, girls are also at risk of discrimination and maltreatment from law enforcement and legal systems (Thomas & Blackmon, 2015) and the fact that Black girls do not receive such messages is in and of itself reflective of gender bias. In essence, while many Black families support mutuality and egalitarianism in family responsibilities patriarchal values in family life can lead to differential socialization of boys and girls (Chavous et al., 2008).

Therapists might ask Black women about their families' strategies to strengthen their positive self-images regarding their Blackness and their womanhood. Hearing these stories may reveal strength and vulnerabilities in women's understanding of themselves regarding race and gender. Women's racial and gender socialization stories may also relate to how women cope in their present lives (Davis Tribble et al., 2019). Therapists should also be aware that exposing Black girls to empowering racial and gendered messages protects their mental health. Black girls who hear oppressive statements about Black women are more likely to report negative feelings about being Black and female. They can have a poor self-image and poor mental health (Anderson & Stevenson, 2019). Therapists might explore communication from adults in the family related to messages that emphasize Black pride, promote mistrust, and prepare girls for race-related encounters. Therapists might also encourage parents to highlight gender discrimination and reinforce egalitarian messages that encourage individual worth and equality regardless of race (Hughes et al., 2006).

When Black women grieve ways in which they were inadequately prepared to understand gendered racism, they may also worry about the next generation of Black girls under their care and influence (e.g., biological, foster children, relatives, and non-kin). Thus, Black women's past, present, and future anxieties and disempowerment are often intertwined in their present distress and suffering. Some Black women may feel mistrust and hypersensitivity, which can color their socialization strategies. Black women who experienced gendered racial discrimination in girlhood may need support to provide positive socialization messages to their daughters.

Helping Black women to craft action-oriented steps that interrupt negative cycles in young people's lives can have an empowering therapeutic effect. Therapists might explore communication patterns among adults in the historical and present family related to racial and gender socialization. For example, a therapist might ask about what messages and experiences fostered or promoted Black pride. Therapists might also explore with Black women how they prepare their daughters and other young women they care for or mentor for encounters with race and gender discrimination, reinforcing egalitarian messages and promoting feelings of individual worth (Hughes et al., 2006). An active past–present–future orientation in therapeutic conversations about Black women's social experiences can increase women's capacity to make peace with the past. We now discuss racial and gender identity development, a concept related to Black girls' socialization that is foundational to how girls and women understand themselves. We continue to emphasize that the seeds of competent Black womanhood are laid down in the tender and developing years.

3.2   Racial and Gender Identity Development

> Growing up as a black girl, I never let anyone tell me I can't achieve greatness because of my skin color. (Watkins, 2016)

We encourage therapists to ask Black female clients about their racial and gender identity and trace how these identities developed in girlhood. Racial identity development centers on two key aspects. The first is *racial centrality*, which is the degree to which a Black woman or girl might emphasize Blackness as a critical aspect of their self-concept. The second aspect is *private regard*: positive or negative attitudes, sometimes unspoken, that a Black person might hold about themselves and other Black people (Sellers et al., 1998). Research confirms that Black girls with higher racial *centrality* and positive *private regard* generally are less stressed. In addition, these girls experience fewer mental health conditions than youth with lower race-central attitudes or those who feel negatively about Black people (Neblett et al., 2013; Rivas-Drake et al., 2014; Sellers et al., 2006). If Black girls hold positive feelings about being Black, they are likely to shrug off negative stereotypes about Black people. Thus, positive racial identity promotes resilience and mental wellness.

Like gendered racial socialization on the part of parents, therapists should be aware of the limitations of only using a racial lens to understand Black girls' identity development. Racial-gender identity development relates to Black girls' feelings of affirmation and pride about being Black *and* female. It also includes Black girls' beliefs and attitudes toward Black women's histories and capacities (Nishina et al., 2010; Sellers et al., 1998; Umaña-Taylor et al., 2014). Therapists should ask about Black women's early memories of being Black and female in different contexts such as the family, school, peer relationships, romantic interests, and in a self-relationship (i.e., Rivas-Drake et al., 2014). For example, for each setting a therapist might ask: "Thinking of your young self, how did people respond to you not just as black or female, but both? What were your experiences as a Black female?" In the social microcosm of schools and other social settings, Black girls may experience forms of marginalization different from those experienced by Black boys, who are privileged in sex and gender. For example, Black girls get negative scrutiny on their hair and are viewed as lowest on the romantic desirability ladder (Crosnoe, 2011). Teachers and peers may also underestimate Black girls in math and science, or Black girls may be stereotyped as loud and unapproachable (Holland, 2012; Lei, 2003; Suárez-Orozco, 2004).

Therapists should support Black women to identify the factors that enhanced and constricted their positive self-image in girlhood. Several interventions can be helpful. Therapists might coach Black women to consider the positive benefits of highlighting Black women's contributions. Being proactive about the future might help Black women regain a sense of agency and empowerment; therapists might help women understand how to mentor young women in activities that bolster pride in their racial and gender identity. For example, Black girls who participate in programs that highlight Black and female role models have increased self-love, positive self-image, and a capacity to withstand stereotypes. Research in two programs for Black girls has shown these effects. "Young Empowered Sisters" (YES!), a 10-week intervention teaching African American history and contemporary culture, increased girls' racial centeredness, and racism awareness (Thomas et al., 2008). Similarly, Black girls who participated in "Sisters of Nia: A Cultural Program for African American Girls," an in-school rite-of-passage program, had greater ethnic identity awareness, engagement, and positive social attitudes than a control group (Aston et al., 2018).

The central theme in these recommendations is helping Black women heal the past through actions that reverse the power of the conditions that disadvantaged them. When Black women break cycles, their empowerment increases, as does their sense of self, a strategy that can mitigate the hurt and pain of underdeveloped racial and gender identities.

3.2.1   Black Girls' Body Image: The Power of Representation

> Growing up as Black girl, guys were never attracted to me because I didn't have long silky hair, blue or hazel eyes, and what they thought was beautiful light skin. (Watkins, 2016)

Watkins (2016) captures well how Black girls battle to love and honor themselves amid everyday encounters that suggest they are unworthy. For Black girls, seeing themselves represented in images and artifacts can make a difference to their self-concepts. Martin (2021) wrote a CBS News Boston story titled "'Representation Matters,' Sales of Diverse Dolls Booming at Mall Kiosk." This report told the story of a young entrepreneur, Widline Pyrame, a Black woman whose business venture, Fusion Dolls, sells dolls that Black girls enjoy. Pyrame's impetus for starting Fusion Dolls was her experience growing up in Haiti; all her dolls were White. In graduate school to complete her social work degree, Pyrame learned about the historical Kent doll studies (described next). She committed to developing a business sponsoring dolls where Black girls might recognize themselves. From Fusion Dolls, people can buy a diverse array of Black dolls with various skin tones and hair types. The dolls' hair can match popular hairstyles of Black women, including braids and natural Afros. Pyrame describes the joy her business brings her.

"It was so exciting for me when I get to meet the kids and see their faces when they see our dolls," she said. "A little girl, her mom had gotten a doll from me for her birthday, and she came back to me and then said, 'Thank you so much for creating a doll that looked like me,' and she gave me a hug. And honestly, that made my day." (Martin, 2021)

The research that compelled Pyrame to design dolls for Black girls – along with a recent replication – demonstrates how persisting negative images of Black girls affect their self-concepts. In the 1940s, psychologists Kenneth and Mamie Clark conducted experiments known as "the doll tests" to study the psychological effects of segregation on Black children (Clark & Clark, 1947). The Clarks used four dolls, identical except for skin color, to test the extent to which children's race and color influence their judgment about themselves, specifically their self-esteem. Black children aged 3–7 years were given White and Black dolls and then asked which dolls were "good," "bad," "nice," and "mean." Most children preferred the White doll and assigned positive qualities to it. The researchers concluded that Black children formed a racial identity by the age of 3. By that age, Black girls can also attach negative traits and feelings of inferiority to their own look's identity, shaped by prejudice and segregation.

In 2010, Margaret Beale Spencer, a leading researcher in child development, replicated the doll study for CNN (CNN, 2010a). Spencer and her team interviewed 133 children from 8 schools in New York and Georgia. The research team worked with children aged 4–5 years and 9–10 years in each school. Team psychologists showed children five identical cartoon pictures of children with skin color ranging from light to dark. Results showed that White children still identified their skin tone with positive comments showing White bias. White children also had negative sentiments toward dark skin tones. Even Black children showed favorability to White skin, but far less than White children, which was an encouraging result. Beale was surprised at the minor changes in White children's attitudes since the 1940s doll studies, noting that White children maintained negative stereotypes about Black children. Spencer was also surprised that older children still held negative attributions about Black children. Spencer concluded that "we are still living in a society where dark things are devalued, and white things are valued" (CNN, 2010b, para. 16).

Therapists should be aware that, consciously and unconsciously, Black girls understand their negative status in a hierarchy whose appearance is considered beautiful, especially in media. Negative media images of Black girls dramatically affect their young self-concepts and confidence (Morris, 2007). Central to this discussion is how popular culture and media misrepresent who girls are. In therapy, Black women may discuss self-esteem challenges that began in girlhood, persisting today (Stephens & Phillips, 2007; Way et al., 2013). Black girls' struggles around self-esteem may manifest in concerns about looks and beauty. Black women may recall girlhood years filled with shame over their skin color, hair texture and length, facial features, and body images. They may have looked longingly at peers whose appearance aligned with White beauty ideals. In addition, Black girls may experience colorism in their communities or even in their families, where feelings about skin color and hair texture reflect bias (Celious & Oyserman, 2001).

Chapter 4 explores stereotypes of Black women that also affect Black girls. In Chapter 12 we discuss the effects of appearance bias. Therapists might also review Chapter 14 on fostering inner healing and thriving in Black women, including several ways Black women might address wounds in the self through strategies that rebuild their self-love, positive regard, and self-compassion.

The doll study offered some encouragement about Black girls' attitudes about Black appearance. Some Black children in the CNN doll study were eloquent in rejecting negative views of their appearance or self-worth. Follow-up interviews with parents of children in the study showed that image-positive children were raised by Black caregivers, teaching them to embrace their ethnic and cultural heritage. Black women who gain a complete understanding of how stereotypes have distorted their self-images can break this cycle in raising their daughters. Women's self-healing can lead to radical change in raising children to love and affirm themselves (Jones et al., 2018).

In another positive outcome, CNN did 11-year follow-ups with 2 young people who, at age 5 and 6 years, were part of the CNN doll test (Cooper, 2021). These individuals saw their young selves identify Black children as bad, ugly, unlikable, and so on. Now older, these young people eloquently rejected any sense of inferiority about their race, skin color, or sense of self. Experiences that changed them include heightened awareness of race and gender stereotypes and positive messages about racial and gender identity. Specifically, for the young Black woman, seeing her young self name the Black child in the doll test as inferior was a transformative moment. Each young person listed experiences that helped them withstand stereotypes, including creative outlets and association with affirming pursuits in the Black community. We found the story of their transformation uplifting and have added it to our list of resources at the end of this chapter (Cooper, 2021).

3.2.2 The Adultification of Black Girls

> Growing up as a black girl, I was always told "Don't be no crazy baby mama, you better keep your legs closed. You gone have 6 babies while your man on child support." (Watkins, 2016)

Therapists should have a solid grasp of a little-understood phenomenon, adultification, that affects the lives of Black girls, sometimes dramatically. Black women, too, may be unaware of this painful childhood and adolescent experience for which they had no name (Gerding & Aubrey, 2018; Morris, 2019). Adultification bias is a unique form of racial and gender prejudice against Black girls that affects how authority figures (i.e., teachers, parents, and law enforcement) comfort, discipline, mentor, and interact with them. Research from Georgetown Law's Center on Poverty and Inequality reveals that adults view Black girls as less innocent and more adultlike than White girls. Adults also view Black girls as more aggressive, more sexually aware, and less in need of support and care than non-Black girls (Epstein et al., 2017). Adultification biases confirm the well-recognized finding that Black girls receive harsher discipline than White girls.

Starting in childhood, adults view Black girls as "sassy" or as having attitude problems. These perceptions are rooted in stereotypes of Black women as angry (Morris, 2019). Experts also link the adultification of Black girls to their disproportionate representation in classroom discipline, school suspension, and referrals to the juvenile justice system. Adultification experiences also directly drive Black girls' school-to-prison pipeline (Epstein et al., 2017).

> In Chapter 5, we discuss adultification as a type of trauma Black girls experience.

We recommend that therapists, when working with Black female clients, label the "adultified" experience and invite Black women to examine their girlhood experiences through this lens. Many women, hearing about adultification bias for the first time, resonate with this description of the dynamics they have experienced in their young lives. We have experienced Black women deconstructing girlhood experiences as being denied comfort, context, or consideration of their choices and motives. These women's stories have been, at times, painful and retraumatizing. But they grieved and healed and feel armed with a solid understanding of the trauma of adultification. Therapists can support Black women to soothe and comfort their inner selves with the comfort and compassion they should have received as girls. Women should be coached to look back with kindness and to understand themselves as adultified girls. Black women are also concerned with ensuring that their daughters do not experience the impact of adultification, and here, too, the therapists' emphasis on past–present–future can be empowering for women.

3.3   Black Girls' Sexual Development

Growing up as a black girl, I was already looked at as a "high school dropout" because of the stereotype that all female African Americans will get pregnant in high school and have to drop out so they could take care of their children. (Watkins, 2016)

On average, Black girls tend to reach puberty earlier than other racial and ethnic groups. Black girls may also grow faster than White girls (Salsberry et al., 2009). Black girls with higher body mass indexes are more likely to reach puberty at younger ages. There are also strong links between obesity and early puberty (Herman-Giddens, 2013). Early puberty maturation may be an underlying reason Black women seek therapy. Many of them may have experienced negative impacts without consciously knowing it. Therapists should be aware of the effect of early pubertal maturation in Black girls to assess how it may play into their clients' historic and present struggles.

Early sexual debuts may be ignored for Black boys or may even draw admiration from parents and other family members. However, for Black girls, the story is different. Their sexual maturation and choices can be subject to ridicule and shame (Roberts, 2013). Negative stereotypes about Black girls' sexual maturation affect how people view Black girls, especially in schools, religious communities, and family systems (Carter, 2015). Black girls experience taunting and teasing about their maturing bodies and receive shaming messages from fearful caregivers about "keeping their legs closed." Black girls who achieve early puberty experience adverse sexual outcomes and negative psychological, academic, and behavioral responses, more than girls experiencing late puberty. Early maturation, directly and indirectly, explains Black girls' depressive symptoms, substance use, and unsatisfactory academic performance (Hamlat et al., 2014; Reynolds & Juvonen, 2012; Tareen, 2015; Tanner-Smith, 2010).

Early maturing Black girls experience more interpersonal harassment than girls of other racial and ethnic groups. Black girls are substantially more likely to be targets of peer sexual advances and unsolicited comments about their changing bodies. In addition, Black girls who mature early are more likely to be approached by and date older boys. They also face the highest rates of threatened violence or injury with a weapon on school property. They are disproportionately vulnerable to child sex trafficking victimization and prosecution for their involvement

(Ross et al., 2012). Early maturing Black girls also experience more sexual harassment, violence, and trauma than White or Latina girls (Crenshaw et al., 2015). These experiences exacerbate poor outcomes for Black girls who are unlikely to receive counseling about the impacts of living in mature bodies.

Early pubertal and sexual maturation can bring even more shocking impacts. Black girls' sexual development links to early ages of sexual initiation and increased risk of unsafe sex, sex with more partners, pregnancy, and sexually transmitted infections (Bachanas et al., 2002; Kaplan et al., 2013). Black girls experience higher rates of sexually transmitted diseases, including HIV, than White and Latina girls. This reality alone can dramatically change their lives (Pflieger et al., 2013). Earlier sex initiation is also associated with a greater likelihood of drug and alcohol use, having ever been forced to have sex, and having experienced dating violence in the past year (Kaplan et al., 2013). Although teen pregnancy and birth rates have dropped in the past two decades, teenage Black girls are more than twice as likely as White teens to become pregnant (Martin et al., 2018).

Black women in therapy may disclose early puberty and early sexual initiation with adverse outcomes such as teen pregnancy and sexually transmitted infections. In addition, these women may carry in their bodies and souls the scars of rejection and shame. Therapists must be poised to embrace Black women's stories of sexual dislocation to help them to heal from painful experiences. Therapists should encourage a discussion on adolescent sexuality and decision-making. They should help women recognize the power of social determinants of behavior and the intersection between race, gender, and privilege. Therapists can also explore the age of puberty, how women felt about their developing bodies, shaming and hurtful memories, and clients' experiences with their fathers and other male relatives. Tracking these experiences with Black women helps them to understand where they carry shame from past choices, a sense of suffering over how people regarded their young developing bodies, and vulnerabilities in self-love and self-acceptance.

See Chapter 14 for strategies to rebuild love of self, including making peace with the past and being proactive about the future.

3.4   Lesbian, Gay, Bisexual, Transgender, and/or Queer Black Girls

While Black lesbian, gay, bisexual, transgender, and/or queer (LGBTQ) girls experience the same dynamics around sexual maturation, their experiences have unique aspects that are important for the therapist to recognize. Black lesbian poet Audre Lorde (1984) writes of "constantly being encouraged to pluck out some aspect of myself and present this as the meaningful whole, eclipsing and denying the other parts of the self" (p. 120). This sentiment highlights the complexity of intersectionality. In the Black community, homosexuality has been a taboo subject that clashes with race and gender role expectations (Kosciw et al., 2018; Stettler & Katz, 2017). Facing multiple oppressions, LGBTQ youth report more depression, anxiety, and other forms of emotional distress than straight, cisgender youth (Kann et al., 2018). LGBTQ youth are also more likely to engage in self-harm, report suicidal thoughts, and attempt suicide. LGBTQ youth also face higher rates of bullying and victimization, feeling unsafe or uncomfortable in school, and discrimination (Kosciw et al., 2018). These dynamics hold for Black LGBTQ youth in addition to other LGBTQ youth.

For Black LGBTQ girls, coming out can be an incredibly challenging task. Major conflicts may occur within the family when a Black girl openly discloses or labels herself as lesbian or queer. Even when family members accept and support her sexual identity, the broader Black community may not be supportive due to homophobia. When Black women reveal their identity as a sexual minority, therapists should uniquely explore coming-out experiences and the messages they received from their family and community. The therapist might carefully probe the impact of ethnic identity, gender, and sexual orientation. Frequently, for Black women, religious identity and bias might be in the mix. Family or community messages rejecting LGBTQ identity may perpetuate women's internal distress and self-loathing. The therapist might explore how clients came out (or plan to come out) to their family members, friends, and social groups. By providing a supportive, nonjudgmental presence, therapists can help clients cope in healthy ways and regain self-acceptance. Therapists might also help Black women locate peer groups and role models to identify and find support. In the resources section we recommend the powerful movie *Pariah* (Rees et al., 2007) that showcases these dynamics of rejection and shaming for Black LGBT girls.

3.5   Therapeutic Support: Understanding Black Women's Girlhood

In this chapter, we hope to increase therapists' capacity to help Black women whose girlhood experiences negatively impact their present lives. To that end, we identify six strategies that therapists might use to help Black women with the pain of girlhood memories or losses. Further, we discuss a case in which a therapist applied these strategies to help a Black female deal with girlhood injuries.

1. *Invite women to tell the stories of their girlhood and connect girlhood themes to present circumstances.* Black women who come to therapy may begin their stories with a discussion of symptoms or concerns. They rarely start their therapy journey with the most vulnerable and painful experiences that may have damaged their self-concepts. But the clues of the deeper story lines are usually present in the early phases, and therapists should listen for them. For example, a conversation about present-day hobbies or recreational pursuits or even about partnership status may reveal clues to a Black woman's self that may be injured or vulnerable. Once self-concept enters the picture, the therapist can and should integrate a developmental emphasis in exploring these experiences. Black women's self-concepts are assaulted by negative images and stereotypes early and often, and girlhood is a vulnerable period. In the case presented here, a client's lack of self-love and positive regard was rooted in painful childhood experiences around colorism that left her vulnerable. The therapist was able to hear these themes and opened up a conversation.

Gloria was a Black woman in her 60s who was diagnosed with depression, which she believed was well under control. Her former therapist had helped assess and treat her for several bouts of moderate to severe depression. Gloria was on antidepression medication under the care of a local psychiatrist. Gloria's primary concern in continuing therapy was an inability to love herself and worries that no one would love her. Hearing Gloria's reason for continuing therapy, the therapist hypothesized that the client struggled with self-love and self-acceptance since childhood. She invited Gloria to discuss her girlhood years. Several bits of information Gloria shared about her girlhood, seemed connected to her self-acceptance concerns. Since her preschool years, Gloria felt unattractive. She vividly recalled overhearing family members discuss her dark skin tone as unusual in the family. She also recalled her mother telling a family member that her father, who did not live in the home, did not claim her as his daughter because she was not his family's "color." Gloria also described herself as a shy child who had few friends in school and whose peers teased her mercilessly about her dark skin tone. In another memory, Gloria recalled her mother as supportive and loving, sewing her fancy clothes. Gloria also remembered her mother's desperation to find the right fabric color to "make her skin look good." Gloria shared these memories in response to the therapist's gentle inquiry about her girlhood years.

---

2. *Help women to name difficult experiences, sometimes for the first time.* Often in therapy, Black women's experiences are globalized and normalized as the experience of "Black people." Whereas in some cases this can be helpful, in other cases the general lens is not specific enough to understand Black women's lives. Black women with girlhood injuries and

vulnerabilities experience beautiful moments in therapy when their suffering gets named. These moments occur when therapists acknowledge and name experiences that have sat privately in women's memories for decades. Cultural knowledge and a good understanding of the Black women's racial-ethnic and gendered experiences intertwined is key to naming and connecting such dots. Black women's experience of mental health conditions and symptoms relate to their historical, social, and cultural circumstances. Gloria's therapist was able to help her name a cultural condition, "internalized colorism," that began in childhood and created gaps in her ability to love herself. The client had some idea of what she struggled with, but the naming of her experience made her hunger to understand more. In and of itself, having a name or label for a lifelong struggle brings relief, curiosity, and a commitment to healing and recovery.

The therapist hypothesized that Gloria's experience of self-loathing was related to hurtful experiences of internalized colorism and the rejection Gloria experienced in her family and in school. The therapist labeled Gloria's experience "colorism trauma" and adopted a trauma framework in working with this client. Treatment involved encouraging the client to recall girlhood experiences of rejection, caring for the pain such memories involved.

This was Gloria's first specific discussion of "internalized colorism" as an adult. In gently offering a name for her experiences, the therapist helped Gloria discover a rather robust theme in her girlhood experiences connected to her present-day self-loathing. Gloria was a voracious reader and started exploring colorism, sharing many new insights with the therapist as she discovered them.

---

3. *Helping women to grieve affirms their girlhood suffering.* There are subtleties of Black girlhood that create ambiguous losses that must be honored in therapy. For example, earlier in this chapter, we discussed the shaming and teasing that can accompany a Black girl's sexually maturing body. The adultification experiences of Black girls can also feel erased because this can occur even in families. Helping Black women to grieve girlhood experiences involves deconstructing the painful experience with precision and care. The therapist becomes a compassionate witness to the suffering of women (in their girlhood years), a listener to story lines that might span multiple years. When Black female clients tell therapists their tender girlhood memories, the experience must be a corrective. The story and storyteller are in sync with the validity of the experience. In Gloria's case, the therapist legitimized and amplified a Black woman's understanding of a part of her relationship to her unloved self.

Gloria's scholarly exploration of colorism in Black families did not immediately improve her capacity to feel more self-accepting. In the process of therapy, there were periods of struggle. The therapist guided Gloria to explore how her relationships with her parents influenced her self-image. She made decisions about addressing these issues with her parents as an adult. Gloria had a respectful but distant relationship with her father and did not feel inclined to deepen it. Peacemaking centered on her mother. Over several conversations, Gloria arrived at a point of forgiving her mother, whom she believed protected her against teasing and bullying in school. She remembered her mother holding meetings with teachers and the principal, and she also felt secure in her mother's friendship. The therapist helped Gloria deconstruct her family members' colorism interactions, which were rooted in historical themes such as the "brown paper bag" test in Black culture (a set of historical discriminatory practices reflecting bias toward people with lighter skin, amid widespread racism affecting all Black people). Gloria decided to mentally release her mother as a source of her childhood pain by determining that her mother was a victim of colonialist thinking. This acknowledgment soothed a sense that her mother had contributed to her self-love struggles.

4. *Helping women to rescue buried joyful girlhood memories.* In revisiting girlhood experiences, Black women often recall memories that add joy or smiles and humor. These memories may have been suppressed or buried under others that were painful or diminishing. The recall of positive girlhood incidents can be uplifting. Therapists might allow this to happen organically as women tell of their experiences of growing up. Some themes are related to pleasant encounters or people. Often, clients keep family memories or rituals in their present lives with no connection to the past. An affirming experience is to help clients "rescue" memories that may help them appreciate parts of their girlhood years that were forgotten. As women recover these stories, therapists should pause to celebrate them like new jewels. In Gloria's case, she recalled the joy of a craft that she loves, which she began as a girl, and these memories brought humor and lightness.

Gloria was an accomplished dressmaker, and in present experiences, she also spent hours looking for fabric that brightened her skin. In linking past to present, Gloria discovered she had inherited from her mother her love of sewing and needlecraft that brought her many hours of fulfillment. Gloria recalled enjoyable girlhood memories of competitions she won, clothing she made that won admiration, and scrapbooks she maintained of her designs. Watching the joys of recovering these memories, the therapist suggested finding other girlhood memories that made her smile or laugh.

5. *Connecting women to culturally informed resources to understand their girlhood experiences.* Therapy conversations may not be enough to help Black women understand their experiences of being Black and female in America. A growing number of resources are available to help therapy clients be aware of experiences they share with other women. Reading up on other Black women's experiences can increase clients' self-understanding and camaraderie with others. Therapists will not find the everyday experiences of Black women well represented in psychological and mental health literature, and we make this point repeatedly in this book. A growing number of Black practitioners and scholars are blogging, creating TED Talks, recording videos and podcasts, hosting online discussions, and so forth. These resources can help Black women connect to aspects of their lives that matter. We encourage therapists to maintain a toolbox of resources related to these experiences, and we provide several at the end of this chapter. Black women may find these resources helpful in that they were created for them. In Gloria's case, the therapist used the client's natural curiosity to amplify her understanding of an internalized condition that she may not have seen or heard much about.

> For her self-work, the therapist connected Gloria to several resources to understand internalized colorism. These resources included blogs, videos, and books.

> See Chapter 12 for a list of resources to address internalized lookism dynamics.

6. *Supporting women to break negative cycles in their young people's lives.* A strategy discussed earlier in this chapter is building Black women's agency and empowerment in breaking cycles in the lives of the next generation. Often heard in women's narratives is their recognition of the multigenerational transmission of values and conditions that can hamper the lives of young people they influence. Black women experience great joy from breaking cycles. A frequent entry to this theme is the client's mention of discussing some condition with their children or other young people. For example, Gloria worried about passing on a damaged self-concept to her daughter. The therapist recognized this not as a casual reflection but as Gloria's heart's desire and anxiety that future generations in her family will not experience the same vulnerabilities of self. With this awareness, the therapist opened up a line of conversation about how Gloria raised her daughter with a solid and positive racial and gender identity.

Gloria regularly talked about her young adult daughter. Gloria described a confident and forward-thinking young woman with whom she related well. Gloria also revealed that her daughter enjoyed a good relationship with her grandmother, brother, and father. The therapist asked specifically about the daughter's sense of self and was able to help Gloria realize that the conditions she had experienced did not replicate in her own family. The therapist affirmed Gloria for raising well-adjusted children who loved themselves and lived with ambition and resilience. Gloria rebuffed but then accepted the affirmation that although she lived with the trauma of colorism, she did not pass this on to her children.

3.6   Conclusion

Growing up as a black girl, I made up in my mind I can do ANYTHING I put my mind to.

Growing up as a black girl, I had a strong black mother who was always there for me and pushed me to do better in life.
(Watkins, 2016)

Black women's interest in breaking generational cycles is one of the most significant impacts of competent psychotherapy for girlhood concerns. As Black women consider their girlhood experiences, frequently they also want to advocate for improved conditions for the Black girls within their sphere of influence. Therapists can help Black women design activities that shape racial and gender pride and encourage their daughters, biological or otherwise, to understand racial and gender stereotyping prejudice and discrimination. Such activities include supporting girls' connection to Black female mentors, taking advantage of community programs and Black cultural celebrations, and reading the work of prominent Black female artists. Therapists can advise Black women on how to engage in open, age-appropriate discussions with their daughters and other girls in their community about puberty, menarche, and sex through role-playing. Developmentally appropriate, accurate resources related to sex education and healthy sexuality provide Black girls with sex-positive and developmentally enhancing choices.

These approaches align well with the Positive Youth Development framework critical for Black girls as they negotiate a social, political, and historical landscape grounded in systemic inequities and racism (Search Institute, 2018). Black girls thrive when connected to their schools and communities, including churches, and when they have supportive adults in their lives (Gooden & McMahon, 2016). In addition, therapists can support Black girls and women to leverage their voices to motivate racial and gender change (Search Institute, 2018). Many Black girls are part of the Black Lives Matter movement, speaking out for social change. When therapists help Black women nullify the impact of girlhood experiences in the present, they help Black women to end cycles in their children's lives. In spite of their difficult childhoods, Black women in our practice express longing to raise their daughters into competent womanhood. In helping to empower their Black girls, our clients heal a part of themselves.

Therapist Reflection Questions

1. How did your caregivers socialize you to understand your race and gender?
2. How did your race and gender impact your experiences of childhood or adolescence?
3. What factors shaped your racial and gender identity?
4. How similar or different were your experiences from the experiences of Black girls as described in this chapter?
5. How does your own racial and gender identity impact your work with Black girls?
6. What are your thoughts and feelings about the results of the CNN doll studies? What are your views of how Black girls are portrayed in media?
7. In your experience, what are the key factors that contribute to girls' success in general, and how might these factors support the development of Black girls?

Resources for Therapists

Books

Bryant-Davis, T. (Ed.). (2019). *Multicultural feminist therapy: Helping adolescent girls of color to thrive*. American Psychological Association.
Gorman, A. (2021). *The hill we climb and other poems*. Penguin Young Readers Group.
Hurston, Z. N. (1937). *Their eyes were watching God*. J. B. Lippincott & Co.
Mans, J. (1982). *Black girl, call home*. Berkeley.
Morris, M. (2016). *Pushout: The criminalization of Black girls in schools*. New Press.
Shange, N. (1974). *For colored girls who have considered suicide/when the rainbow is enuf*. Simon and Schuster.
Thomas, A. (2017). *The hate u give*. HarperCollins.
Walker, A. (1982). *The color purple*. Harcourt Brace Jovanovich.

Films

Berry, D. C., & Duke, B. (Directors). (2011). *Dark girls* [Film]. RLJ Entertainment.
Egbuonu, O. (Director). (2020). *Invisible portraits* [Film]. Independently Published.

Rees, D., Cooper, N., Pierce, W., Oduye, A., Walker, P., Mellesse, S., Wright, G., Wise, D., Lewis, C., Anders, M., & Craig, K. (2007). *Pariah* [Film]. Northstar Pictures.

Media Sources

Cooper, A. (2021, June 2). *Cooper speaks with children years later on effects of racial bias in their childhood* [Video]. CNN. https://www.cnn.com/videos/us/2021/06/02/racial-bias-children-cooper-pkg-ac360.cnn

Watkins, Z. S. (2016, August 2). *Growing up as a black girl*. Odyssey. https://www.theodysseyonline.com/growing-up-as-black-girl

References

Anderson, R. E., & Stevenson, H. C. (2019). RECASTing racial stress and trauma: Theorizing the healing potential of racial socialization in families. *American Psychologist, 74*(1), 63–75.

Aston, C., Graves, S., McGoey, K., Lovelace, T., & Townsend, T. (2018). Promoting sisterhood: The impact of a culturally focused program to address verbally aggressive behaviors in Black girls. *Psychology in the Schools, 55*(1), 50–62.

Bachanas, P. J., Morris, M. K., Lewis-Gess, J. K., Sarett-Cuasay, E. J., Sirl, K., Ries, J. K., & Sawyer, M. K. (2002). Predictors of risky sexual behavior in African American adolescent girls: Implications for prevention interventions. *Journal of Pediatric Psychology, 27*, 519–530.

Benner, A. D., Wang, Y., Shen, Y., Boyle, A. E., Polk, R., & Cheng, Y. P. (2018). Racial/ethnic discrimination and well-being during adolescence: A meta-analytic review. *American Psychologist, 73*(7), 855–883.

Brown, D. L., Rosnick, C. B., Griffin-Fennell, F. D., & White-Johnson, R. L. (2017). Initial development of a gendered-racial socialization scale for African American college women. *Sex Roles, 77*(3–4), 178–193.

Buckley, T. R., & Carter, R. T. (2005). Black adolescent girls: Do gender role and racial Identity: Impact their self-esteem? *Sex Roles, 53*(9–10), 647–661.

Butler-Barnes, S. T., Leath, S., Williams, A., Byrd, C., Carter, R. & Chavous, T. M. (2017a). Promoting resilience among African American girls: Racial identity as a protective factor. *Child Development, 89* (6), e552–e571.

Butler-Barnes, S. T., Varner, F., Williams, A., & Sellers, R. (2017b). Academic identity: A longitudinal investigation of African American adolescents' academic persistence. *Journal of Black Psychology, 43*(7), 714–739.

Butler-Barnes, S. T., Richardson, B. L., Chavous, T. M., & Zhu, J. (2019). The importance of racial socialization: School-based racial discrimination and racial identity among African American adolescent boys and girls. *Journal of Research on Adolescence, 29*(2), 432–448.

Carter, J. (2015). *A call to action: Women, religion, violence, and power*. Simon & Schuster.

Celious, A., & Oyserman, D. (2001). Race from the inside: An emerging heterogeneous race model. *Journal of Social Issues, 57*, 149–165.

Chavous, T. M., Rivas-Drake, D., Smalls, C., Griffin, T., & Cogburn, C. (2008). Gender matters, too: The influences of school racial discrimination and racial identity on academic engagement outcomes among African American adolescents. *Developmental Psychology, 44*(3), 637–654.

Clark, K. B., & Clark, M. K. (1947). Racial identification and preference in Negro children. In T. Newcomb & E. Hartley (Eds.), *Readings in social psychology*. Holt.

CNN. (2010a, April 28). *Pilot demonstration*. http://i2.cdn.turner.com/cnn/2010/images/05/13/expanded_results_methods_cnn.pdf

(2010b, May 14). *Study: White and black children biased toward lighter skin*. http://www.cnn.com/2010/US/05/13/doll.study/index.html

Cooper, A. (2021, June 2). *Cooper speaks with children years later on effects of racial bias in their childhood* [Video]. CNN. https://www.cnn.com/videos/us/2021/06/02/racial-bias-children-cooper-pkg-ac360.cnn

Crenshaw, K., Ocen, P., & Nanda, J. (2015*). Black girls matter: Pushed out, overpoliced and underprotected*. African American Policy Forum & Center for Intersectionality and Social Policy Studies. http://static1.squarespace.com/static/53f20d90e4b0b80451158d8c/t/54dcc1ece4b001c03e323448/1423753708557/AAPF_BlackGirlsMatterReport.pdf

Crosnoe, R. (2011). *Fitting in, standing out: Navigating the social challenges of high school to get an education*. Cambridge University Press.

Davis Tribble, B. L., Allen, S. H., Hart, J. R., Francois, T. S., & Smith-Bynum, M. A. (2019). "No [right] way to be a black woman": Exploring gendered racial socialization among black women. *Psychology of Women Quarterly, 43*(3), 381–397. https://doi.org/10.1177/0361684318825439

Epstein, R., Blake, J., & González, T. (2017). Girlhood interrupted: The erasure of black girls' childhood. *SSRN Electronic Journal,* 3000695.

Gerding, S. A., & Aubrey, J. (2018). Sexualization, youthification, and adultification: A content analysis of images of girls and women in popular magazines. *Journalism & Mass Communication Quarterly, 95*(3), 625–646.

Gooden, A. S., & McMahon, S. D. (2016). Thriving among African-American adolescents: Religiosity, religious support, and communalism. *American Journal of Community Psychology, 57*(1–2), 118–128. https://doi.org/10.1002/ajcp.12026

Hamlat, E. J., Stange, J. P., Abramson, L. Y., & Alloy, L. B. (2014). Early pubertal timing as a vulnerability to depression symptoms: Differential effects of race and sex. *Journal of Abnormal Child Psychology, 42*(4), 527–538. https://doi.org/10.1007/s10802-013-9798-9

Herman-Giddens, M. E. (2013). The enigmatic pursuit of puberty in girls. *Pediatrics, 132*(6), 1125–1126.

Holland, M. M. (2012). Only here for the day: The social integration of minority students at a majority white high school. *Sociology of Education, 85*(2), 101–120.

Hughes, D., Rodriguez, J., Smith, E. P., Johnson, D. J., Stevenson, H. C., & Spicer, P. (2006). Parents' ethnic-racial socialization practices: A review of research and directions for future study. *Developmental Psychology, 42*(5), 747–770.

Jones, J. M., Lee, L. H., Matlack, A., & Zigarelli, J. (2018). Using sisterhood networks to cultivate ethnic identity and enhance school engagement. *Psychology in the Schools, 55*(1), 20–35.

Jones, M. K., & Day, S. X. (2018). An exploration of Black women's gendered racial identity using a multidimensional and intersectional approach. *Sex Roles, 79*(1–2), 1–15.

Kann, L., McManus, T., Harris, W. A., Shanklin, S. L., Flint, K. H., Queen, B., & Lim, C. (2018). Youth risk behavior surveillance – United States, 2017. *MMWR Surveillance Summaries, 67*(8), 1–114.

Kaplan, D. L., Jones, E. J., Olsen, E. C., & Yunzal-Butler, C. B. (2013). Early age of first sex and health risk in an urban adolescent population. *Journal of School Health, 83*, 350–356.

Kosciw, J. G., Greytak, E. A., Zongrone, A. D., Clark, C. M., & Truong, N. L.(2018). *The 2017 National School Climate Survey: The experiences of lesbian, gay, bisexual, transgender, and queer youth in our nation's schools.* Gay, Lesbian and Straight Education Network (GLSEN). https://www.glsen.org/sites/default/files/ 2019-10/GLSEN-2017-National-School-Climate-Survey-NSCS-Full-Report.pdf

Lei, J. L. (2003). (Un) necessary toughness? Those "loud Black girls" and those "quiet Asian boys." *Anthropology & Education Quarterly, 34*(2), 158–181.

Lerner, R. M., Lerner, J. V., Almerigi, J. B., Theokas, C., Phelps, E., Gestsdottir, S., Naudeau, S., Jelicic, H., Alberts, A., Ma, L., Smith, L. M., Bobek, D. L., Richman-Raphael, D., Christiansen, E. D., & Von Eye, A. (2005). Positive youth development, participation in community youth development programs, and community contributions of fifth-grade adolescents: Findings from the first wave of the 4-H study of positive youth development. *The Journal of Early Adolescence, 25*(1), 17–71.

Lorde, A. (1984) *Sister outsider: Essays and speeches.* Crossing Press.

Martin, J. A., Hamilton, B. E., & Osterman, M. J. K. (2018). *Births in the United States, 2017* (NCHS data brief no. 318). National Center for Health Statistics.

Martin, L. (2021, June 8). *"Representation matters," Sales of diverse dolls booming at mall kiosk in Brockton.* CBS Boston. https://boston.cbslocal.com/2021/06/08/ widline-pyrame-fusion-dolls-brockton-westgate-mall-kiosk/

Morris, E. W. (2007). "Ladies" or "loudies"? Perceptions and experiences of Black girls in classrooms. *Youth and Society, 38*(4), 490–515.

Morris, M. W. (2019). Countering the adultification of Black girls. *Educational Leadership, 76*(7), 44–48.

Neblett, E. W., Jr., Banks, K. H., Cooper, S. M., & Smalls-Glover, C. (2013). Racial identity mediates the association between ethnic racial socialization and depressive symptoms. *Cultural Diversity and Ethnic Minority Psychology, 19*(2), 200–207. https://doi.org/10.1037/a0032205

Nishina, A., Bellmore, A., Witkow, M. R., & Nylund-Gibson, K. (2010). Longitudinal consistency of adolescent ethnic identification across varying school ethnic contexts. *Developmental Psychology, 46*(6), 1389–1401.

Peck, S. C., Brodish, A. B., Malanchuk, O., Banerjee, M., & Eccles, J.S. (2014). Racial/ ethnic socialization and identity development in Black families: The role of parent and youth reports. *Developmental Psychology, 50*(7), 1897–1909.

Peters, M. (1985). Racial socialization of young Black children. In H. Pipes McAdoo & J. L. McAdoo (Eds.), *Black children: Social, educational, and parental environments* (pp. 159–174). Sage.

Pflieger, J. C., Cook, E. C., Niccolai, L. M., & Connell, C. M. (2013). Racial/ethnic differences in patterns of sexual risk behavior and rates of sexually transmitted infections among female young adults. *American Journal of Public Health, 103* (5), 903–909.

Rees, D., Cooper, N., Pierce, W., Oduye, A., Walker, P., Mellesse, S., Wright, G., Wise, D., Lewis, C., Anders, M., & Craig, K. (2007). *Pariah* [Film]. Northstar Pictures.

Reynolds, B. M., & Juvonen, J. (2012). Pubertal timing fluctuations across middle school: Implications for girls' psychological health. *Journal of Youth and Adolescence, 41*(6), 677–690.

Rivas-Drake, D., Syed, M., Umaña-Taylor, A., Markstrom, C., French, S., & Schwartz, S. J., & Ethnic and Racial Identity in the 21st Century Study Group. (2014). Feeling good, happy, and proud: A meta-analysis of positive ethnic–racial affect and adjustment. *Child Development, 85*(1), 77–102.

Roberts, S. (2013). *Order and dispute: An introduction to legal anthropology.* Quid Pro Books.

Ross, T., Kena, G., Rathbun, A., KewalRamani, A., Zhang, J., Kristapovich, P., & Manning, E. (2012). *Higher education: Gaps in access and persistence.* National Center for Education Statistics.

Salsberry, P. J., Reagan, P. B., & Pajer, K. (2009). Growth differences by age of menarche in African American and White girls. *Nursing Research, 58*(6), 382–390.

Search Institute. (2018). *Developmental assets among U.S. youth: 2018 update.* https:// www.search-institute.org/wp-content/uploads/2018/01/DataSheet-Assets-x-Gender-2018-update.pdf

Sellers, R. M., Chavous, T. M., & Cooke, D. Y. (1998). Racial ideology and racial centrality as predictors of African American college students' academic performance. *Journal of Black Psychology, 24,* 8–27.

Sellers, R. M., Copeland-Linder, N., Martin, P. P., & Lewis, R. L. H. (2006). Racial identity matters: The relationship between racial discrimination and psychological functioning in African American adolescents. *Journal of Research on Adolescence, 16*(2), 187–216.

Smith-Bynum, M. A., Anderson, R. E., Davis, B. L., Franco, M. G., & English, D. (2016). Observed racial socialization and maternal positive emotions in African American mother–adolescent discussions about racial discrimination. *Child Development, 87*(6), 1926–1939.

Stephens, D. P., & Phillips, L. D. (2003). Freaks, gold diggers, divas, and dykes: The sociohistorical development of adolescent African American women's sexual scripts. *Sexuality and Culture, 7,* 3–49.

Stettler, N. M., & Katz, L. F. (2017). Minority stress, emotion regulation, and the parenting of sexual-minority youth. *Journal of GLBT Family Studies, 13*(4), 380–400.

Stevenson, H. C., Jr., Cameron, R., Herrero-Taylor, T., & Davis, G. Y. (2002). Development of the teenager experience of racial socialization scale: Correlates of race-related socialization frequency from the perspective of Black youth. *Journal of Black Psychology, 28*(2), 84–106.

Stokes, M., Hope, E., Cryer-Coupet, Q., & Elliot, E. (2020). Black girl blues: The roles of racial socialization, gendered racial socialization, and racial identity on depressive symptoms among Black girls. *Journal of Youth and Adolescence, 49*(11), 2175–2189.

Suárez-Orozco, C. (2004). Formulating identity in a globalized world. In M. M. Suárez-Orozco & D. B. Qin-Hilliard (Eds.), *Globalization: Culture and education in the new millennium* (pp. 173–202). University of California Press.

Tanner-Smith, E. E. (2010). Negotiating the early developing body: Pubertal timing, body weight, and adolescent girls' substance use. *Journal of Youth and Adolescence, 39*(12), 1402–1416.

Tareen, R. S. (2015). Substance abuse and adolescent girls. *International Public Health Journal, 7*(2), 191–207.

Thomas, A. J., & Blackmon, S. M. (2015). The influence of the Trayvon Martin shooting on racial socialization practices of African American parents. *Journal of Black Psychology, 41*(1), 75–89.

Thomas, O., Davidson, W., & McAdoo, H. (2008). An evaluation study of the Young Empowered Sisters (YES!) Program: Promoting cultural assets among African American adolescent girls through a culturally relevant school-based intervention. *Journal of Black Psychology, 34*, 281–308.

Umaña-Taylor, A. J., & Hill, N. E. (2020). Ethnic–racial socialization in the family: A decade's advance on precursors and outcomes. *Journal of Marriage and Family, 82*(1), 244–271.

Umaña-Taylor, A. J., Quintana, S. M., Lee, R. M., Cross, W. E., Jr., Rivas-Drake, D., Schwartz, S. J., Yip, T., & Ethnic and Racial Identity in the 21st Century Study Group. (2014). Ethnic and racial identity during adolescence and into young adulthood: An integrated conceptualization. *Child Development, 85*(1), 21–39.

Watkins, Z. S. (2016, August 2). *Growing up as a Black girl.* Odyssey. https://www .theodysseyonline.com/growing-up-as-black-girl

Way, N., Hernández, M. G., Rogers, L. O., & Hughes, D. L. (2013). "I'm not going to become no rapper": Stereotypes as a context of ethnic and racial identity development. *Journal of Adolescent Research, 284*(4), 407–430.

Yasui, M. (2015). A review of the empirical assessment of processes in ethnic–racial socialization: Examining methodological advances and future areas of development. *Developmental Review, 37*, 1–40.

4   Stereotypes of Black Women:
Clinical Implications

On July 14, 2008, *The New Yorker* magazine featured a cartoon image of Michelle and Barack Obama's fist-bumping, which they did at a campaign event. The image depicts Michelle Obama with a large Afro, which is not typically how she wears her hair. She has an assault rifle strapped on her back with a sash of extra bullets across her torso. Barack Obama is depicted as a Muslim terrorist. This cartoon depicted a gesture of support between this Black couple as an expression of anger, aggression, and violence. In it, Michelle Obama fits the stereotype of the angry Black woman ready for battle, a predominant stereotype attached to Black women in the United States. In her memoir, *Becoming*, Michelle Obama describes having to tone down her language and frustration with the country's state while on the campaign trail (Obama, 2018). While campaigning for her husband and throughout her eight years as the first lady, Michelle battled the angry woman stereotype, as she worked to be heard, liked, and taken seriously.

Stereotypes of Black women are pervasive in the United States and show up in everyday life, in families, at work, in media, art, industry, and mental health settings. A stereotype is a belief about a group based on generalizations; these generalizations then get applied to individuals (Kanahara, 2006). Stereotypes are common and caused in part by the brain's attempts to understand, categorize, and make quick decisions in the world. However, some stereotypes have helped to systematically oppress various groups of people throughout history, and Black women have faced some of the worst oppression due to stereotypes. Black women encounter stereotypes that prescribe their behavior and punish them for engaging in behaviors that reflect these stereotypes (Heilman, 2012).

In addition to limiting people externally, stereotypes can also cause harm through internalization. Brown et al. (2002) found that Black people who internalized negative views about themselves were more likely to exhibit low self-esteem. In her qualitative study, Scott (2013) suggests that Black women are "well aware of stereotypes such as 'overbearing, too outspoken, strong, angry, gold diggers, materialistic, oversexed, have lots of children, and unintelligent' as the predominant images of Black women" (p. 319). These stereotypes reflect gendered racism that Black women experience, which causes them psychological distress (Essed, 1991; Thomas et al., 2008).

> Black women's experience of gendered racism is explored further in Chapter 2, on the social determinants of health and mental health for Black women, and in Chapter 9, on the clinical implications of shifting.

Therapists must understand Black women's stereotypes for two primary reasons: First, Black women experience stress and adverse mental health outcomes due to the discrimination when people stereotype them (Jerald, Cole et al., 2017). Stereotypes can reduce Black women's self-esteem when internalized, and therapists must help women to name and depersonalize these distortions to allow women to navigate a biased world. Second, because stereotypes are endemic, therapists are also at risk of holding stereotypes about Black women, which can hinder the therapeutic relationship (Ashley, 2014). To overcome their unconscious negative beliefs about Black women, therapists must first understand and challenge common stereotypes of Black women.

In this chapter, we review historical and contemporary stereotypes of Black women in the United States, driven by histories of race, sex/gender, and social class (Harris-Perry, 2011; Nelson, 2006). We discuss the effects of internalizing these stereotypes on women's sense of self and worthiness. This chapter also examines how therapists might unconsciously hold stereotypes about Black women.

4.1 Overview of Black Women Stereotypes

Here, we review four common stereotypes of Black women present in American culture that have been used to justify racism and systemic oppression of Black women (Jerald, Ward et al., 2017). These stereotypes serve to dehumanize Black women, making it easier for others to harm, neglect, or deny them. We should note that Black women have a history of resisting stereotypical representations using social, political, and communication strategies (Harris-Perry, 2011; Scott, 2013). Yet, in their efforts to actively rebut images that put them in a box and dismantle how others judge them, Black women may suppress emotions and express themselves in ways that can alter and restrict their personalities. Efforts to fight negative connotations of their everyday actions can be destructive to Black women's mental and emotional health.

4.1.1   Black Women as Perpetually Angry

The angry Black woman stereotype characterizes Black women as emasculating, harsh, loud, and ill mannered. This stereotype was first represented as "Sapphire" in the media in the 1940s (Walley-Jean, 2009). The stereotype of Black women being angry is dehumanizing because it represents Black women as demanding and heartless and makes it seem as though they do not need care and tenderness. Despite the widespread acceptance of this stereotype, research has demonstrated that Black women exhibit *less* anger than people from other groups in response to provocation (Walley-Jean, 2009). The stereotype of Black women as overly angry shows up in workplaces, in the Black community, and in intimate relationships with Black men. For example, the portrayal of Black women as angry and aggressive is associated with the belief that they emasculate their Black male partners (Jerald, Ward et al., 2017). Further, people have blamed Black women's anger for their low levels of marriage. In the controversial 1965 "Moynihan Report," *The Negro Family: The Case for National Action*, Black women were deemed partially responsible for the breakdown of the Black family because they were seen as aggressive and overbearing, which the report claimed had pushed Black men out of leadership roles in families (Moynihan, 1965).

Even in the Black community, the perception of Black women as angry and aggressive negatively affects their experiences navigating romantic relationships, with both Black and non-Black men citing their rejection of Black women as potential partners due to these characteristics (Adeyinka-Skold, 2020). The stereotype of Black women being angry causes them to be seen as "unfeminine," not conforming to the traditional, privileged norms of gentle and passive femininity, often ascribed to White women. "Who wants to deal with a bunch of eye-rolling and neck-snapping?" was one Black man's response when asked why he preferred to date non-Black women (Ward, 2019). Black women wanting to date and find long-term partners are rated least desirable on dating apps (Rudder, 2014). The experience of struggling to find love and facing rejection is harrowing for Black women as they search for love. When Black women do find love, their partners may continue to endorse this negative stereotype of them being perpetually angry. There have been instances of famous Black men justifying their mistreatment of their Black female partners by denigrating them as angry and difficult (Harris-Perry, 2011; Jones & Shorter-Gooden, 2003).

See Chapter 11 for more on Black women's experiences in intimate relationships.

In addition to navigating the angry Black woman stereotype in their relationships, Black women frequently navigate this stereotype in workplaces and schools. This everyday reality translates to Black women fearing that their colleagues will label them as angry and aggressive and dismiss their viewpoints if they speak out and advocate for themselves. Black girls experience this stereotype in schools and are more likely to receive punishment than their White classmates (Morris, 2016). These developmental experiences set the stage for Black women to be cautious about how and when they express themselves and the potential consequences they may experience when expressing concerns or grievances.

Further, the angry Black woman stereotype silences Black women's rightful anger regarding personal and community injustice (Ashley, 2014). As we discuss later in this book, Black women have a lot to be angry about: being passed over for jobs they are qualified for, dealing with systems that discriminate against them, experiencing trauma, witnessing family members and friends being unfairly persecuted and even abused by the US justice system; the list could go on. When Black women do get angry, this response is often a reasonable reaction to the harm they are experiencing or witnessing. Yet, people question even their right to feel angry, which represents a denial of their feelings.

Therapists should be aware of how the angry Black woman stereotype plays out in the therapy room. First, there is a history of therapists seeing Black women as paranoid; overlooking their fear, sadness, and anxiety; and generally overpathologizing Black women (Harris-Perry, 2011). Therapists must be careful not to misinterpret their Black female clients' symptomatology as confirming the angry Black woman stereotype (Ashley, 2014). Second, therapists should intentionally make room for Black women to express a range of emotions in the therapy room. One complexity of the stereotype is that anger is one of the few emotions that Black women feel comfortable expressing. As a result, Black women's emotional expressions of sadness and anxiety commonly appear initially as anger or irritability.

To provide emotional space for their Black female clients, therapists should slow sessions down when Black female clients express emotions in order to allow emotions to be described, labeled, and validated. Providing time in therapy to process and understand feelings will let clients know that their feelings are accepted and important. Additionally, if Black women appear in treatment to be overly passive and avoidant of justifiable anger, therapists should explore their Black female clients' thoughts and feelings about expressing anger and help them process any fears that they may be judged or stereotyped. It may be helpful to name the angry Black woman stereotype and explore whether the client is worried that expressing their anger may cause the therapist to stereotype them in this way (Ashley, 2014). Further, to make space for Black women to express their emotions in therapy fully, therapists must examine their values related to "appropriate" emotional expression and work through any countertransference that arises if their Black female clients express anger. Specifically, therapists should examine their feelings and experiences related to anger and expressing anger. Therapists who feel more uncomfortable with the expression of anger are more likely to inhibit or judge Black female clients who express their anger.

We encourage therapists to explore their own relationship with anger and other aspects of themselves and their racial and cultural identity in Chapter 6 on the cultural self-of-the-therapist.

4.1.2   Black Women as Selfless and Self-Sacrificial

Black women are often touted as selfless and self-sacrificing. This historical stereotype depicts Black women as desexualized, caregiving, selfless, and prioritizing caring for White people and their children as a "Mammy." In the media, the Mammy has often been depicted as dark-skinned and overweight, working to care for White families or others with little to no compensation (West, 1995). The Mammy caricature first emerged after slavery, when Black women went to work for White families to earn a living. Modern media depictions of Black Mammy stereotypes are still in play as the overweight, dark-skinned, wise Black woman who is selfless and prioritizes others, guiding White female protagonists to success (Harris-Perry, 2011).

The stereotype of Black women prioritizing everyone else before themselves has evolved beyond just caring for the children in White families. In the Black community, many Black women experience pressure to be selfless and self-sacrificing in their familial relationships and religious communities. For example, while Black churches generally support Black women, they hold expectations that women will always say yes. Church leaders and congregants may view women who set boundaries around their needs and time as selfish. Black women's self-sacrifice keeps many churches running without compensation and full acknowledgment.

The contemporary manifestation of Black women as needing to prioritize other people before themselves can limit Black women's capacity to advocate for their own needs. Therapists should support Black women in identifying where they are overextended, articulating their own needs, and setting boundaries. For example, some Black women who are overly focused on their families' needs may spend time in sessions discussing things that are happening to their family members and avoid talking about themselves. While a relational lens is useful in working with Black female clients, therapists should gently point out when Black women are focused more on other people than themselves. The objective is to support Black female clients to use therapy to make strides related to self-love and self-care.

4.1.3 Black Women as Hypersexual

There is a long history of Black women being stereotyped as hypersexualized, promiscuous, and manipulative or as a "Jezebel" (Jerald, Ward et al., 2017). The Jezebel stereotype originated during slavery, and White men used it to justify their rape and sexual assault of enslaved Black women (Greene, 2000; Jerald, Ward et al., 2017). In modern culture, this stereotype depicts a Black woman as a vixen or stripper who overpowers men trying to resist her sexual advances. In this stereotype, Black women are seen as sexual objects who lack emotion or dynamic personalities. Black women's portrayal as hypersexual has been used to justify violence against them. Stereotypes of Black women as hypersexual make it less likely for the public and justice systems to take crimes of sexual violence against Black women seriously (Greene, 2000). Black men and the Black community's characterization of Black women as promiscuous and hypersexualized has also justified sexual abuse of Black women and girls (Harris-Perry, 2011). Too often, Black girls are labeled as "fast," a term that refers to being easy to engage with sexually, when they are sexually abused or lured into sexual activities at a young age by older boys and men. When Black women do come forward to report their experiences of rape or sexual assault, they are often questioned and blamed for putting themselves in a situation where they provoke such victimization. For example, men and women in the Black community have continued to support and defend the R&B singer R. Kelly after the revelation of his decades of sexual and physical abuse of underaged girls (Hill, 2019). These teenaged girls and their families have been criticized and blamed for the abuse they experienced (Decaille & Hatzipanagos, 2019).

> Additional stereotypes related to Black women's sexuality are discussed in Chapter 11.

One complicated aspect of Black women and girls being seen as overly sexual is that some Black women have utilized their sexual expression to pull themselves out of poverty. Currently, the most famous Black female rappers (Nicki Minaj, Megan Thee Stallion, and Lil' Kim) adopt sexual personas and talk explicitly about sex in their music, mimicking the sexual themes that

Black male rappers often focus on in their music. Additionally, Black women are cast as "video girls" in hip-hop videos, where they are typically barely clothed and dancing in sexually provocative ways. For Black women from low-income backgrounds, being an exotic dancer or a scantily clad woman featured in a music video can feel like a ticket out of a poor neighborhood and a way to care for their family and children. Therapists should consider how Black women gain rewards for pursuing caricatures of this stereotype. With a nuanced understanding of this complexity, therapists can make space for Black women to acknowledge their longings for attention and affirmation and a need to practice healthy ways of embracing their sexuality and the power that comes from this sexuality.

On the other hand, Black women may also try to counter the Jezebel stereotype by suppressing their sexual desire and expression. Black women and girls who are religious (often Christian or Muslim) are often encouraged by elders in their community to "keep their legs closed" to avoid pregnancy. Many Black women grow up hearing these messages, which negatively impacts their appreciation of sex as an avenue to well-being. Black women may counteract the Jezebel stereotype by attempting to be "pure," "clean," or asexual. Such efforts can cause Black women to suppress their sexuality and sexual desire. Asexuality or celibacy can keep Black women safe from sexually transmitted infections and unwanted pregnancies, yet in adopting such postures without self-exploration, Black women deny themselves their full sexual expression. Therapists must be ready to help women understand how their sexual values and behaviors may be related to rebuffing stereotypes.

Black women who identify as lesbian, gay, bisexual, or pansexual may have even more difficulty embracing their sexuality. They may fear that the Black community will shame their sexual desires for another woman or trans or gender-nonconforming person (Hill, 2013). While the Black community in the United States is becoming more accepting of people who identify as lesbian, gay, bisexual, transgender, and/or queer (LGBTQ) and Black queer communities are increasingly visible, homophobia and discrimination against LGBTQ people are still present in the Black community (Greene, 2000). In addition, among many people in the general population, there is a common stereotype that people who identify as bisexual are sexually promiscuous (Klesse, 2005). Thus, Black women who identify as bisexual or pansexual may experience another level of judgment and stereotypes, restricting them from freely expressing their sexuality healthily and authentically.

Therapists should create space in therapy where their Black female clients can openly explore their sexual fears and desires and cultivate a healthy relationship with their sexuality. Therapists should use the following open and nonjudgmental strategies. First, they can name stereotypes that Black women have navigated in relation to their sexuality and support their clients in dismantling them. Second, clinicians can help Black female clients increase their comfort with fully embodying their sexual selves, neither performing a Jezebel caricature nor feeling confined to pure virginity. Third, to support Black women in this self-exploration, therapists need to have a healthy relationship with their own sexuality and an awareness of their beliefs about healthy sexual expression. Therapists who have a more conservative view of sexuality and sexual expression must be careful about the potential judgment of their Black female clients' sexual choices. Additionally, these conversations may be more challenging for male therapists to navigate. We recommend that male therapists ask their Black female clients about how they feel about discussing sex and sexuality with a male therapist.

4.1.4   Black Women as Abusing Systems of Support

In the movie *Precious* (Daniels, 2009), the mother (Mary, who is played by Mo'Nique) reflects the welfare queen stereotype. Mary is on welfare and lies to social workers about the number of children she has to manipulate the government into giving her more money. Additionally, Mary has no interest in working and leaves her daughter, Precious, to fend for herself on the streets of New York. Mary is wholly selfish and is sexually, physically, and emotionally abusive to Precious. This movie made a splash when it came out in theaters in 2009, and Mo'Nique won an Academy Award for best supporting actress for playing Mary. The film honored Precious' resilience against extremely challenging circumstances. Yet, one aspect of the movie's acclaim seemed to emanate from people's hatred of the "welfare queen." We argue that Mo'Nique may have been rewarded because of her depiction of a predominant stereotype of low-income Black women. The movie seemed to endorse a simplistic understanding of Black women as "welfare queens," a viewpoint rooted in racist and sexist belief systems.

The welfare queen stereotype represents a poor Black woman dependent on government assistance who manipulates and abuses aid and support systems. The welfare queen's image is a sociopolitical construction of the 1960s used to denigrate poor Black women and advocate for reducing government support to low-income families (Nadasen, 2007). This stereotype incorporates assumptions about Black women having children out of wedlock and having partners who will not commit to them. When Black women are stereotyped in this way, they are seen as lazy and assumed to manipulate systems that serve them. In a study where African American women watched videos depicting a welfare queen caricature, most participants indicated that Black female job applicants should be directed toward low-wage, low-skill jobs (Monahan et al., 2005). This finding suggests that the welfare queen stereotype can negatively impact Black women's job prospects even when other Black women evaluate them.

This stereotype may show up in therapy in several ways. Black female clients may feel wary of being stereotyped as a welfare queen, and they may challenge this stereotype by demonstrating their self-sufficiency. In particular, Black women who have limited financial resources, receive government aid, or are receiving therapy through a free or reduced payment program may worry about being assumed to be abusing the system. The welfare queen stereotype can also cause therapists to feel that they need to fix or save Black women, which is disempowering to Black female clients. Buying into the stereotype of Black women manipulating and abusing support systems can also cause therapists to be suspicious toward low-income Black women who ask for specific services or service exceptions (e.g., lower fees). Therapists may feel that clients do not deserve the services they are receiving. To combat their own internalized representations of Black women as abusive of governmental, state, or community aid, therapists must pay attention to their own internalized responses to Black female clients. They should notice when their responses reflect a sense that Black women clients are trying to take advantage of a system or service.

4.2   Negative Impact of Stereotypes on Black Women

The negative effects that stereotypes have on Black women relate to how people treat Black women as well as Black women's internal struggles to define or redefine themselves. Stereotypes affect women in three major ways: (a) stereotypes cause Black women to experience stress, (b) stereotypes put Black women in a double bind as they navigate everyday life, and (c) stereotypes can become internalized and cause Black women to see themselves in a negative light.

4.2.1   Stereotype Stress

Black women expend mental energy anticipating discrimination based on negative stereotypes and navigating a world biased against them; this negatively affects their mental health (Jerald, Cole et al., 2017). Jerald, Cole et al. (2017) found that Black women who believe other people hold negative stereotypes about them reported more substance abuse and lower health levels. Stereotype threat is one manifestation of this stress. Stereotype threat is a phenomenon in which people's concern that they will be negatively judged, based on a stereotype, interferes with their performance (Steele, 2010). For example, Spencer et al. (1999) showed that stereotype threat occurs when women who are high achieving in math underperform on math exams. Stereotype threat negatively impacts Black women as they navigate predominantly White fields and contributes to Black women abandoning STEM (science, technology, engineering, and mathematics) majors in college (Beasley & Fischer, 2012). Stereotype threat is also likely to increase blood pressure in testing situations, which may help to explain the high levels of hypertension among Black populations (Blascovich et al., 2001). Further, stereotype threat is connected to the anxiety Black women feel when meeting with health care professionals (Abdou & Fingerhut, 2014), which might keep Black women from seeking medical and mental health care.

4.2.2   Stereotyping as a Double Bind

Stereotypes put Black women in a double bind as they navigate a tension between feeling invisible and hypervisible at the same time (Sesko & Biernat, 2010). Stereotypes keep Black women from being seen as unique human beings and can also cause people to focus on Black women and their behavior. Black women may feel forced to code-switch (change their ways of speaking and their mannerisms) and tone down parts of themselves to avoid being typecast as a stereotype. Black women, like everyone else, want to be seen and acknowledged as individuals, yet often feel that they must hide or represent all Black women or all Black people in predominantly White spaces. This pressure to represent the Black race and community may cause Black women to withdraw or make them feel a need to show the world that Black people are smart, articulate, and hardworking to counter negative stereotypes. As Black women try to dispel these stereotypes, they may feel there is no room for mistakes, rest, or being human, which takes a toll. Shifting is a common way that Black women work to navigate stereotypes. Overall, stereotypes make it more difficult for Black women to be their full selves in various spaces.

In Chapter 9, we delve deeper into the topic of shifting, which is when Black women change their ways of being to accommodate the people they are with at any given time.

4.2.3   Internalized Stereotypes

Internalized racism and negative stereotypes drive depression and lower career aspirations (Brown & Segrist, 2016; Molina & James, 2016). Studies have demonstrated that when Black women cope with sexist and racist events by internalizing these events and blaming themselves, they are more likely to report depression (Carr et al., 2014). When Black women internalize stereotypes, they may feel more negatively about themselves in general and question their ability to be viewed accurately as they navigate everyday life. Black women who internalize these stereotypes may feel constrained in terms of their emotional expression and the possibilities for their personal and professional lives.

4.3   Clinical Strategies to Help Black Women Cope with Stereotypes

We offer three recommendations to help Black women navigate the damaging personal impact of stereotypes in therapy.

4.3.1   Acknowledge and Address Stereotype Stress

Help Black female clients identify and express the stress they experience as a result of navigating and working to dispel negative stereotypes in various aspects of their lives. Encourage Black women to pay attention to shifting and overcompensating in key areas of their lives. As mentioned earlier in this chapter, Black women may overcompensate to prove a high level of competence and show that they can be successful in academic and professional spaces. Scott (2013) conducted a qualitative study with Black women about the communication strategies they use to dispel stereotypes. One participant described: "Oftentimes when I speak, I speak very intelligently. I study hard, get good grades, and I like to let people know. I'll leave my paper out, like, 'Yeah, I got the only A in the class. – it was me.' To let people know we're intelligent" (p. 319). This overcompensation can be exhausting and stressful and can cause Black women to internalize the idea that they do not have the space to rest or take a break.

One resource that can help Black women let go of overworking and overcompensating is The Nap Ministry (https://thenapministry.wordpress.com/), an organization started by a Black woman. Tricia Hersey founded The Nap Ministry to encourage Black people to use rest as a form of resistance. Hersey encourages Black people to step away from the constant need to achieve and prove themselves and to instead engage in social activism through resting and taking care of themselves. Therapists should encourage Black women to balance the need to be seen as competent with claiming their full humanity by embracing physical and mental practices that support rest and freedom. This approach can be a powerful way to help Black women experience mental wellness while navigating stereotypes.

In addition, we recommend that therapists support their Black female clients in engaging in proactive and healthy stress management strategies. Stress-busting strategies include regular exercise, meditation, and fun activities. Therapists can also encourage Black women to find spaces where they feel free to be fully themselves and are not worried about being stereotyped. These spaces, where women can relax and exhale, will be restorative to relieve stress.

Additional physical health and wellness strategies are shared in Chapter 13.

4.3.2   Identify and Challenge Internalized Stereotypes

We suggest that therapists explore their clients' beliefs about Black women using the following questions: (a) When you think of Black women, what images or ideas come to mind? (b) How do you feel about being a Black woman? What are the positive parts of this identity? What are the challenging aspects of this identity? (c) How do you think society sees you as a Black woman? What feels true and untrue about these perceptions? If Black female clients indicate that they hold negative views about Black women and have negative feelings about being Black women, this may signal that they have internalized negative stereotypes.

To address internalized stereotypes, we recommend that therapists guide Black women through a process of challenging and depersonalizing these stereotypes. A central goal in this process is helping Black women to understand that the problem is racism and sexism in society, not their being a Black woman. Black women experience stress as they navigate a world that communicates negative messages about them, resulting in Black women feeling that there is something wrong with being a woman and being Black. Therapists can help clients differentiate between their identity as a Black woman, which is a beautiful thing, and the systemic oppression and discrimination they must navigate due to negative societal views about Black women. Making this distinction does not eliminate the stress of experiencing racial and gender discrimination. Still, it helps to identify any distortions in how Black women view themselves and buffers against stereotypes they face.

Given that stereotypes of Black women are common in mainstream media, therapists might discuss the television, movies, books, and social media that their Black female clients consume. Jerald, Ward, and colleagues (2017) demonstrated a connection between media consumption and endorsement of negative Black female stereotypes. Guiding Black women to name and deconstruct the stereotypes present in the media they consume will likely keep them from internalizing these stereotypes. Further, encouraging Black women to seek out Black women's holistic representations can also be helpful and affirming.

4.3.3   Explore Stereotype Threat in the Therapy Room

One of us, Adia Gooden, recalls her experience of starting therapy with a White female therapist. While the therapist was warm, accepting, and culturally competent, a few months of treatment passed before Adia truly opened up about her struggles and anxieties. Holding back the actual challenges was not her conscious decision; she was a doctoral student training to become a clinical psychologist and understood the importance of being open in therapy. However, at the beginning of therapy she felt the need to perform competence and dispel negative stereotypes by seeming to have it all together. Only when she moved beyond needing to prove that she was okay was she able to fully open up in therapy and begin more in-depth work.

Black women's fears of being stereotyped may show up in the therapy room and relationship, and therapists can explore how stereotypes affect Black women's engagement in therapy. Therapists should be alert to how Black women engage in therapy sessions in a way that seeks to dispel negative stereotypes. This dynamic may be particularly salient for Black women working with non-Black therapists (Scott, 2013). In response to worries about stereotypes therapists may hold about them, Black women may consciously and unconsciously change their way of speaking and engaging to show that they are intelligent and competent in therapeutic conversations (Scott, 2013). They may be especially sensitive in discussions with White therapists or men.

The therapist must demonstrate ease with Black women's identities and help them to name their fears of being transparent and fully present in the presence of therapists who do not share their identities. Therapists may encourage women to resist urges to perform in a way that works to counter stereotypes and to reveal aspects of themselves they may wish to hide. The following case example highlights how a therapist might create a unique space for Black women to navigate challenging stereotypes. It also showcases how therapists can encourage women to fully express anger, sexuality, sadness, power, and generosity without fearing that the therapist will ascribe common stereotypes to them.

Case Example

Tanesha is a 38-year-old, heterosexual, cisgender, married, Christian, Black woman working as a corporate lawyer. She spends most of her life in predominantly White spaces. Having attended a private high school, a prestigious university for college, and one of the top 10 law schools in the United States, Tanesha understands how to navigate White spaces so that she will not be noticed or stand out. She has tried to ignore racism and sexism in these spaces because she believed if she could just make it to one of the prized, high-paying positions at a corporate law firm, she would be successful and could advocate for herself and her community from a place of power. Now, Tanesha has finally made it. She is a senior associate at a top corporate law firm in a major city, yet she is exhausted and angry. Over the years, Tanesha learned to suppress her anger because she was well aware

(*cont.*)

of the angry Black woman stereotype and cautious about doing things that might cause her to be stereotyped or dismissed by her colleagues. Tanesha hoped that when she was promoted, her opinions on cases would be valued and respected. Still, first-year associates who are White have been questioning her decisions and recommendations about cases, which is infuriating to her. The pressure and stress that Tanesha feels at work prompted her to seek therapy.

"How is your experience at work related to your being a Black woman?" the therapist asked after Tanesha shared her feelings of anger and exhaustion at work. Tanesha emphatically agreed that she had been treated differently at work because she is a Black woman. The therapist shared an observation that Tanesha is navigating the tension between feeling anger in response to the racial and gender discrimination that she has experienced at work and avoiding expressing this anger due to not wanting to be stereotyped as an angry Black woman. The therapist suggested that Tanesha's stress has built up over the years while she was in school and as a junior associate at her law firm, when she did not feel she could advocate for herself. Tanesha agreed that her anger reflected past and present experiences of discrimination and injustice.

In sessions, the therapist offered Tanesha space to express her anger, which involved venting and raising her voice. The therapist provided empathy and validated Tanesha's rage in response to the injustice she was experiencing. Together, Tanesha and the therapist acknowledged the real constraints on how she can express herself in her workplace and discussed ways for her to advocate for herself assertively. Tanesha expressed pride in her identity as a Black woman and endorsed positive feelings about herself as a Black woman and support of other Black women, which made it clear that she had not internalized negative stereotypes.

In working with Tanesha, the therapist validated her anger and gave her space to express this anger in the session. The therapist did not communicate discomfort with her anger and did not try to fix or solve the problems or indicate that Tanesha's anger was inappropriate. The therapist also helped Tanesha name the tension she felt related to wanting to express her anger and her fear of being stereotyped as an angry Black woman.

4.4   Therapist Self-Reflection

Stereotypes are endemic in US society, and stereotypes of Black women are prolific, damaging, and hurtful as they play out in everyday life. Stereotypes have been used to justify violence against Black women and are pervasive throughout popular media. It is common for people who have lived in the United States for extended time to unconsciously believe stereotypes about

Black women, and this may also be true for therapists. Stereotypes increase the likelihood that therapists will make assumptions about their Black female clients and make it more challenging for therapists to see their clients fully as individuals. Therefore, we recommend that therapists of all racial and ethnic backgrounds (including Black women) self-reflect to challenge and disrupt any unconsciously held stereotypes. This work is essential as therapists prepare to offer a safe and supportive therapeutic space for Black women to be their full selves without worrying about stereotype threat or performing to counter negative stereotypes in the therapy room. Please refer to the reflection questions at the end of this chapter to begin this self-work. Be gentle with yourself as you reflect on the questions. Unconsciously accepting a stereotype does not make you a racist or evil person. Therapists who combat stereotypes in themselves and create opportunities for clients to combat and address the effects of stereotypes on their mental and emotional health are engaging in culturally competent practice.

4.5   Conclusion

Navigating stereotypes is a common experience for Black women as they operate in a world that so often "misrecognizes" them, as Harris-Perry highlighted in her book *Sister Citizen* (2011). Therapists must ensure that the therapeutic relationship is a safe space where Black women do not have to work to disprove stereotypes. We encourage therapists to examine their own biases and unconsciously held stereotypes to provide a safe therapeutic space for Black women. Therapists need to help Black women acknowledge the stress and constraints they experience as a result of navigating stereotypes, to support Black women in challenging any stereotypes that may have been internalized, and to provide space for Black women to be their full selves both in and outside of therapy.

Therapist Reflection Questions

1. When you think of a Black woman, what images come to mind? If you were to describe Black women, what qualities or characteristics come to mind? Do those characteristics have a theme?
2. What assumptions have you made in the past about Black women?
3. Do you have close friends or family members who are Black women? Why or why not?
4. If you are a Black woman, what stereotypes are you aware of about Black women? How do these stereotypes affect you as a therapist or in your professional roles in general? Are there things you do consciously or unconsciously to combat these stereotypes or show that you are competent?

Resources for Therapists and Clients

Books

Angelou, M. (1969). *I know why the caged bird sings*. Random House.

Harris-Perry, M. V. (2011). *Sister citizen: Shame, stereotypes, and Black women in America*. Yale University Press.

hooks, b. (2001). *Salvation: Black people and love*. HarperCollins Publishers.

Morris, M. W. (2016). *Pushout: The criminalization of black girls in schools*. The New Press.

Morrison, T. (1970). *The bluest eye*. Holt.

Walker, A. (1982). *The color purple*. Harcourt Brace Jovanovich.

References

Abdou, C. M., & Fingerhut, A. W. (2014). Stereotype threat among Black and White women in health care settings. *Cultural Diversity and Ethnic Minority Psychology, 20*(3), 316–323. https://doi.org/10.1037/a0036946

Adeyinka-Skold, S. (2020). Barriers in women's romantic partner search in the digital age. In R. Kalish (Ed.), *Young adult sexuality in the digital age* (pp. 113–137). IGI Global. http://dx.doi.org/10.4018/978-1-7998-3187-7.ch007

Ashley, W. (2014) The angry Black woman: The impact of pejorative stereotypes on psychotherapy with Black women, *Social Work in Public Health, 29*(1), 27–34. https://doi.org/10.1080/19371918.2011.619449

Beasley, M. A., & Fischer, M. J. (2012). Why they leave: The impact of stereotype threat on the attrition of women and minorities from science, math and engineering majors. *Social Psychology of Education, 15*(4), 427–448. https://doi.org/10.1007/s11218-012-9185-3

Blascovich, J., Spencer, S. J., Quinn, D., & Steele, C. (2001). African Americans and high blood pressure: The role of stereotype threat. *Psychological Science, 12*(3), 225–229. https://doi.org/10.1111/1467-9280.00340

Brown, D. L., & Segrist, D. (2016). African American career aspirations: Examining the relative influence of internalized racism. *Journal of Career Development, 43*(2), 177–189. https://doi.org/10.1177/0894845315586256

Brown, T. N., Sellers, S. L., & Gomez, J. P. (2002). The relationship between internalization and self-esteem among Black adults. *Sociological Focus, 35*(1), 55–71.

Carr, E. R., Szymanski, D. M., Taha, F., West, L. M., & Kaslow, N. J. (2014). Understanding the link between multiple oppressions and depression among African American women: The role of internalization. *Psychology of Women Quarterly, 38*(2), 233–245. https://doi.org/10.1177/0361684313499900

Daniels, L. (Director). (2009). *Precious* [Film]. Lee Daniels Entertainment.

Decaille, N., & Hatzipanagos, R. (2019, January 11). What "Surviving R. Kelly" tells us about race and sexual abuse. *The Washington Post*. https://www.washingtonpost.com/nation/2019/01/11/what-surviving-r-kelly-tells-us-about-race-sexual-abuse/

Essed, P. (1991). *Understanding everyday racism: An interdisciplinary theory*. Sage.

Greene, B. (2000). African American lesbian and bisexual women. *Journal of Social Issues*, *56*(2), 239–249. https://doi.org/10.1111/0022-4537.00163

Harris-Perry, M. V. (2011). *Sister citizen: Shame, stereotypes, and Black women in America*. Yale University Press.

Heilman, M. E. (2012). Gender stereotypes and workplace bias. *Research in Organizational Behavior*, *32*, 113–135.

Hill, J. (2019, January 11). R. Kelly and the cost of Black protectionism. *The Atlantic*. https://www.theatlantic.com/entertainment/archive/2019/01/r-kelly-and-cost-black-protectionism/580150/

Hill, M. J. (2013). Is the Black community more homophobic?: Reflections on the intersectionality of race, class, gender, culture and religiosity of the perception of homophobia in the Black community. *Journal of Gay & Lesbian Mental Health*, *17*(2), 208–214. https://doi.org/10.1080/19359705.2013.768089

Jerald, M. C., Cole, E. R., Ward, L. M., & Avery, L. R. (2017). Controlling images: How awareness of group stereotypes affects Black women's well-being. *Journal of Counseling Psychology*, *64*(5), 487–499. http://dx.doi.org/10.1037/cou0000233

Jerald, M. C., Ward, L. M., Moss, L., Thomas, K., & Fletcher, K. D. (2017). Subordinates, sex objects, or Sapphires? Investigating contributions of media use to Black students' femininity ideologies and stereotypes about Black women. *Journal of Black Psychology*, *43*(6), 608–635. https://doi.org/10.1177/0095798416665967

Jones, C., & Shorter-Gooden, K. (2003). *Shifting: The double lives of Black women in America*. HarperCollins.

Kanahara, S. (2006). A review of the definitions of stereotype and a proposal for a progressional model. *Individual Differences Research*, *4*(5), 306–321.

Klesse, C. (2005). Bisexual women, non-monogamy and differentialist anti-promiscuity discourses. *Sexualities*, *8*(4), 445–464. https://doi.org/10.1177%2F1363460705056620

Molina, K. M., & James, D. (2016). Discrimination, internalized racism, and depression: A comparative study of African American and Afro-Caribbean adults in the U.S. *Group Processes & Intergroup Relations*, *19*(4), 439–461. https://doi.org/10.1177/1368430216641304

Monahan, J. L., Shtrulis, I., & Givens, S. B. (2005). Priming welfare queens and other stereotypes: The transference of media images into interpersonal contexts. *Communication Research Reports*, *22*(3), 199–205. https://doi.org/10.1080/00036810500207014

Morris, M. (2016). *Pushout: The criminalization of Black girls in schools*. The New Press.

Moynihan, D. P. (1965). *The Negro family: The case for national action* (No. 31-33). U.S. Government Printing Office.

Nadasen, P. (2007). From widow to "welfare queen": Welfare and the politics of race. *Black Women, Gender & Families*, *1*(2), 52–77.

Nelson, C. A. (2006). Of eggshells and thin-skulls: A consideration of racism-related mental illness impacting Black women. *International Journal of Law and Psychiatry*, *29*(2), 112–136.

Obama, M. (2018). *Becoming*. Crown Publishing Group.

Rudder, C. (2014, September 10). *Race and attraction, 2009–2014*. OKTrends. https://www.gwern.net/docs/psychology/okcupid/raceandattraction20092014.html

Scott, K. D. (2013) Communication strategies across cultural borders: Dispelling stereotypes, performing competence, and redefining Black womanhood. *Women's Studies in Communication, 36*(3), 312–329. https://doi.org/10.1080/07491409.2013.831005

Sesko, A. K., & Biernat, M. (2010). Prototypes of race and gender: The invisibility of Black women. *Journal of Experimental Social Psychology, 46*(2), 356–360. https://doi.org/10.1016/j.jesp.2009.10.016

Spencer, S. J., Steele, C. M., & Quinn, D. M. (1999). Stereotype threat and women's math performance. *Journal of Experimental Social Psychology, 35*(1), 4–28. https://doi.org/10.1006/jesp.1998.1373

Steele, C. M. (2010). *Whistling Vivaldi: How stereotypes affect us and what we can do.* WW Norton & Company.

Thomas, A. J., Witherspoon, K. M., & Speight, S. L. (2008). Gendered racism, psychological distress, and coping styles of African American women. *Cultural Diversity and Ethnic Minority Psychology, 14*(4), 307–314. https://doi.org/10.1037/1099-9809.14.4.307

Walley-Jean, J. C. (2009). Debunking the myth of the "angry Black woman": An exploration of anger in young African American women. *Black Women, Gender & Families, 3*(2), 68–86.

Ward, T. (2019, December 30). *I asked 5 Black men why they don't date Black women and their answers were shocking but not surprising.* Praise 102.5. https://mypraiseatl.com/1692779/i-asked-5-black-men-why-they-dont-date-black-women-and-their-answers-were-shocking-but-not-surprising/

West, C. M. (1995). Mammy, Sapphire, and Jezebel: Historical images of Black women and their implications for psychotherapy. *Psychotherapy: Theory, Research, Practice, Training, 32*(3), 458–466.

5   Black Women and Trauma

with Candice Norcott[*]

> We are Black women born into a society of entrenched loathing and contempt for whatever is Black and female. We are strong and enduring. We are also deeply scarred.
>
> Audre Lorde (1984)

On August 6, 2004, Johnny Allen, a 43-year-old man, solicited Cyntoia Brown, a 16-year-old Black girl, for sex. According to Cyntoia, he picked her up in his truck and brought her to his house. She reported that she shot the man, taking money and two guns from his home and fearing for her life when she left. In terms of background, Cyntoia was born with fetal alcohol syndrome to a teenage mother struggling with alcohol and cocaine addictions. By 8 months of age, she was no longer in her mother's care. As a teenager, she ran away from her foster placement, was repeatedly raped, and subsequently was trafficked for sex by a man named "Kut-throat." Cyntoia told a judge in her 2012 appeal hearing that this man would tell her that "some people were born whores, and that I was one. I was a slut, and nobody'd want me but him, and the best thing I could do was just learn to be a good whore" (Victor, 2017).

In the trial for Johnny Allen's death, Cyntoia was tried as an adult, convicted of murder, and sentenced to life in prison. Throughout her trial and in the media coverage of this story, Cyntoia was referred to as a "prostitute" despite her status as a minor. Her defense highlighted that her portrayal as a Black woman engaged in sex work was prejudicial. She served 15 years before her sentence was commuted in 2019, thanks to the #MeToo movement and celebrities such as Rihanna, who first tweeted about Cyntoia in 2017. Since she was convicted, Tennessee law has changed so that girls under 18 cannot be tried for prostitution. In her 30s, Cyntoia Brown Long (her married name) is an author and advocate for social justice and founder of the Foundation for Justice, Freedom, and Mercy. Cyntoia's story is not unique. It is just one example of how gender-based violence and systemic racism can devastate Black girls' lives.

---

[*] C. Norcott & Gooden, A. (2023). Black women and trauma. In D. Baptiste & A. Gooden, *Promoting Black women's mental health: What practitioners should know and do*. Cambridge University Press.

As demonstrated in Cyntoia Brown Long's case, the traumas that Black girls and women experience are often layered. Black women exist at the intersection of traumatic sexism and racism and experience historical, systemic, and individual traumas. Even in Black-led movements, Black women can experience sexism in response to their trauma experiences. It is the victimization of the Black male that has galvanized the Black community with the most fervor. It was the murders of Mike Brown and George Floyd that made individuals take to the streets, not those of Sandra Bland, Breonna Taylor, or Tony McDade. In fact, the call and response for women who have been victimized by police is "Say her name" and "Remember Breonna," as if pleading for acknowledgment. It is as if the atrocities enacted on Black women are expected and do not alarm us as much as the violence enacted upon any other body. This suggests a dehumanization of the Black woman and makes it more likely that Black women will be overlooked and denied care at every level. For Black women, this reality takes a psychological toll.

This chapter is aimed at helping therapists to provide trauma-informed support for their Black female clients. Many Black women may not even recognize the trauma and victimization they have experienced. Therapists can support Black women in prioritizing their own healing and self-advocacy. One of our study participants appreciated "being able to talk through past trauma and work through a plan for healing." For clinicians to effectively support Black women on their healing journeys, it is essential to understand the context of her pain.

5.1   Historical Trauma

Historical trauma refers to the cumulative physical and psychological wounding that occurs over a life span and across generations. Sotero's (2006) framework shows that historical trauma involves the intentional subjugation of a population that results in psychological and physiological harm in the first generation. This trauma is passed to subsequent generations through in-utero exposure to stress, maladaptive parenting, and vicarious trauma. Historical trauma serves as the backdrop for many Black women's lives, and it is important for therapists to understand the legacies of historical trauma in order to effectively help Black women heal in the present. We discuss some trauma experiences affecting Black women that therapists should know about.

5.1.1   Slavery

Although many years have passed since the abolition of slavery, the transatlantic slave trade and subsequent chattel slavery in the United States fit within Sotero's (2006) framework of historical trauma. In the transatlantic slave trade,

African people were taken against their will, shipped across the world in horrific conditions, and sold to slave owners in the Americas. Enslaved Africans in the United States were treated as property, and children were born into slavery. Further, slavery went on for centuries and White slave owners used racist views of Black people to justify slavery and their inhumane treatment of enslaved Black people. The violence, separation of families, harsh physical labor, rape of many enslaved women, and general lack of power enslaved people experienced were traumatic. Some theorists have suggested that Black people continue to struggle directly and indirectly with the multi-generational impact of slavery. Poussaint and Alexander (2000) describe Post-Traumatic Slave Syndrome: "the persistent presence of racism, despite the significant legal, social, and political progress made during the last half of the twentieth century, has created a physiological risk for black people that is virtually unknown to white Americans" (p. 15). In regard to Post-Traumatic Slave Syndrome, therapists should know that Black people can exhibit anger, a sense of inferiority, and lowered self-esteem (Wilkins et al., 2013). Contemporary experiences that visually depict the brutality of the US slave trade, such as movies about slavery or visiting the slavery exhibits in the National Museum of African American History and Culture in Washington, DC, can be incredibly validating and also trigger Black women to relive slavery trauma in their ancestry.

5.1.2   Segregation and Mass Incarceration

Traumatizing conditions for Black people in America did not end with slavery; the segregated south and Jim Crow laws subjected Black people to violence through lynchings, terrorization by police, and poverty (Graff, 2014). While the civil rights movement was a triumph, many forms of oppression, particularly those that affect poor Black Americans, did not disappear. They just changed conditions. In *The New Jim Crow: Mass Incarceration in the Age of Colorblindness*, Michelle Alexander (2010) highlights the collective trauma Black people have experienced through policing and incarceration policies that target Black communities. While Black women are incarcerated at lower rates than Black men, they are incarcerated at higher rates than White women. They endure the pain of losing fathers, sons, and brothers and caring for children and families without partners and parents.

Mass incarceration is also connected to the high rates of police violence that Black communities endure. In the last 10 years, the murders of Black people by police have entered public awareness. Black people experience trauma by witnessing these killings on video and feeling a sense of emotional proximity to the victims. Most Black people have had at least one negative encounter with police. When another incident of police violence surfaces, Black people often think the person harmed could have been them or someone they know. It is important for therapists to be aware that this trauma affects Black women in their daily lives and is exacerbated when police shootings of Black people occur. Therapists should be prepared to create space for Black women to process their experience and responses to this trauma.

5.1.3   Effects of Historical Trauma

Violence and trauma are painful and challenging when they occur and often do not end with the person experiencing them. Research has demonstrated that trauma can be passed down intergenerationally, and trauma can influence how all people parent (Sotero, 2006). One way trauma can be passed from one generation to the next is through shame-induced parenting. When Black parents experience racial violence and shame, they may have trouble attuning to their children and engaging in empathic, supportive parenting (Graff, 2014). Trauma is often dysregulating emotionally and can cause people to suppress their emotions and avoid being vulnerable in relationships. Parenting involves high levels of vulnerability, empathy, and emotional connection, which may be difficult for parents who have experienced and not healed from trauma. Specifically, Black women may become overprotective or overly strict and harsh with their children in response to trauma (Jenkins, 2002). Supporting Black women in healing from trauma involves exploring the legacies of trauma that may have played out in their lives through the parenting they received and other challenges they might have experienced.

Additionally, Black parents are often concerned with the safety of their children. They fear their children may experience the same traumas as they have. At times, to protect their children, Black parents can become overly harsh and strict to make sure their children follow directions and listen to authority. The fear is that if Black children do not listen to authority in their households, they may talk back or end up in a violent encounter with police outside the home. Black women are often in mothering roles, and therapists can support Black women in processing their anxiety for their children's safety while also fostering a loving and supportive home environment.

> Black women's mothering and caregiving roles are discussed further in Chapter 10.

Trauma is also passed down intergenerationally through the womb (Sotero, 2006). In 2012, the American Academy of Pediatrics highlighted the fact that "toxic stress" can negatively impact gene expression and development (Garner et al., 2012). Individual and collective trauma can certainly create toxic stress. Black women experience physiological and psychological effects of this trauma passed down from their parents. Further, personal experiences of racial and gendered violence compound the traumas they carry forward from their heritage, creating a complex profile that requires equally unique and responsive care to support their posttraumatic growth and healing. Historical trauma can feel overwhelming to address, and therapists working with Black women have the opportunity to help Black women heal from this trauma and break the cycles of trauma being passed down through generations. As Resmaa Menakem (2017) says, "the trauma response can look like part of the person's personality. As years and decades pass, reflexive traumatic responses can lose context" (p. 9). The therapist can help Black women recontextualize their trauma, helping them understand the true source of responses or reactions that they may have come to believe were part of their own nature.

5.2   Systemic and Institutional Trauma

The framework of systemic trauma examines how trauma occurs within families, schools, communities, and institutions, focusing on prevention and treatment. Goldsmith and colleagues (2014) developed the concept of systemic trauma to encompass the full range of traumatic experiences, not just events or acts of violence. Contextual factors create the conditions for trauma, maintain trauma, and influence how trauma is experienced (Goldsmith et al., 2014, p. 117). Systemic trauma is rooted in the historical traumas of slavery, and Black women are uniquely vulnerable to this type of trauma in their families, communities, schools, and other institutions. Understanding the influence of systems on Black women's experience of trauma is vital for providing therapy to Black women and facilitating their posttraumatic growth.

5.2.1   Adultification of Black Girls

Adultification, explored in Chapter 3, is a term used to describe the perception of Black girls as more adultlike, more responsible for their actions, and less innocent than their white counterparts. A study by the Georgetown Law Center on Poverty and Inequality (Epsteinet al., 2017) found that participants perceived Black girls as needing less nurturing, protection, comforting, and support when compared with same-aged White girls. Adultification can lead to Black girls experiencing trauma: Black girls receive more punitive punishment for developmentally normative behavior and are more likely to be criminalized. In other words, Black girls are more likely to be punished and are punished more harshly than White girls. Research shows that Black girls are disproportionately arrested and harassed by public safety officers at all levels of schooling (Morris, 2016). What happened to Cyntoia Brown, who was tried as an adult, is a clear example of the harm adultification can cause. Therapists working with Black women must be aware of the stress and trauma Black women likely experienced in their youth as they navigated harsher punishment. Further, Black women may not have been given the space to be kids as they were expected to be older and more mature than their biological age. Guiding Black women to re-parent their inner child can be a powerful intervention to heal the trauma of adultification.

Chapter 3 offers strategies to help Black women address lingering memories and effects of their girlhood.

5.2.2   Sexual Abuse to Prison Pipeline

The Human Rights Project for Girls, the Georgetown Law Center on Poverty and Inequality, and the Ms. Foundation detailed the criminalization of Black girls' trauma response in *The Sexual Abuse to Prison Pipeline: The Girls' Story* (Saar et al., 2015). This report describes how Black girls in particular become involved with the juvenile justice system because their response to sexual abuse is criminalized. The systemic links become clear when we look at the data showing that Black girls and women are more likely to be treated punitively in our criminal justice system. Black girls are almost three times as likely to be referred to juvenile justice as their White counterparts (Epstein et al., 2017). This trend continues into adulthood as Black people are 25% more likely than White people to be detained before trial.

Further, Black women and girls are more likely to have to pay bail (Sawyer, 2019). As a result of this and other factors, often including the inability to pay bail and afford private lawyers, Black women are incarcerated at a rate double that of White women, with disproportionate sentences for the same crimes. These biased systemic inequalities set the stage for Black girls and women to be treated violently by figures of authority, to have their victimization disregarded, and instead to be routed through a disproportionately punitive legal system that is costly and further interrupts their ability to engage with their families. Nowhere along this pathway are they offered counseling or treatment for the violence they have experienced.

5.2.3   Trauma in the Medical System

In addition to our judicial system, the medical system has a long history of enacting harm to Black women via their bodies. J. Marion Sims, a nineteenth-century surgeon historically referred to as the "father of modern gynecology," conducted vaginal fistula surgeries on enslaved women without anesthesia. He conducted similar surgeries on White women but with anesthesia; it was a commonly held belief that Black women did not experience pain in the same way as White women. This belief exists to this day and has been linked to discriminatory prescriptive and health care practices. According to a study published in *Proceedings of the National Academy of Sciences of the United States of America*, 40% of first- and second-year medical students endorsed the belief that "Black people's skin is thicker than white people's" (Hoffman et al., 2016). The same study found that medical trainees who believed that Black people are not as sensitive to pain as White people were less likely to treat Black people's pain appropriately (Hoffman et al., 2016).

Black women's reproductive rights have been the subject of racist practices as well. Between 1929 and 1974, Black women in North Carolina were sterilized without their consent as part of the eugenics movement (Nittle, 2020). A disproportionate number of incarcerated Black women have been given decreased sentences if they agree to have tubal ligation surgeries to prevent them from having children in the future (Roth & Ainsworth, 2015). In psychiatric institutions, many Black women were sterilized involuntarily, and as recently as 2017, some judges offered reduced sentences if Black people agreed to birth control implants or other sterilization (Perry, 2017). This systemic trauma in medical and health care systems creates a context of danger for Black women in these spaces, and it is important for therapists to be aware of this context. Therapists can work to ensure that Black women feel safe working with them in therapy by utilizing a trauma-informed approach to treatment, as we discuss later in this chapter.

In Chapter 13 we share recommendations for how therapists can support Black women in caring for their health and wellness and navigating health systems that are not always welcoming.

5.2.4   Effects of Systemic and Institutional Trauma

When Black women and girls experience trauma as they navigate systems that are supposed to protect them, they are likely to mistrust and not to benefit from those systems. Specifically, when school becomes an unsafe place, Black girls may have a harder time learning and pursuing their academic goals. When people do not complete high school, their career trajectory is often hampered, which also impacts their ability to earn money to support themselves and their families. Therefore, traumatic experiences in school may contribute to Black women being stuck in poverty. We also see the impact of Black women experiencing trauma within medical systems when Black women put off seeking medical care due to concern about being mistreated.

We explore trauma in the medical system in detail in Chapter 13 on Black women's health and wellness.

5.3   Individual Experiences of Trauma

The contexts of historical, systemic, and institutional trauma place Black women at increased risk for exposure to individual traumatic events, including adverse childhood experiences of sexual victimization (i.e., gender-based violence as well as racist attacks and interpersonal violence). During childhood, the rates and risks for violence are similar across genders. The most common victimization experiences for girls up to age 10 include maltreatment by a family member, witnessing family violence, and bullying. Important gender differences begin to emerge as individuals enter adolescence. Girls and young women between ages 14 and 24 are at greatest risk for sexual assault and other forms of intimate partner violence (Snyder, 2000). Many trauma survivors recount a pattern of violence, including childhood sexual abuse, dating violence and sexual assault in adolescence, and sexual assault and relationship violence in adulthood. Women experience higher rates of rape and sexual assault compared to men (Morgan & Oudekirk, 2019). This pathway for abuse and victimization highlights that women are most likely to experience sexual and physical violence from someone to whom she is related and says, "I love you." As a result, violence, violation, and intimacy can become intertwined in her life (Covington, 2008). In addition to experiencing more violence due to gender, according to the Institute for Women's Policy Research (DuMonthier et al., 2017), Black women experience significantly higher rates of psychological abuse, including humiliation, insults, name-calling, and coercive control.

Gender and sexual minorities are often overlooked in discourses about gender-based abuse. While there is limited research on the experiences of violence for women who identify as a sexual minority, the research suggests that they are at greater risk for violence exposure than heterosexual women and sexual minority men (Roberts et al., 2010). According to a study exploring multiple types of discrimination on mental health, 40% of lesbians and 12% of bisexual women reported being harassed in public about their sexual orientation (Bostwick et al., 2014). Additionally, Black transgender women are more likely to experience violence and sexual assault than Black cisgender women. Further, Black transgender women account for 66% of all transgender and gender nonconforming people murdered in the United States (Human Rights Campaign Foundation, 2020). We encourage clinicians to consider gender and sexual minority status when exploring how intersectional identities influence the experience of trauma. The experience for women of being both a racial and sexual minority presents a meaningful context that therapists need to understand. For example, sexual minority women of color were significantly more likely than their White counterparts to report experiences related to discrimination in public, related to admission to school or a training program, in the courts, and related to obtaining housing (Bostwick et al., 2014).

The negative impact of traumatic events on physical and emotional wellness has been well established (McCann et al., 1988; Myers et al., 2015; Shonkoff et al., 2012). Racial, gender, and sexual discrimination has also been found to increase the risk for reporting a mental health disorder (Bostwick et al., 2014). However, the same traumatic events can impact two people very differently. McCann et al. (1988) suggested that how an individual responds to a traumatic event is shaped by the experience of the event, beliefs about the self and the world, and expectations of future events (Pearlman & MacIan, 1995). Trauma can affect one's beliefs about the future via loss of hope, limited expectations about life, fear that life will end abruptly or early, or anticipation that normal life events will not occur (e.g., access to education, ability to have a significant and committed relationship, good opportunities for work). These beliefs often become barriers to seeking help after trauma. Further, historical and systemic trauma make it less likely that Black women will receive help, support, and compassion even when they ask for it. As a result, Black women have not had access to and utilized mental health counseling as frequently as their White counterparts.

Black women often cite not feeling understood or feeling judged as reasons that they do not seek therapy. These are also trauma reactions that compound the emotional distance a Black woman may experience in therapy. While there is no monolithic experience for Black women, therapists need to understand how the client's experiences and identities can increase risk, can lead to unique symptom presentations, and also can be a source of strength.

5.4   Treating Trauma in Black Women: An Intersectional Framework

We encourage therapists to work with Black women's trauma through the lens of Black feminist theory, which illuminates how Black women's life experiences are shaped by race and gender dynamics that are intertwined. A Black feminist view of Black women's trauma amplifies the interconnections of Black women's experience of racism and sexism simultaneously with their trauma experiences. This type of racial-gendered lens on Black women's lives averts the shortsightedness of interventions that treat race or gender as discrete identities. Rooted in the work of abolitionism, suffrage, civil rights, and Black power, early Black feminism was marked by Black women, like Sojourner Truth and Harriet Tubman, who rejected their subjugation. In *Black Feminist Thought*, Patricia Hill Collins (2002) writes that "such [Black feminist] thought can encourage collective identity by offering Black women a different view of themselves and their world than that offered by the established social order" (p. 186). Working within a Black feminist orientation encourages therapists to stress self-definition and self-valuation in their Black women clients. Black women's feminist practice can "teach us about the complex interworkings of changing structures of power" (Mahmood, 2011, p. 9). Further, drawing on intersectionality, which is rooted in Black feminism, emphasizes the importance of understanding the systems and structures that contribute to Black women's experience and urges therapists to advocate roles for social justice both in and outside of the therapy room (Settles et al., 2020).

Therapists are encouraged to explore with clients (and with themselves) the externally imposed images and stereotypes as well as their unique intersectional identities. Self-identification and self-valuation, therefore, become powerful tools in working with Black women toward instilling posttraumatic resilience and growth (Collins, 1986). Further, we encourage therapists to be aware of how the systems they operate within and services they provide may discriminate against or even traumatize Black women and advocate for these systems to be more equitable and just. Adopting an intersectional lens on Black women's trauma paves the way for a more holistic approach to trauma-informed therapy.

5.5 Therapeutic Safety for Black Women: Establishing the Context for Trauma Work

Given that trauma, by its nature, threatens an individual's safety, it is essential that the therapeutic environment, including the therapeutic relationship, feels safe for the client. Trauma-informed care (TIC) is a model of care that guides therapists and mental health systems to provide safe environments for clients. TIC is a strengths-based service delivery approach grounded in understanding the pervasive impact of trauma, which allows survivors to successfully access services and thrive. It asks the survivor "What happened to you?" instead of "What's wrong with you?" TIC offers individual as well as systemic and organizational guidance for service delivery transformation. The Substance Abuse and Mental Health Services Administration (SAMHSA) outlines six core principles of TIC and suggests that by adhering to these principles, therapists and organizations can understand the widespread impact of trauma, see paths to recovery, better recognize signs and symptoms of trauma, and create policies and procedures to actively avoid retraumatizing clients as well as employees (SAMHSA, 2014). Here we share recommendations for how to apply the six principles of TIC with Black women.

5.5.1   Safety and Trustworthiness

Building trust and making sure the therapeutic relationship is safe are the first two important components of TIC. The gold standard and fundamental principle of TIC involves creating safety for clients and support for clinicians and other staff at all levels of the organization. Fostering safety for clients is an ongoing process, and it is important to give clients time to develop trust. Survivors of trauma often have trouble trusting other people, and therapists working with Black women who have experienced trauma will need to focus on building trust. Microaggressions are one thing that can cause Black women to feel unsafe, and it is important to prevent these subtle, unintentional slights and indignities in health and mental health systems. Therapists can work to create safety for Black female clients by engaging in training to address the bias that they and other members of the health care system may hold toward Black women. Showing up authentically and engaging in appropriate self-disclosure can be an important part of helping Black female clients to build trust with the therapist over time.

> We discuss building a safe therapeutic relationship further in Chapter 7.

As with building a strong, trusting therapeutic environment with all clients, therapists are encouraged to provide a warm and welcoming environment. Initial sessions should be focused on fostering good rapport and building a relationship with the client. Fostering connections between the therapist and the client is an important pillar in providing TIC (Bath, 2008). Therapists are encouraged to pay special attention to creating authentic connections with their clients and avoiding the traditional "expert" stance in therapy. The conventional "blank slate" approach to therapy is likely not a good fit for trauma work with Black female clients, particularly if you are a White therapist. Lack of responsiveness can be easily interpreted as judgment or dislike, which can exacerbate any shame your clients may be experiencing. Further, most Black people are aware of the pervasive negative views that White society holds about Black people, and a highly boundaried and emotionally withdrawn approach to the therapeutic relationship may leave Black women wondering whether you hold negative views toward them.

Building a strong therapeutic alliance is discussed in more depth in Chapter 7.

5.5.2   Peer Support

Trauma commonly causes victims to feel ashamed and isolated. The third component of TIC, peer support, refers to the support of other individuals with shared, lived traumatic experiences. Peer networks provide a powerful tool for victims of violence to feel less alone and begin to reconnect after their trauma. For Black women, whose trauma is often minimized and overlooked, peer support can be an important and powerful place for validation. As a result, Black women have connected in this way for years in the form of sister circles. Sister circles are informal, naturally occurring support groups for Black women that build upon existing friendships, family networks, and community. Sister circles can emerge when women connect around shared health concerns, such as diabetes, exercise, mental well-being, or heart health. Women also form sister circles through shared activities such as church, social clubs, sororities, or workplaces (Boyd, 1993; Giddings, 1984). Not all women, however, have such circles or experience forming connections, and some may need help finding such circles. We encourage therapists to talk with their Black female clients about how to find and cultivate supportive peer relationships that can support them in their healing journey.

5.5.3   Collaboration and Empowerment

The fourth and fifth core principles of TIC urge therapists and organizations to encourage collaboration and mutual effort toward empowerment of the survivor by elevating her voice and choice. The trauma that Black women experience often involves someone using their power over them, and it is essential not to replicate these power dynamics in the therapy room. Therapists must acknowledge the power dynamic inherent in the therapeutic relationship and take a feminist/womanist approach to flatten that hierarchy. For White therapists, an additional layer of power dynamics at play in the therapeutic relationship may contribute to Black female clients feeling less safe and empowered in therapy, and this should be acknowledged and addressed. It is also important for Black women to decide to process their trauma. The therapist should not make this decision for them. We encourage therapists to provide psychoeducation about processing trauma, including what this entails and what benefits their clients might experience through this process. Ultimately, the decision about whether or not to revisit and reprocess painful experiences must be made by the client.

See Chapter 7 for more specific recommendations on how to address power dynamics in the therapeutic relationship.

The principles of collaboration and empowerment also have implications on the organizational level. Trauma-informed mental health centers and clinical practices should have a flattened hierarchy with shared decision-making and inclusion of a diversity of opinions (Madsen et al., 2003). If therapists work at an agency, hospital, or group practice, it is important to foster healthy communication and relationship dynamics between clinical and nonclinical staff members because these relationships are likely to be reflected in the clinical services provided to clients (Madsen et al., 2003).

5.5.4   Attending to Culture, History, and Gender

Finally, the sixth principle of TIC is attending to cultural, historical, and gender issues. The decision to seek therapy is not made lightly by Black women. Black women and mothers of Black girls share fears of further victimization and traumatizing interactions with non-Black therapists. The aforementioned historical and systemic trauma that Black women experience as well as negative stereotypes (discussed further in Chapter 4) that Black women navigate serve as barriers to them seeking therapy.

Once a Black woman engages in therapy, she may be apprehensive about sharing negative or traumatic experiences she has had within her families and the Black community for fear of perpetuating stereotypes about Black people to a non-Black therapist. She may be reluctant to disclose her victimization or the full extent of the violence to manage the public perception of Black men. Aligned with this thinking, Black women often feel that a positive public image of the Black community relies on her silence. Black women may feel torn between speaking their truth and processing their pain and staying silent to protect the reputation of members of their community. Black women who do speak out publicly about the harm they have experienced at the hands of Black men are harshly criticized by Black men and women (e.g., Anita Hill and Megan Thee Stallion). This results in tension for a Black woman as she thinks about disclosing abuse. As a result, it is important for therapists to make room for a wide range of trauma reactions and expressions. Menakem (2017) asserts that when trauma is decontextualized and has not been processed can look like personality and even culture. Given the history of overpathologizing Black women, we suggest that therapists look at the symptoms and behaviors of their Black female clients through a trauma lens. A therapist will ultimately be more successful, understanding, and compassionate by seeking to understand how historical, systemic, and personal trauma may have contributed to the symptomatology that Black women exhibit. This approach will also support Black women in being compassionate with themselves.

Attending to this sixth core principle will help therapists ensure their treatment system does not traumatize or retraumatize their clients. Many therapists are accustomed to focusing solely on what happens inside of the therapy room and may mistakenly believe that those are the only factors that influence the effectiveness of treatment. However, just as trauma always happens in context, we must increase our awareness of the context of the treatment for our clients. This is particularly important for Black women, who often experience microaggressions in health and mental health care systems, which causes them to feel unheard, invalidated, and unsafe. Therapists striving to provide trauma-informed treatment are encouraged to attend to the experiences Black women may have with their entire system, including interactions with reception, billing, and other aspects of the system with which a client might interact. We recommend that therapists who work in organizations or group practices regularly check in with their clients about experiences with the whole therapeutic process, including reception and billing.

5.6   Trauma Interventions: Best Practices for Black Women

The term *best practices* refers to reliance on evidence-based programs. While the literature on evidence-based trauma interventions for Black women is sparse, several interventions in general practices can be adapted for Black women trauma survivors. Trauma-specific therapy interventions should target alleviation or prevention of traumatic stress in Black women. The case example later in this chapter illustrates how a therapist worked with a Black client's trauma, highlighting how these recommendations might be applied.

5.6.1   Address the Reluctance to Disclose

A key aspect of healing for survivors is sharing the narrative of their trauma. However, a number of barriers may make a Black female survivor reluctant to share her story. For example, survivors of trauma may fear they will not be believed. The perpetrator may have some standing in the community (e.g., campus athlete, teacher, pastor, authority figure), which can make it more likely for people to assume the perpetrator could do no harm. A woman may also feel that circumstances such as her socioeconomic status or substance use when she was assaulted may erode her credibility. Women, and Black women in particular, may have also had prior experiences of trauma that were dismissed or disbelieved. This can make a survivor feel that disclosing trauma to her current therapist may be futile at best or harmful at worst. Additionally, Black women may be reluctant to disclose trauma experienced at the hands of a Black man, as they may worry about reinforcing stereotypes of Black men if they report this. They may fear that their disclosure will result in another Black man being victimized by a racist judicial system. Therapists must be aware of this tension for Black survivors. We recommend that therapists help Black female clients place responsibility for their victimization on the perpetrator while being careful not to cast all Black men as perpetrators or harmful. It can be helpful for therapists to normalize the tension Black women feel between advocating for and protecting themselves and protecting Black men. For example, a non-Black therapist might comment: "As you share what you experienced, I hear you downplaying what happened to you. It also sounds like you don't want me to think he is a bad person. Some Black women I have worked with in the past worried about how I might judge Black men. They worried that because I am a White woman, I might come away thinking that all Black men are rapists. Is this something you might be worried about?"

5.6.2   Believe the Black Woman's Trauma Narrative

As stated earlier, survivors are often reluctant to disclose for many reasons. Black women commonly have experienced numerous racist and gender-based harassment instances over their lifetime. It is important for therapists to believe the stories that Black women share. Therapists must notice if they feel compelled to question the veracity of Black women's reports of the trauma they have experienced. In particular, therapists whose privileged identities and backgrounds have protected them from racial, systemic, and gender-based trauma may find it difficult to believe the many traumatic experiences that Black women report. The desire to "fact check" may be a cue that the experiences a Black woman is describing are so foreign to your own lived experience that it is easier to interrogate her veracity than to sit with her violent reality. It is essential for therapists to prioritize validating the experiences of their Black female clients and explore any questions about their clients' experiences in their own supervision or consultation.

5.6.3   Acknowledge How Trauma Influences Behavior

Trauma and societal messages shape the decision-making practices of girls and women about Black female sexuality. Research has shown that one of the most devastating effects of childhood sexual abuse for girls and women is that it increases the risk for victimization later in life. Many Black women grew up in a context where Black girls who were victims of sexual assault were seen as "fast," which is connected to the stereotype of Black women being hypersexual. If a survivor of childhood sexual abuse has internalized the narrative that she is "fast" she may believe that she "asked for" her abuse. She may also rely on sexualized behavior to get attention, resulting in an increased risk for revictimization, unplanned pregnancy, and sexually transmitted infection. A culturally appropriate, gender- and trauma-responsive approach guides us to look at the ways in which we interpret the behaviors our clients engage in and the challenges they face. We recommend therapists ask: "What are the systems and structures that are affecting you?" The therapist should inquire about the narratives about abuse and victimization that the client grew up with, what aspects of these narratives she rejects, and what parts she believes.

5.6.4   Coach Black Women in Self-Soothing

Emotion regulation is an important skill that supports survivors in healing from their trauma. Trauma lives in our bodies and is intimately connected to our innate tendencies to respond to threatening experiences by fighting, running away (fleeing), or getting stuck (freezing). These reactions often continue in response to activating events, and one of the central tasks of therapy is to support clients in calming their nervous systems through emotion regulation practices when they are not faced with immediate threats to their safety. One way to support Black female clients' emotion regulation is to guide them in strategies that help to ground themselves in their bodies.

Humming is a culturally responsive grounding strategy that helps Black people to soothe themselves (Menakem, 2017). Black women who grew up in the Black church will likely have memories of older women in the church humming in response to a painful event that occurred in the community. This deep, vibrational humming is soothing to the ears and to the soul. Therapists can encourage their Black female clients to practice humming as a grounding technique by sitting in a comfortable position, noticing how their body feels sitting in the chair with their feet on the floor, taking a few slow deep breaths down into their bellies, and then humming on an out-breath. Clients can hum to a familiar song or melody that is comforting or just hum whatever tone or tune arises for them. Therapists should guide their clients to attend to the gentle vibration they feel as they hum. After doing this for a couple of minutes, therapists can guide Black women to stop humming, notice how their body is feeling, and identify any shifts or changes they have experienced. Another common grounding technique is the "Notice 5 Things" activity, in which clients are guided to look around the room and name five things they can see, four things they can hear, three things they can feel physically in their body, two things they can smell, and one thing they can taste. Therapists can also guide clients in slow, deep belly breathing to help calm their bodies. All of these strategies are designed to help Black women slow down and communicate to their bodies that they are safe.

Because trauma lives in the body, taking care of the body is an important aspect of healing for Black women (Menakem, 2017). Often, the trauma that Black women experience happened to their physical bodies, and healing this trauma involves helping them to cultivate a safe and healthy relationship with their bodies through self-care. Further, somatic-focused therapies that support Black women to process the physical manifestation of emotions and care for their bodies can be especially helpful for healing historical trauma as well as trauma that occurred for Black women before they could speak. Therapists can support Black women in taking care of their health and bodies as a means of healing.

> Supporting Black women's health and wellness through self-care is discussed extensively in Chapter 13, and we encourage readers to use that chapter as a guide for ways to support Black women in taking care of their health and bodies.

As Black women become more comfortable and settled in their bodies, they will be able to be present with painful experiences without engaging in the trauma response of trying to run away from these memories. Clinicians can support the emotion regulation of their Black female clients by helping them to sit with and accept difficult emotions while offering compassion for themselves and their feelings. Self-compassion resources are included in the resource list at the end of this chapter. Clinicians are encouraged to use this exercise with their clients during emotionally difficult moments in therapy sessions. This exercise experientially demonstrates to clients that their emotions will not overwhelm them.

Overall, helping Black women soothe and comfort themselves aligns with what we know about the neurobiology of trauma. When we experience a threatening circumstance, our amygdala takes over from our prefrontal cortex (the decision-making part of our brain). This makes it difficult to function and make decisions. When a therapist guides a Black female client in these soothing practices, they support her in healing her trauma and making empowered decisions in her life.

5.6.5   Encourage Religious and Spiritual Coping

Faith, spirituality, and the community offered through the Black church can be great sources of strength and support for many Black survivors. Black women of various religious traditions often use their faith and religious community to seek help, cope, and make sense of the trauma they have experienced. Specifically, Black Christian women commonly seek counsel from their spiritual leaders before seeking professional therapy. It is important not to be dismissive of the counseling and support offered through the church. Black women may also have had negative and sometimes even traumatic experiences with their church families or in past church communities. Therapists should not assume that the church has been a refuge for Black female survivors of sexual assault. In her book, *Thriving in the Wake of Trauma: A Multicultural Guide,* Dr. Thema Bryant-Davis (2005) provides clients and therapists with a nuanced understanding of the opportunities and challenges religion can provide for survivors. We encourage therapists to inquire about the client's relationship with her spiritual and religious beliefs as well as her church homes. Ask her how the church treated sexuality, sexual violence, and abuse. Was it talked about? Were girls and women burdened with the responsibility of protecting sexuality and purity? Black female clients' relationship with religion and the church may be complicated and require disentangling. Attending to these questions in therapy is important because if these issues are salient for Black female clients, leaving them unaddressed may lead to premature termination.

See Chapter 15 for further discussion of religion and spirituality in the context of Black women's therapy.

5.6.6   Support Communal Coping

In addition to practices that support Black women in responding individually to their trauma, it is important for therapists to remember that Black women often hold communal values and heal through connection and close relationships with other people. Therapists should support Black women in prioritizing and deepening (if necessary) their relationships with other Black women or loved ones in general. Therapists should guide Black women through an assessment of their social support networks to identify people in their lives that they can turn to for support and connection. This assessment should also identify how and when Black women can reach out to people for support and any barriers to seeking support they might face. As mentioned earlier, Black women are often involved in sister circles or informal groups of close female friends who they laugh and cry with and can turn to for support. These groups of friends will often offer to pray for each other and commiserate and empathize with each other. This support can also be fostered in the context of group therapy. One of us (Adia Gooden) facilitated a group for women of color for several years and witnessed the powerful healing that took place as these women connected, supported, and encouraged each other.

5.6.7   Encourage Activism

Research demonstrates that activism promotes posttraumatic growth in survivors (Fields et al., 2020; Strauss Swanson & Szymanski, 2020). Trauma can cause people to question their worth and the purpose of life. An important aspect of healing trauma is helping people reconnect to their self-worth and the meaning of life. Having a sense of purpose and meaning promotes resilience (Alim et al., 2008). Therapists are encouraged to guide Black women to identify and explore their purpose and connect to things that remind them of this purpose. This exploration can involve Black women sharing their religious, spiritual, and political views. Therapists should work to collaborate with survivors, activist groups, researchers, and other providers to challenge systems of power and oppression that promote, enact, and sustain violence against Black women. For example, a therapist may work with a campus sexual assault advocacy group to support survivors beyond the context of therapy and expand their understanding of survivors' experiences. Additionally, therapists can have supportive materials about surviving trauma available around the office or on the practice website for their clients.

Case Example

Nia is a 43-year-old, heterosexual, cisgender, single, "spiritual" Black woman employed in security for an upscale apartment high-rise. Nia presented to therapy in considerable distress. Nia is the youngest of three children and was raised by her mother, whom she describes as a strong and powerful woman. She reported seeing her mother being treated violently by boyfriends. Despite the abuse she endured, her mother always worked to make sure that Nia and her two siblings had everything they needed. Nia also described a significant history of sexual trauma that began in her childhood and continued into her adolescence, with experience of dating violence, and into adulthood. She shared that she is the most stable she has been in her life but feels that she is emotionally falling apart.

She is the sole provider for her children, ages 10, 8, and 6. She takes great pride in her role as mother. She has secure employment and housing, but when her youngest daughter started elementary school, Nia started having flashbacks, had trouble feeling connected to her kids, had difficulty sleeping, and generally felt irritable. She reported having unexpected bouts of crying, and in therapy sessions she apologized whenever she began to tear up. Nia shared that she felt "crazy," didn't know why she couldn't stop thinking about her past, and just wanted to get control again. Nia made it clear that she did not see herself as a victim and shared that she could not afford to be weak for her children. She felt that therapy is a White person's luxury that she never thought she could afford, financially or timewise.

As Nia's therapy journey began, the therapist identified several factors could be a threat to Nia's emotional safety. The therapist asked if this was her first experience with therapy, and Nia confirmed that it was. She in fact had never talked about her abuse with anyone other than the father of her children. With that in mind, the therapist provided psychoeducation about the therapeutic process and clinic procedures. The therapist also sought to maintain an egalitarian relationship with Nia so as to minimize any dynamics of hierarchy and not recreate aspects of her experiences of disempowerment (e.g., child sexual abuse, dating violence, and employee role in an upscale setting). The therapist invited Nia to ask questions and gave her options of how to use the session time. Another factor impacting safety was Nia's feeling that she was "going crazy." Providing psychoeducation about the impact of trauma and trauma activators was an important foundational step. The therapist shared with Nia that it is common for women to have their trauma experiences activated when they have children that are near the age at which they experienced their own trauma. For Nia, the youngest of three, her own abuse began when she was in first grade, the same age as her youngest daughter at the time of therapy. Learning about this helped Nia understand her own symptoms better and feel in more control.

Nia also seemed to have beliefs about emotional expression that defined crying as weakness and self-care as indulgent. She saw her mother as a self-sacrificing matriarch and sought to replicate that in her children's lives. Early sessions were spent challenging Nia's notions of strength and weakness and emotional expression. The therapist encouraged Nia to see widening her range of emotional expression as a good lesson to teach her children.

In working with Nia, it was important to make her feel like an equal partner in her therapy. Her trauma experiences caused her to feel powerless, and she worked to avoid that feeling in her job, her role as mother, and her personal relationships. The therapist worked with her to disentangle vulnerable and emotional expression from powerlessness and lack of control. Nia gained an understanding of her symptoms as connected to her trauma and the ways in which avoidance sustained her distress. Nia learned to recognize her symptoms as signals she could use as cues to engage in grounding and mindfulness techniques to help soothe herself. Nia learned to recognize trauma activators in her life, such as her children's development stage and even her job, in which she experienced microaggressions triggering her to recall past experiences of powerlessness. Nia's understanding of the role of power and control in abuse and violence helped her to recognize those elements in her workplace and her relationships. Nia found that these tools gave her a greater mastery over her emotional experience so she could "risk" being emotional when she wanted to.

5.7   Conclusion: Posttraumatic Growth

Acknowledging and addressing trauma can be overwhelming and can cause therapists and clients to feel a sense of despair regarding the horrific things that happen in this world. However, healing from trauma can present opportunities for survivors to grow mentally and emotionally. Research on posttraumatic growth has shown that trauma survivors can experience positive psychological adjustment in five areas: appreciation for life, relationships with others, new possibilities in life, personal strength, and spiritual change (Tedeschi & Calhoun, 1996). Posttraumatic growth diverges from the deficit reduction approach to trauma recovery that previously dominated the literature and offers a strength- and resilience-based model. Posttraumatic growth suggests that even after traumatic events, it is possible for individuals to be compassionate with themselves and give themselves permission for self-care in ways they did not before their trauma. Through the process of healing, survivors can learn to be more attuned to their emotions than they were before their adversity.

Additionally, individuals who have experienced trauma may feel that they are a part of a new community of survivors. This sense of belonging can offer a powerful and new sense of connection and source of support. A survivor may become connected spiritually or emotionally in ways that they had not prior to the trauma and develop a sense of a larger purpose or meaning for their life. Finally, the experience of victimization and recovery may motivate survivors to seek ways to improve their communities and engage in activism around issues related to their trauma. These efforts can be a powerful redirection of a survivor's energy away from self-deprecation and self-blame. Of course, as therapists we wish we could take the client's pain away. Yet while we cannot turn back time, we can provide culturally relevant tools so they can manage their recovery and invite them to open their own powerful gift of empowerment.

Therapist Reflection Questions

1. Have you had experiences of trauma? How did you make sense of them?
2. How has your racial and gender identity shaped your trauma experiences?
3. What are your thoughts on the idea of Post-Traumatic Slave Syndrome as a unique experience for Black people?
4. How might Black women be impacted by watching a movie or visiting an exhibit about slavery?
5. What hesitations might Black women feel about sharing trauma stories with non-Black or male-identified therapists?
6. What are societal and media messages that may make Black women hesitant to disclose sexual trauma? What lessons have you learned (or what information do you need) related to treating Black nonbinary or Black trans women trauma survivors?

Resources for Therapists

Hotlines and Websites

Me too. (n.d.). https://metoomvmt.org/. Founded by Tarana Burke.

Rape, Abuse, & Incest National Network. (n.d.). https://www.rainn.org/. National hotline, resources for survivors, family members, and providers, statistics, and other resources.

The National Center on Violence Against Women in the Black Community. (n.d.). Ujimacommunity.org. Ujima is a clearinghouse for research literature, webinars, national issue forums, regional trainings, community-specific roundtables, blogs, articles, and on-site technical assistance.

The National Organization of Sisters of Color Ending Sexual Assault (SCESA). (n.d.). https://sisterslead.org/. An advocacy organization of Women of Color dedicated to working with our communities to create a just society in which all Women of Color are able to live healthy lives free of violence.

Self-Compassion. (n.d.). https://self-compassion.org/. Self-compassion meditations, scripts, and other resources.

Books

Bryant-Davis, T. (2005). *Thriving in the wake of trauma: A multicultural guide* (No. 49). Greenwood Publishing Group.

Buirski, N. (Director). (2018). *The rape of Recy Taylor* [Film]. Augusta Films LLC. https://www.therapeofrecytaylor.com/the-film/. A documentary about Mrs. Recy Taylor who was gang raped by six White boys in 1944 Alabama. Unbroken, she spoke up and fought for justice with help from Rosa Parks and legions of women.

Herman, J. L. (2015). *Trauma and recovery: The aftermath of violence – from domestic abuse to political terror*. Hachette UK.

hooks, b. (1993). *Sisters of the yam: Black women and self-recovery*. South End Press.

Lorde, A. (1984). *Sister outsider*. Crossing Press.

Morris, M., & Atlas, J. (Directors). (2019). *PUSHOUT: The criminalization of Black girls in schools* [Film]. A Woman in the Room Productions. https://pushoutfilm.com/. PUSHOUT is a feature-length documentary that takes a close look at the educational, judicial, and societal disparities facing Black girls.

Ritchie, A. J. (2017). *Invisible no more: Police violence against Black women and women of color*. Beacon Press.

Roberts, D. E. (1997) *Killing the Black body: Race, reproduction, and the meaning of liberty*. Pantheon Books.

Films

Simmons, A. S. (Director). (2006). *No! The rape documentary* [Film]. AfroLez Productions. https://notherapedocumentary.org/home. NO! The Rape Documentary is the 2006-released Ford Foundation-funded, groundbreaking, film about intraracial rape, accountability, and healing in Black communities. Produced, written, and directed over a period of 12 years, by child sexual abuse and adult rape survivor Aishah Shahidah Simmons, this internationally acclaimed, award-winning film also explores how rape is used as a weapon of homophobia.

References

Alexander, M. (2010). *The new Jim Crow: Mass incarceration in the age of colorblindness*. The New Press.

Alim, T. N., Feder, A., Graves, R. E., Wang, Y., Weaver, J., Westphal, M., Alonso, A., Aigbogun, N. U., Smith, B. W., Doucette, J. T., Mellman, T. A., Lawson, W. B., & Charney, D. S. (2008). Trauma, resilience, and recovery in a high-risk African-American population. *American Journal of Psychiatry, 165*(12), 1566–1575.

Bath, H. (2008). The three pillars of trauma-informed care. *Reclaiming Children and Youth, 17*(3), 17–21.

Bostwick, W. B., Boyd, C. J., Hughes, T. L., West, B. T., & McCabe, S. E. (2014). Discrimination and mental health among lesbian, gay, and bisexual adults in the United States. *American Journal of Orthopsychiatry, 84*(1), 35–45.

Boyd, J. (1993). *In the company of my sisters: Black women and self-esteem*. Dutton.

Bryant-Davis, T. (2005). *Thriving in the wake of trauma: A multicultural guide* (No. 49). Greenwood Publishing Group.

Collins, P. H. (2002). *Black feminist thought: Knowledge, consciousness, and the politics of empowerment*. Routledge.

Collins, P. H. (1986). Learning from the outsider within: The sociological significance of Black feminist thought. *Social problems, 33*(6), s14–s32.

Covington, S. S. (2008). Women and addiction: A trauma-informed approach. *Journal of Psychoactive Drugs, 40* (Suppl. 5), 377–385.

DuMonthier, A., Childers, C., & Milli, J. (2017). *The status of Black women in the United States*. Institute for Women's Policy Research.

Epstein, R., Blake, J., & González, T. (2017). Girlhood interrupted: The erasure of black girls' childhood. *SSRN Electronic Journal, 3000695*.

Fields, L., Valdez, C. E., Richmond, C., Murphy, M. J., Halloran, M., Boccellari, A., & Shumway, M. (2020). Communities Healing and Transforming Trauma

(CHATT): A trauma-informed speakers' bureau for survivors of violence. *Journal of Trauma & Dissociation, 21*(4), 437–451.

Garner, A. S., Shonkoff, J. P., & Committee on Early Childhood, Adoption, and Dependent Care. (2012). Early childhood adversity, toxic stress, and the role of the pediatrician: Translating developmental science into lifelong health. *Pediatrics, 129*(1), e224–e231.

Giddings, P. (1984). *When and where I enter: The impact of Black women on race and sex in America.* Morrow.

Goldsmith, R. E., Martin, C. G., & Smith, C. P. (2014). Systemic trauma. *Journal of Trauma & Dissociation, 15*(2), 117–132.

Graff, G. (2014). The intergenerational trauma of slavery and its aftermath. *The Journal of Psychohistory, 41*(3), 181–197.

Hoffman, K. M., Trawalter, S., Axt, J. R., & Oliver, M. N. (2016). Racial bias in pain assessment and treatment recommendations, and false beliefs about biological differences between Blacks and Whites. *Proceedings of the National Academy of Sciences of the United States of America, 113*(16), 4296–4301.

Human Rights Campaign Foundation. (2020). *An epidemic of violence: Fatal violence against transgender and gender non-conforming people in the United States in 2020.* https://hrc-prod-requests.s3-us-west-2.amazonaws.com/FatalViolence-2020Report-Final.pdf

Jenkins, E. J. (2002). Black women and community violence: Trauma, grief, and coping. *Women & Therapy, 25*(3–4), 29–44.

Madsen, L., Blitz, L., McCorkle, D., & Panzer, P. (2003). Sanctuary in a domestic violence shelter: A team approach to healing. *Psychiatric Quarterly, 74*(2), 155–171.

Mahmood, S. (2011). *Politics of piety: The Islamic revival and the feminist subject.* Princeton University Press.

McCann, I. L., Sakheim, D. K., & Abrahamson, D. J. (1988). Trauma and victimization: A model of psychological adaptation. *The Counseling Psychologist, 16*(4), 531–594.

Menakem, R. (2017). *My grandmother's hands: Racialized trauma and the pathway to mending our hearts and bodies.* Central Recovery Press.

Morgan, R. E., & Oudekerk, B. A. (2019). *Criminal victimization 2018. National Crime Victimization Survey.* Bureau of Justice Statistics. https://www.bjs.gov/index.cfm?ty=pbdetail&iid=6686

Morris, M. (2016). *Pushout: The criminalization of Black girls in schools.* The New Press.

Myers, H. F., Wyatt, G. E., Ullman, J. B., Loeb, T. B., Chin, D., Prause, N., Zhang, M., Williams, J. K., Slavich, G. M., & Liu, H. (2015). Cumulative burden of lifetime adversities: Trauma and mental health in low-SES African Americans and Latino/as. *Psychological Trauma: Theory, Research, Practice, and Policy, 7*(3), 243–251. https://doi.org/10.1037/a0039077

Nittle, N. K. (2020, August 26). *The U.S. government's role in sterilizing women of color.* ThoughtCo. https://www.thoughtco.com/u-s-governments-role-sterilizing-women-of-color-2834600

Pearlman, L. A., & MacIan, P. S. (1995). Vicarious traumatization: An empirical study of the effects of trauma work on trauma therapists. *Professional Psychology: Research and Practice, 26*(6), 558–565.

Perry, D. M. (2017, July 27) *Our long, troubling history of sterilizing the incarcerated.* The Marshall Project. https://www.themarshallproject.org/2017/07/26/our-long-troubling-history-of-sterilizing-the-incarcerated

Poussaint, A. F., & Alexander, A. (2000). *Lay my burdens down.* Beacon Press.

Roberts, A. L., Austin, S. B., Corliss, H. L., Vandermorris, A. K., & Koenen, K. C. (2010). Pervasive trauma exposure among US sexual orientation minority adults and risk of posttraumatic stress disorder. *American Journal of Public Health, 100* (12), 2433–2441.

Roth, R., & Ainsworth, S. L. (2015). If they hand you a paper, you sign it: A call to end the sterilization of women in prison. *Hastings Women's Law Journal, 26,* 7–50.

Saar, M. S., Epstein, R., Rosenthal, L., & Vafa, Y. (2015). *The sexual abuse to prison pipeline: The girls' story.* Human Rights Project for Girls and Center for Poverty and Inequality at Georgetown University Law Center.

Sawyer, W. (2019). *How race impacts who is detained pretrial.* Prison Policy Initiative https://www.prisonpolicy.org/blog/2019/10/09/pretrial_race/

Settles, I. H., Warner, L. R., Buchanan, N. T., & Jones, M. K. (2020). Understanding psychology's resistance to intersectionality theory using a framework of epistemic exclusion and invisibility. *Journal of Social Issues, 76*(4), 796–813.

Shonkoff, J. P., Garner, A. S., & Committee on Psychosocial Aspects of Child and Family Health, Committee on Early Childhood, Adoption, and Dependent Care, and Section on Developmental and Behavioral Pediatrics. (2012). The lifelong effects of early childhood adversity and toxic stress. *Pediatrics, 129*(1), e232–e246.

Snyder, H. N. (2000). *Sexual assault of young children as reported to law enforcement: Victim, incident, and offender characteristics: A statistical report using data from the National Incident-Based Reporting System.* U.S. Department of Justice, Office of Justice Programs, Bureau of Justice Statistics.

Sotero, M. (2006). A conceptual model of historical trauma: Implications for public health practice and research. *Journal of Health Disparities Research and Practice, 1*(1), 93–108.

Strauss Swanson, C., & Szymanski, D. M. (2020). From pain to power: An exploration of activism, the #Metoo movement, and healing from sexual assault trauma. *Journal of Counseling Psychology, 67*(6), 653–668.

Substance Abuse and Mental Health Services Administration. (2014). *SAMHSA's concept of trauma and guidance for a trauma-informed approach.* SAMHSA's Trauma and Justice Strategic Initiative. https://ncsacw.samhsa.gov/userfiles/files/SAMHSA_Trauma.pdf

Tedeschi, R. G., & Calhoun, L. G. (1996). The Posttraumatic Growth Inventory: Measuring the positive legacy of trauma. *Journal of Traumatic Stress, 9*(3), 455–471.

Victor, D. (2017, November 22). Why celebrities have rallied behind Cyntoia Brown, a woman spending life in prison. *The New York Times.* https://www.nytimes.com/2017/11/22/us/cyntoia-brown-sex-trafficking.html

Wilkins, E. J., Whiting, J. B., Watson, M. F., Russon, J. M., & Moncrief, A. M. (2013). Residual effects of slavery: What clinicians need to know. *Contemporary Family Therapy, 35*(1), 14–28.

Part II

Therapy Contexts

6   Therapists' Cultural Self-Awareness

with Kesha Burch*

My therapist does research on black culture and experiences to help identify and affirm me as a client. Sometimes she asks me but more often, she uses other resources. She doesn't always get it, but I see her efforts to understand. She affirms black women's feelings and experiences as real without comparing them to general female experiences. I do want a black therapist but I'm sticking with the white Protestant woman because it works.

Study participant

Our work rests on the belief that therapy can be an arena of recovery and healing for Black women in the hands of a committed and skilled psychotherapist. To achieve this goal, therapists must be *self-aware* especially of their social and cultural identities that make them privileged or disadvantaged in their societies. Therapists must then use their social and cultural self awareness to deepen their *other-awareness* (Sue et al., 2019). Other-awareness helps therapists to conceptualize and intervene with clients in the context of client's personal, social and cultural histories, especially of oppression and marginalization. Armed with deep social and cultural self- and other-awareness, therapists must adopt a multicultural orientation in practice while working with their clients whose social and cultural identities are different from their own. Should a therapist display awareness, humility and using opportunities therapy affords to bond with Black female clients, we predict these clients will feel culturally comfortable. Clients will trust and engage and a strong therapist–clients alliance will produce useful outcomes. We write this chapter to assist therapists wanting these core qualities in their work (Sue et al., 2019).

Overwhelmingly, Black female clients want to work with Black therapists, and our study confirms this. In our sample of 227 women, around 90% indicated a preference for a Black therapist (Cabral & Smith, 2011). The reasons behind Black women's ubiquitous requests for a same-race therapist

---

* K. Burch, D. Baptiste, & A. Gooden (2023) Therapists' cultural self-awareness. In D. Baptiste & A. Gooden, *Promoting Black women's mental health: What practitioners should know and do.* Cambridge University Press.

are straightforward. Many want a racially similar therapist who they believe has an "insider lens" on what it means to be a Black woman in America (Cabral & Smith, 2011; Constantine, 2007; Townes et al., 2009). Our qualitative data suggest that in seeking a Black therapist, Black women also feel protective toward the Black race. This protectiveness shows up as not wanting to add negative story lines in discussing Black life with non-Black people (Sanders-Thompson et al., 2004).

For the same reasons they want a Black therapy, some Black women have reservations about working with non-Black ones. In our study, 44% of Black women indicated discomfort with non-Black therapists. Our research suggests this relates to worries about being misunderstood or a sense that the therapist has a superficial understanding of Black women. Black women may also experience microaggressions or bias in therapy and such ruptures lead them to hold the belief that therapies or therapists are not useful, worth their time or money (Constantine, 2007; Owen et al., 2011, 2014).

The real-world dynamics of mental health practice reveals the limitations of matching Black women with Black therapists. First, the sparsity of Black mental health practitioners suggests that Black women are unlikely to find a Black therapist easily. There are not enough Black therapists in practice (Burch, 2018). This reality can discourage Black women, and some drop out of the mental health marketplace. Second, Black client-therapist matching may be helpful in some aspects of therapy, for example, building rapport with clients and producing a sense of comfort that comes from shared cultural meanings in the dyad (Burch, 2018; Goode-Cross & Grim, 2016). However, the benefit of race matching for treatment outcomes is less clear (Cabral & Smith, 2011). Ultimately, the quality of the alliance between client and therapist is directly and indirectly related to therapy effectiveness and client satisfaction. The working partnership between the client and therapist is one of the most significant sources of change and positive therapeutic outcomes in therapy relationships (Wampold, 2015).

> See Chapter 7 for a detailed discussion of the therapeutic alliance.

Third, other client–therapist identities, such as personalities, social class, religious/spiritual affiliations, and sexual identity, may be misaligned even with race matching (Cabral & Smith, 2011). These dimensions also present challenges to alliance building. Given these real-world dynamics and our interest in helping Black women to find therapy, we also make the following arguments.

Our study suggests that while Black women might prefer a Black therapist, more than 55% would be neutral to quite comfortable working with a non-Black therapist. This speaks to our purpose in writing this book. We believe culturally informed and culturally aware non-Black therapists can help Black women meet their mental health goals. Any therapist who works with a Black female client must be adept at navigating the personal, interpersonal, and cultural dynamics of the relationship (Davis et al., 2016).Therapists should also respect, embrace, and connect with Black women's vibrant mixtures of identities and experiences. A therapist's empathy, genuineness, and collaboration on treatment goals (i.e., common factors) can earn a Black woman's trust (Wampold, 2015). Numerous scholars have also shown the damaging effects when these therapist dynamics are absent (Hook et al., 2016; Owen et al., 2011, 2014). Disruptions in the working alliance with Black people often occur because of microaggressions. Microaggressions are often based on common stereotypes of Black women, which makes them all the more harmful (Constantine, 2007; Sue et al., 2019).

In Chapter 7 we discuss the impact of microaggressions on the therapeutic alliance and how to address microaggressions in therapy.

Effective work with Black women requires deep and sustained *cultural self-awareness*. This self-awareness must begin with a therapist's intentional gaze on all aspects of the self as a culturally defined being. This chapter indicates where therapists can begin this journey.

6.1   The Use of Self-Awareness in Therapy

Black women in our study have a preference to work with someone who has engaged in cultural competence training as part of their clinical professional training. Despite some differences among the professional specialties within the psychotherapy field, each mental health profession places the *therapist's self-awareness* at the foundation of multicultural counseling skills, and therapists are encouraged to pursue a lifelong journey toward cultural competence (American Counseling Association [ACA], 2014; American Psychological Association [APA], 2017; National Association of Social Workers [NASW], 2015). Table 6.1 displays excerpts and examples from professional codes of conduct and multicultural practice guidelines that address the importance of the therapist's self-awareness and self-reflection. The policies and principles listed demonstrate that therapist self-awareness is a necessary aspect of multicultural counseling and developing a multicultural orientation to practice.

This chapter discusses a framework to understand what cultural self-awareness entails and how it effectively expands a therapist's capacity to ally with Black women. The cultural selves of both the client and the therapist

Table 6.1 *Guiding principles for self-awareness in mental health professions*

Counseling	ACA Code of Ethics (ACA, 2014)	"Counselors also explore their own cultural identities and how these affect their values and beliefs about the counseling process." (Section A)
	Multicultural and Social Justice Counseling Competencies (Ratts et al., 2016)	"Privileged and marginalized counselors develop self-awareness, so that they may explore their attitudes and beliefs, develop knowledge, skills and action relative to their self-awareness and worldview." (Section I: Counselor Self Awareness)
		Counselors "acquire reflective and critical thinking skills to gain insight into their assumptions, worldviews, values, beliefs, biases, and privileged and marginalized status." (Section I: 3, Counselor Self Awareness, Skills)
Psychology	Multicultural Guidelines: An Ecological Approach to Context, Identity, and Intersectionality (APA, 2017).	"Psychologists aspire to recognize and understand that as cultural beings, they hold attitudes and beliefs that can influence their perception of and interactions with others as well as their clinical and empirical conceptualizations. As such psychologists strive to move beyond conceptualizations rooted in categorical assumptions, biases, and/ or formulations based on limited knowledge about individuals and communities." (Guideline 2)
Social work	NASW Standards and Indicators for Cultural Competence in Social Work Practice (NASW, 2015).	"Social workers shall demonstrate an appreciation of their own cultural identities and those of others. Social workers must also be aware of their own privilege and power and must acknowledge the impact of this privilege and power in their work with and on behalf of clients. Social workers will also demonstrate cultural humility and sensitivity to the dynamics of power and privilege in all areas of social work." (Standard 2)

shape beliefs about the nature of issues brought to therapy, the methods employed in treatment/healing, and the character of the counseling relationship (Chang & Yoon, 2011). Cultural beliefs of both the client and the therapist are activated in the deeply personal work of therapy. While people often think of culturally responsive therapy as solely about the client's culture, the cultural self of the therapist is important in the therapeutic relationship too (DiAngelo, 2013; Zhang & Burkard, 2008). In this chapter we discuss why a therapist's lack of cultural self-awareness can lead to deleterious therapeutic ruptures and how to avoid these ruptures (Constantine, 2007). We present case vignettes to illustrate how cultural self-awareness expands the therapist's readiness to engage with stated and unstated culturally nuanced material that clients present.

6.2   Understanding Cultural and Social Identities

6.2.1   Culture

Falicov (1988) defines culture as "those sets of shared world views, meanings and adaptive behaviors derived from simultaneous membership and participation in a multiplicity of contexts, such as rural, urban or suburban setting; language, age, gender, family configuration, race, ethnicity, religion, nationality, cohort, sexual orientation, socioeconomic status, employment, education, occupation, political ideology, and stage of acculturation" (p. 336). A modern definition defines culture as, "the way of life, especially the general customs and beliefs, of a particular group of people at a particular time" (Cambridge International Dictionary of English, 1996). The cultural beliefs and values of therapists shape their attitudes and actions about most matters key to the therapy relationship. Culture is a powerful and invisible force in all psychotherapies. The cultural lens shows up in the therapist's theories on causes, progression and treatments of mental, emotional, and behavioral dynamics and symptoms (Sue et al., 2019). Therapists' cultural beliefs also frame explanations of what causes mental illness and wellness, strategies for therapy conversations, treatment and healing, and the nature of the therapeutic relationship. Cultural meanings on the part of both the client and the therapist, although invisible or unspoken, are influential in therapy encounters and activated in the deeply personal work in sessions. For this reason, we strongly suggest that therapists have a solid understanding of their cultural and social identities (Baumann et al., 2020; Sue et al., 2019).

6.2.2   Cultural Identity

Therapists, like other individuals, acquire a cultural imprint and template based on experiences within their ethnic groups, families, nations, regions, sociopolitical and economic affiliations, and more (Adams, 2013). While culture develops collectively, it also shapes people's worldviews and personal identities that unfold individually. Therapists derive personal meaning from their cultural backgrounds, which shows up in their lived experiences every day in multiple settings and contexts. Involuntary processes such as the beliefs, traditions, and practices passed down through family life shape the therapist's cultural identities. Cultural identity is also a matter of volition or choice, in that therapists choose what aspects to maintain and revitalize (Settles & Buchanan, 2014).

For example, one coauthor of this book and chapter, Donna Baptiste, identifies culturally as Caribbean American. Mentioned before is that Donna grew up in Trinidad and Tobago in the Caribbean. Donna was shaped by this region's unique heritage and by the traditions of the Trinidadian people and her family. Donna also currently maintains links to Caribbean heritage through affiliations with organizations like the Caribbean American Family Network in Illinois. While therapists such as Donna express their cultural identities personally, their cultural beliefs and actions have meaning within a social context. In these contexts, living out one's cultural values can affect the beliefs and values of others (Falicov, 1988).

Another coauthor on of this chapter, Kesha Burch, identifies racially as Black and ethnically as African American. Kesha is aware of how her beliefs, behaviors, and social relationships are imbued with cultural meanings shaped by the legacy of slavery, racial segregation, oppression, and racism in the United States. Kesha derives a sense of pride and purpose from her cultural roots. She identifies African American traditions of resistance to oppression and indigenous forms of coping as integral to her personal life and professional work as a therapist.

As a foundation for deep cultural self-awareness, therapists should be curious and seek knowledge about aspects of their cultural backgrounds, including ethnic affiliations and traditions. Therapists should also be keenly aware of areas in which cultural similarities and differences with clients play out. We center a solid understanding of cultural similarities and differences in notions of social identities.

6.2.3   Social Identities

Social identities refer to the individual's self-perception of being a member of a societal collective or group (e.g., Black race or biracial). Social identities are determined by what people believe or claim about themselves (e.g., "I'm a Muslim woman"). Social identities can also be forced on individuals by other entities (e.g., government description of who qualifies as an immigrant). Renowned Black psychologist Beverly Tatum wrote a seminal article explaining the concepts of social identities. The article, titled "The Complexity of Identity: 'Who Am I?'," describes the diversity and interconnectedness of social identities that people hold. Social identities include a person's sense of belonging to groups based on race, ethnicity, gender, sexual orientation, class, religion, or ability. Other social identity groupings center on nationality or regional backgrounds, or language. Social identity groups can also be related to more subtle dimensions of self, including physical appearance (e.g., body size).

Social identities may vary based on life experiences, individual decisions about social group affiliations, social status, and more. External factors also influence how people affiliate with various social identities (Settles & Buchanan, 2014; Tatum, 2000). Social identities have both intrapersonal and interpersonal significance. The salience of various social identities may fluctuate throughout a person's life span. Therapists must be fully aware of the unique and individual dimensions of their own social identities. Therapists must also firmly understand the social identities of their clients (APA, 2017). In Table 6.2, we provide a tool to assist the therapist with social identity exploration. To demonstrate the importance of knowledge of client identities, we invite the therapist to think about a recent client and address the queries provided in the tool. Therapists should make the time to engage in a robust discussion with a peer or mentor to build social identity self-awareness.

Social identity groups are often based on physical, social, mental, and other characteristics. Sometimes our identities are clear to us and others and sometimes not. For example, government agencies, colleges, and employers often ask us what racial identity group we claim, or they simply assign them to us based on how we look.

For this activity, what identities do you claim based on how you see yourself? You can also base your answers on familiar groupings that people use to describe you. Feel free to use your own language for your identities.

6.2.4   Social Identity Privilege and Disadvantage

Social identity groups hold unequal power, status, and influence in society. The concept of social identity privilege is made visible by examining current life. The social identity framework shines a light on "isms" that drive tensions and ferment in areas of life. Racial privilege and "racism" might be the most

Table 6.2 *Social identities of therapists and clients*

Social Identities	Examples	How Do You Describe Yourself?	Think of a Recent Black Female Client	
			Which of your client's identities were *you* most aware of?	Which of your identities did your *client* seem most aware of?
Race	Asian, Pacific Islander, Native American, Latin, Black, White, bi/multiracial, etc.			
Ethnic background	Irish, Chinese, Puerto Rican, Italian, Mohawk, Jewish, Guatemalan, Lebanese, European-American, Jamaican, etc.			
Sex	Female, male, intersex, etc.			
Gender	Woman, man, transgender, post-gender, etc.			
Sexual attraction/ orientation	Lesbian, gay, bisexual, pansexual, heterosexual, queer, questioning, etc.			
Religion/spirituality	Hindu, Muslim, Buddhist, Jewish, Christian, pagan, agnostic, atheist, secular humanist, etc.			
Social class/income	Poor, working class, lower middle class, upper middle class, owning class, ruling class, low income			
Age	Child, young adult, middle-age adult, elderly, etc.			
(Dis)ability	Person with disabilities (cognitive, physical, emotional, etc.), blind, Deaf/deaf, temporarily disabled, etc.			
National origin/ citizenship	United States, Nigeria, Korea, Turkey, Argentina, etc.			
Body size/type	Fat, plus-size, thin, slender, heavy, short, tall, etc.			
Tribal or Indigenous affiliation	Mohawk, Aboriginal, Navajo, Santal, etc.			
Other				

Note. Adapted from Thompson, M. C., Brett, T. G., & Behling, C. (2001). Educating for social justice: The program on intergroup relations, conflict, and community at the University of Michigan. In D. Schoem & S. Hurtado (Eds.), *Intergroup dialogue: Deliberative democracy in school, college, community and workplace* (pp. 99–114). University of Michigan.

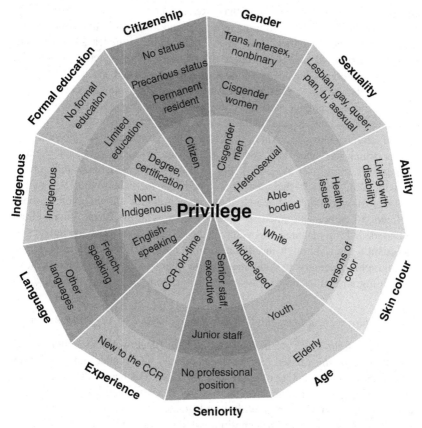

Figure 6.1 Oppression based on social group identity and status

straightforward framework to understand (DiAngelo, 2013; Long & Van Dam, 2020). The national unrest in the United States about the killings of George Floyd and Breonna Taylor shines a light on anti-Black racism. Figure 6.1 shows the wide range of privileges or "isms" and biases based on social identity differences. It is imperative for therapists to become familiar with their social identity backgrounds, affiliations, advantages, or disadvantages (Sue et al., 2019). For the non-Black therapist, this self-examination is critical to fully grasp the gendered racism, classism, and other "isms" that Black women experience (DiAngelo, 2018). Over many years, in our workshops training therapists we have encouraged radical awareness of this dynamic. Where therapists are privileged in terms of social identities, they are likely to commit microaggressions towards their clients of different identities. Also, where therapists are disadvantaged or targeted in social identities, they are more likely to experience client bias. Remembering the principle of social identity privilege guides us to remain humble and aware of both our privileged and disadvantaged identities (Hook et al., 2016). This posture leads to our strong encouragement to therapists to become deeply aware of all aspects of their social identities and how values of these identities are internalized and lived out.

Therapists' stated or presumed identities (e.g., race, gender, class) play a role in how they engage with all clients, especially those with marginalized identities. The client's social identities also explain how they relate to therapists of any background. Also, social identity formation has personal and interpersonal relevance and can be significant from the onset of therapy (Sanders-Thompson et al., 2004). For example, a Black woman may prefer to work with a Black therapist of a specific gender identity or age range. A therapist who may not match these demographics should explore these preferences, without judgment or defensiveness, with the Black female client to understand the meaning and value of these social identity characteristics in the client's life. Although the therapist may not match the client's preferred demographic, openness to understanding the client's viewpoints can be crucial to building a relationship of trust and collaboration.

6.2.5   Intersecting Identities: A Lens through Which to View Black Women

Repeatedly in this book we have discussed how Black women simultaneously experience dynamics based on their race/ethnicity and gender and this creates more intense circumstances of oppression (Settles & Buchanan, 2014). Here we are referring to ways in which on the basis of Black women's underprivileged status in terms of race (non-White) and gender (non-male) they are apt to experience biases. Imagine a scenario in which women hold other underprivileged social standing such as being poor, uneducated, disabled, non-English speaking, non-Christian, lesbian, gay, bisexual, transgender, and/or queer (LGBTQ), and the like. The main point is that Black women who hold multiple underprivileged statuses in society are apt to experience the greatest oppressions and therapists must be aware of this. Therapists much hold an *intersectional lens* on cultural and social identities to fully grasp how oppressive institutions (e.g., racism, sexism, homophobia, transphobia, ableism, xenophobia, classism, etc.) affected people (Settles et al., 2020). When people experience these multiple and intersecting form of oppressions, these experiences cannot be examined separately from one another. A wealth of research on Black women's lives in the United States show the multiple dangers they experience by their belongingness to marginalized social groups. In the words of Audre Lorde (1982), Black feminist lesbian poet, writer, and activist, "There is no such thing as a single issue struggle because we do not lead single issue lives" (para. 14). This is a quote from a speech "Learning from the 60s," delivered to honor Malcolm X at Harvard University in February 1982. This sentiment typifies Black women's lives.

6.3   Intersectional Cultural and Social Identity Awareness in Practice

Our main point is that a therapist's deep understanding of their social identities and experience with privilege and oppression is a foundation for building cultural self-awareness. Here, we identify several social identity dimensions that therapists should examine closely in themselves to become fully aware of these identities in their clients. A solid understanding of the social identity's history, belief systems, biases, and societal privilege or disadvantage helps the therapist to understand their potential preferences and gaps in understanding when working with clients (Sue et al., 2019). We discuss the dimensions of social identities including race, gender, ethnicity, religion and spirituality, sexual orientation, and socioeconomic background. We will discuss the intersectionality of identities and illustrate how therapy encounters with Black women around social identity differences can lead to ruptures or opportunities that impact trust.

6.3.1   Racial Identity

In the United States, the sociocultural legacy includes the history and continuing presence of anti-Black racism(DiAngelo, 2013). Anti-Blackness is a devaluation of Black identities and Black culture. It also drives the systemic marginalization of Black individuals and communities. Anti-Blackness is also reflected in indifference to the social inequalities in US society and the institutional and systemic racism that perpetuates racial inequality. We emphasize anti-Black racism here because of its associated biases, prejudices, negative beliefs, and relevance to clinical work with Black women. These sentiments are endemic in the United States, and institutions and practices that serve Black people must address the cultural reality of US history and social relations. Anti-Blackness can be seen in the mass incarceration of Black people that is out of proportion to the crimes committed in comparison to the incarceration rates of White people. Anti-Blackness can be seen in the school-to-prison and trauma-to-prison pipelines for Black children, where in-school punishment is harsh and often leads to school dropout and later incarceration (DiAngelo, 2018). Anti-Blackness can be seen in negative stereotypes about Black people and Black neighborhoods and the lack of investment in Black communities. Current national dialogues and unrest showcase the proliferation of anti-Black sentiments. The imprint of anti-Blackness in US culture is experienced and internalized by Black and non-Black individuals, therapists, and clients alike (Townes et al., 2009). Therapists seeking self-awareness around their race and racial identity must scrutinize themselves for anti-Black thoughts and beliefs that they may have internalized.

Case Example

This case vignette demonstrates how anti-Blackness and lack of awareness of White racial privilege can harm the therapeutic relationship. A White cisgender female therapist in her early 40s worked in a college counseling center on a predominantly White college campus. Her client, a 20-year-old cisgender African American woman, sought counseling concerning life stressors related to the transition from college to career. When the therapist greeted her client in the waiting room, she overheard her client on a phone call with a friend. The client's voice was elevated, and she spoke in a casual, conversational tone using African American English (AAE; Green, 2002). Later during the session, the therapist explored the client's communication using AAE and suggested that this style of communication would not be appropriate in her desired workplace settings. The therapist also asked why the client was speaking on the telephone call in this manner. The therapist suggested that the client avoid "trying to fit in by using slang" and instead focus on "being herself" and representing her "best self" in all circumstances.

In this scenario, the therapist did not fully recognize her discomfort with the client's use of AAE. The therapist also ignored the fact that the Black female client was code-switching. Code-switching, for Black women, is an intentional shift in language, style, and expression to match Black peer groups or to conform to norms of expression in White spaces. Instead, the therapist relied on dominant cultural norms about communication and speech and injected these values into the therapy relationship. Although the therapist may have rightly assessed that AAE may be viewed negatively in a corporate workplace, the therapist also denied this aspect of the client's identity (Dickens & Chavez, 2018). The therapist communicated judgment on the client's use of AAE in the therapy space. The therapist seemed unaware of her White racial privilege and valued her comfort over the client's. In this way, the therapist may have caused harm to the therapeutic relationship with the client by imposing her White cultural norms.

6.3.2   Ethnic Identity

Race and ethnicity can be confounded in discussions about identity. Therapists need to understand the distinctions between race and racial identity, and ethnicity and ethnic background. While race is usually associated with the biological makeup and physical traits of a person, ethnicity is linked to how individuals identify and express their cultural affiliations. For example, a client might be racially Black but culturally and ethnically tied to a country or people (e.g., Black or Afro Brazilian). Clients may equally value their racial and ethnic heritage and want therapists to see them through a racial-ethnic lens (e.g., Black Latina). An understanding of these subtleties helps the therapist to avoid ethnic bias against Black female clients (Zhang & Burkard, 2008). The subtleties of race and ethnicity distinctions are especially critical for women who are racially Black and also have ethnic affiliations outside the United States, such as with Latin American or African countries. Even in same-race therapeutic relationships, ethnic differences between the client and therapist may require the therapist to be specifically aware of their ethnic heritage and their client's heritage.

Case Example

A 29-year-old Black woman came to therapy with mild symptoms of social anxiety. The client was a first-generation American whose parents immigrated from Nigeria. The client recently relocated to a central metropolitan area for employment and felt disconnected and lonely in her new city. The client's social anxiety was a problem in the past, but with the relocation, the anxiety was even more of a barrier to her social adjustment. The client sought therapy with a Black therapist, specifically after a negative experience with a non-Black therapist. The therapist, in this case, was a 34-year-old African American woman who enjoyed working with other Black women. The therapist had been able to forge positive alliances with Black female clients due to shared values, shared interests, and similar identities. The therapist prided herself on being inclusive and collaborative toward clients of any identity and cultural background.

The client complained that she found it difficult to build a community in the new city because she did not fit in with African Americans in their social settings. The client believed that neither African Americans nor Whites understood the unique influence of her Nigerian upbringing. The client's Nigerian heritage was robust and influential in her life. This heritage, nurtured by her immigrant parents, helped the client maintain strong linkages with a predominantly Nigerian immigrant religious community. The client identified as a bicultural Black woman. The therapist recognized that she had little knowledge about the experiences of Black people in the African diaspora and said as much to the client. With a sense of curiosity, the therapist broached with the client a need to better understand Nigerian ethnic affiliations and values. The therapist knew that shared race was not enough and did not want to rely on the client's racial similarities. Through self-reflection, the therapist realized how much she needed to understand her ethnic identity background, something she had not thought of much. Working with the client instigated the therapist to explore her ethnic heritage as African American. This strategy led to a deep appreciation for the power of ethnic affiliation, which helped the therapist work with clients of other ethnic heritages.

6.3.3   Gender and Sex Identity and Expression

Black women experience gendered racism or intersectional biases based on their racial and gender social identities. Other identities (e.g., LGBTQ status or social class) also interact with race and gender to deepen Black women's experience of bias in multiple settings (Baumann et al., 2020). Sex and gender identity are not the same, and therapists should know the difference. Sex refers to a person's physical characteristics at the time of birth. Physical sexual characteristics may lead to an individual being classified as male, female, or intersex based on genitalia or chromosomes. Therapists should be aware of multiple controversies centered around intersex infants at birth being "assigned a sex" by a physician or parent (Human Rights Watch, 2017).

On the other hand, individuals may identify with and express roles, norms, and behaviors associated with their gender. In addition to binary expressions (e.g., woman or man), the therapist should be aware of the broad spectrum of gender identities and expressions, including nonbinary, gender-neutral, gender nonconforming, and transgender. Gender and gender expression, in and of themselves, can create powerful biases in therapy, as the following vignette illustrates (Settles & Buchanan, 2014). All therapists should seek to understand how their gender and gender expression function in the context of their therapeutic relationships. Male-identified therapists should know how gender privilege may shape their worldview and relationships with women clients. This vignette involving a Black male therapist and a nonbinary Black client showcases the importance of understanding clients' gender and gender expression.

Case Example

A 27-year-old Black client with a diagnosed depressive disorder sought therapy for personal growth. The client self-identified as genderqueer. The therapist was a 48-year-old Black cisgender male. The Black male therapist was highly respected for his work with men and boys in the community; he even wrote books and gave lectures about the role of gender in mental health. While working with men and boys was a primary passion, the therapist also saw women in clinical practice, many of whom appreciated the perspectives the therapist could offer about relationships with their sons, husbands, and fathers. This client, however, required the therapist to move beyond a binary understanding of gender into a more expansive and affirming therapeutic stance.

The client's depressive disorder was well managed with medication. This allowed the client to be open for personal growth work around their personal identity and social relationships. When the client entered therapy, they had been

(cont.)

out as genderqueer to their family for two years. They felt acceptance of their gender identity at home but not completely understood. The client enjoyed live music and dancing. However, they often felt rejected or experienced harassment in nightclubs and parties. For example, at nightclubs there is often an expectation of dancing with a partner, and the client was often rebuffed when asking individuals to dance. In another instance, the client was harassed with catcalls and derogatory statements as they left a party.

The therapist was humbled by his lack of sophistication when it came to an understanding of the risks of sexism and heteronormativity in the Black community for nonbinary persons. The therapist used peer consultation to explore his gendered and binary worldview. The therapist sought realized that much of the work he had done relied on binary thinking about gender in Black families, individuals, and communities. Fortunately, the therapist was able to build an effective alliance early in treatment. This development allowed the therapist to conduct an assessment on the client and then search the professional literature and other resources to support the client.

6.3.4 Religious and Spiritual Identity

Our study echoes the findings of many others that Black women are highly religious and spiritual. Almost 70% of our sample described themselves as very religious/spiritual. In therapy, a predominantly secular domain, spiritual and religious faith matters can create discomfort and tension for both clients and therapists (Boyd-Franklin, 2010). Therapists do not need to embrace their client's religious faith. They must fully understand their own religious and spiritual identities or lack of religious and spiritual affiliation to have the type of self-awareness needed to understand and respect their clients' faith identities. When therapists are not religious or spiritual themselves, they may risk overlooking the importance of religion and spirituality in their Black female client's life. This can also cause missed opportunities to integrate the client's religious beliefs and coping into therapy as appropriate (Boyd-Franklin, 2010). This vignette demonstrates how a therapist's religious values and background became activated when working with a Black female client facing an unplanned pregnancy.

Chapter 15 explores definitions of religion and spirituality and the ways Black women express these identities.

Case Example

A 34-year-old Black cisgender woman worked as a case manager in a religiously affiliated social service agency. The therapist was a middle-aged, White cisgender woman from an employee assistance program affiliated with the client's employer. The client's agency was conservative, and no other employees were Black, Indigenous, or people of color. The client sought therapy to discuss her pregnancy. The client was not married; however, she was in a committed heterosexual partnership with the father of her unborn child. Along with preparing for mother-hood, the client struggled with judgmental comments from her conservative Christian coworkers. The comments were about the pregnancy, the relationship, and her decision to live with her partner. The client liked her job and needed financial stability for her growing family. However, the client, a woman of faith herself, felt sad and rejected by her coworkers, whom she once considered friends.

Working with this Black woman, the therapist recalled her own conservative evangelical Christian religious upbringing and felt triggered by conflicting feelings about faith. While the therapist respected the client's faith and religious beliefs, her own experience of distancing from what she considered a harmful faith community threatened to override her clinical judgment. Both the therapist's and client's religious background were present in this encounter. The client reported feeling harmed by her coworkers' comments and hostility. The therapist felt triggered by her memories of what she considered a cult-like style in her former congregation. The therapist set aside her belief systems and reflected on the intersection of race and faith in Black women. The therapist knew that the client's faith could be a strength, especially during such tumultuous times. She "bracketed" her triggers and memories in deference to the client's values. Further, the therapist was mindful of the ways that race and faith intersect.

The therapist connected several dots that helped the client to understand the distress she felt. The therapist knew the client was the only woman of color in the small agency. She also knew that Black women experience bias toward their reproductive and family life decisions. In this instance, the client seemed to be experiencing familiar stereotypes of Black women as promiscuous and hypersexual. This bias was accompanied by religious judgments about the client's pregnancy while being unmarried. The therapist recognized the racial, gender, and religious complexities in this case and how the social and cultural identities of herself and the client played into the situation. The therapist was keenly aware of the influences, both positive and negative, of her upbringing in a conservative religious community. The therapist was also knowledgeable about how racialized stereotypes might make the client's experience in a religious work environment difficult considering the pregnancy. The therapist broached these thoughts and feelings with the client, who opened up a deep conversation around boundaries of faith and religious coping, rejection of stereotypes, and feedback to colleagues.

6.3.5   Socioeconomic Status

Socioeconomic status or social class refers to the standing of an individual or group based on a combination of education, income, wealth, and occupation. There are well-documented socioeconomic status differences between White and Black people in the United States related to educational achievements, income, and distribution of wealth (Gittleman & Wolf, 2004; Kochhar et al., 2011). Many social class differences are rooted in slavery and policies that structurally keep Black people in poverty (Long & Van Dam, 2020). Even though Black people face disproportionate financial and economic hardships, some attain financial success in this society. It is important for therapists to be aware of any stereotypes they might hold about the social class of Black people and not make assumptions about the social class of their Black female clients. The following case vignette shows how social class differences can impact the therapy relationship.

Case Example

The client was a 45-year-old, financially successful Black woman. The client worked hard in college and in graduate school to achieve her professional goals. She gained two professional degrees and became the leader in a technology firm. The client, however, experienced these successes as bittersweet. Academic, professional, and financial security put emotional distance between her family and herself. The client had grown up in a single-parent home with seven brothers and sisters. The client's siblings had not achieved the same success. The client used some of her wealth to support her mother and siblings, who had unstable income and inconsistent employment.

The client reached out for therapy because of low energy and motivation to excel at work. While work was the stated reason for coming to treatment, the client had an unstated need related to childhood trauma and frustrations with her family members. The client was reluctant to name these underlying concerns due to family loyalties and fears of betraying them. The client was assigned a White male therapist who had built a reputation working with C-suite professionals. The therapist, a 52-year-old White man in a heterosexual marriage with two children in college, felt quite prepared to meet the client's request to get to the bottom of her lack of motivation and challenges with executive leadership. In this situation, it was helpful for the therapist to recognize his lens of self and what he brought to the therapeutic relationship. The therapist was familiar with the individualistic and competitive environment of the client's workplace, having been a C-suite executive before becoming a therapist. The therapist's racial and gender socialization primed him to relate well in such environments.

Fortunately, the therapist was mindful of the client's race and gender socialization as a Black woman, aligned with collectivistic and relational ways of seeing the

---

(cont.)

world. The client revealed that she was giving away a significant portion of her earnings to support struggling family members. The therapist realized that this behavior reflected the client's worldview, different from his own. The therapist's individualistic cultural influences meant that he expected financial self-sufficiency in his college-age children and was accustomed to having more boundaries in relationships with nuclear and extended family. The therapist's self-awareness allowed him to tread carefully in helping the client explore how to maintain close ties and responsibilities within her family while setting financial boundaries.

Further, the therapist also demonstrated self-awareness of his social identity as a White man. He knew that this would impact his view of the client, who was struggling professionally in a work environment with several White men who challenged her competence and authority. The therapist disclosed his present thoughts and feelings about the client in the service of the therapeutic relationship. This disclosure led the client and therapist to explore how race, gender, and class differences impact their working alliance. Then, the client was able to explore the racialized aspects of her career difficulties more freely. The therapist supported the client by connecting with professional leadership organizations that promoted diversity, equity, and inclusion within her field as an external resource to address some of the ongoing concerns at work.

6.3.6   Worldview

In the preceding case we see clear differences between the client and therapist with respect to worldview. A person's worldview relates to how they see and make sense of the world. Worldviews are shaped by our individual, familial, religious, spiritual, social, cultural, and societal experiences. The client's and therapist's worldviews in the preceding case are quite different as the client and therapist are different in terms of race, gender, and socioeconomic background. In therapy, some alignment between the client's worldview and the therapeutic approach is important (Sue et al., 2019). Fortunately, the differences in worldview in this case were overcome by the therapist being aware of his own worldview, and being sensitive enough to work from the knowledge of the client's worldview in treatment. In this case the therapist made space for collectivist notions of sharing resources while helping the client to process feeling burdened and angry at times. This led to her setting new, healthy boundaries that were created on her own terms. Therapists should not put their worldviews onto their clients. In keeping with the theme of this chapter, an effective way for therapists to explore their own worldviews is included in the reflection questions at the end of this chapter.

6.3.7   Sexual Orientation

Black women who identify as members of the LGBTQ community may experience intense marginalization, discrimination, and stress from being minoritized. For this reason, LGBTQ persons may seek out a specifically queer-affirming clinician who can understand psychotherapy through this lens (Baumann et al., 2020). It is essential for therapists who promote themselves as queer affirming to examine themselves to understand how their own sexual identity influences their clinical work. Self-scrutiny is warranted to unlearn pervasive homophobia and heteronormativity that is present in society.

Case Example

A 37-year-old Chinese woman therapist worked with a 27-year-old Black woman diagnosed with anxiety and attention-deficit/hyperactivity disorder (ADHD). After experiencing unstable adolescence and early adulthood, the client made tremendous strides to complete her education and gain employment while working with this therapist. A greater sense of stability and improved self-esteem influenced the client, who identifies as lesbian, to become more invested in dating and exploring intimate relationships. For the client, this also means sharing her identity in social relationships where she has yet to come out. The therapist, who identifies as a bisexual woman, benefits from her self-awareness about her affectional orientation as LGBTQ. However, the therapist must continue to assess her own biases and internalized homophobia. The therapist should understand her comfort level with self-disclosing her affectional orientation to the client and should do so only if it benefits the client (Baumann et al., 2020). Whether self-disclosure occurs or not, the therapist should continuously monitor how her own identity and experiences are relevant to the therapeutic relationship.

6.3.8   Intersecting Identities

In the previous case vignette, both the client and the therapist were identified with at least three historically marginalized and oppressed identities: race, gender, and affectional/sexual orientation. Identity itself is multifaceted and is shaped in multiple contexts (Settles & Buchanan, 2014). Most individuals are aware of numerous identities and roles salient to them, such as occupation, geographical origin, race, gender, and educational level. In addition to acknowledging multiple identities, the concept of intersectional identities is powerful for understanding the self. Specific identities may be intersectional. A combination of identities creates a unique experience of oppression or privilege that cannot be untangled (Settles et al., 2020). Gendered racism is an example of how intersectionality can be experienced by Black women. The therapist and client discussed in this case are likely to have qualitatively unique experiences in their identities as queer women of color. The intersectional lens is helpful to explore identities that experience discrimination, oppression, or privilege. For therapists who possess multiple privileged identities, recognizing how those cumulative advantages impact their worldview and the counseling process and practice is an essential area of self-awareness. Using the concept of intersectionality is a way therapists can analyze crucial implications of the identities they hold.

Other social identity differences between therapists and clients are potential areas of differences and ruptures (Owen et al., 2016). Appearance bias, for example, is an unexamined belief that may affect how therapists respond to a Black woman's body size, shape, hair texture, skin color, and the like. While therapists may be knowledgeable about their racial, gender, or class identities, they may be relatively unaware of their body size biases.

Chapter 12 addresses lookism and appearance biases therapists may hold.

6.4   A Framework for Building Trust with Black Female Clients

One of the benefits of a therapist's deep cultural self-awareness is a capacity to forge strong bonds culturally with people who hold different social identities and worldviews. While cultural sensitivity or cultural competence are common descriptors for what Black women say they need in their therapy (e.g., "I have had some therapists who were not culturally aware and sensitive"), a more apt framework is a therapist's *multicultural orientation* (Owen et al., 2011). A therapist's multicultural orientation is demonstrated through three features: (a) cultural humility, (b) use of cultural opportunities, and (c) cultural comfort. We discuss each element of a multicultural orientation and show how they can be enacted in a relationship with a Black client.

6.4.1   Cultural Humility

Hook and colleagues (2013) have researched cultural humility and its process within the past decade. Specifically, they define cultural humility as "the ability to maintain an interpersonal stance that is other-oriented (or open to the other) in relation to aspects of cultural identity that are most important to the client" (p. 254). Cultural humility includes (a) a lifelong motivation to learn from others,

(b) critical self-examination of cultural awareness, (c) interpersonal respect, (d) a capacity to develop a mutual partnership that addresses power differentials, and (e) an other-oriented stance open to new cultural information (Mosher et al., 2017). Cultural humility is the foundation of a multicultural orientation.

Cultural humility can be challenging to operationalize and demonstrate. Mosher et al. (2017) proposed a four-part framework to guide how therapists can implement cultural humility in practice. The first part, "engaging in critical self-examination and self-awareness" (p. 225), directs therapists to intentionally examine how their own cultural identities shaped their worldviews and biases. Such deep exploration prepares therapists to delve similarly into their clients' cultural identities. The next aspect of the framework, "building the therapeutic alliance" (p. 226), highlights the critical importance of humility to forge a trusting relationship built on a foundation of welcoming and validating a client's cultural identities. The third component, "repairing cultural ruptures" (p. 227), directly addresses the cultural mistakes therapists make, including microaggressions. Maintaining cultural humility affords the therapist opportunities to recognize and identify when a rupture has occurred and, most importantly, take action to repair the client-therapist relationship. The final framework element, "navigating value differences" (p. 228), requires the therapist to be aware of their own values while always focusing treatment to work for and within the client's values.

Building a trusting therapeutic relationship is discussed extensively in Chapter 7.

6.4.2   Cultural Opportunities

Cultural opportunities are instances in therapeutic relationships that create openings to explore salient aspects of a client's identity and worldview (Owen et al., 2016). Such moments are plentiful in sessions and require ongoing vigilance by the therapist to listen and watch for interactions that might offer opportunities for exploration of the client's cultural background. For example, sharing about family of origin, perceptions of gender roles, faith traditions, and career and vocational pursuits all hold cultural contexts that a counselor may broach to explore further. While these moments can lead to deepening understanding in the therapist–client relationship, missed cultural opportunities consequently can lead to distancing within the relationship. Owen and colleagues (2016) found that clients who perceived their therapists as missing cultural opportunities also perceived the therapists to be low in cultural humility.

6.4.3   Cultural Comfort

Owen and colleagues (2017) described *cultural comfort* as the ease and fluidity with which therapists engage in topics related to cultural identities. A multicultural orientation requires therapists to demonstrate comfort when working with clients to assist in managing discussions centered around clients' salient identities (Owen et al., 2017). It stands to reason that such cultural comfort aids in building a stronger therapeutic relationship. Owen et al.'s research found that therapists who displayed consistent cultural comfort were successful at retaining both clients of racially/ethnically diverse backgrounds and White clients in counseling, underscoring the importance of this tenet of a multicultural orientation. Cultural comfort, when paired with cultural humility, frees a therapist to lean into discussions about race, ethnicity, cultural, and other salient client identities without the risk of saying the wrong thing, mainly because they are seeking to fully understand the other without a judgmental or preconceived worldview lens.

Research demonstrates that the stakes are high if therapists do not create conditions related to a multicultural orientation. A significant body of research highlights how Black women may prematurely terminate counseling, feel misunderstood, and even experience racism and microaggressions in therapy if the therapist is not culturally attuned. A respondent in our study reported such an experience:

She [the therapist] was interested in my professional history and surprised [by] my knowledge of mental health issues and terminology. So, while it was friendly, I felt she saw me as different and was "entertained" when we met. My sharing my life history and issues of concern was like a soap opera where she was waiting for the next episode. So, I walked away feeling she was not skilled enough or equipped to help me. She was White, I'm Black, it felt as if she was in awe of my intellect. I came to resent that and distrusted her and questioned her ability to help me. So, I just stopped going without saying why.

Chang and Yoon (2011) highlighted how Black clients, among other clients of color, end therapy prematurely if a therapist does not display cultural sensitivity. Zhang and Burkard (2008) reported that therapists who seek to learn more about their client's racial identity were rated more credible by clients of color than those who do not. A predominant need for Black women is to understand and cope with being Black women in the United States. Thus, Black women need encouragement to explore their racial-gender and other cultural identities and how these identities impact their lived experiences (Cardemil & Battle, 2003; Davis & Gelsomino, 1994).

6.4.4   Broaching

While multicultural framework can be considered a roadmap to guide travel, the technique of *broaching*, is the signal that begins the journey with clients. Day-Vines and colleagues (2021) described *broaching* as an intervention to engage in therapist and client discussions on meaningful aspects of the client's personal and social identities that impact their work together. Broaching simply describes the process by which a therapist learns what social identities are important to the client. Day-Vines et al. (2020) found that therapists may demonstrate a broad spectrum of comfort related to broaching ranging from avoidant to achieving an infused status whereas multiculturalism and social justice are woven into a therapists' overall "way of being" if you will. Branco and Jones (2021) suggested broaching as cultural humility in action. Their idea was discussed within the context of the clinical supervision relationship; however, the same concept applies to therapists and clients. Further, frequent broaching consistently reinforced their attempts to remain culturally humble and adhere to Mosher et al.'s (2017) framework of *building the therapeutic alliance* (p. 226) and *navigating value differences* (p. 228). One participant in our study echoed *broaching* as a recommendation for therapists:

Have a cultural conversation early on. Diversity of experience among people of color means that we do not all experience being black early on. If I sense that my therapist doesn't "get me" due to a difference in age or experience, I won't trust them readily.

Even if relationship ruptures occur in the therapeutic experience, broaching creates an opportunity to discuss missteps that needed to be repaired on the therapist's part stemming from their own biases. Broaching conversations around ruptures in the alliance can create some powerful and intimate therapy moments with Black women. We illustrate this in our case discussion.

6.5   Strategies for Development of Cultural Self-Awareness

A well-rounded therapist develops constructive forms of self-awareness that can support culturally responsive therapy. Further, self-awareness is embedded in models of cultural competence and cultural humility. Gaining knowledge of the self within cultural identities should happen as early as possible in education and clinical training. The process of cultivating self-awareness begins at the outset of a career as a therapist and should also be an ongoing and consistent part of professional and personal development. What follows are tried-and-proven strategies therapists can employ to develop their cultural self-awareness.

Therapists should thoroughly explore their race, ethnicity, culture, gender and gender expression, religion, affectional or sexual orientation, socioeconomic status, ability status, language, and educational status. In resources for therapists we provide several questions to begin such explorations. Therapists can conduct this exploration alone or with others through supervision or consultation. The following are some strategies for deep cultural self-discovery.

1. **Set aside regular time for personal self-reflection.** Current events and everyday experiences in diverse communities offer ample material to reflect on essential understandings of our own cultural identities and the byproducts of interacting within a diverse society. Journaling about significant multicultural relationships and experiences is one method of self-reflection. In response to contemporary matters such as news stories involving social identity dynamics, therapists can ask themselves: What am I thinking? What am I feeling? What feels similar to my life narratives? What feels different? In-depth process recording or psychotherapy notes concerning the multicultural considerations of practice with diverse clients is another practice that could be beneficial.

2. **Engage in cross-racial and intergroup dialogue.** Therapists committed to deepening their self-awareness and learning more about the importance of culture in all manner of interpersonal relationships should intentionally dialogue and invite conversations with a wide range of individuals and communities. These conversations can take place organically or in a structured way. Therapists should stretch themselves beyond their narrow and culturally encapsulated views of self. Interacting with others who are different allows us to observe our social identities across various types of relationships. This awareness can be beneficial for understanding cultural dynamics in clinical relationships. Professional opportunities and dialogues are increasing across the mental health spectrum. Most recently, virtual participation in a rich array of events deepens the therapist's capacity for self-evaluation. Generalized or focused conversations are useful for example, on antiracist viewpoints, gender bias, LGBTQ themes, immigration issues, men's concerns, women in leadership, and so forth.

3. **Become familiar with the historical and sociological foundations of the concepts of cultural and social identities and intersectionality.** Explore race, ethnicity, gender, religion, sexual orientation, socioeconomic status, age, and physical or mental ability. The resource list at the end of this chapter includes several books, articles, blogs, and movies that invite consideration of identity dynamics and "isms." Remember that the exploration of cultural dynamics in society is a lifelong pursuit and will have relevance to your thinking beyond clinical practice. Culturally responsive therapists do their

own work of building knowledge about cultures and social problems such as violence, oppression, and structural barriers to mental health. Culturally responsive therapists use knowledge of the historical and cultural foundations related to their clients' identities to contextualize their presenting concerns and interpersonal dynamics in the therapeutic relationship.

4. **Use formal supervision and peer consultation to exchange ideas with others.** Ensure that your supervisory relationships and peer consultation experiences actively explore cultural and social identity. We should feel comfortable initiating and benefiting from critical dialogue on multiculturalism in our professional development experiences. This strategy includes creating a rich network of multiculturally diverse colleagues and peers with whom to dialogue, consult, and exchange ideas.

5. **Use therapy.** Psychotherapy is an excellent pathway for understanding more about oneself. Therapists should engage in their own therapy experiences as clients to explore and unpack aspects of their social and cultural identities.

6.6   Conclusion

Therapists who work with clients whose cultural backgrounds are different from their own may be eager to obtain knowledge about their clients' cultural identity and background to assist in connecting with their clients and understanding clients' worldviews. However, therapists should first explore how their own culturally derived attitudes, beliefs, and worldviews influence their relationships with clients. This chapter emphasizes the importance of cultural self-awareness for the therapist and highlights that cultural and social identities are simultaneously internally and externally derived and maintained. The reflection questions and resources at the end of this chapter will assist with exploring your cultural self and other attitudes relative to treating Black women. The resources have been selected to assist therapists in exploring their cultural identity and learning more about critical social identities that are relevant when working with Black women.

Therapist Reflection Questions

1. How do you identify yourself? What aspects of your identity are most important to you and why? What parts of your identity have the least importance in the way you see yourself? What have been the major influences on your worldview?

2. What do you think causes good things to happen in your life and in the world? Is it due to fate? Luck? God? A higher power? Karma? Personal effort or perseverance? People working together? Help from someone else?

3. How do you believe that racism, sexism, homophobia, transphobia, class-ism, ableism, ageism, or any other discrimination was at play?
4. What parts of yourself do you have an awareness of bringing into the therapy room? How or why do these parts of yourself matter to you? What parts of your identity get enacted in clinical work with Black women?
5. Which of your social identities confer privilege to you? Which of your social identities are marginalized or oppressed? (See Table 6.2 and Figure 6.1.)
6. What are the implications of your marginalized identities in your clinical work? How do your privileged or dominant identities interact with those of Black women? What are the implications of your privileged identities in your clinical work? How can you become more aware of power dynamics in clinical relationships?
7. Do you have close personal relationships with Black women, apart from your work as a therapist? If yes, reflect on these experiences. What are the circumstances or barriers that have prevented such relationships from forming? How might these dynamics impact your professional relationships with Black female clients?
8. What stereotypes and biases do people of your racial and ethnic background hold about Black people? What stereotypes and prejudices are explicitly held about Black women? What do you notice about your thoughts and reactions when you perceive a Black woman exhibiting stereotypical behavior?

Resources for Therapists

Books

Adams, M. E., Bell, L. A. E., & Griffin, P. E. (2016). *Teaching for diversity and social justice.* Routledge.

Adams, M., Blumenfeld, W. J., Chase, D., Catalano, J., Dejong, K., Hackman, H. W., Hopkins, L. E., Love, B., Peters, M. L., Shlasko, D., & Zuniga, X. (Eds.). (2018). *Readings for diversity and social justice* (4th ed.). Routledge.

Cooper, B. (2018). *Eloquent rage: A Black feminist discovers her superpower.* St. Martin's Press.

DiAngelo, R. (2013). *What does it mean to be white? Developing white racial literacy* (rev. ed.). Peter Lang International Academic Publishers.

(2018). *White fragility: Why it's so hard for white people to talk about racism.* Beacon Press.

(2021). *Nice racism: How progressive white people perpetuate racial harm.* Beacon Press.

Emerson, M. O., & Smith, C. (2001). *Divided by faith: Evangelical religion and the problem of race in America.* Oxford University Press.

Helms, J. E. (2020). *A race is a nice thing to have: A guide to being a white person or understanding the white persons in your life*. Cognella.

Hook, J. N., Davis, D., Owen, J., & DeBlaere, C. (2017). Exploring your cultural identity. In *Cultural humility: Engaging diverse identities in therapy* (pp. 43–64). American Psychological Association.

Irving, D. (2016). *Waking up white: And finding myself in the story of race*. Author's Republic.

Kendi, I. X. (2016). *Stamped from the beginning: the definitive history of racist ideas in America*. Nation Books.

Singh, A. A. (2019). *The racial healing handbook: Practical activities to help you challenge privilege, confront systemic racism, and engage in collective healing*. New Harbinger Publications.

Tatum, B. D. (2000). The complexity of identity: "Who am I?" In M. Adams, W. J. Blumenfeld, R. Castañeda, H. W. Hackman, M. L. Peters, & X. Zuniga. (Eds.), *Readings for diversity and social justice* (pp. 9–14). Routledge.

(2019). In living color: Reflections on race, racialization, and identity. *Equity & Excellence in Education, 52*(1), 89–92.

Blogs, Websites, and Poetry

Academics for Black Survival and Wellness. (n.d.). https://www.academics4blacklives.com

Lorde, A. (2020). *Sister outsider: Essays and speeches*. Penguin Classics.

Racial Equity Tools. (n.d.). https://www.racialequitytools.org

Stovall, N. (2019, August 12). *Whiteness on the couch*. https://longreads.com/2019/08/12/whiteness-on-the-couch

The National SEED (Seeking Educational Equity and Diversity) Project. (n.d.). https://nationalseedproject.org/

References

Adams, M., Blumenfeld, W., Castaneda, C., Hackman, H. W., Peters, M. L., & Zúñiga, X. (Eds.). (2013). *Readings for diversity and social justice* (3rd ed.). Routledge Taylor & Francis Group.

American Counseling Association. (2014). *ACA code of ethics*. https://www.counseling.org/resources/aca-code-of-ethics.pdf

American Psychological Association. (2017). *Multicultural guidelines: An ecological approach to context, identity, and intersectionality*. https://www.apa.org/about/policy/multicultural-guidelines.pdf

Baumann, E. F., Ryu, D., & Harney, P. (2020). Listening to identity: Transference, countertransference, and therapist disclosure in psychotherapy with sexual and gender minority clients. *Practice Innovations, 5*(3), 246–256. https://doi.org/10.1037/pri0000132

Boyd-Franklin, N. (2010). Incorporating spirituality and religion into the treatment of African American clients. *The Counseling Psychologist, 38*(7), 976–1000.

Branco, S. F., & Jones, C. T. (2021). Supporting Black, Indigenous, and People of Color counselors: Considerations for counselor skills training and practice. *Journal of Mental Health Counseling*, *43*(4), 281–300. https://doi.org/10.17744/mehc.43.4.01

Burch, K. S. (2018). *A qualitative study of African American mental health professionals: Exploring rewards and opportunities of same-race counseling relationships* (Publication No. 10932027) [Doctoral dissertation, The Chicago School of Professional Psychology]. ProQuest.

Cabral, R. R., & Smith, T. B. (2011). Racial/ethnic matching of clients and therapists in mental health services: a meta-analytic review of preferences, perceptions, and outcomes. *Journal of Counseling Psychology*, *58*(4), 537–554. https://doi.org/10.1037/a0025266

Cambridge International Dictionary of English. (1996). Cambridge University Press.

Cardemil, E. V., & Battle, C. L. (2003). Guess who's coming to therapy? Getting comfortable with conversations about race and ethnicity in psychotherapy. *Professional Psychology: Research and Practice*, *34*(3), 278–286.

Chang, D. F., & Yoon, P. (2011). Ethnic minority clients' perceptions of the significance of race in cross-racial therapy relationships. *Psychotherapy Research*, *21*(5), 567–582.

Constantine, M. (2007). Racial microaggressions against African American clients in cross-racial counseling relationships. *Journal of Counseling Psychology*, *54*, 1–16. https://doi.org/10.1037/0022-0167.54.1.1

Davis, D. E., DeBlaere, C., Brubaker, K., Owen, J., Jordan, T. A., Hook, J. N., & Van Tongeren, D. R. (2016). Microaggressions and perceptions of cultural humility in counseling. *Journal of Counseling and Development*, *94*(4), 483–493. https://doi.org/10.1002/jcad.12107

Davis, L. E., & Gelsomino, J. (1994). An assessment of practitioner cross-racial treatment experiences. *Social Work*, *39*(1), 116–123.

Day-Vines, N. L., Cluxton-Keller, F., Agorsor, C., & Gubara, S. (2021). Strategies for Broaching the Subjects of Race, Ethnicity, and Culture. *Journal of Counseling and Development*, *99*(3), 348–357. https://doi.org/10.1002/jcad.12380

Day-Vines, N. L., Cluxton-Keller, F., Agorsor, C., Gubara, S., & Otabil, N. A. A. (2020). The multidimensional model of broaching behavior. *Journal of Counseling & Development*, *98*(1), 107–118.

DiAngelo, R. (2013). *What does it mean to be white? Developing white racial literacy* (rev. ed.). Peter Lang International Academic Publishers

(2018). *White fragility: Why it's so hard for white people to talk about racism*. Beacon Press.

Dickens, D. D., & Chavez, E. L. (2018). Navigating the workplace: The costs and benefits of shifting identities at work among early career U.S. Black women. *Sex Roles*, *78*(11–12), 760–774. https://doi.org/10.1007/s11199-017-0844-x

Falicov, C. J. (1988). Learning to think culturally. In H. A. Liddle, D. C. Bruenlin, & R. C. Schwartz (Eds.), *Handbook of family therapy training and supervision* (pp. 335–357). Guilford Press.

Gittleman, M., & Wolff, E. N. (2004). Racial differences in patterns of wealth accumulation. *Journal of Human Resources*, *39*, 193–227.

Goode-Cross, D. T., & Grim, K. A. (2016). "An unspoken level of comfort": Black therapists' experiences working with Black clients. *Journal of Black Psychology, 42*(1), 29–53.

Green, L. J. (2002). *African American English: A linguistic introduction.* Cambridge University Press.

Hook, J., Davis, D., Owen, J. J., Worthington, E., & Utsey, S. (2013). Cultural humility: Measuring openness to culturally diverse clients. *Journal of Counseling Psychology, 60*(3), 353–366.

Hook, J. N., Farrell, J. E., Davis, D. E., DeBlaere, C., Van Tongeren, D. R., & Utsey, S. O. (2016). Cultural humility and racial microaggressions in counseling. *Journal of Counseling Psychology, 63*(3), 269–277. https://doi.org/10.1037/cou0000114

Human Rights Watch. (2017, July 25). *"I want to be like nature made me."* https://www.hrw.org/report/2017/07/25/i-want-be-nature-made-me/medically-unnecessary-surgeries-intersex-children-us#

Kochhar, R., Fry, R., & Taylor, P. (2011). *Wealth gaps rise to record highs between whites, blacks and Hispanics (Social and demographic trends report).* Pew Research Center. https://www.pewresearch.org/wp-content/uploads/sites/3/2011/07/SDT-Wealth-Report_7-26-11_FINAL.pdf

Long, H., & Van Dam, A. (2020, June 4). The black-white economic divide is as wide as it was in 1968. *Washington Post.* https://www.washingtonpost.com/business/2020/06/04/economic-divide-black-households

Lorde, A. (1982). *Learning from the 60s.* Speech delivered at Harvard University in honor of Malcolm X. https://www.blackpast.org/african-american-history/1982-audre-lorde-learning-60s/

Mosher, D. K., Hook, J. N., Captari, L. E., Davis, D. E., DeBlaere, C., & Owen, J. (2017). Cultural humility: A therapeutic framework for engaging diverse clients. *Practice Innovations, 2*(4), 221–233.

National Association of Social Workers. (2015). *Standards and indicators for cultural competence in social work practice.* https://www.socialworkers.org/LinkClick.aspx?fileticket=7dVckZAYUmk%3D&portalid=0

Owen, J., Drinane, J., Adelson, J. L., Hook, J. N., Davis, D., & Fookune, N. (2017). Racial/ethnic disparities in client unilateral termination: The role of therapists' cultural comfort. *Psychotherapy Research, 27*(1), 102–111.

Owen, J., Imel, Z., Tao, K. W., Wampold, B., Smith, A., & Rodolfa, E. (2011). Cultural ruptures in short-term therapy: Working alliance as a mediator between clients' perceptions of microaggressions and therapy outcomes. *Counselling & Psychotherapy Research, 11*, 204–212. http://dx.doi.org/10.1080/14733145.2010.491551

Owen, J., Tao, K. W., Drinane, J. M., Hook, J., Davis, D. E., & Kune, N. F. (2016). Client perceptions of therapists' multicultural orientation: Cultural (missed) opportunities and cultural humility. *Professional Psychology: Research and Practice, 47*(1), 30–37.

Owen, J., Tao, K. W., Imel, Z. E., Wampold, B. E., & Rodolfa, E. (2014). Addressing racial and ethnic microaggressions in therapy. *Professional Psychology, Research and Practice, 45*, 283–290. http://dx.doi.org/10 .1037/a0037420

Ratts, M. J., Singh, A. A., Nassar-McMillan, S., Butler, S. K., & McCullough, J. R. (2016). Multicultural and social justice counseling competencies: Guidelines for the counseling profession. *Journal of Multicultural Counseling and Development, 44*(1), 28–48. https://doi.org/10.1002/jmcd.12035

Sanders-Thompson, V. L., Bazile, A., & Akbar, M. (2004). African Americans perception of psychotherapy and psychotherapists. *Professional Psychology, Research, and Practice, 35*(1), 19–26. https://doi.org/10.1037/0735-7028.35.1.19

Settles, I. H., & Buchanan, N. T. (2014). Multiple groups, multiple identities, and intersectionality. In V. Benet-Martínez & Y.-Y. Hong (Eds.), *The Oxford handbook of multicultural identity* (pp. 160–180). Oxford University Press.

Settles, I. H., Warner, L. R., Buchanan, N. T., & Jones, M. K. (2020). Understanding psychology's resistance to intersectionality theory using a framework of epistemic exclusion and invisibility. *Journal of Social Issues, 76*(4), 796–813.

Sue, D. W., Sue, D., Neville, H. A., & Smith, L. (2019). *Counseling the culturally diverse: Theory and practice.* John Wiley & Sons.

Tatum, B. D. (2000). The complexity of identity: "Who am I?" In M. Adams, W. J. Blumenfeld, R. Castañeda, H. W. Hackman, M. L. Peters, & X. Zuniga. (Eds.), *Readings for diversity and social justice* (pp. 9–14). Routledge.

Thompson, M. C., Brett, T. G., & Behling, C. (2001). Educating for social justice: The program on intergroup relations, conflict, and community at the University of Michigan. In D. Schoem & S. Hurtado (Eds.), *Intergroup dialogue: Deliberative democracy in school, college, community and workplace* (pp. 99–114). University of Michigan.

Townes, D. L., Chavez-Korell, S., & Cunningham, N. J. (2009). Reexamining the relationships between racial identity, cultural mistrust, help-seeking attitudes, and preference for a Black counselor. *Journal of Counseling Psychology, 56*, 330–336.

Wampold, B. E. (2015). How important are the common factors in psychotherapy? An update. *World Psychiatry, 14*(3), 270–277.

Zhang, N., & Burkard, A. W. (2008). Client and counselor discussions of racial and ethnic differences in counseling: An exploratory investigation. *Journal of Multicultural Counseling and Development, 36*(2), 77–87.

7 Building Strong and Effective Alliances with Black Female Clients

The therapeutic relationship is one of the most significant sources of transformation in therapy. Ample literature on the therapeutic process has highlighted that the therapeutic alliance accounts for a substantial portion of positive therapeutic outcomes (e.g., Lambert & Barley, 2001). This reality is no different for therapy with Black women. Black women prioritize relationships in their lives, making the therapeutic relationship a particularly significant aspect of therapy for Black female clients. Cultivating a solid therapeutic alliance with Black female clients is essential because Black women are less likely to seek therapy than White women (McGuire & Miranda, 2008). When Black women engage in therapy, they are less likely to receive the highest quality of care and are more likely to drop out than White clients (King & Canada, 2004; McGuire & Miranda, 2008). Research has demonstrated that fearing judgment based on negative stereotypes can cause dropout (Johnson et al., 2014), and as we discussed in Chapter 4, Black women constantly navigate negative stereotypes. This chapter will explore the unique challenges that arise in building strong therapeutic alliances with Black women. We provide recommendations to help therapists overcome these challenges and cultivate strong, authentic, therapeutic connections with their Black female clients.

7.1 Therapeutic Alliance

Vasquez (2007) defines the therapeutic alliance as the "quality of involvement between therapist and client or patient, as reflected in their task, teamwork, and personal rapport" (p. 879). The therapeutic alliance is an essential component of successful therapy regardless of the therapeutic orientation. A "good enough" alliance early in therapy is critical for success with most clients (Horvath et al., 2011; Sharf et al., 2010). Cultural differences between therapist and client can lead to a greater likelihood of empathic failure and contribute to a poor alliance (Asnaani & Hofmann, 2012; Comas-Díaz, 2006). In an article on cross-cultural working alliance, Shonfeld-Ringel (2001) emphasizes the importance of empathy in therapeutic relationships. Likely, one reason ethnic minority populations do not engage in psychotherapy is anticipation of feeling uncomfortable and feeling unable to make a strong connection with their therapist (Castonguay et al., 2006; Vasquez, 2007). Further, while more research needs to be done, once clients of color engage in therapy, the quality of the therapeutic alliance may be a primary factor that contributes to ethnic minority clients dropping out of therapy (Castonguay et al., 2006). Research on cultural humility has demonstrated that the clients of therapists who practice cultural humility rate the therapeutic alliance more highly and that these clients also have better therapeutic outcomes (Hook et al., 2013). Cultural humility involves therapists being focused on understanding their client's experiences and showing respect and not demonstrating superiority toward clients of a different cultural group than the therapist (Hook et al., 2013).

7.2   Pillars of Strong Therapeutic Alliances with Black Female Clients

Modern conceptualizations of the therapeutic alliance see strong alliances as collaborative and focused on building consensus between the therapist and client (Horvath et al., 2011). Bordin's (1979) popular definition specifies three components of the therapeutic alliance: (a) tasks, which are the behaviors and processes within therapy sessions that constitute the work of therapy; (b) goals, which are objectives of therapy that both the client and the therapist endorse; and (c) bonds, which include positive interpersonal attachment between the client and the therapist with mutual trust, confidence, and acceptance. We use this framework to guide our discussion of creating strong therapeutic alliances with Black female clients. In our discussion of various strategies, keep in mind that tasks, bonds, and goals are not entirely separate. Building a strong therapeutic relationship should permeate the treatment (Horvath et al., 2011).

7.2.1   Therapeutic Tasks

Tasks are behaviors and processes within therapy sessions that constitute the work of therapy. The literature on therapeutic alliance highlights the importance of clients and therapists having the same understanding of therapy tasks. One study with African American clients found they were concerned that their therapists did not explain how therapy could help and the expected length of therapy (Thompson et al., 2004). We encourage therapists to be clear about their approach to treatment and expectations of how Black female clients should engage in the therapeutic process. It may be helpful for therapists to explain the tasks of therapy and how therapeutic interventions work to alleviate clients' mental and emotional distress.

For a strong therapeutic alliance, therapists and clients need to be aligned on what will happen in therapy. When there is misalignment on therapy tasks, the therapist and client may have difficulty moving together toward goals. Some Black female clients may enter therapy familiar with the process, while other Black women may be unsure about what to expect. After assessing whether a new Black female client has had treatment previously, we recommend that therapists take the time to share their approach to therapy. Therapists should also explore what the client expects from therapy and the therapist specifically. Questions can include "What is your understanding of how therapy works?" and "How do you hope to use our time together?" These types of questions can open conversations about the tasks of therapy.

The therapeutic relationship and therapeutic processes should be collaborative. A collaborative approach reduces the power differences between therapists and Black female clients (Evans et al., 2005; Jones & Harris, 2019). In keeping with a womanist and Black feminist approach, we recommend that therapists signal their desire to collaborate by soliciting clients' agreement on the tasks of the therapy (Evans et al., 2005; Horvath et al., 2011; Jones & Harris, 2019; Williams, 2000). Therapists should be mindful of the power differences in relationships with clients and create opportunities to ensure that clients' hopes and goals drive therapy tasks.

When therapists invite Black women to shape their therapy experiences, they send an important message. Black communities often have a culture of deference, which involves respecting and prioritizing the wisdom of elders and authority figures. This cultural dynamic can lead Black female clients to agree to tasks for therapy due to the power difference rather than their assessment of what they need. We recommend that therapists encourage Black female clients to express any disagreement on the suggestions and interpretations that therapists share. For example, a therapist might ask their Black female client if she is uncertain about or uncomfortable with any aspects of the ideas or tasks being discussed. We also encourage therapists to be mindful of a Black female client who seems to agree too quickly. The client might agree to try something outside of the session and then return week after week saying that she never got to it. This dynamic may be a sign of passive dissent that the client does not feel comfortable expressing directly. Therapists can help a Black female client feel more comfortable expressing dissent by highlighting that they see the client as the expert on her life and what is best for her.

7.2.2   Therapeutic Goals

Goals are the objectives of therapy that both the therapist and client agree upon. Goal setting should be a collaborative process. Following a thorough assessment, therapists should engage the Black female client in a discussion about what she hopes to get out of therapy. Therapists can share their observations related to the challenges she has shared and how therapy can help her address these challenges. Collaboratively establishing the goals of therapy helps to ensure the therapist and client are in agreement on the direction in which therapy is headed. There may be times when a therapist identifies potential goals for therapy that the client may not yet be ready to pursue, and we recommend the therapist openly share their thoughts about potential therapeutic goals when the client is ready. For example, Adia Gooden has some Black female clients who experience ongoing challenges related to depression and anxiety. Adia has shared her hypothesis with these clients about how their symptoms may be in part connected to trauma they have experienced in the past and has also shared ways that they can use therapy to help process and heal the trauma. These clients have indicated a willingness to address their trauma at some point but have expressed that they are not ready yet. Adia has respected their assertion that they are not yet ready for this to be a goal of therapy, and she has supported them in focusing on other therapeutic goals.

Conversations about goals and tasks are intertwined because it can be helpful to talk with clients about how goals will be accomplished through the process of therapy. For example, if a client indicates that her goal is to be free from anxiety, a therapist could share that the process of working toward this goal might involve the therapist asking her to engage in behaviors both in and outside of the session that temporarily increase her anxiety. Therapists should provide psychoeducation about how anxiety works and the mechanism by which exposing ourselves to anxiety helps to reduce anxiety in the long run. This explanation, offered either at the time of setting the goal or before engaging in tasks to help reduce anxiety, would be important in order to inform the client of what to expect and to ensure that she is willingly engaging in the tasks involved to reach her therapeutic goals.

7.2.2.1 Client Worldviews and Therapy Goals

Clients' worldviews and beliefs should be considered in the process of establishing goals for therapy. Black women have unique life experiences that shape their worldviews and beliefs. Our worldviews are the way that we see and make sense of the world; they shape our engagement in the world and our experience of the world. Black women may be more likely to endorse Afrocentric worldviews (Jackson & Sears, 1992). An Afrocentric worldview is characterized by seeing an interconnection between the spiritual and material world, a value for connection and communalism, and a flexible view of time (Jackson & Sears, 1992). Communalism involves a sense of interdependence, responsibility for others, and focus on social identity (Boykin et al., 1997).

An effective way for therapists to explore their client's worldviews is by asking the following questions, similar to those recommended for therapists at the end of Chapter 6: What do you think causes good things to happen in your life and in the world? Is it due to fate? Luck? God? A higher power? Karma? Personal effort? Perseverance? People working together? Help from someone else? Did you question the positive experience? Did you expect that things will go well for you? How do you make sense of the challenging things that have happened in your life and the world? Do you believe they were caused by fate? God? A higher power? Karma? Personal failure? Other people or systems getting in your way? Do you believe that racism, sexism, homophobia, transphobia, classism, ableism, ageism, or any other discrimination was at play? How did you make sense of what happened and how it turned out? These questions will not only help the therapist understand how the client makes sense of the world; they will also help the client reflect on their own worldview.

Guided by the practice of cultural humility, we encourage therapists to display openness and respect when exploring a client's worldviews (Hook et al., 2013). We encourage therapists to make room for their Black female clients' worldviews to be different from theirs, particularly if the therapist is not a Black woman. To make room for differing worldviews, therapists must spend time examining their own worldviews. It is possible for a client's worldview to conflict with a therapist's worldview, and it is important for therapists to be aware of their own worldviews so they do not unintentionally impose their beliefs onto their client. Chapter 6 provides guidance in this process. Additionally, at the end of this chapter, we provide therapist reflection questions along with questions adapted from an article by Collins and colleagues (2010), which guide therapists to consider how their worldviews intersect with their client's worldviews.

An example of how conflicting worldviews could play out in therapy with a White, upper-class, cisgender, female therapist who is working with a Black working-class woman. The therapist might have the value of individualism as part of her worldview and prioritize people taking care of themselves and their own needs before offering help or support to others. In contrast, the Black female client might see herself and her well-being as intimately connected to the well-being of members of her family and community. The client might identify the goals of reducing stress and anxiety in her life, and the therapist might think the best way for her to do this is by limiting time spent with her family and community because they always seem to ask so much of her. However, this intervention would likely be misaligned with the Black female client's worldviews and could cause her to feel the therapist does not understand her or what is important to her. In this example, having a collaborative conversation with the client about what she thinks would help reduce her stress would be most effective. The therapist could suggest that the client might benefit from setting firmer boundaries with her family and, if the client is open to this, discuss ways to establish boundaries while also maintaining the strong connection with her family. The therapist could also guide the client to articulate both the benefits and challenges of being so close to her family and to affirm that the value of family in her life can make it challenging but not impossible to set healthy boundaries with her family.

7.2.2.2 Social and Political Factors and Therapy Goals We encourage therapists to talk with their Black female clients during the goal-setting process about the social, political, and cultural factors they may want to process or address during therapy (Evans et al., 2005; Jones & Harris, 2019; Williams, 2000). Black women may find it helpful to use therapy to address their social, political, and cultural experiences in addition to interpersonal and intrapersonal concerns. For Black women, the political is often personal. Greene (1997) asserts that it is important for clinicians to balance their understanding of a Black female client's personal problems with the challenges she faces related to race, gender, and sexuality and not to minimize the influence of the personal or societal influences on Black women. As discussed throughout this book, we encourage therapists to help Black female clients contextualize their concerns in order to understand the societal contributions to challenges they experience (Williams, 2005).

A colleague who is also a Black female therapist shared her experience of seeking therapy during the summer of 2020, when there were protests throughout the United States in response to the killings of Black people by police. She engaged in a few sessions with a skilled and accomplished White therapist but terminated prematurely after this therapist did not bring up race or provide space to discuss the distress this woman was experiencing in the context of this very present racial trauma. A therapist's skill and good intentions may be overshadowed by not checking in with a Black female client about her experience with social and political issues that reflect ongoing racial trauma. Ultimately, this can cause a rupture in the therapeutic relationship and make a Black woman feel she cannot address all of her concerns in therapy.

To be able to support Black women in navigating racism and sexism, it is essential for therapists to include these experiences in their assessment. We recommend therapists begin by assessing their Black female client's identities, being sure not to assume identities based on appearance. Further, we encourage therapists to explore their client's experiences with oppression and discrimination. This exploration should happen throughout therapy and can be initiated during the assessment phase of therapy by asking whether clients have had pivotal positive or negative experiences related to their identities that have influenced their experiences with other people and how they see the world. It is possible that the client will not have a specific experience to share at that time, and we encourage therapists to continue to check in with the client about whether she feels any negative experience she may bring up later is connected to her identity as a Black woman.

A sociocultural/political framework informed by womanist approaches to therapy includes addressing racism and sexism in the client's life. For therapists to support Black women in therapeutic goals that involve managing the role of oppression and discrimination in their lives, therapists must examine their own experiences with power, privilege, and oppression. Greene (1997) captures this well: "Therapists cannot explore the role of oppression in clients' lives without having explored the role of oppression and privilege in their own, particularly where they are positioned on the spectrum of privilege and oppression relative to the client" (p. 318).

> For more details on developing this type of self-awareness, see Chapter 6 on the cultural self of the therapist.

7.2.3   Client-Therapist Bonds

Bonds are positive interpersonal attachments between the client and the therapist, characterized by mutual trust, confidence, and acceptance. Therapists of all racial and ethnic backgrounds must be aware of cultural transference and countertransference. These dynamics play out at the beginning of therapy in the initial stages of developing a therapeutic relationship with Black female clients (Shorter-Gooden & Jackson, 2000). For example, cultural transference can initially support a therapeutic connection between a Black female client and a Black therapist. Cultural transference might hinder a connection between a White therapist and Black female client (Shorter-Gooden & Jackson, 2000). However, Black therapists cannot assume that initial connection and comfort with a Black female client due to shared racial identities negates the need to build a therapeutic alliance in other aspects of the relationship.

7.2.3.1 Addressing Racial Differences Therapists who are not Black should address racial/ethnic differences with their Black female clients to support the bonds in therapy (Coleman, 2000). Bringing up these differences early in the therapeutic relationship provides space for the client to share how she feels about working with a therapist of a different race or ethnicity. A discussion of differences also sets the stage for the client or therapist to return to this topic in future sessions as it is relevant for the therapy. Race and racial differences are often avoided as topics in therapy. Non-Black therapists and particularly White therapists may not have engaged in many conversations about race. They may feel uncomfortable naming the racial differences between them and the client. Therefore, it is essential for therapists who feel uncomfortable talking about race to reflect on their own racial identity and racialized experiences (as described in Chapter 6) through supervision and consultation groups. We also encourage Black therapists to check in with their Black female clients about working with a Black female therapist. This will help the therapist get a solid understanding of Black female clients' hopes and dreams for building a therapeutic relationship with another Black woman. In our study on Black women's experiences of and perspectives on psychotherapy, many participants expressed a preference for working with a Black female therapist because they assumed that this would help the therapist understand their experiences as a Black woman.

Research has demonstrated that clients of color rate therapy more highly when the therapist demonstrates knowledge about race (Coleman, 2000). Further, Black clients rate therapy and therapists more poorly when they avoid conversations about race (Constantine, 2007). Given these findings, we encourage therapists to be willing to be uncomfortable. We recommend that therapists broach conversations about race with their clients. Therapists can broach the topic of race with clients initially by asking the client how they identify racially, ethnically, and culturally in the assessment phase of treatment. Therapists can then ask: "How do you feel about working with a therapist who is _____ race?" During the course of treatment, when a client shares an experience that seems connected to race, it can be useful to ask a question such as "Do you think the experience you just described is related to your being a Black woman?" These questions open the conversation about the client's racialized experiences and give her an opportunity to share her interpretation of these experiences. The questions also demonstrate the therapist's willingness to discuss race in therapy.

Note that not all Black women see their racial identity as primary. While we encourage therapists to bring up racial differences with all Black female clients, some Black women may dismiss therapist–client racial differences as insignificant. The racial differences may be more significant than the client imagines. However, the therapist should not try to convince the client that their racial identity is salient.

7.2.3.2 Ensuring Safety Safety is another significant aspect of a strong therapeutic bond. It is essential for Black female clients to feel safe in the therapy room and to know they can share their experiences without fear of judgment or rejection by the therapist. As discussed in previous chapters, Black women frequently experience rejection and judgment as they navigate sexism and racism in their workplaces and communities. Some Black women may be particularly sensitive to encountering similar judgments or rejection by their therapists. This happens especially with therapists who are non-Black. While most therapists are generally well intentioned, social psychological research on implicit bias demonstrates that people, including therapists, have biases of which they are unaware. Implicit biases influence how people from different racial backgrounds interact (Vasquez, 2007). Therapists must be mindful of the ways in which their biases influence their interactions with Black female clients, making these clients feel unsafe in the therapy room. Implicit biases are one reason for the self-of-the-therapist work we recommend in Chapter 6. This work is an essential part of practicing cultural humility when providing therapy for Black women (Hook et al., 2013). We encourage therapists to work to ensure Black female clients feel safe. This could involve an explicit conversation about how safe she feels with the therapist and what could help her to feel safer. For example, therapists could ask their Black female clients the following questions: "Do you feel comfortable sharing your experiences of being a Black woman with me?" "Do you have any concerns about opening up and being vulnerable in therapy?" "What can I do to help you feel safer sharing in our sessions?" Further, adopting Carl Rogers's unconditional positive regard may be particularly helpful in ensuring that Black female clients feel accepted without judgment in therapy.

7.2.3.3 *Therapeutic Stance*

7.2.3.3 Therapeutic Stance Therapeutic stance refers to how the therapist shows up in the therapy room and engages with the client. The therapeutic stance can also foster or potentially inhibit bonds in the therapeutic relationship. A traditional, highly boundaried therapeutic stance in which therapists disclose little of their reactions and thoughts may work against building trust and connection with Black women (Thompson et al., 2004). Western psychotherapy, designed by White, cisgender, straight, upper-class men, suggests a boundaried stance as the optimal therapy style. This rigid, "blank slate" traditional approach to psychotherapy may not be a good fit for Black female clients. Such a stance creates distance in the therapeutic relationship, something that works against Black women's healing. Black female clients may assume their non-Black therapist is judging or discriminating against them in the absence of clear communication of compassion, affirmation, and acceptance. We encourage therapists to be mindful about how they bring themselves into therapy. We advocate for appropriate therapist self-disclosure that does not overshadow the clients' opinions and experiences in the process. We encourage therapists to share their thoughts and emotional responses honestly, inviting clients to provide feedback on these disclosures. Research suggests that when therapists engage in limited self-disclosure, clients from different backgrounds than the therapist rate the therapeutic alliance more highly (Coleman, 2000).

Our final recommendation related to facilitating strong bonds in therapy is for therapists to acknowledge and address the asymmetry of the therapeutic relationship (Shonfeld-Ringel, 2001). In all therapeutic relationships, the therapist has more power than the client. This asymmetry of power increases when the therapist is a member of a dominant culture and the client, in this case a Black woman, has multiple marginalized identities. Further, therapists must be thoughtful about how their own intersecting identities and experiences of power and privilege interact with and influence the power dynamic in therapeutic relationships with Black female clients. Drawing from feminist therapeutic approaches, therapists can take a stance and explicitly communicate that they see their clients as experts on themselves and their experience. While the therapist supports the client's healing, they do not have the authority on everything that will be most helpful for the client (Brown, 2008). Therapists can also empower their Black female clients to engage in the therapeutic process willingly, highlighting the strengths they already possess for self-advocacy (Brown, 2008).

Overall, a healthy alliance is a collaborative relationship, which is impossible if the power difference is so significant that there is no capacity for mutual participation and voice. A collaborative therapeutic relationship empowers a Black woman by affirming that she knows what she needs most, with the therapist supporting her healing and growth. Black women's history of negative experiences with medical and mental health systems is a cautionary tale for therapists. Therapists must avoid treating Black women as sick patients that need fixing. Emphasizing the wisdom of Black female clients will help foster collaboration and address some of the power differences present in the therapeutic relationship.

7.3   Impact of Microaggressions on the Therapeutic Alliance

In addition to the need to attend to tasks, goals, and bonds in therapy to build strong therapeutic alliances with Black female clients, therapists must also be mindful of how microaggressions damage the therapy relationship with Black women. In this section, we discuss how therapists can become aware of the potential for microaggressions, how to avoid them, and how to address them if they occur. These recommendations are aligned with practicing cultural humility, which guides clinicians to practice self-awareness and critique (Foronda et al., 2016).

We have discussed how a therapist's biases can negatively affect the therapeutic relationship. Studies show that therapists are more likely to have negative countertransference with Black clients when they internalize negative messages and stereotypes about Black people (Vasquez, 2007). Therapists should critically examine negative countertransference or judgments to maintain a capacity to empathize with the Black women seeking help.

One way that biases emerge in therapy is through microaggressions. According to Sue and colleagues (2007), "Microaggressions are brief, everyday exchanges that send denigrating messages to people of color because they belong to a racial minority group" (p. 3). Microaggressions communicate one person's feelings of power and dominance over another person based on identity or group membership (Vasquez, 2007). Microaggressions are often committed unconsciously and are invisible to the person who commits them. People may resist acknowledging microaggressions they commit because they did not intend to cause harm. Additionally, people might be concerned about admitting to a microaggression because they do not want to be labeled racist or bad. Microaggressions cause mental and emotional damage to the person who experiences them. After experiencing a microaggression, people often wonder if what they experienced was biased behavior based on their identity group or if they did something wrong to provoke their mistreatment. Adia Gooden remembers experiences of being treated rudely by store clerks who dismissed her presence or seemed to follow her around the store with their eyes to ensure she would not steal anything. After such experiences, she was left wondering if the way she was dressed and the way she carried herself prompted this treatment. She also wondered if she should say something to the clerk or the store manager to advocate for herself and then worried that she would not be believed if she spoke up. This left her with a feeling of frustration and not knowing how best to advocate for herself in the situation. These concerns are common for people who have experienced microaggressions, and it is easy to imagine how difficult it would be for a client to navigate these worries in the context of therapy. In a study of Black clients being treated by White therapists, Constantine (2007) found that when clients experienced racial microaggressions from their therapists, they reported weaker therapeutic alliance and lower satisfaction with counseling overall.

To be aware of microaggressions in the therapy room, it is important to know what microaggressions look and sound like since they can be unintentional and subtle. One example of a microaggression is expressing surprise at how articulate a Black female client is and how much competence she demonstrates in her work. When a therapist is overly impressed or seems to communicate that their Black female client's competence was unexpected, the therapist is sending a message that they assume their Black female client is unintelligent and uneducated, reflecting a negative stereotype about Black people. In Table 7.1, we provide examples of microaggressions adapted from Sue and colleagues (2007) to be specific to Black women. We encourage therapists to familiarize themselves with the types of microaggressions Black women commonly experience as they navigate daily life. These microaggressions can also occur in therapy. What follows are four recommendations for how to address microaggressions in treatment.

Table 7.1 *Common microaggressions in therapy with Black women*

Theme	Example	Message
Assumptions about intelligence	Being surprised by the achievements of your Black female clients	It's unusual for a Black woman to be so intelligent and accomplished
Color blindness	Telling a client that she is being too sensitive when she brings up an experience of being treated differently as a Black woman	Invalidating the racial experiences of the client and indicating that race is not that significant in daily interactions
Assumptions of criminality	Therapist asking a client how she might have contributed to someone assuming that she stole something	Assumption that she is a criminal
Denial of individual racism	A therapist indicates that they understand their Black female client's experience because of their own oppressed identity	Indicating that racial oppression is the same as gender or sexual orientation oppression
Myth of meritocracy	Communicating to a client that their fears of being passed over for a promotion will be assuaged if they work harder	Black people are not successful because they are lazy
Pathologizing cultural values	Diagnosing a Black female client for being loud and emotional	Communicating differently than the way White society thinks you should communicate is pathological

Note. Adapted from Sue et al. (2007).

7.3.1   Validate the Client's Experience

Our first recommendation is to validate the Black female client's experiences of microaggressions in and outside of therapy sessions. Black women experience microaggressions based on their race and gender frequently. Microaggressions may leave a Black woman questioning her experience and whether she did something wrong to cause the poor treatment she experienced. Validation can be a powerful intervention related to microaggressions because it helps to interrupt the self-questioning and will help her acknowledge that her feelings are valid. This validation will help reduce her stress pertaining to figuring out whether she should feel the way she did in response to the microaggression.

Sometimes, a client will share an experience of negatively biased treatment but fail to link this treatment to being a Black woman. When this happens, the therapist might suggest that the experience may be a result of racial or gender bias. This comment could be posed as "I wonder if you think people are not acknowledging your contributions in meetings because of their perception of you as a Black woman." Broaching the topic in this way opens the door for the client to share her experience of feeling invisible in the workplace because she is a Black woman. Validating the client's experience and normalizing it as what many Black women experience helps the client to know that she is not at fault for racial and gender microaggression or other biases.

7.3.2   Avoid Committing Microaggressions

Our second recommendation is for therapists to avoid committing microaggressions themselves. Microaggressions occur unintentionally, but therapists can be intentional about reducing the microaggressions they commit. Microaggressions are often subtle and go unnoticed by the person who commits them. Therefore, preventing microaggressions starts with addressing any negative beliefs or biases that you may have about Black women. This book is intended to support you in understanding the nuanced experiences of Black women, and reading the book in its entirety will likely help you understand Black women at a depth that challenges unconsciously held stereotypes about Black women. The more you know about the diverse experiences of Black women, the less likely you are to make assumptions and believe negative stereotypes, which can lead to microaggressions. Further, actively practicing cultural humility through demonstrating respect, a lack of superiority, and seeking to prioritize understanding your Black female client's life experiences over relying on your own knowledge will support you in avoiding microaggressions (Hook et al., 2013).

In addition to learning more about Black women, therapists should explore their own experiences with race, privilege, and oppression. Therapists are encouraged to examine the narratives you have internalized about race, gender, and class, as this exploration will also help prevent you from committing microaggressions. This work is essential because good intentions do not eliminate biases. Proactively working through your own experiences and assumptions related to race is essential in being aware of when these implicit biases may emerge with a Black woman in therapy. At their core, microaggressions against Black women are connected to the biased belief that Black women are "less than," which is a narrative that is unfortunately promulgated in mainstream media.

We guide you through the self-work of examining your internalized narratives about race, gender, and class in Chapter 6.

7.3.3   Acknowledge Microaggressions in Therapy

Our third recommendation is for therapists to intentionally monitor and acknowledge the occurrence of microaggressions. Even if you do your best to avoid committing microaggressions, they may still occur, and it is important to be willing to acknowledge them when they do occur. To monitor microaggressions that you commit, we recommend that you closely attend to your Black female client's reactions to what you say. If she shuts down or seems withdrawn after you say something, this may be because she experienced what you said as a microaggression. Your client's verbal and nonverbal responses can be helpful cues that you may have done or said something that caused a rupture in the relationship.

Additionally, therapists working in mental health or medical systems should be aware that microaggressions might occur in other parts of the system. For example, a member of the reception or billing department could commit a microaggression against a Black female client. Therapists should take responsibility for addressing microaggressions Black female clients experience with these departments as well as in the therapy room.

7.3.4   Address and Repair When Microaggressions Occur

Our fourth recommendation is to address microaggressions with clients when you become aware of them. As with any rift or tear in the therapeutic relationship, it can feel vulnerable to address our mistakes with our clients and opportunities to address and repair mistakes are powerful interventions that ultimately strengthen the therapeutic relationship. Suppose you become aware that you committed a microaggression in therapy with your Black female client through observation of their reactions, in your reflection after a session, or through consultation or supervision. In that case, it is vital that you proactively bring this up in a session with the client. You can say something like this: "After our session, I thought about what I said to you about whether or not you had prepared well enough for the interview for the job that you didn't end up getting, and I realized that was a hurtful and racially biased comment. I committed a microaggression. I want to apologize for saying that and for potentially causing you to feel judged in our session. If you are willing, I would like to talk about how what I said made you feel and to repair our relationship. How would you feel about talking about what happened?" This statement acknowledges the microaggression, apologizes without defensiveness, and allows the client to decide whether to revisit the conversation. The client may respond by indicating that she is not interested or ready to talk about what happened. She may also suggest that she did not feel what you said was a microaggression. We encourage you to honor your client's response and not force her to discuss what happened. You can let her know that if she would like to talk about it in a future session, you are always willing to return to the conversation. When you address microaggressions you might have committed, it is crucial to stay calm and grounded and to soothe yourself. Black women are often implicitly or explicitly asked to care for the feelings of White people, White women in particular. If you are a White therapist, it is vital that this dynamic not arise when you are discussing a rupture in the therapeutic relationship. We encourage therapists to express sadness or disappointment related to committing a microaggression with their clients but without crying or indicating that you need to be taken care of.

A client might also bring a microaggression experienced in therapy to your attention. In that case, it is essential for you to be nondefensive and communicate openness to addressing what happened. It takes a lot of courage for a client to bring up a rupture in the therapeutic relationship and to call a therapist out on a microaggression. Bringing up a microaggression committed by the therapist is particularly challenging considering the power differential present in therapy and the additional imbalance of power if the therapist is White. The first thing we encourage a therapist to do if a client brings up a microaggression they experienced with the therapist is to thank the client for having the courage to bring it up and to validate the client's experience and emotional response to what happened. You can then ask the client to share how they understood what you said and what made it hurtful for them. If you do not know why the client is upset or offended, do not make them convince you of the validity of their experience. Use outside consultation or supervision to work through and make sense of what happened on your end. Make sure that you apologize and commit to avoiding microaggressions in the future. Also, encourage the client to let you know in the future if they feel you have committed other microaggressions.

7.4 Guiding Principles for a Strong Therapeutic Alliance with Black Women

Earlier in this chapter, we provided specific recommendations for cultivating strong therapeutic alliances with Black women. Here, we share five guiding principles for therapists seeking to build strong therapeutic relationships with Black female clients.

7.4.1 Proactively Build Trust

We recommend that therapists working with Black female clients proactively and intentionally work to build trust with these clients. Creating a trusting relationship is important for all clients. It is particularly important for Black women, who may take longer to trust their therapist. There is a legacy of mistrust between Black communities and medical and mental health professionals due to the mistreatment Black people have experienced at the hands of medical and mental health professionals (Washington, 2006). Thompson and colleagues (2004) found that trust was a significant barrier to African Americans seeking therapy.

> The history of mistreatment of Black people in medical and mental health care is detailed in Chapters 2, 5, and 13.

Additionally, Black women may be wary of the intentions and beliefs of White therapists due to past negative experiences with White people and while interacting with White systems. Specifically, Adams (2000) argues that trust is a significant issue in the therapeutic relationship between White therapists and Black clients. Black female clients may wonder whether their therapist will understand them and their experience. Given these historical and systemic barriers to trust between Black women and therapists, it is important for therapists to understand that Black women's apprehension about trusting them is understandable and to proactively build trust with their Black female clients.

To build trust, we recommend therapists talk to their Black female clients about what they can expect in therapy, explain confidentiality, and take the time to solicit and answer any questions clients may have (Thompson et al., 2004). We also recommend therapists strive to be consistent. Black women may assess whether a therapist is trustworthy based on what they say and based on their behavior and interactions with the client and the interactions the client witnesses between the therapist and their coworkers. For example, suppose a therapist working in a mental health practice is kind and gracious to their Black female client but short and dismissive with the Black female receptionists for the practice. In that case, the client will be wary of trusting that the therapist truly respects Black women. Additional qualities therapists can exhibit to build trust with Black female clients are compassion, empathy, and nonjudgment. Further, helping the client know that you truly care about them, paying attention to what they share, and respecting that it may take time for them to open up and address some of their concerns in therapy foster trust (Borba et al., 2012). Additionally, research has linked being honest and making sure that clients are satisfied with the service they are receiving to clients trusting their provider (Gaebel et al., 2014).

7.4.2   Be Patient in the Relationship

Our second guiding principle goes hand in hand with building trust because it is important for therapists be patient with the time it takes for Black women to connect and open up in therapy. Given the sociohistorical and cultural factors discussed elsewhere in this book (e.g., Chapters 2, 5, and 8), Black women may be slow to open up and be vulnerable in therapy. Cultural norms in the Black community discourage Black people from sharing private information with strangers. Therefore, most Black women will want to get to know their therapist and no longer feel they are strangers in order to share personal experiences.

We encourage therapists to be patient in developing the therapeutic relationship with Black women and give clients time to share more of themselves and their experiences throughout treatment. Greene (1997) highlights the importance of clinicians taking the time to build trust with their Black female clients. Once trust is established, therapists can guide them to explore how their emotional patterns and characteristics may be at play in navigating challenges. As therapists, we may be eager to rush into interventions we think will benefit our clients. Still, if our clients are not ready to engage in these interventions or to address those concerns, we can end up eroding trust in the therapeutic relationship. We encourage therapists to allow their Black female clients to set the pace of therapy to feel safe and know they have the choice about what to focus on at various stages of the therapy. Therapists can check in with their clients about the pacing of therapy by asking if they are ready to share certain things about themselves or explore or process specific concerns. Therapists should always respect any boundaries a client sets around what they are and are not ready to talk about. It can be helpful for the therapist to discuss with clients what is keeping them from feeling ready to talk about their concerns and what would help them to feel ready to discuss these issues.

7.4.3   Practice Curiosity

Curiosity is the third guiding principle because even as therapists read this book and learn more about the nuanced experiences of Black women, it is essential to be curious about the specific experiences of each Black female client. Curiosity involves seeking to understand what is valid for the client and is essential in practicing cultural humility (Hook et al., 2013). Curiosity helps to counter our human tendency to make quick assumptions and buy into stereotypes as we try to make sense of a world with many stimuli. When we stereotype people, we stop seeing them as individuals, but curiosity helps us pause and slow down to take in the person in front of us fully. Curiosity is critical to avoid stereotyping in the therapy room.

One way that clinicians can put curiosity into practice is through dynamic sizing, which involves knowing when to generalize and when to individualize (Sue, 1998). Dynamic sizing is sensing when to connect a client's experience to other people's experiences with shared identities and when to explore the unique experiences of a client. Here, we offer two key recommendations to support therapists in practicing curiosity. First, therapists can put dynamic sizing into practice by balancing an acknowledgment of the experiences common to many Black women with an exploration of the unique experiences of each of their Black female clients. To practice curiosity, therapists must listen to what their clients have to say. In our study of Black women's views of and experiences with psychotherapy, many participants expressed a desire for their therapist to listen to them and hear what they had to say. The second essential component of practicing curiosity is for therapists to examine themselves, their reactions, and the assumptions they make about Black women. Practicing self-curiosity in this way will help therapists to slow down and center their attention on the woman in front of them as they share their lived experiences.

7.4.4   Communicate with Respect

The fourth guiding principle for strong therapeutic relationships with Black women is showing respect, this is in line with recommendations for cultural humility (Hook et al., 2013). Black women experience a lot of disrespect in their daily lives. Therapists need to communicate their respect for the Black women they work with. Specifically, therapists can respect their Black female clients by honoring their boundaries and acknowledging their wisdom. When a client indicates they are not comfortable talking about something or engaging in an intervention, therapists must respect the boundary she is establishing. Further, as discussed previously, the womanist approach to therapy sees the client as an expert on her own life. We encourage therapists to respect and highlight the internal wisdom of their Black female clients. Numerous narratives in mainstream media depict Black people being saved by White people, and this should not be the dynamic in therapy. We encourage therapists to prioritize their Black female client's wisdom over the therapist's opinions.

We recommend that therapists working with Black women over the age of 50 or doing family interventions begin by addressing their adult Black female clients formally with *Mrs.*, *Ms.*, or *Dr.* as appropriate. You can then ask the client what they prefer to be called and follow their request. There is a legacy in the United States of Black men and women being called "boy" and "girl" by racist White people attempting to demean their personhood. Even today, Black women may be less likely to be addressed formally and respectfully. We have heard examples of Black women being called "girl" or "girlfriend" by medical professionals to try to relate to them. This casual approach to connecting to a client is inappropriate, can communicate disrespect, and may be experienced as a microaggression. Therapists have the opportunity to ensure that their clients feel respected by using formal titles at the beginning of the therapeutic relationship.

We also encourage therapists to consider how Black women's experiences in the systems where they are receiving care might be respectful or disrespectful. How do the receptionists and other providers treat Black women? Is there an assumption that she has public insurance or cannot afford to pay her bill? Is there a tendency to overlook her needs and prioritize serving other clients first? These things could all be classified as microaggressions, and they communicate a lack of respect for Black women.

7.4.5   Make Room for High-Context Communication

Our fifth and final guiding principle is to make room for high-context communication styles in therapy with Black women. Communication is an essential component of a healthy therapeutic alliance, especially when the therapist and the client are from different cultures (Shonfeld-Ringel, 2001). Therapists should know that the communication styles of Black women can vary by socioeconomic status. Overall, Black women tend to engage in high-context communication (Gooden, 2019). High-context communication can include tone, volume, and use of slang that is unique to African American communities (Adams, 2000). Given the pervasive narratives about how African Americans talk, therapists should work to be aware of their internalized stereotypes or negative beliefs about the communication styles of their Black female clients (Adams, 2000). We recommend therapists ask for clarification when they do not understand what a client is trying to communicate. Many Black women feel the need to shift, which involves changing language, behavior, and tone when they are in non-Black spaces. While this is an adaptive strategy, it can take a toll on the people who do it (Jones & Shorter-Gooden, 2003) and prevent clients from showing up authentically in the therapy room. Black female clients may shift (as discussed in Chapter 9) even when working with a Black therapist because the culture of therapy is often White, as Western therapy was developed by White, heterosexual, upper-class men and psychotherapy often reflects the culture of its founders. Therapists need to create a space where Black female clients can feel comfortable expressing themselves without shifting. As part of making room for different communication styles, we also encourage therapists to make room for displays of emotional expression. Black women are stereotyped as being angry and may feel apprehensive about expressing emotions in the therapy room. Yet, we know that fully processing emotions in therapy is a powerful intervention that facilitates healing, and therapists should help clients to connect to and express the full range of their emotional experience.

In Chapter 9 we discuss in detail how to address Black women shifting in therapy.

Case Example

Denise is a 49-year-old African American woman who is divorced and does not have children. Denise came to therapy with concerns about ongoing depression. Denise was matched with the therapist when she requested to work with a Black female therapist, although she did not know the therapist specifically. Denise's initial demeanor in therapy was reserved; she seemed almost annoyed with the therapist during the first couple of sessions and did not smile. Although Denise's reservations made the therapist wonder whether she had done something wrong, the therapist remembered that her Black female clients often take longer to warm up in therapy, and she continued to show warmth to Denise and was patient as Denise took her time to feel safe and open up in therapy. Initial sessions focused on Denise's frustrations with her job and her desire to find another job. The therapist provided space for Denise to vent her frustrations about work. Together, they explored whether Denise attributed some of her challenges to being one of the few Black women at her job. In giving Denise space to process her frustrations with work, the therapist aligned the sessions with her initial goals and tasks for therapy, which involved having the space to vent her frustrations with life.

The therapist practiced patience and allowed Denise to lead the pace of the therapy, and over time, as Denise began to feel more comfortable, she began to talk about the challenging relationship she had with her late father, who died in his 50s due to complications related to alcoholism. Denise shared that she spent a lot of time imagining what would have been different about her life and her parents' lives if he had not been an alcoholic. The therapist gave Denise space to express her sadness, anger, and frustration at her father for not taking care of himself or being the parent she needed. The therapist validated the pain Denise experienced in her relationship with her father. Denise and the therapist explored how the unresolved issues in Denise's relationship with him contributed to the anger, frustration, and disappointment she was experiencing in her life. The therapist helped Denise to see that holding on to the wounds from her relationship with her father was contributing to her depression and holding her back in life. Denise was initially resistant to the idea of forgiving her father. The therapist helped her explore what felt safe about holding on to her anger toward him and what it might be like to release this anger through forgiving him. Providing Denise with time to get to know the therapist and ensuring a safe

(cont.)

and trusting therapeutic relationship enabled the therapist to provide her with this feedback and helped her to be willing to begin the process of forgiveness.

As therapy progressed, it became evident that Denise was comfortable with the therapist. She would laugh in sessions and seemed more at ease and authentic. Building this trust also enabled Denise and the therapist to explore Denise's dreams of owning her own business. Denise had longed to work for herself and build a business but had let go of that dream, worrying that she was too old or would not be successful. Through the safe and nonjudgmental therapeutic relationship, therapy became a space where Denise could explore her dreams. The therapist held space for Denise's dreams, empowered her to take courageous steps to pursue building a business, and supported her in managing her anxiety during this process.

This therapeutic relationship highlights the importance of patience and allowing Black women to lead the pace of therapy, being aligned on the goals and tasks of therapy, and building trust and a strong therapeutic bond. This case demonstrates how the therapist carefully nurtured the alliance with a Black female client. It shows the power of the therapeutic relationship to enable Black women to acknowledge their true hopes and dreams for their lives. While subtle, this case illustrates how a solid therapeutic alliance serves as a foundation for interventions and client progress in therapy.

7.5   Conclusion

A final note on building therapeutic alliances with Black women: Therapists must not buy into the myth of the strength of Black women (Jones & Shorter-Gooden, 2003) when setting goals and cultivating therapeutic relationships with Black female clients. As discussed extensively in Chapter 8, Black women are socialized to appear strong and push through challenges. Seeing Black women as having mythical strength can cause therapists to overlook mental illness, emotional pain, and other challenges Black female clients experience. Building a solid therapeutic relationship involves therapists fully acknowledging their clients' pain and suffering. Therapists should be aware that Black women may report symptoms of depression, anxiety, and other diagnoses in a way that may be less readily identifiable. A qualitative study found that African American women talk about depression differently from the literature (Waite & Killian, 2007). Black women may be less likely to use words like *hopeless*, *sad*, and *depressed* to describe their symptoms. They may be more likely to share their feelings of fatigue and exhaustion, express feeling like they are struggling in life, and share that they feel irritable, resentful, and angry (Waite & Killian, 2007). We urge therapists to be attuned to these differences so they do not overlook Black female clients' core concerns when identifying the goals and tasks of therapy.

Therapist Reflection Questions

1. How do you assess the quality of your alliance with clients in therapy?
2. How are the recommendations in this chapter aligned with your approach to developing a therapeutic alliance with clients?
3. What has helped or hindered your capacity to build strong therapeutic alliances with Black female clients?
4. How have you managed therapeutic ruptures with clients?
5. What are your experiences around microaggressions in therapy with Black female clients or with clients who have different identities than your own?
6. What takeaways from the chapter might you apply in your work with Black female clients?

Questions adapted from "Enhancing Reflective Practice in Multicultural Counseling Through Cultural Auditing" by Collins et al. (2010):

- What assumptions am I making about my Black female client and her culture?
- What aspects of my own beliefs, values, and worldview do I anticipate might be challenged or in conflict in my work with this client?

Resources for Therapists

Books

Burke, T., & Brown, B. (Eds.). (2021). *You are your best thing: Vulnerability, shame resilience, and the black experience*. Random House.

Helms, J. E. (2017). Counseling Black women: Understanding the effects of multilevel invisibility. In M. Kopala & M. Keitel (Eds.), *Handbook of counseling women* (pp. 219–233). Sage Publications, Inc. https://doi.org/10.4135/9781506300290.n22

Higgins, N. (2021). *Purposeful perspectives: Empowering black women towards spiritual alignment, self-mastery, & joy*. Paper Raven Books.

Winters, M. F. (2020). *Inclusive conversations: Fostering equity, empathy, and belonging across differences*. Berrett-Koehler Publishers.

Articles

Asnaani, A., & Hofmann, S. G. (2012). Collaboration in multicultural therapy: Establishing a strong therapeutic alliance across cultural lines. *Journal of Clinical Psychology, 68*(2), 187–197.

Coleman, D. (2000). The therapeutic alliance in multicultural practice. *Psychoanalytic Social Work, 7*(2), 65–91. http://dx.doi.org/10.1300/J032v07n02_04

Collins, S., Arthur, N., & Wong-Wylie, G. (2010). Enhancing reflective practice in multicultural counseling through cultural auditing. *Journal of Counseling & Development, 88*(3), 340–347. https://doi.org/10.1002/j.1556-6678.2010.tb00031.x

Podcasts

Crenshaw, K. (Executive Producer). (2019–present). *Intersectionality matters!* [Audio podcast]. African American Policy Forum. https://www.aapf.org/imkc-podcast-episodes

Media Resources

Stovall, N. (2019). *Whiteness on the couch.* Longreads. https://longreads.com/2019/08/12/whiteness-on-the-couch/

References

Adams, J. M. (2000). Individual and group psychotherapy with African American women: Understanding the identity and context of the therapist and patient. In L. C. Jackson & B. Greene (Eds.), *Psychotherapy with African American women: Innovations in psychodynamic perspective and practice* (pp. 33–61). Guilford Press.

Asnaani, A., & Hofmann, S. G. (2012). Collaboration in multicultural therapy: Establishing a strong therapeutic alliance across cultural lines. *Journal of Clinical Psychology, 68*(2), 187–197.

Borba, C. P., DePadilla, L., McCarty, F. A., von Esenwein, S. A., Druss, B. G., & Sterk, C. E. (2012). A qualitative study examining the perceived barriers and facilitators to medical healthcare services among women with a serious mental illness. *Women's Health Issues, 22*(2), e217–e224. https://doi.org/10.1016/j.whi.2011.10.001

Bordin, E. S. (1979). The generalizability of the psychoanalytic concept of the working alliance. *Psychotherapy: Theory, Research & Practice, 16*(3), 252–260. https://doi.org/10.1037/h0085885

Boykin, A. W., Jagers, R. J., Ellison, C. M., & Albury, A. (1997). Communalism: Conceptualization and measurement of an Afrocultural social orientation. *Journal of Black Studies, 27*(3), 409–418.

Brown, L. S. (2008). Feminist therapy. In J. Lebow (Ed.), *Twenty-first century psychotherapies: Contemporary approaches to theory and practice* (pp. 277–306). John Wiley & Sons, Inc.

Castonguay, L. G., Constantino, M. J., & Holtforth, M. G. (2006). The working alliance: Where are we and where should we go? *Psychotherapy: Theory, Research, Practice, Training, 43*(3), 271–279.

Coleman, D. (2000). The therapeutic alliance in multicultural practice. *Psychoanalytic Social Work, 7*(2), 65–91. http://dx.doi.org/10.1300/J032v07n02_04

Collins, S., Arthur, N., & Wong-Wylie, G. (2010). Enhancing reflective practice in multicultural counseling through cultural auditing. *Journal of Counseling & Development, 88*(3), 340–347. https://doi.org/10.1002/j.1556-6678.2010.tb00031.x

Comas-Díaz, L. (2006). *Cultural variation in the therapeutic relationship.* In C. D. Goodheart, A. E. Kazdin, & R. J. Sternberg (Eds.), *Evidence-based psychotherapy: Where practice and research meet* (pp. 81–105). American Psychological Association. https://doi.org/10.1037/11423-004

Constantine, M. G. (2007). Racial microaggressions against African American clients in cross-racial counseling relationships. *Journal of Counseling Psychology, 54*(1), 1–16. https://doi.org/10.1037/0022-0167.54.1.1

Evans, K. M., Kincade, E. A., Marbley, A. F., & Seem, S. R. (2005). Feminism and feminist therapy: Lessons from the past and hopes for the future. *Journal of Counseling & Development, 83*(3), 269–277.

Foronda, C., Baptiste, D. L., Reinholdt, M. M., & Ousman, K. (2016). Cultural humility: A concept analysis. *Journal of Transcultural Nursing, 27*(3), 210–217. https://doi.org/10.1177/1043659615592677

Gaebel, W., Muijen, M., Baumann, A. E., Bhugra, D., Wasserman, D., van der Gaag, R. J., Heun, R., Zielasek, J., & European Psychiatric Association. (2014). EPA guidance on building trust in mental health services. *European Psychiatry, 29*(2), 83–100.

Gooden, A. (2019). Black women in couples and families. In J. L. Lebow, A. L. Chambers, & D. C. Breunlin (Eds.), *Encyclopedia of couple and family therapy* (pp. 285–289). Springer. https://doi.org/10.1007/978-3-319-49425-8_702

Greene, B. (1997) Psychotherapy with African American women: Integrating feminist and psychodynamic models. *Smith College Studies in Social Work, 67*(3), 299–322. https://doi.org/10.1080/00377319709517495

Hook, J. N., Davis, D. E., Owen, J., Worthington E. L., Jr., & Utsey, S. O. (2013). Cultural humility: Measuring openness to culturally diverse clients. *Journal of Counseling Psychology, 60*(3), 353–366. https://doi.org/10.1037/a0032595

Horvath, A. O., Re, A. C. D., Flückiger, C., & Symonds, D. (2011). Alliance in individual psychotherapy. In J. C. Norcross (Ed.), *Psychotherapy relationships that work: Evidence-based responsiveness* (pp. 25–69). Oxford University Press. https://doi.org/10.1037/a0022186

Jackson, A. P., & Sears, S. J. (1992). Implications of an Africentric worldview in reducing stress for African American women. *Journal of Counseling & Development, 71*(2), 184–190.

Johnson, S., Price, M., Mehta, N., & Anderson, P. L. (2014). Stereotype confirmation concerns predict dropout from cognitive behavioral therapy for social anxiety disorder. *BMC Psychiatry, 14*(1), 1–6. https://doi.org/10.1186/s12888-014-0233-8

Jones, L. V., & Harris, M. A. (2019). Developing a Black feminist analysis for mental health practice: From theory to praxis. *Women & Therapy, 42*(3–4), 251–264. https://doi.org/10.1080/02703149.2019.1622908

Jones, M. C., & Shorter-Gooden, K. (2009). *Shifting: The double lives of Black women in America.* Harper Collins.

King, A. C., & Canada, S. A. (2004). Client-related predictors of early treatment drop-out in a substance abuse clinic exclusively employing individual therapy. *Journal of Substance Abuse Treatment, 26*(3), 189–195. https://doi.org/10.1016/s0740-5472(03)00210-1

Lambert, M. J., & Barley, D. E. (2001). Research summary on the therapeutic relationship and psychotherapy outcome. *Psychotherapy: Theory, Research, Practice, Training, 38*(4), 357–361. https://doi.org/10.1037/0033-3204.38.4.357

McGuire, T. G., & Miranda, J. (2008). New evidence regarding racial and ethnic disparities in mental health: Policy implications. *Health Affairs (Project Hope), 27* (2), 393–403. https://doi.org/10.1377/hlthaff.27.2.393

Sharf, J., Primavera, L. H., & Diener, M. J. (2010). Dropout and therapeutic alliance: a meta-analysis of adult individual psychotherapy. *Psychotherapy: Theory, Research, Practice, Training, 47*(4), 637–645.

Shonfeld-Ringel, S. (2001). A re-conceptualization of the working alliance in cross-cultural practice with Non-Western clients: Integrating relational perspectives and multicultural theories. *Clinical Social Work Journal, 29*(1), 53–63. https://doi.org/10.1023/A:1005258511296

Shorter-Gooden, K. & Jackson, L. C. (2000). The interweaving of cultural and intrapsychic issues in the therapeutic relationship. In L. C. Jackson & B. Green (Eds.), *Psychotherapy with African American women*. Guilford Press.

Sue, D. W., Capodilupo, C. M., Torino, G. C., Bucceri, J. M., Holder, A. M. B., Nadal, K. L., & Esquiline, M. (2007). Racial microaggressions in everyday life: Implications for clinical practice. *American Psychologist, 62*(4), 271–286. https://doi.org/10.1037/0003-066x.62.4.271

Sue, S. (1998). In search of cultural competence in psychotherapy and counseling. *American psychologist, 53*(4), 440–448.

Thompson, V. L. S., Bazile, A., & Akbar, M. (2004). African Americans' perceptions of psychotherapy and psychotherapists. *Professional Psychology: Research and Practice, 35*, 19–26.

Vasquez, M. J. (2007). Cultural difference and the therapeutic alliance: An evidence-based analysis. *American Psychologist, 62*(8), 878–885. https://doi.org/10.1037/0003-066X.62.8.878

Waite, R., & Killian, P. (2007). Exploring depression among a cohort of African American women. *Journal of the American Psychiatric Nurses Association, 13*(3), 161–169. https://doi.org/10.1177/1078390307304996

Washington, H. A. (2006). *Medical apartheid: The dark history of medical experimentation on Black Americans from colonial times to the present.* Doubleday Books.

Williams, C. B. (2000). African American women, Afrocentrism and feminism: Implications for therapy. *Women & Therapy, 22*(4), 1–16.

(2005). Counseling African American women: Multiple identities – Multiple constraints. *Journal of Counseling & Development, 83*(3), 278–283.

Part III

Core Themes in Black Women's Stress and Distress

8   Strong Black Woman Persona: Mental Health Impacts

Strong is a term ubiquitously applied to Black women, and they hear it across our life spans. "You are a strong Black woman" can convey different sentiments, mostly positive. *Strong* can be a compliment honoring a Black woman's selflessness. *Strong* might refer to a Black woman's poise and emotional control, a posture of grace and overcoming in the face of crises. *Strong* might also convey admiration for a Black woman's choice to turn the other cheek when faced with hostilities. To us, *strong* is an apt descriptor for many Black women who understand their power and influence and show physical and psychological resilience in the face of challenging circumstances. In these scenarios, Black women persevere, demonstrate self-efficacy, and exert influence with faith, good humor, and humility to make good things happen. Many Black women, ordinary and extraordinary, embody strengths (Black & Peacock, 2011; Black & Woods-Giscombe, 2012). Black women's strengths appear in song, media, and art, but the qualities of strength as described in this paragraph are *not* our focus in this chapter.

This chapter discusses the Strong Black Woman persona or lifestyle (hereafter SBW) that some Black women adopt, with little reflection on how it threatens their mental and emotional health. Participants in our study talked about the SBW. One stated: "Historically Black women are taught (erroneously) that we are supposed to be able to handle everything (the myth of the superwoman) and if we can't, then there is something wrong with us ... this might prevent people from seeking support because it can be hard to admit that we can't do it all." The reasons Black women assume and live out SBW values are complex (Beauboef-Lafontant, 2005). The SBW lifestyle is driven by a historical and cultural *archetype* (a generalized model of how to be) and also a *stereotype* (an oversimplified image or caricature) that is poorly understood even among Black women themselves (Beauboeuf-Lafontant, 2009; Walker-Barnes, 2016). Racial stereotypes drive the SBW identity, especially views of Black people as unimaginably tough and hardy. Historically, this imagery harkens to Black enslaved bodies that were seemingly undaunted by hard labor (Abrams et al., 2014; Simms, 2001). A large body of research highlights the stress of racism and intergenerational trauma on Black people in America.

The impact on Black women – the subject matter of this book – is indisputable. Black women's self-perception of being tough and invincible causes many to refrain from seeking help in life's difficult circumstances. Gendered stereotypes also maintain SBW lifestyles (Abrams et al., 2014; Beauboef-Lafontant, 2007). Frequently, Black women are assumed to have unending reserves of energies to care for others, sometimes well beyond their own physical and emotional capacities and with the abandonment of their self-needs. In such situations, Black women can mute themselves to avoid painful stereotypes of being overbearing, selfish, or emasculating (Black & Peacock, 2011).

We aim to increase therapists' awareness and skill in working with Black female clients whose mental and emotional symptoms reflect SBW values. Therapists should understand the historical origins of the SBW persona and why some Black female clients might adopt SBW lifestyles. Therapists should become familiar with crucial SBW traits to uncover how they may be barely visible in a client's everyday routines, even to the clients themselves. Therapists should know what to look for in women's narratives to formulate SBW hypotheses and link such assumptions to concrete interventions. Therapists must also help their clients celebrate positive aspects of their SBW identities while replacing features that endanger their health and wellness (Settles et al., 2008). We also present a resilience framework to help SBW appreciate their tenacity and service to others while prioritizing their need for self-care, support, and rejuvenation.

8.1   Recognizing the SBW Persona

SBW traits reflect an internalized dimension of some Black women's lives from which they derive great significance (Beauboeuf-Lafontant, 2009; Woods-Giscombé & Black, 2010). An SBW often embodies four traits that might show up in a client's narrative and demeanor: (a) visible emotional composure and regulation; (b) emotional stoicism and resignation toward stress and suffering; (c) radical acts of caregiving, sometimes well beyond personal capacity; and (d) a sense of independence and a dogged refusal to seek help (Walker-Barnes, 2016). These SBW traits can hide a turbulent inner world. Walker-Barnes describes the SBW as having "extraordinary capacities for caregiving and suffering without complaint . . . a particular and fixed way of being in the world . . . a scripted role into which Black women are socialized, usually beginning in childhood. Rather than being a genuine expression of personality, [the SBW] . . . stifles authenticity . . . behind a singular wall of self-sacrifice and emotional stoicism" (2016, p. 14). In other words, Black women have a way of being in the world that masks their internal suffering.

SBW traits can show up as a lifestyle or persona (as discussed in this chapter). Others may also refer to SBW values as an ideology, a mask, a schema, a script, a personality trait, or part of identity (Walker-Barnes, 2016). First identified in published literature in the 1970s, the SBW trait has received other labels, including the Superwoman (Wallace, 1999) and the Sisterella Complex (Jones & Shorter-Gooden, 2003). The social and emotional "DNA" of most Black women embeds SBW pressures, and SBW values hover over Black women's identity, roles, and self-perceptions (Donovan, 2011; Romero, 2000). Black women learn how to become SBWs from their female caregivers and role models, who themselves may have lived (and died) from such lifestyles (Harris-Lacewell, 2001). What makes the SBW lifestyle so compelling is the admiration it commands in both majority cultures and Black social and cultural microcosms (Parks, 2010). The SBW lifestyle, which is powerfully endorsed in pop culture, movies, books, media, art, and influential Black institutions (e.g., sororities, Black media, and churches), inspires this kind of admiration and respect. For Black women, the SBW persona is a powerful pathway to significance, meaning, and social standing (Romero, 2000).

Hence, the SBW persona has both positive and negative features. It reflects Black women's nurturance and uplift of families and communities. These qualities are precious in a world of narcissism and self-centeredness, rightly deserving of admiration and respect (Collins, 2000). But research also suggests that the SBW persona comes with a steep price. Such lifestyles produce systemic fatigue in Black women after years of expending themselves with little attention to their own needs (Beauboeuf-Lafontant, 2007, 2009). SBW lifestyles are negatively associated with chronic stress, depression, anxiety, and obesity; chronic health conditions such as heart disease and diabetes; and mortality and morbidity (Donovan & West, 2015). Most critically, SBW values, deeply embedded in the psyches of Black women, cause them to struggle in silence, even in dire situations, and to avoid seeking help (Beauboeuf-Lafontant, 2003, 2005; Harrington et al., 2010; Mitchell & Herring, 1998). Therapists must be alert to certain conditions that may indicate a Black woman with underrecognized SBW values. Table 8.1 is a checklist of traits the therapist might use to understand if clients' narratives hint at SBW values.

8.2   Origins of the SBW Archetype and Stereotype

An important starting point for understanding the SBW persona is to uncover why it has become so valuable in contemporary culture (Walker-Barnes, 2016). In the late 1990s, Wallace (1999) criticized the Black women involved in the Black Power movement and Black politics as living "Superwoman" lifestyles driven by patriarchal biases. The Black "Superwoman" caricature was a larger-than-life woman of great emotional tenacity and a capacity to withstand harsh labor and suffering (Wallace, 1999). In the 2000s, several

Table 8.1 *Strong Black Woman checklist*

Traits or Values	Definitely Present	Maybe Present	Definitely Not Present	Examples
Constantly self-sacrificing on behalf of others				
The go-to woman for assistance, counsel, comfort (church, job, family, children)				
A deeply ingrained desire to be helpful and caring				
Finds it hard to say "no" without feeling guilty and worthless				
Willing to be perpetually available				
Can feel and is overcommitted				
Wears a suit of "armor"				
Carries burdens for many lives				
Worried about doing too much				
Difficulty asking for help				
Overemphasis on independence and self-sufficiency				
Prioritizes being a "giver" and not a receiver				
May demonstrate self-sacrifice with religious or moral fervor				
Invests considerable attention to maintain appearance of strong women				
A tendency to suppress behaviors, emotions, and thoughts that might threaten the Strong Black Woman image				
Even in the face of psychological distress, maintains a façade of holding it together				
Romanticism or stoicism around suffering				
Substance abuse and addictions				
Poor sleep				
Emotional eating, obesity				
Perfectionism				
Stress (significant events, daily hassles)				
Migraines or headaches				
Hypertension (high blood pressure)				
Feelings of emptiness, joylessness				
Limited capacity for sexual or romantic intimacy				
Depressive symptoms				
Anxiety symptoms				
Victim of intimate partner violence				
Somatization				
Soul weariness and inertia				

authors picked up themes related to Black women destroying their physical, mental, and emotional health by living as superwomen or as SBWs (Jackson & Greene, 2000). Since then, dozens of articles and blogs have discussed the downsides of embracing SBW values, yet such values persist.

Black women may internalize SBW personas to fight depictions of their femininity as inferior, unattractive, and deficient. Collins (2020) discusses the power of privileged groups to manipulate ideas of Black womanhood through old and new stereotypes. For example, Black women are seen as hypersexual, and the stereotypical Black Mammy is sacrificial and self-abasing. The "Black matriarch" remains a powerful stereotype that shows up in the "sassy" qualities of Black women characters in television and movies. This stereotype portrays Black mothers as aggressive and angry, whipping their children into compliance and emasculating their men (Harris-Perry, 2011; Thomas et al., 2004).

> Chapter 4 describes vicious stereotypes that still haunt Black women today.

To fight these caricatures of themselves, subconsciously, Black women may cling to images that positively represent their resilience, thoughtfulness toward others, emotional composure, and independence (Walker-Barnes, 2016). Black women's spirituality and religious values may also relate to their attraction to SBW lifestyles. Black women's love of their deity, affinity to religious communities, and living a life of self-denial and esteem align with sacred literature. Black women can internalize these religious values as endorsements of SBW lifestyles (Walker-Barnes, 2016).

Why might contemporary Black women cling to SBW values, often without realizing it? The SBW persona enjoys credibility as a Black feminine ideal. The idealized image of Black femininity still is that of "a Strong Black Woman – autonomous, industrious, reliable, and capable, a devoted and selfless worker on behalf of Black families, churches, and communities, always emotionally composed and prepared to serve" (Walker-Barnes, 2016, p. 55). A sentiment of one of our study participants seems to support this view: "The negative aspects of the myth of the 'Strong Black Woman' [seem] to include the belief that we can/should 'take care of business' on our own/with limited assistance."

SBW lifestyles invite wide acceptability, and the SBW identity fits comfortably with dominant and Black ideologies of Black femininity (Collins, 2000; Harris-Perry, 2011). Black women have seen SBW identities in their mothers and grandmothers who have garnered admiration and respect from family and community. Romero (2000) notes that the SBW is "a mantra for so much a part of US culture that it is seldom realized how great a toll it has taken on the emotional wellbeing of the African American woman. As much as it may give her the illusion of control, it keeps her from identifying what she needs and reaching for help" (p. 225). In a positive sign of change, however, the steep price of the SBW lifestyle is becoming more apparent.

8.3   Mental and Emotional Impacts of SBW Lifestyles

Studies link internalized SBW values directly and indirectly to Black women's adverse physical and emotional health outcomes (Beauboeuf-Lafontant, 2007, 2009; Woods-Giscombé, 2010). Three particular features of the SBW lifestyle stand out as the most destructive. The first is *tolerance for chronic stress conditions*. Stress can come from moderate to significant one-time events or, more insidiously, multiple daily hassles. The physiological stress response threatens physical and mental health (Beauboeuf-Lafontant, 2007, 2009). The second feature is *self-silencing*. In this posture, SBW barely acknowledge, even to themselves, that they are struggling. Black women may channel their struggles through negative coping, spiritual talk, a pretense at humor, and emotional stoicism (Beauboeuf-Lafontant, 2007, 2009; Watson & Hunter, 2016). The third SBW feature is *low help-seeking and prioritization of mental health needs*. Black women might feel overwhelmed for years without conscious recognition of erosion in their mental and emotional wellness. Frequently, a health crisis is the first recognition of a need for treatment. Even then, the SBW may find ways to suppress the problem without professional support (Waite & Killian, 2009; Watson & Hunter, 2016).

8.3.1   Stress, Depression, and Negative Coping

The links between chronic stress and mental and emotional vulnerability are well known. This finding is critical for Black women, who are more likely than women of other racial/ethnic groups to live stressful lives (Beauboeuf-Lafontant, 2008; Woods-Giscombé & Black, 2010). Black women are more likely than White women and Latinas to battle poverty, which contributes to an accumulation of stressors. A majority of Black women are raising children in households with significant economic and caregiving demands. Black women are also more likely than women of other racial identities to experience stress emanating from gender and racial oppression in almost every societal setting, including employment, worship, education, personal grooming, and legal environments (Parks, 2010). Studies show that Black women's stress response may include overeating, self-silencing, and reduced help-seeking and self-care (Donovan & West, 2015; Donovan & Williams, 2002; Harrington et al., 2010; Romero, 2000; Woods-Giscombé, 2010).

Chapters 2 and 13 explain how Black women's chronic stress connects to their high rates of preventable diseases. For example, chronic diseases have lowered Black women's years of wellness and life expectancy as a group. In the United States, Black women number highly among those with type 2 diabetes, cardiovascular disease, hypertension, stroke, and heart disease (Chinn et al., 2021; Woods-Giscombé & Black, 2010). The consequences of chronic health conditions in the morbidity and mortality of Black people could not be more alarming, as the COVID-19 pandemic revealed. Studies show a disproportionate burden of COVID-19 deaths among some racial and ethnic minority groups. An analysis of selected states and cities with data on COVID-19 deaths by race and ethnicity showed that 34% of deaths were among non-Hispanic Black people. However, this group accounts for only 12% of the total US population (Chinn et al., 2021). The prevalence of chronic health conditions among Black people increases their vulnerability to COVID-19 death.

Stressful lives are more prone to mental health vulnerabilities, and for Black women who experience high levels of stress, this is the case. For example, some Black women, especially those who are poor, have health conditions such as obesity, hypertension, and diabetes; or experience high levels of personal, family, or environmental stress, also have elevated rates of depression and anxiety (Holden et al., 2015). Chinn et al., 2021 reported depression was almost twice as common among women as among men. The proportion of adults with depression also increased with decreasing family income (Brody et al., 2018). This finding is vital to understanding socio-economically disadvantaged Black women who live well below the poverty line. As highlighted by other studies, psychological distress and depression often go unnoticed because Black women mask it well and become even more self-reliant (Beauboeuf-Lafontant, 2007).

8.3.2   Self-Silencing

A primary feature of the SBW lifestyle is self-silencing, and this is rooted in women's construction of self. In describing women generally, Surrey (1985) suggests that a key to understanding women's self-concept is how they view themselves in relationships. The relational self has three features: (a) building emotional connections through interest and attention to others; (b) wanting and expecting a mutual empathic process in relationships; and (c) placing a high value on relational intimacy. The emphasis on relationships in this framework may explain Black women's tendency to self-silence, a strategy they use to mute feelings, thoughts, and actions to avert relational tensions (Jack & Dill, 1992). Gendered norms for women such as passivity, niceness, and submission also reinforce self-silencing (Beauboeuf-Lafontant, 2009).

In Black women, self-silencing relates to gendered racial oppression in various contexts (Parks, 2010). Black women stay silent to protect their children and themselves from relational turbulence (Tillman-Meakins, 2017). They hide their inner voice to defend themselves from being devalued by others. Black women also self-silence to avert the stereotyping or censure resulting from sharing their honest thoughts and feelings. For example, in intimate relationships Black women may not speak up about things that bother them. They may fear that speaking up would invite stereotypical depiction as being "angry and aggressive" (Whitton et al., 2007). Self-silencing averts conflict, forcing Black women to tolerate rejection, abuse, and maltreatment that lowers their self-esteem.

To this end, Black women bite their tongues to avoid rejection, loss, and alienation, and this can show up in four ways: (a) not directly asking for what they want or telling others how they feel; (b) presenting a demure exterior to the public despite feeling hostility, dissent, and anger; (c) putting needs and emotions of others ahead of their own; and (d) shifting their behaviors because of stereotype threat (Jack & Ali, 2010). Remaining silent in the face of difficulties might protect a Black woman's image of managing things with ease. But over time muted self-expression can have severe mental and physical health consequences (Jack & Ali, 2010; Jones & Shorter-Gooden, 2003). Research suggests that self-silencing is a good predictor of depression (Cramer et al., 2005; Whiffen et al., 2007). For example, Beauboeuf-Lafontant's (2007) study linked Black women's internalizing of SBW values with self-silencing and depression symptoms. Black women may believe that what they feel inside is less valuable than what others feel. Thus, in self-silencing, Black women reinforce their values of competent and admirable womanhood.

8.3.3   Low Help-Seeking

Our study suggests that Black women may not seek professional psychotherapy services for reasons such as a fear of seeming weak, stigma, and family pressures to seek natural sources of help. One study participant stated: "I think some black women avoid therapy because we feel like we don't need it. Black women are raised to be strong, fierce, brave, and solid. We are taught to fight through whatever we go through alone. That's what we have always seen." Another said: "Black women are seen as strong and able to take care of themselves. I am seen as a strong woman, not in need of support."

Our study findings (discussed in Chapter 1) support previous literature that identifies four principal reasons for Black women's low professional help-seeking: (a) Black women's cultural obligations to avoid contributing to negative perceptions of Black womanhood (Watson & Hunter, 2015); (b) perceived pressures to refrain from inconveniencing others with their emotional issues and needs; (c) mistrust of professional helping systems as being White and privileged and lacking a solid understanding of the historical conditions of Black people in America; and (d) reasons related to a lack of resources to find help, such as time, cost, and convenience (e.g., location; Watson & Hunter, 2015).

Even when an SBW tries therapy, she may present as composed and unaffected by various stressors (Romero, 2000). Black women may underreport their symptoms and downplay the degree of their distress, which may lead to inconsistencies in the results of screening and diagnostic tools (Watson & Hunter, 2015). With its emphasis on facilitating emotional expression, professional therapy services may be at odds with Black women's value of displaying strength and self-reliance (Neufeld et al., 2008; Watson & Hunter, 2015).

Romero (2000) describes the invincibility mask of the SBW schema as a double-edged sword. On the one hand, it helps Black women surround themselves with an illusion of control, which allows them to fulfill their daily routines. This reality helps Black women avoid being crippled by a sense of victimization despite the difficulty of their circumstances. But invincibility also masks vulnerabilities. We believe that this dynamic process underscores the importance of therapists being welcoming and authentic with a Black female client even before therapy begins. For the SBW, doing therapy may come at a great expense to her self-concept. The act of seeking professional help might also engender identity confusion and cultural shame. If the therapist were to parrot the stereotypical "you are a strong Black woman" sentiment, this might be self-fulfilling, inviting early termination (Romero, 2000).

8.4   Treating the SBW: A Culturally Informed Framework

In treating women with SBW lifestyles, the therapist must work from a culturally attuned framework. This framework includes five components to establish the therapy climate and six intervention strategies that might prove successful with Black women.

8.4.1   Establishing the Climate for Therapy for the SBW

The therapists should create an environment for work with SBWs, with five features.

1. *View SBW phenomena as a culturally reinforced dynamic.* SBW values have complex historical and social underpinnings connected to Black women's gendered-racism and classism experiences. The therapist must showcase a robust understanding of these sociocultural context dynamics to gain their client's trust.

> Understanding the themes of social determinants of health (Chapter 2), trauma (Chapter 5), and shifting (Chapter 9) will support therapists in this contextual understanding.

2. *Diagnose and treat symptoms from a culturally informed framework.* Stress, depression, and other mental health conditions in an SBW typically resemble the symptoms of the general population (e.g., women) (Walton & Payne, 2016). However, many Black women who experience depression and adopt the SBW persona are unlikely to have difficulty getting out of bed or engaging in daily tasks because they push themselves to keep going even amid depression. To fully understand and treat depression in an SBW, therapists must assess and diagnose clients through a cultural lens. This lens allows the therapist to explore the complex self-schemas that Black women may present. Such features include a posture of pseudo-wellness and avoidance of support, even when distress increases (Thomas, 2009).

3. *Identifying positive and negative characteristics of the SBW lifestyle.* SBW values are typically well integrated into Black women's identities and self-concepts. Narrative interventions can reveal the quality of SBW impacts. Such interventions include deconstructing and reconstructing a client's view of self, self in relation to others, self in cultural context, and so forth. The narrative approach requires skillful use of questions to amplify and expand the client's understanding of their inner world (Drustrup & Baptiste, 2019). This approach will reveal aspects of the client's SBW values that they may wish to retain, reconstruct, or replace.

4. *Avoid subtle endorsements of SBW values in therapy conversations.* Hearing a client's burden of caregiving, therapists may show admiration for their client's resilience. But a therapist's casual commentary on Black women's strengths or courage can parallel stereotypical compliments that Black women often receive (e.g., "You are so strong"). This sentiment might stroke a woman's pride in her capacity to self-sacrifice, further risking SBW pride. We encourage therapists to support the Black female client in identifying her strengths but not to invalidate the challenges she experiences. The therapist is tasked with helping her to hold both her strengths and vulnerabilities together in an integrated way.

5. *Work through the client's intersecting social identities.* The intersectionality of identities compounds oppression (Crenshaw, 2017). Black women with multiple disadvantaged identities may find it extremely difficult to prioritize their own needs. They may also hesitate to enact boundaries or get others to respect their need for support (Buchanan &

Fitzgerald, 2008; Myers & Anderson, 2013; Parks, 2010). Therapeutic interventions to address SBW lifestyle must be adaptive to the range of personal, family, and community situations of Black women. Therapists must be prepared to work outside the walls of therapy to advocate for their clients. The following six intervention strategies can be helpful for SBW clients.

8.4.2   Interventions to Examine SBW Themes in the Client's Narratives

An SBW may be a reluctant participant in the initial stages of therapy. The client may be conservative in sharing details about self and may seem polite but distant. The therapist's warm, friendly, and businesslike presence is likely to help build trust. We encourage therapists to explore their Black female client's experience by initially focusing on specific symptoms they report. Exploring the manifestation and context of these symptoms will reveal more information. Black women may experience emotionally focused assessment prompts such as "Have you felt depressed for most of the day?" as threatening. Such prompts may contradict a Black woman's view of herself as strong and self-reliant. Somatic prompts, such as "Have you felt slowed down?" (Watson & Hunter, 2015, p. 610), may be more welcoming. In this phase, the therapist should have brief and useful materials on stress and links between stress, anxiety, and mental health symptoms. Use the checklist in Table 8.1 to assess the potential for SBW values. The therapist should set up a time for the next appointment to show the high value of a subsequent encounter. Pay attention to strategies discussed in Chapter 7 on building a solid therapeutic alliance. The therapist can consider the following intervention strategies when working with SBW clients.

1. *Increase the client's awareness of SBW values.* Merely hearing that she may be living the SBW lifestyle may not make an SBW want to change, and some may even resist increasing their self-care. Examining the SBW identity via some well-designed narrative deconstruction techniques can be useful because a narrative examination externalizes an internal discourse (Drustrup & Baptiste, 2019; White et al., 1990). Therapists can start by concentrating on a client's proximal life contexts to understand how she functions. For example, how does she function in her family and especially in parenting, at church, at work, in friendship networks, and as a confidante? Start with a genogram for family context (McGoldrick et al., 2005). Explore these areas to uncover stress, burden, and self-silencing. The therapist could also introduce the SBW construct using an externalized tool such as a brief reading or video, inviting the client to consider how the SBW framework may apply in her life. This approach is invitational and

aimed at helping the client think about whether she may fit the SBW designation. The reality is that some Black women may never fully accept the SBW framework and terminology. However, therapy can still help women learn to prioritize self-care, strengthen their agency and voice, and protect their mental health (Donovan & West, 2015).

2. *Deconstruct endorsements and reinforcements of SBW values.* Woods-Giscombé's (2010) study suggests that Black women learn SBW behaviors and values from female role models in the family. The generational family transmission of SBW, as well as its media reinforcement, explains its perpetuation. Therapists should help clients discover how caregivers modeled SBW values and how this dynamic has become normalized in families and communities. The goal is to avoid demonizing loved ones who themselves could have lived the SBW lifestyle without knowing it. Talking openly with women about SBW role transmission will help Black women to understand how they may live as SBWs in their homes, workplaces, and communities. During this work, reinforce ways to help clients retain their attachment to an idea of strong Black womanhood while embracing wellness. The following questions may be helpful: Why is the SBW persona so automatic? Why do Black women adopt SBW values? Who may have modeled the SBW lifestyle in your life? What are the challenges of adopting the SBW lifestyle? What do you enjoy about being an SBW? How might you help your daughters to understand the challenges of being an SBW? When have you had to be an SBW when you didn't necessarily want to be?" Encourage women to use resources such as blogs and documentaries that have discussed the SBW phenomenon. See the resources section at the end of this chapter for some examples.

3. *Reconnect clients to silenced or denied aspects of self.* Unsurprisingly, when clients get in touch with their denied or suppressed aspects of self, they can grieve deeply about what was lost or what could have been. Mourning or grieving is an integral aspect of therapeutic work with the SBW. Black women may mourn the loss of adolescence, educational pursuits, career advancement, travel, hobbies, and other opportunities. These losses can bring up feelings of anger toward the partners, family members, clergy, or children who asked or required them to sacrifice their wants and needs. Black women's anger and sadness may also be directed toward the universe, a deity, or themselves. Therapists must prepare to be a compassionate witness to a unique kind of loss and suffering. Therapists must help the client imagine new ways of living that make peace with the old while welcoming the new. Therapists should help clients maintain an appreciation for how their contributions of sacrifice and peacemaking have enriched others' lives, including their own.

We encourage therapists to prepare for a range of responses that may reflect grief about a loss of opportunities. Guide the client to connect failures to possibilities for living differently with self-compassion and loving-kindness to self. Therapists should encourage SBW clients to find a way to ritualize thinking about and treating themselves. This could involve connecting self-love to sacred literature (e.g., Bible verses) for those who are religious. For others, new beginnings may be expressed through writing, storytelling, song, poetry, or testimony. Therapists should work gently and steadily to help Black women focus on the present circumstances of their lives while also looking toward their futures (Collins, 2000; Donovan & West, 2015). A note of caution: Change is not linear, and even with fresh ways of showing self-love, Black women may still prioritize others. The aim is to support Black women in making agentic choices and follow their values in deciding when it feels healthy to prioritize themselves and when prioritizing loved ones is aligned with their values.

Strategies for approaching inner-healing work are highlighted in Chapter 14.

---

4. *Promote rest, recovery, and reinvigoration.* Often, SBW discover a deep layer of weariness that may overwhelm the body, soul, and spirit. SBW women may represent this as emptiness, inertia, depersonalization, or being cut off from loved ones and others. Black women may be living perfunctorily at home and work without meaning and joy. Depressive symptoms can show up as anhedonia, negative mood, and even thoughts of self-harm. The therapist must find ways to help Black women rest, recover, and reinvigorate (Beauboeuf-LaFontant, 2007). One strategy is to negotiate periods in which all activities, even routine household ones, are downsized. Recommend taking "psychological vacations," possibly a sabbatical from leadership activities or commitments. In friendship circles, resting requires setting boundaries around accepting calls, dispensing advice, and other actions. Promote a decrease in the use of social media and a suspension of dating activities. Downsizing activities can help Black women increase sleep and exercise, find moments of silence, and listen to music. This strategy allows the mind and body to recover. A period of three–six months of downsized activity can be restorative.

   Mindfulness meditation is another tangible and sustainable practice to help Black women cope with stress (Dutton et al., 2013). By targeting moment-to-moment awareness with self-compassion and loving-kindness (Grossman et al., 2004), the SBW can become gradually aware of moment-to-moment "mental responses to external and internal stimuli" (p. 36). Black women can learn to modify their responses and replace them with healthy coping (Grossman et al., 2004). A small qualitative study with Black women found that mindfulness was an effective intervention for depressive symptoms (Burnett-Zeigler et al., 2019). The SBW will benefit from mindfulness interactions that address guilt in prioritizing self-care behaviors. To this end, the therapist should be mindful of the role guilt plays among Black women who embody the SBW role.

5. *Coach boundary setting and other assertiveness skills.* Black women are socialized to set fewer boundaries in care for others. Poor boundary setting causes them to be less protective of their emotional energy or connected to their personal needs (Jones & Shorter-Gooden, 2003). Therapists should work with Black women to navigate feelings of guilt when identifying how boundaries impact family members, community members, and coworkers. Black women may not automatically understand boundaries, why they are necessary, or how to set them. Excellent resources like *Set Boundaries, Find Peace* by Nedra Glover Tawwab (2021) make the concept of boundaries accessible. Therapists should help Black women use these resources. We have also provided other valuable resources for boundary discussions in the resources section at the end of this chapter. Once Black women understand the value of boundaries in their own lives, the therapist should coach them on how to apply boundaries in a way that de-escalates conflict situations and maintains a connection. The goal is to support Black women in getting better at boundary setting over time.

6. *Promote a resilience framework.* Resilience involves an intentional cognitive, narrative, and behavioral shift in understanding self and life events. Resilience is consistent with the SBW values in reframing problems away from notions of damage, destruction, and devastation to overcoming, thriving, persevering, and getting over. Therapists should coach Black women to understand what resilience is and is not and how they can use it to fit their strengths and adaptive traits. For example, resilience is not ruggedness, invincibility, or toughness. Resilience acknowledges vulnerability and is associated with allowing others to help (Walsh, 2012). Resilience has both individual and relational features and a contextual view of crises, symptoms of distress, and adaptation. Therapists should reframe help-seeking as an act of personal resilience. When challenged with a complicated and seemingly tenuous list of personal and social demands, clients can prioritize their self-care without guilt or worry. A handout on resilience is provided in Figure 8.1. Therapists can use this framework to show the connections between strength and resilience and emphasize resilience as seeking help when needed.

BUILDING RESILIENCE

RESILIENCE IS NOT	RESILIENCE IS MORE THAN	RESILIENCE IS
• Invulnerability or self-sufficiency • Toughness in the face of stress • Inner fortitude • Steely character • Rugged individualism	• A display of competence • An ability to breeze through • Something entirely dependent on competent functioning • Simply surviving	• A capacity to rebound • Endurance and self-righting • Recalibrating well • Growth in the face of crisis and challenge • Fueled by supportive intimate relationships

Resilience is built by…

1) Shifting the narrative around the problem:

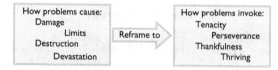

2) Identifying individual and relational features of resilience:

INDIVIDUAL	RELATIONAL
• Easy-going temperament • Solid self-esteem • A sense of hopefulness and optimism • Ability to feel deeply and commit to activities • Anticipation of change as exciting • Moral and spiritual courage • Ability to live with some unknowns and ambiguity	• Access to *at least* one caring family member, kin or non-kin • Capacity to give and receive warmth, affection, and emotional support in relationships • Capacity to create or adapt to a new normal or reasonable structure • Access to "cheerleaders": relatives, friends, teachers, neighbors, coaches, clergy, mentors who show consistent positive regard

3) Creating "Bouncing Forward" Strategies:

Identify disruptions/ life cycle events/transitions   Adapt proactively to changing conditions   Create a new normal

Figure 8.1 Resilience handout (adapted from Walsh, 2002, 2015)

BUILDING RESILIENCE

TARGET BELIEFS

MAKING MEANING OF ADVERSITY	POSITIVE OUTLOOK	FAITH AND SPIRITUALITY
• Crisis as a *shared* challenge • Normalizing distress • Honest appraisal of the situation • Causal explanations without blaming and shaming • Acknowledging fears and anxieties in present and future	• Hope and optimism • Courage and encouragement • Affirming strengths • Initiative and perseverance • Seizing opportunities • Belief in what's *possible* • Accepting what may not change	• Larger values, sense of purpose • Faith, healing rituals, reflection, meditation, spiritual community • Inspiration, creative expression, awe, social action • Reassessment of personal priorities • Articulating growth

STRENGTHEN BUFFERS

CONNECTEDNESS	RESOURCES
• Mutual support, collaboration, and commitment • Respect for individual needs, differences and boundaries • Reconciling wounded relationships • Offering forgiveness and grace	• Family, friends, social networks, and community support • Mentors or faith partners • Balancing work and personal stressors • Institutional or structural supports

IMPROVE COMMUNICATION

CLARITY	EMOTIONAL EXPRESSION	CREATIVE PROBLEM SOLVING
• Clear, consistent messages in words and deeds • Decreased ambiguity around crisis • Truth speaking as antidote to secrecy, distortions, cover-ups, or falsehoods	• Displaying range of emotions • Showing mutual empathy • Owning feelings and behavior • Avoiding blaming, scapegoating • Leaning into humor or respite	• Problems, stressors, Constraints, and options • Goals and concreteness • Proactive approach toward future challenges

Figure 8.1 (*cont.*)

Case Example

Yvonne is a 42-year-old Black woman who sought therapy on her physician's advice. Yvonne described classic depression and anxiety symptoms, including low energy, poor sleep, and negative affect. Her primary health care provider ruled out specific health concerns and recommended psychotherapy. Yvonne expressed reluctance about therapy but also felt so unwell she wanted to try. In the initial sessions, the therapist listened as Yvonne sobbed, raged, doubted and judged herself, questioned her faith, and told of pervasive unhappiness, not visible to many on the outside, even those close to her. Yvonne lived a stress-filled life. She seemed adrift, especially from immediate and close extended family, and described existential anxiety around her life's purpose and goals. She seemed burnt out in a demanding job and narrated how she felt taken for granted in her kindness and support for others. She also questioned her faith and seemed to be experiencing a spiritual crisis. The therapist hypothesized that Yvonne had lived an SBW lifestyle for more than a decade, and this lifestyle explained some symptoms of depression.

In searching for a clinical roadmap to support Yvonne, the therapist diagnosed a current depressive episode of moderate severity, comorbid with nonspecific anxiety. The therapist also explored Yvonne's narratives to evaluate whether SBW values explain the depth of fatigue Yvonne presented. Since adolescence, Yvonne has performed daily acts of instrumental and emotional care for others. At the time of seeking therapy, she reported weekly support of three adult children who sought her out for counsel and encouragement. While the kids were doing relatively well, Yvonne continued offering help even before they asked, and they gladly accepted it (e.g., loans, meals, borrowing her vehicle, pickups, and drop-offs). Yvonne also volunteered to care for the children of nieces and nephews. She was a lay counselor to girlfriends, exercise buddies, and other people in her life. Yvonne felt loved and appreciated, and she enjoyed her role as a confidant.

Yvonne worked faithfully in her church, holding several leadership positions requiring multiple weekly discussions. She loved these experiences, which were central to her faith, although they were stressful. Meanwhile, she was heavily stressed in a demanding job, working with a boss who assigned tasks many times outside of typical work hours. Yvonne felt upset about her workload for years but rarely complained. She appeared pulled together but often felt hassled and overwhelmed. A formal diagnosis of depression and treatment to support it seemed inadequate to address Yvonne's nuanced pressures and well-hidden mental and emotional depletion. Yvonne had diminished capacity spanning several years to acknowledge her own emotional needs.

Yvonne described having SBW traits since adolescence, and yet such features remained unnamed in her life. In answer to the therapist's questions about women who were most influential in her life, Yvonne named her grandmother and two elderly aunts. She did not admire her mother, whom she thought of as "immature" and "selfish," until she died. She wanted to be the opposite of her mother, and her grandmother's example was alluring. Yvonne's grandmother was a tireless and influential woman of faith. Her grandmother's house was perpetually open to relatives and others who dropped by for food and shelter. In addition to her service in the home, Yvonne's grandmother was a devoted member of a local congregation who spent hours working in several ministries. Yvonne could not recall her grandmother ever leaving her town even when people offered vacations as gifts. Her big-heartedness was legendary. The grandmother also did not appear to have much faith in doctors or people who try to "get into your business." Through reflexive questioning, the therapist helped Yvonne recognize that she had patterned her life after her grandmother's and judged herself for saying "no" to others. Even with this new recognition that some of her own choices contributed to her unwellness, Yvonne felt reluctant to see SBW values in herself.

The therapist used the culturally attuned framework described in this chapter, including viewing Yvonne's depression as driven by SBW values. The therapist did not spend much time persuading Yvonne of the SBW diagnosis or discussing caregivers who may have modeled these values. The therapist conveyed a sense of acceptance that a part of Yvonne enjoyed and celebrated her esteem of others. She was especially gratified in her service at church. The therapist invited Yvonne to embrace the "care for others and care for self" approach. Audits of predominant areas of fatigue showed that these areas generated the most stress: incredible work from her boss, feeling overinvolved in friends' emotional issues, guilt for enabling her children, and wanting more time for weekly rest, vacations, and personal body care. Armed with a list of areas for focused work, the therapist worked with Yvonne around boundaries with the boss, family, and friends. Yvonne also committed to schedule self-care services (nails, salon, foot massages) twice over the next 2 months and at least once monthly after that. She also discussed sleep hygiene with her physician and received a low-dose prescription to improve her sleep. Yvonne committed to continuing therapy twice weekly for 6 months, after which she agreed to evaluate her therapy needs. Yvonne was more successful in some areas than in others, and over time her depression lifted. Yvonne also began to pay attention to the media on SBW values. She even came to accept that aspects of her life may reflect SBW choices.

8.5   Conclusion

Professional counseling services are not the only resources available to help Black women uncover and address SBW traits. Black women can find resources such as books, articles, and podcasts on the subject as awareness of the SBW lifestyle's detrimental impacts on Black women's mental health is growing. Blogs and personal testimonials about SBW conditions are also growing louder. Besides therapy, Black women can find support in their community and in religious discussion groups, virtual groups, sister circles, and other sources. Therapists should have a handy list of community resources available to empower Black women to better understand their SBW values and to find support in other women who are also gaining awareness of their SBW lifestyles. The resources shared at the end of this chapter will be a good starting place.

Working with the SBW condition in Black women is not meant to limit Black women's contributions to families, communities, and cultural groups. Instead, SBW work is most impactful in helping Black women reconstruct their internal working models to value their own social and emotional needs. This reformulation enhances Black women's influence and capacity to go the distance in service to others. In this framework, Black women can be strong, influential, and also resilient. That means living life on their terms and defying racial and gendered pressures, including internalized negative images of themselves. Strong and resilient Black women prioritize and defend a right to rest and recover and seek others' help to meet life's burdens.

Therapist Reflection Questions

1. How have you used the term *Strong* in describing Black women?
2. What media stereotypes have you encountered about the SBW?
3. If you have worked with Black female clients, what are your experiences with SBW values or lifestyles?
4. How do you think superwoman qualities apply to your racial-ethnic group?
5. How have you personally related to your Black female client's expressions of SBW identity?
6. What SBW ideas in this chapter do you find personally useful?
7. How do you prioritize rest and rejuvenation in your own life?

Resources for Therapists and Clients

Organizations

Black Girl in Om. (n.d.). https://www.blackgirlinom.com/
No More Martyrs. (n.d.). https://www.nomoremartyrs.org/

Books

Barnes, C. W. (2014). *Too heavy a yoke: Black women and the burden of strength*. Cascade Books.
Burnett-Zeigler (2021). *Nobody knows the trouble I've seen: The emotional lives of Black women*. Harper Collins.
Tawwab, N. G. (2021). *Set boundaries, find peace: A guide to reclaiming yourself*. TarcherPerigee.

Podcasts

Cole, M. (Executive Producer). (2018). *Black girls don't cry* [Audio podcast]. BBC Radio 4. https://www.bbc.co.uk/programmes/b0b9zfws

References

Abrams, J. A., Maxwell, M., Pope, M., & Belgrave, F. Z. (2014). Carrying the world with the grace of a lady and the grit of a warrior: Deepening our understanding of the "Strong Black Woman" schema. *Psychology of Women Quarterly, 38,* 503–518.

Beauboeuf-Lafontant, T. (2003). Strong and large Black women? Exploring relationships between deviant womanhood and weight. *Gender & Society, 17,* 111–121.

(2005). Keeping up appearances, getting fed up: The embodiment of strength among African American women. *Meridians: Feminism, Race, Transnationalism, 5*(2), 104–123.

(2007). You have to show strength: An exploration of gender, race, and depression. *Gender & Society, 21*(1), 28–51.

(2008). Listening past the lies that make us sick: A voice-centered analysis of strength and depression among Black women. *Qualitative Sociology, 31*(4), 391–406.

(2009). *Behind the mask of the strong Black woman: Voice and the embodiment of a costly performance.* Temple University Press.

Black, A. R., & Peacock, N. (2011). Pleasing the masses: Messages for daily life management in African American women's popular media sources. *American Journal of Public Health, 101*(1), 144–150. https://doi.org/10.2105/AJPH.2009 .167817

Black, A. R., & Woods-Giscombé, C. (2012). Applying the stress and "strength" hypothesis to Black women's breast cancer screening delays. *Stress and Health, 28*(5), 389–396.

Brody, D. J., Pratt, L. A., & Hughes, J. P. (2018). *Prevalence of depression among adults aged 20 and over: United States, 2013–2016.* Centers for Disease Control and Prevention. https://www.cdc.gov/nchs/products/databriefs/db303.htm

Buchanan, N. T., & Fitzgerald, L. F. (2008). Effects of racial and sexual harassment on work and the psychological well-being of African American women. *Journal of Occupational Health Psychology, 13*(2), 137–151.

Burnett-Zeigler, I., Satyshur, M. D., Hong, S., Wisner, K. L., & Moskowitz, J. (2019). Acceptability of a mindfulness intervention for depressive symptoms among African-American women in a community health center: A qualitative study. *Complementary Therapies in Medicine, 45,* 19–24. https://doi.org/10.1016/j.ctim .2019.05.012

Chinn, J. J., Martin, I. K., & Redmond, N. (2021). Health equity among Black women in the United States. *Journal of Women's Health, 30*(2), 212–219.

Collins, P. H. (2000). *Black feminist thought: Knowledge, consciousness, and the politics of empowerment.* Routledge.

(2020). Defining black feminist thought. In C. McCann, S. Kim, & E. Ergun (Eds.), *Feminist theory reader* (5th ed., pp. 278–290). Routledge.

Cramer, K. M., Gallant, M. D., & Langlois, M. W. (2005). Self-silencing and depression in women and men: Comparative structural equation models. *Personality and Individual Differences, 39*(3), 581–592.

Crenshaw, K. W. (2017). *On intersectionality: Essential writings.* The New Press.

Donovan, R. A. (2011). Tough or tender: (Dis) similarities in White college students' perceptions of Black and White women. *Psychology of Women Quarterly, 35*(3), 458–468.

Donovan, R. A., & West, L. M. (2015). Stress and mental health: Moderating role of the strong Black woman stereotype. *Journal of Black Psychology, 41*(4), 384–396.

Donovan, R. A., & Williams, M. (2002). Living at the intersection: The effects of racism and sexism on Black rape survivors. *Women and Therapy*, 25, 95–105.

Drustrup, D., & Baptiste, D. R. (2019). Problem-saturated stories in narrative couple and family therapy. In J. Lebow, A. Chambers, & D. C. Breunlin (Eds.), *Encyclopedia of couple and family therapy* (pp. 2334–2336). Springer.

Dutton, M. A., Bermudez, D., Matas, A., Majid, H., & Myers, N. L. (2013). Mindfulness-based stress reduction for low-income, predominantly African American women with PTSD and a history of intimate partner violence. *Cognitive and Behavioral Practice, 20*(1), 23–32.

Grossman, P., Niemann, L., Schmidt, S., & Walach, H. (2004). Mindfulness-based stress reduction and health benefits: A meta-analysis. *Journal of Psychosomatic Research, 57*(1), 35–43.

Harrington, E. F., Crowther, J. H., & Shipherd, J. C. (2010). Trauma, binge eating, and the "Strong Black Woman." *Journal of Consulting and Clinical Psychology, 78*, 469–479.

Harris-Lacewell, M. (2001). No place to rest: African American political attitudes and the myth of Black women's strength. *Women & Politics, 23*, 1–33.

Harris-Perry, M. V. (2011). *Sister citizen: Shame, stereotypes, and Black women in America*. Yale University Press.

Holden, K. B., Belton, A. S., & Hall, S. P. (2015). Qualitative examination of African American women's perspectives about depression. *Health, Culture and Society, 8* (1), 48–60.

Jack, D. C., & Ali, A. (Eds.). (2010). *Silencing the self across cultures: Depression and gender in the social world*. Oxford University Press.

Jack, D. C., & Dill, D. (1992). The Silencing the Self Scale: Schemas of intimacy associated with depression in women. *Psychology of Women Quarterly, 16*(1), 97–106.

Jackson, L. C., & Greene, B. (Eds.). (2000). *Psychotherapy with African American women: Innovations in psychodynamic perspectives and practice*. Guilford Press.

Jones, C., & Shorter-Gooden, K. (2003). *Shifting: The double lives of African American women in America*. Harper Collins.

McGoldrick, M., Giordano, J., & Garcia-Preto, N. (Eds.). (2005). *Ethnicity and family therapy*. Guilford Press.

Mitchell, A., & Herring, K. (1998). *What the blues is all about: Black women overcoming stress and depression*. Perigee Trade.

Myers, L. J., & Anderson, M. (2013). Mental health assessment and treatment of African Americans in cultural context. In F. A. Paniagua, & A. M. Yamada (Eds.), *Handbook of multicultural mental health. assessment and treatment of diverse populations* (2nd ed., pp. 265–281). Academic Press.

Neufeld, A., Harrison, M. J., Stewart, M., & Hughes, K. (2008). Advocacy of women family caregivers: Response to nonsupportive interactions with professionals. *Qualitative Health Research, 18*(3), 301–310.

Parks, S. (2010). *Fierce angels: The strong Black woman in American life and culture.* Random House of Canada.

Romero, R. E. (2000). The icon of the strong Black woman: The paradox of strength. In L. C. Jackson & B. Greene (Eds.), *Psychotherapy with African American women: Innovations in psychodynamic perspectives and practice* (pp. 225–238). Guilford Press.

Settles, I. H., Pratt-Hyatt, J. S., & Buchanan, N. T. (2008). Through the lens of race: Black and White women's perceptions of womanhood. *Psychology of Women Quarterly, 32*(4), 454–468.

Simms, R. (2001). Controlling images and the gender constructions of enslaved African American women. *Gender and Society, 15,* 879–897.

Surrey, J. L. (1985). *The "self-in-relation": A theory of women's development.* Wellesley College, Stone Center for Developmental Services and Studies.

Tawwab, N. G. (2021). *Set boundaries, find peace: A guide to reclaiming yourself.* Tarcher Perigee.

Thomas, A. J., Witherspoon, K. M., & Speight, S. L. (2004). Toward the development of the stereotypic roles for Black women scale. *The Journal of Black Psychology, 30*(3), 426–442.

Thomas, K. A. (2009). *A sistah's legacy of strength: A mixed methods investigation of gender attitudes among African American women* [Unpublished doctoral dissertation]. University of Michigan.

Tillman-Meakins, P. J. (2017). *The strong Black woman and depression: A scoping review* [Unpublished doctoral dissertation]. University of Michigan.

Waite, R., & Killian, P. (2009). Perspectives about depression: Explanatory models among African-American women. *Archives of Psychiatric Nursing, 23*(4), 323–333.

Walker-Barnes, C. (2016). *Too heavy a yoke: Black women and the burden of strength.* Wipf and Stock Publishers.

Wallace, M. (1999). *Black macho and the myth of the superwoman.* Verso.

Walsh, F. (2002). A family resilience framework: Innovative practice applications. *Family Relations, 51*(2), 130–137.

(2012). Family resilience: Strengths forged through adversity. In F. Walsh (Ed.), *Normal family processes: Growing diversity and complexity* (pp. 399–427). Guilford Press.

(2015). *Strengthening family resilience.* Guilford Press.

Walton, Q. L., & Payne, J. S. (2016). Missing the mark: Cultural expressions of depressive symptoms among African-American women and men. *Social Work in Mental Health, 14*(6), 1–21.

Watson, N. N., & Hunter, C. D. (2015). Anxiety and depression among African American women: The costs of strength and negative attitudes toward psychological help-seeking. *Cultural Diversity & Ethnic Minority Psychology, 21* (4), 604–612.

(2016). "I had to be strong": Tensions in the strong Black woman schema. *Journal of Black Psychology, 42*(5), 424–452.

Whiffen, V. E., Foot, M. L., & Thompson, J. M. (2007). Self-silencing mediates the link between marital conflict and depression. *Journal of Social and Personal Relationships, 24*(6), 993–1006.

White, M., Wijaya, M., & Epston, D. (1990). *Narrative means to therapeutic ends*. WW Norton & Company.

Whitton, S. W., Stanley, S. M., & Markman, H. J. (2007). If I help my partner, will it hurt me? Perceptions of sacrifice in romantic relationships. *Journal of Social and Clinical Psychology, 26*(1), 64–91.

Woods-Giscombé, C. L. (2010). Superwoman schema: African American women's views on stress, strength, and health. *Qualitative Health Research, 20*(5), 668–683.

Woods-Giscombé, C. L., & Black, A. R. (2010). Mind-body interventions to reduce risk for health disparities related to stress and strength among African American women: The potential of mindfulness-based stress reduction, loving-kindness, and the NTU therapeutic framework. *Complementary Health Practice Review, 15*(3), 115–131.

9   Shifting in Black Women: Clinical Implications

with Kumea Shorter-Gooden[*]

> Black women . . . shift to accommodate differences in class as well as gender and ethnicity. From one moment to the next, they change their outward behavior, attitude, or tone, shifting "White," then shifting "Black" again, shifting "corporate," shifting "cool." . . . shifting has become such an integral part of Black women's behavior that some adopt an alternate pose or voice as easily as they blink their eyes or draw a breath – without thinking, and without realizing that the emptiness they feel and the roles they must play may be directly related.
>
> (Jones & Shorter-Gooden, 2003, p. 7)

Adia was around age 12 when she first learned a painful lesson on what happens when a Black woman does not shift her behavior in the way that Jones and Shorter-Gooden (2003) describe. Adia was invited to join a choir organized by the White parents of a classmate. She attended a small, predominantly White private school, and almost everyone in the class was in the choir. Adia was the only Black girl and one of two Black children in the choir. She was confident in her singing abilities because she had been part of the youth choir at her Black church since she was around 5 years old. Adia enjoyed singing, and she was excited that this new choir was going to be recording songs. Adia's confidence quickly dimmed as she was told repeatedly that she was too loud, that her voice was too bold, that it did not blend into the rest of the choir. Adia was confused by this; her choir director at church had affirmed her bold singing voice, and she was never chastised for her voice standing out too much. Adia tried her best to tone it down, to make her voice sound softer, to blend in, but her efforts were not enough. When the choir regrouped for a second season, she was the only person not invited to return to the choir. Adia felt hurt and rejected; she felt like there was something wrong with her and the way she sang. She had not done a good enough job fitting in, assimilating, shifting. She learned that her full voice, her full self, would not always be

---

[*] A. Gooden & K. Shorter-Gooden. (2023). Shifting in Black women: Clinical implications. In D. Baptiste & A. Gooden, *Promoting Black women's mental health: What practitioners should know and do*. Cambridge University Press.

214

welcome and that if she wanted to be included in predominantly White spaces, she would need to change the way she acted and engaged. This was Adia's introduction to why and how Black women and girls shift.

As Black girls and women navigate racism and sexism, they learn to shift, changing how they act or present themselves at school, work, and in other aspects of their lives. Sometimes the message that Black women and girls must shift comes explicitly from family members warning them against the perils of being too open at school or work. Sometimes Black women learn shifting as Adia did, through the pain of rejection and the implicit communication that being herself was not okay. Shifting is both a strategy that helps Black women to navigate environments where Black women are expected not to take up space and a burden that weighs Black women down and can cause them to feel disconnected from their true selves (Jones & Shorter-Gooden, 2003). In this chapter, we explore what leads Black women to shift, provide a nuanced understanding of how Black women shift in their lives, and discuss the costs and benefits of shifting. We share strategies for working with Black women clients to identify shifting and its impact, and we offer recommendations for therapists to enhance their effectiveness in working with Black women in a culturally responsive manner.

9.1   What Is Shifting?

Shifting is defined as the myriad ways – affective, cognitive, behavioral – that Black women respond to racial and gender bias (Jones & Shorter-Gooden, 2003; Jones et al., 2021). It includes a focus on the Black woman's feelings and mood; her confidence, sense of agency, and aspirations; and her behavior (e.g., how she styles her hair, how she performs in job interviews, whether she extricates herself from an abusive relationship, whether she marches for racial justice). At times, shifting is consciously elected and enacted; at other times, shifting occurs unconsciously. The phenomenon of shifting is not unique to Black women but rather is a way of understanding the experiences of all social identity groups that experience societal marginalization (Jones & Shorter-Gooden, 2003).

9.2   Black Women's Shifting in Context

We have mentioned before that Black women living at the intersection of racism and sexism navigate two marginalized identities – being Black and female – which incurs the double marginalization of gendered racism (Essed, 1991; Reid, 1988). The uniqueness of gendered racism can be overlooked in discussion of the racial oppression or racial animus experienced by "Black people" – often meaning Black men. Much of the discourse spotlights Black men, who often experience racism in particularly overt, violent, and lethal ways (Crenshaw, 2017). The May 2020 murder of George Floyd by a Minneapolis police officer galvanized the nation, as it well should! Yet, the somewhat quieter, more subtle ways in which many Black women experience racism and sexism in multiple contexts are sometimes missed or overlooked. It should be noted that Black women also experience overt, violent, deadly racism, as in the March 2020 killing of Breonna Taylor (Crenshaw, 2017).

Who Black women are, and how they function emotionally in response to gendered and racist contexts, has to do with internal psychological factors, which are largely a function of childhood experiences with primary caregivers and family members (Shorter-Gooden & Jackson, 2000). And yet, these two categories – sociocultural and internal psychological – are not fully distinct; for example, caregivers' capacity, competence, strengths, and challenges are influenced by their own experiences of bias and discrimination, including, in many cases, socioeconomic disadvantage and exposure to stress. Psychological theories have typically done little to incorporate these two categories and make sense of the impact of the sociocultural context on Black people (Greene, 1997). Meanwhile, Afrocentric approaches have tended to focus on static, group-level characteristics purported to be applicable to all Black people, but these approaches pay little attention to how cultural factors intersect with a person's individual psychology (Braun, 1999). As a result, therapists who aspire to treat Black women in a culturally responsive manner are often on their own in discerning how to integrate personal-emotional and sociocultural factors appropriately and effectively. The concept of shifting provides a lens that brings together these two categories. Therapists should understand why and how Black women shift to manage racist or sexist situations or other marginalization (Jones et al., 2021). This understanding can lead to assessment and therapeutic interventions to help Black women clients live authentic lives, finding other strategies to manage the pain and suffering of marginalizing experiences.

9.3   Why Black Women Shift

Black women engage in shifting to help them navigate the racism and sexism they experience in spaces and places where White people and men are centered. Black women report experiencing high levels of stress in their workplaces and using the strategy of shifting to navigate the stereotyping and discrimination they experience in their professional lives (Dickens et al., 2019; Hall et al., 2012; Jones & Shorter-Gooden, 2003). Black women who identify as lesbian, gay, bisexual, transgender, and/or queer (LGBTQ) may engage in shifting such as changing their tone or pitch of their voice and their general way of expressing themselves to protect themselves as they navigate the world (Holden, 2019). Black women also report shifting in their home communities, with family, and in romantic relationships (Jones & Shorter-Gooden, 2003). Black women who identify as LGBTQ may shift in response to homophobia and transphobia they experience within the Black community, which has historically not been welcoming of people who identify as sexual minorities. As with women from other racial groups, the demands, at home and in public, for Black women's time and attention and to present themselves in narrowly defined ways can be high, and Black women often shift to make their loved ones and colleagues feel comfortable. In summary, many Black women employ mental strategies to hold their heads high as they learn, work, love, and interact in a world that diminishes them and their accomplishments. They use an array of shifting strategies to avoid being marginalized and diminished and to find ways to thrive.

To provide a clearer picture of how shifting manifests, we discuss four core themes in Black women's shifting that emerged from the African American Women's Voices Project, a qualitative study of 333 Black women, exploring their experiences and perceptions of the impact of racism and sexism in their lives (Jones & Shorter-Gooden, 2003). The four themes are inferiority, image, invisibility, and invincibility. These themes will serve as helpful guides to therapists who are seeking to identify and understand shifting practices and patterns.

9.3.1   Inferiority

Black women live in the shadow of the myth of inferiority. Many Black women talk about the impact of the long-standing stereotype that they are not intelligent or competent. For example, Black professional women talk of how weary they are, after delivering an excellent speech or otherwise demonstrating their intellectual prowess, of seeing a look of amazement and hearing "You're so articulate!" or even "You don't seem Black." These backhanded compliments clearly convey that "Blackness" and "competence" are seen as mutually exclusive.

Particularly in settings where they are in the minority or where few Black people are present, Black women are frequently hypervigilant, often scanning and scrutinizing the environment, keenly attuned to how they are being perceived and whether they are outpacing the myth of inferiority. A 26-year-old single mother and college student at a predominantly White university reported:

I was the only one from my family to go to college. I had to adapt to Whites' expectations of me. I felt I had to change my external appearance – the way I talk, the way I walk, the way I carried myself, the way I wore my hair. I had to create all of this hype in order to be perceived as an intelligent Black woman. (Jones & Shorter-Gooden, 2003, p. 68)

Like many other Black women, she may not have come to *believe* that she was inferior, but she appeared to utilize significant emotional resources to counter the notion in the eyes of others – to prove them wrong.

We encourage therapists to be aware of how their Black female clients may be working to combat the stereotype that they are inferior in the therapeutic relationship itself by intellectualizing their issues or using language that is not how they typically speak. As discussed in Chapter 4, it is important for therapists to examine their beliefs about Black women and ensure that they are not holding negative assumptions or stereotypes about Black women. For example, if a therapist assumes that Black women typically do not attend graduate school, they may express surprise when a client shares that she has earned a graduate degree and reinforce the client's feelings that she must shift in therapy to disprove the myth that Black women are inferior.

9.3.2   Image

The intersection of racial and gender bias is particularly evident in the arena of beauty. We live in a society with a strong demand for women to be beautiful and where beauty continues to be defined as "White, thin, and blonde" (Cotter et al., 2015; West, 1995). As a result, many Black women wrestle with feeling good about how they look. Some speak of being ashamed of the darkness of their skin, the kinkiness and short length of their hair, the breadth of their noses, the fullness of their behinds. One woman said: "It's taken me 41 years to get to accepting the package I'm in – to be okay with my skin tone, my weight, my hair, with just me. For a long time, I walked in a lot of shame; I walked in a lot of low self-esteem" (Jones & Shorter-Gooden, 2003, p. 176). Although the Black Power movement of the late 1960s, with its slogan "Black is beautiful," helped to transform the beauty aesthetic of many Black women from a Eurocentric to an Afrocentric ideal, and thus to facilitate a shift from feeling unattractive to feeling beautiful (Cotter et al., 2015; Russell et al., 1992), contemporary experiences convey that the transformation is not yet complete.

Related to image, hair is a powerful symbol of Black women's beauty and self-expression. Hair has also been the source of discrimination for Black women, with Black girls being banned from school for their locs or Afros and Black women being barred from wearing braids or twists in the military (Griffin, 2019). Black women's hair has become a primary way that White society has communicated that Black women's appearance is not acceptable. Because of this, many Black women shift through the way they wear their hair. Most Black women's hair is naturally kinky and curly, and many women spend hours in beauty salons straightening their hair through chemicals or intense heat. It is a ritual of sorts for Black women, who range from genuinely preferring their hair straight to feeling obligated, consciously or unconsciously, to straighten their hair to experience professional success. Adia can clearly remember the last time she straightened her hair for an interview and the nervousness she felt when she wore her natural hair without straightening or adding extensions for the next professional interview she had. This choice not to shift her appearance felt bold and vulnerable.

The challenges that Black women experience related to their physical appearance and the judgment they experience based on their appearance are explored further in Chapter 12 on lookism, also known as appearance bias.

We encourage therapists to pay attention to how their Black female clients show up to therapy in terms of their physical appearance. For example, Black women may feel pressure to have their hair, nails, makeup, and clothing just right even when they are going to a therapy session. This may represent a deliberate strategy to increase the likelihood that they will be taken seriously and receive excellent care. However, therapists need to be attuned to this possibility and the problem of the client needing to "perform" for the therapist. Therapists should support their Black female clients in exploring the pressures they feel to shift their appearance in and outside of the therapy room.

9.3.3   Invisibility

Many Black women feel invisible – unseen, discounted, dismissed, especially in situations where they are one of a few Black people or women. Professional women report that they are often unrecognized by White people as fellow professionals and instead are routinely assumed to be support staff or wait staff. Others report that at work their comments and ideas are not taken seriously. Some women describe being "ghettoized" at work, for example, being given only the accounts of Black clients or being consulted or listened to only with regard to Black issues or concerns. As a prominent C-suite leader at a university and the only Black woman among a high-level cabinet, one of the coauthors of this chapter had the experience at her first meeting of being instructed to sit at the far end of a very long rectangular conference table, along with lower-ranked cabinet members. At first, thinking this was a joke, she ignored the instruction and chose a seat. Later she was pulled aside and told that this was no joke. This overt marginalization may not have been based primarily on race or gender, but not surprisingly the one other Black person on the cabinet was also at the far end, requiring more effort to get the attention of the presiding officer and join the conversation. And it was not clear that a White man or woman would have been instructed so vigorously about where to sit. In contrast, when diversity-related crises occurred on campus, this coauthor's experience of invisibility morphed into hypervisibility, and the message from leadership was that she was critical to fixing things.

Some Black women experience themselves as shrinking, in effect, colluding with the external message of invisibility. Marva, a 23-year-old college student, said:

One of my biggest adjustments is that when I'm around other Black people, I think I'm the most outgoing, most outspoken. But at school, I don't feel as free to just voice my opinions. I feel like I have to think about what I'm going to say before I just say it. I seem so much more reserved, painfully shy. This semester I have a chemistry lab and I'm the only Black person there. I almost feel my voice just shrink. (Jones & Shorter-Gooden, 2003, p. 115)

And yet, the irony is that many Black women, especially those in the minority at school or at work, often experience a heightened sense of visibility. They feel they are in the spotlight, their every move observed and judged. A compelling body of research has documented the increased visibility, scrutiny, and demands placed on "tokens" in the workplace – those who are in the numerical minority with respect to race or gender (Reskin et al., 1999). Ironically, the sense of invisibility and the heightened sense of visibility often seem to coexist. Black women may feel torn between wanting to stand out and be seen as an individual and wanting to shift in order to fly under the radar and avoid additional scrutiny. We suggest therapists explore the times when their Black female clients feel invisible or hypervisible and how this experience impacts them.

9.3.4   Invincibility

Many Black women have internalized the notion that they must always be strong: that they are invulnerable, that they never need help, that they can and must do it all. The myth of invincibility is seductive, as it is far more attractive than being seen as unintelligent or unattractive. Yet, the myth of always being strong is a potential trap, especially if it makes a woman feel that she must be superhuman and that she does not deserve love and care from others. The underside of the sense of invincibility is the feeling that one is undeserving or unworthy. One woman, in her late 30s, said:

The superwoman stereotype – we've embodied that. And we think we have to be all things to everybody. And we go about doing that, but we are nothing to ourselves. We are nurturing; we're taking care of our kids. We're taking care of our brother, our sister, our parents, our man, but not taking care of ourselves. I think that just about every Black woman I know is doing that. . . . I really feel guilty if I do something for myself. I think that a lot of us have been beat down by life, that even though outwardly, we may be the most sophisticated, the most together sister there is, we're not sure we're worth the self-nurturing. (Jones & Shorter-Gooden, 2003, pp. 20–21)

Black women who subscribe to the myth of invincibility have difficulty acknowledging their pain or distress and thus have difficulty in seeking therapeutic help (Romero, 2000). Moreover, even when these women seek therapy, they may have difficulty in engaging, disclosing, and acknowledging their vulnerability. However, a sense of invincibility can, in moderation and when unaccompanied by a feeling of undeservedness, be a valuable resource for the client as she tackles obstacles in her life. While affirming Black women's resilience, we caution therapists not to use language such as "you are strong" with Black women, which may invalidate the pain they experience and inadvertently reinforce the Strong Black Woman persona.

The pressure Black women feel to be invincible is discussed further in Chapter 8, on the Strong Black Woman phenomenon.

9.4   Benefits of Shifting

Shifting has helped Black women adapt to the demands of different environments and succeed academically and professionally (Jones & Shorter-Gooden, 2003; Jones et al., 2021). Shifting enables Black women to sense what is expected of them in various spaces and meet these expectations. In a qualitative study, early-career Black women identified that shifting enabled them to develop relationships with colleagues that would benefit them in their careers (Dickens & Chavez, 2018). The ability to change their use of language, tone of voice, and overall presentation allowed these Black women to connect with coworkers and supported them in moving forward in their careers. In other words, shifting helps Black women to live and work effectively across differences – to function biculturally. Shifting can even enable Black women to bring an often needed "outsider" perspective into an organization, bringing fresh eyes and new perspectives (Gamst et al., 2020; Shorter-Gooden, 2012).

Shifting helps Black women to effectively navigate challenging environments where racial and gender bias are prevalent. Johnson et al. (2016) found that Black women who demonstrate higher levels of acculturation to African American culture also report anticipating bias and engaging in shifting behaviors to protect themselves from this bias. Black women have also reported that shifting is one strategy they used to combat negative stereotypes about Black women and to represent the Black community in a positive way (Dickens & Chavez, 2018), which many Black people are forced to do when they are the only Black person or one of few Black people in a work or educational environment.

In predominantly White environments, Black people often feel compelled to shift in order to maintain White people's comfort because when White people feel comfortable, Black people are usually safer around them (Menakem, 2017). Many Black people have had the experience of being blamed or attacked when White people are uncomfortable with their presence or behavior (DiAngelo, 2018). Extreme examples of this are the harsh punishment that Black children receive in schools and police shootings of unarmed Black people. More subtle examples involve being passed over for a promotion, ignored in a board meeting, and unfairly accused of being aggressive or angry. Thus, shifting can help Black women protect themselves and buffer White racism; it can help Black women to survive and to succeed. Yet this raises the question – at what cost?

9.5   Costs of Shifting

While shifting is one way that Black women cope with the gendered racism they experience and can help them in navigating school, career, and relationships, it comes with mental and emotional costs. In a qualitative study, Black women shared that losing their voices and ability to advocate for themselves and others was one cost of shifting (Dickens & Chavez, 2018). Specifically, Black female participants shared that shifting made them feel that they were being inauthentic at work and that they needed to assimilate to the White culture in their workplaces (Dickens & Chavez, 2018). Overall, Dickens and Chavez found that their participants reported experiencing significant psychological stress from shifting across various work and personal settings. This stress can show up as feelings of exhaustion, irritability, and burnout. In another qualitative study of Black women's experience in the workplace, participants expressed that shifting took a toll on them mentally and emotionally (Hall et al., 2012).

Shifting in the context of romantic relationships can also be problematic. As discussed in Chapter 11, romantic relationships between Black women and Black men can be challenging for a number of reasons. Black women may feel compelled to shift in their relationships with Black men and downplay their assertiveness and achievements to avoid outshining their Black male partners. In the African American Women's Voices Project, Jones and Shorter-Gooden (2003) found that 40% of the survey participants acknowledged hiding their strengths and accomplishments in relationships with Black men. Due to systemic racism and the gendered racism that Black men experience, many of their paths to success have been blocked, making it difficult for them to achieve in mainstream American society (Franklin, 1998). African Americans' relationships are known to be more egalitarian than those of their White peers (Marks et al., 2008). However, it is not uncommon for patriarchal gender norms to influence the relationship, and Black women's academic and financial success can sometimes be a threat to harmonious relationships with Black male partners. Black women who shift in their relationships may experience cumulative exhaustion over the course of the relationship and may even be in danger of staying in harmful or abusive relationships. We encourage therapists to support Black women in exploring the ways they may be shifting in their romantic relationships and help them identify ways to create space in their relationships to be their full selves.

Overall, shifting can limit the times and spaces in which Black women feel that they can be their authentic selves, and over time Black women may lose touch with their true selves as they contend with both demanding and limiting expectations at work, at home, and in their communities. Not being grounded in their sense of self and purpose can lead to feelings of anxiety and depression. Additionally, as Black women shift to accommodate the people in their lives, it can be easy for them to internalize the belief that who they are is not okay.

9.6   Recommendations for Therapists

Shifting is a normative, complex process that most Black women engage in, which impacts their well-being. Given that shifting is such a common experience and has significant costs for Black women, it is important to integrate discussions of shifting into therapy. We encourage therapists to be attuned to, assess, and be aware of shifting that may occur inside and outside the therapy room, and to support awareness of shifting and the development of healthy shifting strategies for their Black female clients. An important aspect of the therapeutic work related to shifting is focused on supporting Black women in loving and accepting themselves as they are and reducing the amount of emotional energy they spend shifting to make other people feel comfortable. Here, we provide five recommendations for therapists to take a strengths-based approach to supporting Black women in navigating shifting: (a) discuss issues of racial and gender bias, (b) assess shifting, (c) support Black women in cultivating authenticity, (d) help Black women manage the stress of shifting, and (e) explore and address how shifting shows up in the therapy room.

9.6.1   Discuss Race and Gender Bias

Therapists can begin the process by bringing issues of racial, gender, and other relevant biases into the room. During the assessment phase of treatment, therapists should ask Black female clients about how they identify with respect to race, ethnicity, and gender. Additionally, it is helpful for therapists to guide clients in exploring and processing their experiences related to racism, sexism, and gendered racism and normalize the stress that results from experiencing discrimination.

Black female clients may not feel comfortable talking about race with non-Black therapists, and it is especially important for non-Black therapists to communicate their willingness to talk about race-related stress and discrimination by asking about whether these experiences are salient for their Black female clients. Many Black people have had the experience of sharing stories of race-based discrimination with White friends or colleagues and having their experiences invalidated by questions about whether they did something to provoke the poor treatment or suggestions of other explanations for the discrimination they experienced. We encourage therapists to accept their Black female clients' experiences at face value and trust their perceptions of what happened. In addition to overt discrimination, the more subtle slights and microaggressions that Black women experience often leave them questioning whether they are being treated poorly due to their race and gender. Black women often wrestle with questions: Is this bias? Maybe he's just having a bad day? Am I overreacting? Evidence shows that the ambiguity of subtle or implicit bias is emotionally taxing and negatively impacts mental health (Nadal et al., 2014). We encourage therapists to listen for what might not be stated explicitly and to prompt exploration of difficult experiences by asking Black female clients if they believe that they were treated in a particular way because of their race, gender, or other intersecting marginalized identities, like being queer or Muslim. And we encourage therapists to create space for their clients' uncertainty and unsureness about these experiences.

9.6.2   Assess Shifting

Our second recommendation is for therapists to guide Black women through a shifting assessment to help the client identify ways that they are shifting in their lives. See Table 9.1 for an assessment that can be used in session with clients. As therapists conduct this assessment, they can ask about some items on the list directly and should listen for others. We encourage therapists to keep in mind the four themes of gendered racism (inferiority, image, invisibility, and invincibility) as a useful lens for exploring the ways that Black women shift in their lives. Begin this assessment by asking Black female clients about their experiences at school, at work, and in their family and community. Continue the assessment by exploring how and when Black women feel they need to change their behavior, language, and mannerisms and the impact this has on their internal experiences – their feelings and thoughts. Clients' answers to the shifting assessment questions will help the therapist begin to understand their experiences in various spaces in their lives and how they shift as they navigate these environments.

Table 9.1 *Shifting assessment*

Clinical Assessment of Shifting
Opening Questions

- How do any other marginalized identities – based on socioeconomic status, sexual orientation, gender expression, nationality, immigration status, religion/spirituality, disability, age – intersect with being Black and being a woman and impact your experiences?
- Are there ways that you change your communication style or mannerisms when you are at work, at school, with friends, with a partner, at home? In what ways?
- Are there ways that you downplay your strengths and accomplishments to make your partner feel comfortable?
- What makes you feel more or less comfortable fully expressing yourself in your romantic relationship?

Costs and Benefits of Shifting
Preface these questions with an explanation of what shifting is: Shifting occurs in response to stereotypes and biases. It involves changes in your sense of agency and empowerment and can manifest as different communication styles, mannerisms, appearance, ways of being, and interacting, as well as differences in how you think and feel about yourself. Shifting can be helpful in some ways but harmful in others.

- How has shifting helped you to navigate experiences at work? In school? and in relationships?
- In what ways have you benefited from being able to shift in various aspects of your life?
- How has shifting taken a toll on you? Mentally? Emotionally? Physically?

If Black female clients indicate that they shift in their romantic relationships, we encourage therapists to further explore these dynamics with a sensitivity to the unique pressure and anxiety Black women feel related to finding and maintaining romantic relationships. As mentioned earlier, Black women may shift in their relationships, hiding parts of themselves and downplaying their strengths (Gamst et al., 2020; Jones & Shorter-Gooden, 2003). Exploring the ways that Black women shift in their relationships may bring up truths about the relationship that are difficult for Black women to face, and therapists are encouraged to be gentle with their probing.

Once therapists have supported Black women in identifying how they shift in their lives, the next step in the shifting assessment is to guide their clients in identifying the ways that shifting is helpful to them as well as how shifting can be a burden in their lives. As discussed earlier in this chapter, Black women report benefits of shifting, which can help them to be successful in academic and professional spheres. We also encourage therapists to support their Black female clients in exploring the emotional toll that shifting has on their lives, as certain types of shifting likely contribute to the exhaustion, emotional fatigue, and clinical symptoms that Black women report. Acknowledging the problematic impact of shifting and supporting Black women in considering the spaces and places in their lives that offer rest and restoration can be a powerful intervention.

A shifting assessment will help Black female clients to name the shifting they do in their lives and acknowledge how it affects their lives. Shifting can be automatic and unconscious, and many Black women may not be aware of the shifts they make as they navigate different environments. Helping Black women to identify the ways that they shift in their lives can increase their awareness and set the stage for them to make intentional choices about whether, when, and how they want to shift in their lives moving forward. During this exploration process, therapists should name and normalize the shifting as a necessary and, at times, adaptive response to racism and sexism. Using the term *shifting* can be helpful in providing a name for the client's experiences.

9.6.3   Support Black Women in Cultivating Authenticity

Our third recommendation is for therapists to help their Black female clients cultivate authentic ways of being in multiple spaces. In a qualitative study, Dickens and Chavez (2018) found that Black women who engage in shifting end up feeling inauthentic. When Black women shift in several areas of their lives, they may become disconnected from their authentic selves. Therapy provides an opportunity to help Black women cultivate their authenticity.

At its core, authenticity is about being honest and true to ourselves, including what we believe in and who we are. When we are authentic, we are guided by our internal values, by what is meaningful to us, and by what feels right to us, rather than by external expectations and demands (Thacker, 2016). Authenticity is important for each of us, but it can be harder to achieve when we are bombarded by negative stereotypes and constricting messages.

To begin the process of helping Black women cultivate authenticity, we recommend guiding Black female clients to reflect on times when they feel most at home, relaxed, and comfortable with themselves. Therapists should then guide clients to share how they communicate and behave during these times and discuss what helps them feel comfortable in the spaces where they are being true to themselves. Identifying how Black women show up and engage with others when they feel most comfortable will serve as an indicator of what it looks like for them to be their most authentic selves.

Another helpful exercise to support Black women in connecting to their authenticity is by exploring values through an Acceptance and Commitment Therapy (ACT) framework. Within ACT, values are seen as guides for ongoing action and behavior; values reflect who you want to be in the world and the legacy that you want to leave. ACT posits that our values guide us to live rich and meaningful lives and serve as a counterpoint to being guided by fear or anxiety (Grumet & Fitzpatrick, 2016; McCracken & Keogh, 2009). We encourage therapists to engage their Black female clients in values-oriented conversations with these guiding questions: What do you want to be remembered for in your life? What do you want your life to be about? When do you feel most alive and present in your life and what are you doing in those moments? What is most important to you in your life? These questions are intended to help clients connect to who they want to be without focusing on the demands of the other people in their lives.

Once Black female clients have articulated what it looks and feels like for them to be authentic, we recommend that therapists encourage their clients to identify ways that they can bring their full selves into various aspects of their lives. Explore what it would look like for the client to live out her values and be true to herself at work, at school, and in relationships. How would her behavior in these places and relationships be different? In what ways does she want to choose to continue to shift and how would she like to let go of shifting in these environments? As part of this exploration, the client may need to process fears related to expressing her authentic self in professional spaces and talk through ways to determine if it will be safe to bring her full self to various environments. Guiding Black women to identify the real risks of being authentic in predominantly White professional environments is an important part of this process. Further, related to relationships, therapists should understand that discussing the ways a Black female client might be more authentic in her romantic relationships could lead her to consider ending relationships. These conversations can be difficult and painful, and therapists must be careful not to encourage their Black female clients to stay or leave relationships, jobs, or academic programs. The aim of this work is for therapists to empower Black women in making informed and conscious choices about how they want to show up and engage in various parts of their lives.

9.6.4   Stress Management for Shifting

As mentioned, gendered racism and shifting can take a physical and emotional toll on Black women and cause them to experience stress. Our fifth recommendation is for therapists to support Black women in actively managing the stress related to shifting. The shifting assessment guides Black women to identify the mental and emotional toll that shifting can take on them, which is an important first step toward working to mitigate stress caused by shifting. Specifically related to managing stress connected to shifting, we suggest encouraging Black women to spend time with people with whom they can be their full and authentic selves. Additionally, it can be helpful for Black women to have restorative time alone when they feel grounded in themselves and not pulled to meet anyone's expectations. We encourage therapists to explore with their clients whether engaging in artistic or creative pursuits like singing, dancing, or painting, alone or with other people in accepting spaces, are activities that would help them feel free to express themselves and also relieve stress.

> General stress management and coping strategies are discussed further in the chapters on Black women's health (Chapter 13) and resources for Black women thriving (Chapter 14).

9.6.5   Explore and Address How Shifting Shows Up in the Therapy Room

Our sixth and final recommendation relates to how shifting might show up in the therapy room for Black female clients. As mentioned, Black female clients may feel compelled to shift to overcompensate and appear competent to their therapists. With White therapists in particular, Black female clients may shift in order to make their therapist feel comfortable. We encourage therapists to explore with Black female clients how they may be shifting with the therapist. During this exploration, it is important for therapists to be open and accepting of what their clients share. Therapists may feel guilt and want to defend themselves in response to hearing that their clients do not feel completely comfortable with them, and it is important for therapists to manage their emotional reactions to any feedback Black female clients provide. Therapists should be curious about their Black female client's experience in therapy and explore what keeps them from being their full selves in therapy and how the therapist can increase the comfort and safety in the therapeutic relationship.

> Building a strong therapeutic relationship with Black female clients is discussed further in Chapter 7.

Therapists can guide their Black female clients to identify the parts of themselves they are bringing into therapy and the parts of themselves they are leaving outside of the therapy room. We encourage therapists to discuss what it would look like for clients to bring all parts of themselves into therapy and how it would feel to be vulnerable with the therapist in this way. Focusing on the therapeutic relationship and facilitating an interpersonal process discussion about shifting in therapy can be a powerful intervention for Black female clients. We recommend that therapists utilize the therapeutic space and relationship as an opportunity for the client to practice being their authentic selves. This approach will also enable therapists to further support their Black female clients as they bring their authentic selves to other aspects of their lives.

Case Example

Latrice is a 25-year-old, heterosexual, cisgender Black woman. Latrice grew up on the west side of Chicago, which is a predominantly Black and economically disadvantaged area. Latrice excelled academically and got into a magnet high school located close to downtown Chicago; she commuted to school by bus while many of her friends in the neighborhood attended the local high school. Latrice was the first in her family to attend college, and while she stayed in Illinois for school, she lived on campus and only saw her family a few times a semester. When she was in college, she had a hard time finding a community and fitting in, and she began feeling somewhat separate from her family and her community when she returned home for visits.

After college and back in Chicago, Latrice, who had always been an athlete, decided to pursue a career in personal training and wellness coaching. Latrice continued to feel like an outsider in the upscale gym where she works as a personal trainer and wellness consultant. She is one of the few women offering personal training and the only Black woman working at the gym who is not part of the maintenance staff. Latrice feels pressure to look the part and makes sure to wear expensive workout gear and always have her hair and nails done. Latrice feels like she has to be "on" when she is at work and interacting with her clients as well as her colleagues. She notices that clients and coworkers seem to question her competence and are surprised when she does things well. Latrice feels demeaned when her coworkers and clients call her "girl" in an attempt to sound cool and connected to Black culture. Latrice feels that she is constantly navigating microaggressions, and she finds herself stressed and exhausted at the end of her workdays.

Latrice longs for the comfort of home and community connection, but when she visits home and spends time with her family she feels like she cannot be completely herself there either. Her cousins tease her about talking "White" and forgetting where she came from. Latrice feels caught between two worlds; at work people assume she is uneducated, and at home people think she considers herself too good for them because she has a college degree and a job in a wealthy neighborhood.

Latrice came to therapy because she was not sure how to handle the microaggressions and stress she was experiencing and noticed that she had been feeling anxious. In the initial sessions, the therapist, a Black woman, worked to build a strong therapeutic relationship with Latrice and did a thorough assessment to understand Latrice's experience of stress. The therapist helped Latrice to name the pattern of shifting that she was using to cope with the racism, sexism, classism, and micro-aggressions she was experiencing. This approach helped to normalize the stress and exhaustion Latrice experienced as a result of being the only Black woman working in a professional capacity at her gym and no longer feeling like she fits in at home. The therapist guided Latrice to explore the ways that she shifts when she is at work and the emotional energy this takes. Latrice was able to identify the benefits that she experiences when she shifts at work as well as the toll this takes on her and how this makes it more difficult for her to be her authentic self.

Together, Latrice and the therapist also explored whether Latrice felt the need to shift in the therapy room. Latrice acknowledged that she has always wanted to make people like her. Latrice expressed that she looks up to the therapist, sees her as having it all together, and has a hard time talking with her about the ways in which she is struggling. Latrice noted that what she assumed are the class differences in their backgrounds make her feel like it is important for her to speak "proper English." The therapist acknowledged the class differences in their backgrounds and normalized the pressure Latrice felt to disprove the myth of inferiority with the therapist due to their class differences. The therapist offered empathy related to how challenging it is to be vulnerable in therapy and expressed hope that therapy would be a space where Latrice could be her full self. The therapist asked if she could do anything to help Latrice feel more comfortable in the space; Latrice said she did not know, and the therapist encouraged her to tell her if she thought of something in the future. The therapist also briefly disclosed some of her own past struggles and challenges that were relevant to Latrice's experiences, to help her know that she was not alone in struggling.

To help increase the amount of time Latrice spends being her authentic self, the therapist explored with her when she feels most like herself and what helps her to feel most comfortable in these moments. Latrice shared that she feels most authentic with a few of her close girlfriends from college who are also Black and come from similar low-income backgrounds. The therapist guided Latrice to share what she is like when she is with these friends. Latrice and the therapist then discussed what it could look like for Latrice to bring more of herself into the therapy room as a way to practice being her authentic self in more places. Eventually, they expanded this discussion to identify ways for Latrice to bring more of herself into work and at home with her family. They acknowledged that sometimes Latrice still feels it is necessary to shift, particularly at work or in environments that have a history of gendered racism. The therapist used the values-oriented questions from ACT to help Latrice identify ways that she could engage her values at work even when she feels it is still necessary to shift. Latrice found this conversation helpful because pursuing a career in fitness was aligned with her passion and her desire to help people live healthy lives, and revisiting what she most valued about work helped her to feel more empowered in a challenging environment. Finally, the therapist guided Latrice to identify self-care practices to help her relieve her stress and manage her anxiety on days when shifting felt necessary. She also encouraged Latrice to spend more time with her college friends whom she feels most comfortable with.

This case example highlights the balance we encourage therapists to strike between helping Black female clients to reduce the amount of time they spend shifting while also acknowledging when and where shifting is adaptive in their lives. Normalizing and validating Latrice's experience without rushing to fix or change her behavior was important. Therapists must remember that there are no easy solutions to shifting and that the goal is to support Black female clients to be aware of how and when they shift in their lives and make conscious choices about when they choose to shift and when they can be their authentic selves.

9.7   Therapist Self-Awareness and Authenticity

To work effectively with Black female clients, therapists must develop their awareness, knowledge and skills. In particular, therapists should explore and examine their own identities and privileges, acknowledge their own assumptions and biases, and have strategies to mitigate their impact. This means that White therapists need to wrestle with Whiteness and White privilege (DiAngelo, 2018), particularly the often invisible (to them) ways that Whiteness shows up and impacts the therapeutic relationship. It means that male therapists need to wrestle with sexism and the often subtle ways in which sexism can marginalize women, and how this can be exacerbated with women of color. But this work of self-examination is not limited to White and male therapists. Black women therapists need to be attuned to how they might inadvertently privilege particular shifting strategies that they themselves have adopted or used, and how they might have difficulty creating space for alternative ways in which Black female clients can be authentic and thrive.

Therapist self-examination is discussed further in Chapter 6.

Therapists can do their own "shifting assessment" as part of the self-examination process. In addition to answering questions from the shifting assessment for clients (Table 9.1), we encourage therapists to consider the reflection questions at the end of this chapter. To support clients in cultivating authenticity, it is important for therapists themselves to be on a path toward authenticity.

9.8   Conclusion

Shifting is an important framework for understanding the behaviors and experiences of Black women. Shifting is a complex and at times adaptive response to the gendered racism that Black women navigate on a daily basis. However, shifting can also take an emotional toll on Black women, and therapy provides an opportunity for Black women to explore and examine their shifting and make empowered choices about how and when to engage in shifting and to cultivate their authenticity. An important caveat: When addressing shifting as a psychological coping mechanism, with positive but mostly negative impacts on mental health, the therapist needs to fully grasp why Black women shift in the first place. Indeed, even in the therapy environment Black women can display shifting dynamics, which may be subtle yet visible to the discerning therapist. Asking a Black female client about shifting dynamics requires therapists to be culturally self-aware and attuned to the therapy environment as one in which Black women can feel racial and cultural discomfort. When Black female clients collaborate with a therapist to name and explore shifting dynamics, this is a powerful signal of trust and confidence that can pave the wave for corrective emotional experiences. In any scenario, Black women's mental health is protected by their confidence to show up as their authentic selves, without having to code-switch or shift to avoid being stereotyped or marginalized.

Therapist Reflection Questions

1. What are your privileged and marginalized identities?
2. How do you deal with your marginalized identities based on race, gender, sexual orientation, and other characteristics? What are your shifting strategies?
3. How might your approach impact your capacity to discuss these issues with clients and your sense of *how* one should shift? To what extent have you explored these issues?
4. What additional work do you need to do to become more aware of your own standpoint and the lens through which you work with Black female clients?
5. What are your biggest takeaways from this chapter that might impact your conversations with Black female clients?
6. What experiences have your Black female clients discussed with you that makes you wonder if they shift to manage dynamics in some settings?

Resources

Books

Anderson. C. (2021). *Intelligence isn't enough: A black professionals guide to thriving in the workplace.* Jonathan Ball Publishers.

Jones, C., & Gooden, K. S. (2003). *Shifting: The double lives of black women in America.* HarperCollins Publishers.

Tatum, B.D. (2017). *Why are all the black kids sitting together in the cafeteria?: And other conversations about race* (2nd ed.). Basic Books.

Podcasts

Hodson, T. (Executive Producer). (2020, July 28). Code-switching is a form of systemic racism against blacks [Audio podcast episode]. In *Spectrum.* WOUB Public Media. https://woub.org/2020/07/28/code-switching-is-a-form-of-systemic-racism-against-blacks/

Pharm, J. (Host). (2020–present). Blackness and the workplace [Audio podcast]. https://www.blacknessandtheworkplace.com/podcast

Films

Melfi, T. (Director). (2016). *Hidden figures* [Film]. Fox 2000 Pictures.

Media Resources

Netflix. (2018, May 18). *What had happened was. Episode 2: Code switching* [Video]. YouTube. https://youtu.be/5iQuATmEbVw

References

Braun, C. B. (1999). African American women, Afrocentrism and feminism: Implications for therapy. *Women & Therapy, 22*(4), 1–16.

Cotter, E. W., Kelly, N. R., Mitchell, K. S., & Mazzeo, S. E. (2015). An investigation of body appreciation, ethnic identity, and eating disorder symptoms in Black women. *Journal of Black Psychology, 41*(1), 3–25. https://doi.org/10.1177/0095798413502671

Crenshaw, K. W. (2017). *On intersectionality: Essential writings.* The New Press.

DiAngelo, R. (2018). *White fragility: Why it's so hard for White people to talk about racism.* Beacon Press.

Dickens, D. D., & Chavez, E. L. (2018). Navigating the workplace: The costs and benefits of shifting identities at work among early career US Black women. *Sex Roles, 78*(11–12), 760–774. https://doi.org/10.1007/s11199–017-0844-x

Dickens, D. D., Womack, V. Y., & Dimes, T. (2019). Managing hypervisibility: An exploration of theory and research on identity shifting strategies in the workplace among Black women. *Journal of Vocational Behavior, 113*, 153–163.

Essed, P. (1991). *Understanding everyday racism: An interdisciplinary theory.* Sage.

Franklin, A. J. (1998). Treating anger in African American men. In W. S. Pollack & R. F. Levant (Eds.), *New psychotherapy for men* (pp. 239–258). John Wiley.

Gamst, G., Arellano-Morales, L., Meyers, L. S., Serpas, D. G., Balla, J., Diaz, A., Dobson, K., Feller, C., Rought, S., Salazar, B., Garcia, S., & Aldape, R. (2020). Shifting can be stressful for African American women: A structural mediation model. *Journal of Black Psychology, 46*(5), 364–387.

Greene, B. (1997). Psychotherapy with African American women: Integrating feminist and psychodynamic models. *Smith College Studies in Social Work, 67*(3), 299–322. https://doi.org/10.1080/00377319709517495

Griffin, C. (2019, July 3). *How natural Black hair at work became a civil rights issue.* JSTOR Daily. https://daily.jstor.org/how-natural-black-hair-at-work-became-a-civil-rights-issue/

Grumet, R., & Fitzpatrick, M. (2016). A case for integrating values clarification work into cognitive behavioral therapy for social anxiety disorder. *Journal of Psychotherapy Integration, 26*(1), 11–21. https://doi.org/10.1037/a0039633

Hall, J. C., Everett, J. E., & Hamilton-Mason, J. (2012). Black women talk about workplace stress and how they cope. *Journal of Black Studies, 43*(2), 207–226.

Holden, M. (2019, August 12). *LGBTQ people are forced to constantly code-switch and it's exhausting.* Vice. https://www.vice.com/en/article/evj47w/the-exhausting-work-of-lgbtq-code-switching

Johnson, J. C., Gamst, G., Meyers, L. S., Arellano-Morales, L., & Shorter-Gooden, K. (2016). Development and validation of the African American Women's Shifting Scale (AAWSS). *Cultural Diversity and Ethnic Minority Psychology, 22*(1), 11–25. http://dx.doi.org/10.1037/cdp0000039

Jones, C. & Shorter-Gooden, K. (2003). *Shifting: The double lives of Black women in America.* HarperCollins.

Jones, M. S., Womack, V., Jérémie-Brink, G., & Dickens, D. D. (2021). Gendered racism and mental health among young adult US Black women: The moderating roles of gendered racial identity centrality and identity shifting. *Sex Roles, 85*, 221–231.

Marks, L. D., Hopkins, K., Chaney, C., Monroe, P. A., Nesteruk, O., & Sasser, D. D. (2008). "Together, we are strong": A qualitative study of happy, enduring African American marriages. *Family Relations, 57*(2), 172–185.

McCracken, L. M., & Keogh, E. (2009). Acceptance, mindfulness, and values-based action may counteract fear and avoidance of emotions in chronic pain: An analysis of anxiety sensitivity. *The Journal of Pain, 10*(4), 408–415. https://doi.org/10.1016/j.jpain.2008.09.015

Menakem, R. (2017). *My grandmother's hands: Racialized trauma and the pathway to mending our hearts and bodies.* Central Recovery Press.

Nadal, K. L., Griffin, K. E., Wong, Y., Hamit, S., & Rasmus, M. (2014). The impact of racial microaggressions on mental health: Counseling implications for clients of color. *Journal of Counseling & Development, 92*(1), 57–66.

Reid, P. T. (1988). Racism and sexism: Comparisons and conflicts. In P. A. Katz & D. Taylor (Eds.), *Eliminating racism: Profiles in controversy* (pp. 203–221). Plenum Press.

Reskin, B. F., McBrier, D. B., & Kmec, J. A. (1999). The determinants and consequences of workplace sex and race composition. *Annual Review of Sociology, 25*(1), 335–361.

Romero, R. E. (2000). The icon of the strong Black woman: The paradox of strength. In L. C. Jackson & B. Greene (Eds.), *Psychotherapy with African American women: Innovations in psychodynamic perspectives and practice* (pp. 225–238). Guilford Press.

Russell, K. Y., Wilson, M., & Hall, R. E. (1992). *The color complex: The politics of skin color among African Americans.* Anchor.

Shorter-Gooden, K. (2012). The paradox of the margin: Advantages for institutional transformation. In H. Curtis-Boles, D. Adams, & L. Jenkins-Monroe (Eds.), *Making our voices heard: Women of color in academia* (pp. 165–175). Nova Science.

Shorter-Gooden, K., & Jackson, L. C. (2000). The interweaving of cultural and intrapsychic issues in the therapeutic relationship. In L. C. Jackson & B. Greene (Eds.), *Psychotherapy with African American women: Innovations in psychodynamic perspectives and practice* (pp. 15–32). Guilford Press.

Thacker, K. (2016). *The art of authenticity: Tools to become an authentic leader and your best self.* John Wiley & Sons.

West, C. M. (1995). Mammy, Sapphire, and Jezebel: Historical images of Black women and their implications for psychotherapy. *Psychotherapy: Theory, Research, Practice, Training, 32*(3), 458–466.

10   Black Women's Mothering and Caregiving

with Yolande Cooke[*]

In 1997, for the movie *Soul Food* (Tillman, 1997), Boyz II Men performed "A Song for Mama" (Flick, 1997), which has become an ode to the fierce and tenacious love of Black mothers everywhere. The film *Soul Food* shows Mother Jo, a matriarch who helps to hold a Black family together as tensions and conflicts threaten the family's values and traditions. Mother Jo's insistence on family members attending a weekly soul food dinner is more than just a family gathering around a good meal. A soul food dinner is an event symbolic of family togetherness that showcases Mother Jo's influence on her three daughters, their partners, children, and a host of other extended members of a large and complex family system. So powerful is Mother Jo's role in the family that when she becomes gravely ill, the withdrawal of her care and wisdom shakes the family's center of gravity. Mother Jo's gift of nurturing and steady caregiving in her family is beautifully represented in the lyrics of the song, which express how maternal love deeply feeds the soul.

"A Song for Mama" and *Soul Food* won accolades across the film and music industries for their powerful and positive depictions of the strengths and challenges of Black families and the role and influence of Black mothers as parents, caregivers, mentors, wise women, truth speakers, and burden bearers. Both song and movie are precious reminders of the reverence in which Black mothers are held and how much Black women strive to keep families connected amid conflicts and tragedies.

Our own mothers are great examples of the enduring care of Black mothers. Adia's mother, Kumea, is a dynamic and influential woman helping to improve diversity and inclusion infrastructures across the United States. Donna's mother, Florina, has passed on and, in her time, was a major influence in the lives of Donna, her sister Tessa, and several non-kin daughters who claimed her as their own. Yolande's mother, Myrtle, passed away more than 20 years ago. She was a beloved community organizer who touched the lives

---

[*] D. Baptiste, Y. Cooke, & A. Gooden. (2023). Black women's mothering and caregiving. In D. Baptiste & A. Gooden, *Promoting Black women's mental health: What practitioners should know and do*. Cambridge University Press.

236

of many in her neighborhood. She passed on a love of social advocacy to her daughters. Our mothers represented role models for how to pattern our lives, and they loved us consistently and deeply, which grounds our personalities and identities.

The picture of Black women as influential and competent mothers and caregivers depicts only one side of the story. In therapy we hear of other aspects of Black mothering and caregiving in family life and the high toll these critical identities can take on Black women's physical and mental health and wellness. In the Introduction to this book, we discuss the "both/and" perspective therapists must hold as they work with Black women about their mental and emotional needs. Therapists must be able to celebrate the joys and beauty of Black mothering and caregiving while also helping their clients to audit and alleviate caregiving burdens, which can be multifaceted. This chapter explores Black women's experiences as mothers and caregivers in family systems. We discuss the contexts in which Black women parent and care for others and the factors that affect their maternal anxieties and efficacy. We highlight a range of roles and responsibilities that Black mothers take on in households, extended families, and communities. Throughout, we identify themes around which therapists might support Black women in these important identities of mother and caregiver. We amplify therapists' strategies to support Black women's efforts to have positive family and generational influences and impacts while also protecting their own lives. We begin with a consideration of the importance of motherhood and mothering in Black culture, and ways in which this plays out in family life. While *mothering* and *caregiving* are intertwined, we also consider Black women's caregiving for other family members (such as their own parents or caregivers or extended family members).

Black women also provide care for intimate partners, a dynamic we discuss further in Chapter 11.

10.1 Black Motherhood: Cultural Contexts

We use an inclusive definition of Black motherhood that includes cisgender, transgender, and gender-nonconforming Black women who give birth biologically, adopt, are foster mothers, have children through surrogates, or help to raise children. In Black homes, mothering roles are fulfilled by biological maternal parents, grandmothers, or other women who take on the care of children. In Black culture, motherhood is a precious and celebrated identity. Yet Black mothering may not fit the dominant cultural motherhood ideals. To fully understand the complexities of Black mothering, we provide a few themes that therapists should grasp in working with Black female clients.

10.1.1 Mothering in Black Culture

In American culture, motherhood is sacred, and women of different cultural backgrounds may attach unique meanings to their mothering identity. Black cultural understandings of motherhood have some differences from how motherhood is understood in mainstream American culture (Bezusko, 2013; Hill, 1987; Nelson, 2011). Traditionally, motherhood is presented as one of life's highest callings, centered on giving birth and raising children well, even if that means not working outside the home. Traditional motherhood also means caring for family members and households. This picture of motherhood aligns with the myth of the ideal mother based predominantly on White and middle-to upper-class women and their families (Hill, 1987).

Feminist scholars make clear that this picture of idealized motherhood has been shaped by patriarchal gender norms, gender role expectations, and the myth of ideal womanhood mostly constructed on the experiences of White women (Johnston & Swanson, 2003). As mothers, women labor in households in a manner that can seem invisible. Mothers are assigned the moral weight for children's well-being and competence. Feminist scholars also debunk the ideal that women are incomplete if they do not want children or do not want to give birth (Kendall-Tackette, 2001; Nelson, 2011). The feminist discourse about the meaning of motherhood has been helpful to women generally. Yet Black women's motherhood has not necessarily been included in these conversations (Hill, 1987).

Therapists must understand the unique and salient themes of Black motherhood. First, stereotypes distort an understanding of Black women as mothers. In brief, the stereotypical Black mother has been characterized as a "Mammy" – a cheerful, loving, asexual, and hardworking domestic worker caring for White children as if they were her own (Parks, 2010). The Black Mammy is not as visible a role in contemporary culture but subtly exists in representations of Black women as self-sacrificing in families, living as "strong Black women" with little attention to their own needs (Nichols et al., 2015; Parks, 2010). Even the positive and influential character of Mother Jo in *Soul Food* (Tillman, 1997) has features reminiscent of the Black Mammy stereotype.

Chapter 4 discusses stereotypes in more depth. See Chapter 8 for a full discussion of the Strong Black Woman persona.

Second, a contemporary and often stereotypical representation of Black motherhood is the Black matriarch on welfare. The Black matriarch is often cast as overly aggressive and controlling while raising undisciplined and unsuccessful children. The stereotype of the Black matriarch as a hustler and dependent on welfare is not a redemptive or kind representation of Black women (Bezusko, 2013). Stereotypes of Black motherhood present simplistic tropes that drive biases and prejudices. Stereotypes of Black mothering negate a holistic and complex understanding of Black women's maternal identity and roles (Harris-Perry, 2011; Parks, 2010).

Black women may mother in complex family arrangements, and many work outside the home. Historically, enslaved Black women were forced to work throughout their pregnancies and to resume work shortly after giving birth. After slavery, Black women had to work outside of the home due to financial necessity and were not afforded the privilege of staying home like White women (Collins, 2005). The history of Black women working outside of the home has supported more egalitarian relationships between Black women and their partners. Black mothers may share domestic responsibilities, including caregiving, with intimate partners who may or may not reside in the home. Grandmothers, aunts, and others who live in and outside the house may be part of caregiving circles (Hill, 1987). The hustling of Black women as working mothers must not be denigrated. It must be celebrated as Black women's honest and powerful striving to make ends meet, to provide for their families, and to keep poverty at bay.

Third, Black women may assume a mothering role without biological ties to children they care for. Black women make room for "other mothering," or being part of networks and communities that care for other people's children as their own (Chatters et al., 1994; Wane, 2000). This dynamic can happen inside and outside of primary families. Black women's maternal influence might extend well beyond the dominant culture's understanding of "launched adults" in their own nuclear families. Maternal mentoring is an essential contribution of Black women and vital to Black culture. In this posture, Black women take on the voice and cadence of a mother to children, adolescents, or adults, providing guidance, counsel, rebuke, or scaffolding to those who need it. This aspect of mothering not necessarily unique to American culture, yet Black women who provide such aid to their families and others often go unrecognized for their deep service and contribution. At the funerals and celebrations of life of Black mothers, family members often learn of the extent of mothering that Black women provided for children who were not biologically their own (Wane, 2000).

Fourth, Black motherhood is revered in Black culture in a fashion that goes well beyond raising children, homemaking, or caregiving. Black mothers' roles in generational stability and success have sustained Black families through difficult periods in US history (Elliott & Reid, 2019; Goodman & Silverstein, 2002; Hill, 1987). Hence, Black mothering is an enduring resource and strength of Black families (Boyd-Franklin, 1989); the mother's influence is celebrated in helping her children to adapt to the sociocultural realities of the United States. The beauty and influence of Black mothering are serenaded in music, the arts, and pop culture, as captured in a song by Kanye West in 2005. The song, "Hey Mama," offers a tribute to the Black mother whose style is tender, yet tough and enduring.

Finally, Black mothering has transcended Black family life to wield political and social influence. Most recently, the voices of Black mothers calling for social and political change in the face of gun violence and killings by police have been influential (Morgan, 2018). In George Floyd's killing, a pivotal moment captured in the horror of his death is his call for "Mamma." O'Neal (2020) writes, "George Floyd's mother was not there, but he used her as a sacred invocation." Black motherhood in the pursuit of social and political influence and the advancement of justice is increasing (Morgan, 2018).

10.1.2   Single Black Mothering

Black single mothers and their households are fraught with stereotypes and overgeneralizations. In the Black community, a high percentage of Black women may appear to be single parents, but therapists should be aware of nuances around this depiction (Taylor & Conger, 2017). Black maternal single parents include a diverse range of family forms, experiences, and outcomes. For example, some Black mothers may be formally designated as single parents. However, they may have unmarried partners that are part of parenting arrangements (Barnes, 2001). Though sometimes invisible, single Black mothers can have parenting support from others residing outside the home. Black single mothers may share responsibilities across various households, with kin and non-kin family members taking on co-parenting roles (Chatters et al., 1994). Black single mother households may also include co-parenting adults such as grandparents who offer guidance and support for the parenting responsibility. We advise therapists to ignore one-dimensional storylines about children's maladjustment growing up in the households of "single Black mothers."

Nonetheless, for many single Black mothers the burden of parenting can be severe: The entire burden of parenting is theirs to bear financially, emotionally, physically, and spiritually. Single Black mothers often take on the *psychological* responsibility for their children, and their role demands the equivalent of both roles in a two-parent household (Elliott & Reid, 2019). For such women, parenting is exhausting and draining. Resources may be scarce, especially when the mother is young, not highly educated, or maintains a minimum-wage job. Emotions of shame and guilt can also accompany such parenting, which includes having to live with the thought of what one cannot provide for their children. The social and emotional risks for children's well-being may be more significant for children in single-mother households than for children in two-parent homes (Taylor & Conger, 2017).

10.1.3   Black Teen Mothering

Although the numbers have decreased over the past few decades, Black women are overrepresented as teenage mothers (Elliott & Reid, 2019). Here, again, a "both/and" perspective is needed. Black teen mothering must be viewed with complexity. Where a teen mother's story may begin in risky circumstances, that is not necessarily where it ends. Young Black women who become mothers often have complicated developmental histories that lead to compromised choices about motherhood. While their early years as parents can be difficult for their children and themselves, they can go on to be accomplished and successful (Leadbeater & Way, 2007). Iyanla Vanzant, a motivational speaker and *New York Times* best-selling author, offers a picture of the complex circumstances that can lead to a Black teen's pregnancy and how life can improve in time (Vanzant, 1999). Vanzant describes a girlhood of loneliness and abuse beginning at age 2, when her mother died of breast cancer; her father was unavailable. Paternal relatives raised Vanzant, one of whom raped her at the age of 9. Vanzant was a teenage mother by age 16, and by 21, she had three children with a physically abusive husband. As a single mother, Vanzant raised her three children on public assistance. Yet, she fought to become a practicing attorney, serving nearly three years as a public defender in Philadelphia. Vanzant's story is one of struggle, strength, perseverance, and triumph (Vanzant, 1999).

For other Black teens the risks associated with adolescent pregnancy and parenthood negatively impact their social, mental, and financial health, with effects lasting a lifetime (Assini-Meytin & Green, 2015). Black teen mothering may also usher in decades of underdeveloped caregiving. Teens may mother in complex and unsupported caregiving situations. Often, teen mothers are held to low expectations for caregiver responsibilities. Many fathers, some of whom are older men who have victimized underage girls, do not claim parentage (Forte et al., 2016). Thus, the responsibilities of caregiving fall solely on the teen mother, impacting her ability to thrive (Paschal et al., 2011). Thus, lack of support in teen parenting may affect a teen's capacity to finish high school or gain a college degree. The effects of these early experiences may make women feel bitter and ashamed (Forte et al., 2016). Often heavily subsidized by government resources, Black teen mothers might endure years of shame, embarrassment, ridicule, and loneliness (Murray, 2010).

Research also suggests that some teen mothers are more likely to have multiple births before age 20 (Kan & Ramirez, 2020), and many teen mothers provide care without adequate education, employment, and financial support. Some teens strive to take care of their own children with the added responsibility of caring for their younger siblings. The task is massive, and the mistakes made in their duties as parents are sometimes irreversible and possibly even life threatening to themselves and their children. Black female clients who began caregiving as teens may present in therapy with anxiety, shame, and suffering for how they have affected their children's lives. Even clients who overcome difficult circumstances as teen mothers may present a complex early history that affects their capacity to advance professionally. Many struggle with self-acceptance and self-respect as they examine their pasts (Elliott et al., 2015).

Finally, teen parenting may negatively impact grandmothers called upon to mother their grandchildren (Goodman & Silverstein, 2002). Numerous studies have shown the impact this second round of motherhood has on grandmothers. Women who became teen mothers, and their mothers who supported them, may seek therapy to deal with the past's legacies (Elliott et al., 2015; Whitley et al., 2001).

10.1.4   Black Non-kin Mothering

Being socialized from a young age to give back and care for others, Black women may take on a maternal role for neighborhood kids, close family friends, and others. Often Black women take it upon themselves to help financially, to supplement schooling, to provide tutoring or college application guidance, to serve as positive role models through mentorship; they do the emotional labor of supporting others (Neal-Barnett et al., 2011; Wane, 2000). Black women may take on roles in churches, local park districts, professional business organizations, sorority membership, and more. Driven by a sense of personal and cultural contribution, such caretaking responsibilities, while beneficial to recipients, can significantly roil Black women's wellness. A therapist's understanding of the cultural significance of Black women's call to mothering is key to alliance building. A goal is not to have women end these activities, which have offered culturally sanctioned scaffolding for Black youth. Instead, discussions should help Black women balance their contributions in such roles to protect their own physical and mental health and to recognize and prioritize rest (Kendall-Tackett, 2001).

10.2   Black Mothering: Therapy Themes

First, Black women may be mothering in complex family arrangements. The families in which they perform these roles exist in many forms (Boyd-

Franklin, 1989). Black family systems include blood-related immediate and extended family members, with many Black people growing up in close relationships with aunts, uncles, and cousins; this differs from the mainstream White American nuclear family. Black families also include non-kin families living in varying arrangements, sometimes across multiple households. In Black families, the structure and expectations of non-kin members can parallel those of nuclear and blood-related ones. A capacity to live adaptively in complex family constellations is a well-established strength of Black culture. Black women are central to such arrangements (Chatters et al., 1994).

In families, Black women take on parental caregiving roles and responsibilities that are expected (e.g., raising their biological children), unexpected or unplanned (e.g., raising incapacitated family members' children), demanded (e.g., becoming default caregivers with little support or help from others), or forced (e.g., girls caring for younger siblings). In any of these situations, Black women may be expected to provide care well beyond their capacities and in denial of their own needs (Goodman & Silverstein, 2002; Nichols et al., 2015; Rosenthal & Lobel, 2016). They may also feel pressure, shame, or disempowerment that forces them to choose options at odds with their own needs. Therapists should abandon restrictive vocabulary such as "immediate" family to track Black women's caregiving influence even across geographically dispersed locations. Understanding a Black woman's family contexts will provide clues about her strengths, resources, and challenges.

Second, Black mothers carry powerful anxieties about protecting their children, and therapists should ally with them around their profound fears about racism (and other "isms") in the United States. For example, massive anxiety in Black mothers centers around the US criminal justice system and policing. Systemic racism drives stereotyping and discrimination against Black children. The killings of George Floyd and Breonna Taylor, among countless others, represent a Black mother's worst nightmare (Morgan, 2018). Some Black mothers worry that they will receive "that phone call" about their child being shot by the police. This awareness drives a deep psychological tension in Black women that mothers of White children do not experience. We recommend therapists show radical understanding and acceptance of the anticipatory losses and passion of Black mothers to seek justice for Black people killed by rogue police (Morgan, 2018). We validate these fears and use empathy and compassion to bond with our Black female clients about the mental trauma of the *potential* for the racially charged killings of their loved ones. Black women report this fear as so powerful that it robs them of peace and sleep, and therapists should find ways to hold space for Black mothers to process this anxiety and pain.

Third, for many Black women, motherhood can create severe role strain (Nichols et al., 2015). Black women's mothering knowledge may come from socialization, misinformation, or lack of training. Women may have inadequate preparation for the role. Frequently, Black women sign on to provide maternal care without realizing the depths of the responsibility required (Losada et al., 2010). Once they take on the task, it is difficult to give it up, leading to being overwhelmed. Other heavy responsibilities may accompany mothering, such as caring for a family member requiring long-term medical care. Black women may love their children but may not feel equipped to continue to be the primary caregiver (Nelson, 2011). They may find it difficult to create personal boundaries and express complex beliefs without erecting walls that could disconnect a family (Tsuruta, 2012). Therapists can help Black mothers name their thoughts and feelings and dissect them without self-judgment and with self-compassion. Therapists might coach women to share their feelings with trusted family members without appearing disrespectful, unreliable, and uncaring (Querusio, 2015).

Fourth, Black women may have conflicted thoughts and feelings about how they were mothered or parented. Black women can come into adulthood with psychosocial and emotional wounds related to how people took care of them. These old hurts can connect to how Black women understand their current caregiving roles. Showing radical empathy for their clients' developmental experiences, therapists can help Black women explore the impact of their care. Black women often carry scars and traumas from receiving and providing care (SmithBattle, 2018). Many of their concerns may be rooted in the past. Their maladaptive behaviors and coping may be heavily internalized, requiring a specific kind of intervention. Therapists can help women to grieve and make peace with these painful legacies. Numerous anxieties, fears, and traumas from the past interrupt Black women's joys and caregiving rewards in the present. Therapists should prepare to support Black women to honor and explore a sense of dissonance and resentment, but not inappropriately, as a necessary step in recovery.

See Chapter 3 for further exploration of Black women's girlhood.

10.3   Black Women as Caregivers in Families

While Black *mothering* focused primary on the needs of children, *caregiving* is an expanded role that goes well beyond children to the needs of many others. Therapists should be alert to the range of tasks women accomplish and the worries and anxieties that arise. Black women may be fully supported in caregiving tasks, sharing responsibilities with other adults such as husbands or partners in a household. Caregiving tasks may splay across homes, such as providing shelter and food while an aunt in another home takes on education responsibilities. Black women may be the sole caregiver in a household. Such arrangements explain women's fatigue, and stress increases the potential for health and mental health incidents (Kendall-Tackett, 2001). What exacerbates the emotional strain on Black women is the vast amount of caregiving work (Nichols et al., 2015). Women do multiple daily tasks in providing care for biological family members and close and extended kin, neighbors, and friends or colleagues that need support. Women may struggle with internal pressure to "step up" to help people going through a crisis. Therapists' emphasis on the joys and the burdens and anxieties of normative and non-normative caregiving is essential to help women manage role demands and personal needs. In this section, we discuss some areas in which Black women can experience caregiving pride and anxiety.

10.3.1 Supporting Children's Education

Supporting Black children's education takes a village of collaborators. A Black female caregiver is often at the center of such networks. Educational caregiving includes working with school choices or a lack of them, supervising daily homework, working with teachers or administrators regarding children's progress, seeking funding for private schools, monitoring online school (e.g., during the COVID-19 pandemic), managing tutoring experiences for a struggling child, guiding college and financial aid applications, providing moral and spiritual education, and promoting the children's developmental assets (Dilworth-Anderson et al., 2005).

Despite the heroic contributions of Black women in supporting their children's education, data suggest that many Black children, especially those born to single mothers and low-income families, trail behind their White, Asian, and lately even Latinx peers (Ayodeji et al., 2021; Bowman et al., 2018). In addition to lower academic performance, Black children have higher referral rates for discipline concerns in school, which reflects the discrimination Black children experience in schools (Ayodeji et al., 2021). The educational system avoids structural-level changes that will address these discrepancies, often placing the responsibility back on the caregiver (Farkas, 2003).

10.3.2 Providing Shelter and Homemaking

Black women proudly tout their capacity to care for their households, including shopping, cooking, cleaning, creating attractive spaces, entertaining, and so forth. Every day, women perform tasks that can contribute to an efficient home, leaving them with both a sense of accomplishment and fatigue

(Nichols et al., 2015). A frequent complaint from women in general, including Black women, is the sheer number of tasks each week. Women may be working inside and outside the home and with scant support even when others are present. The Strong Black Woman persona (Beauboeuf-Lafontant, 2009) discussed in Chapter 8 is one factor that can drive Black women to overachieve as heads of households. Compounded with women's experience of stress, these expectations may lead them to self-silence and internalize a sense of invincibility. Black women may internalize the Strong Black Woman persona as a form of coping with the burdens of household management; because they care about their children and their family's perceptions, they take on home and family obligations without complaint. When women feel overburdened, stressed, and anxious about jarring situations, they hide these emotions or ignore them. They often do not allow themselves to express vulnerability or ask for help (Beauboeuf-Lafontant, 2009).

Chapter 8 details how women may adopt the Strong Black Woman lifestyle, leading to chronic stress that affects their health and mental health.

Black women may encounter a "you owe me" stance from extended family members with demands to open their households to care for others. If they were a teen mother, they may have experienced relative foster care or family support, with others assisting them with child-rearing responsibilities, household chores, and more. When they have their own homes, family members may suggest a need for payback: "You owe me for helping to take care of you when you were younger." Black women may feel pressure to honor such requests, despite not having the resources to support them (Woods-Giscombé, 2010). Some women may have just entered a phase of attending to their own needs or may themselves be living in arrangements supported by others. Women may just be making progress after dropping out of high school or forging their way in life with the help of government and community resources. Feeling guilty or needing to pay back, a Black woman may allow family members or family friends to move in. A few weeks progresses into months of temporary or permanent housing (Pashos & McBurney, 2008). If that person does not have a job, the Black woman now provides meals and other "necessities" for her "tenant." We raise this as an example of the unique internal conflicts that Black women face. Without an adequate understanding of cultural and family loyalties, therapists may be quick to solve problems or suggest solutions for women who choose to self-silence in the face of these expectations. We encourage appreciation for the internal value conflicts that women may feel about caring for others while caring for themselves.

10.3.3   Giving Health-Related Care to Others

Caring for others' health needs is another category of caregiving that places a heavy burden on Black women. As a racial group, Black people are over-represented among people with debilitating conditions such as high blood pressure, diabetes, asthma, and strokes (Braithwaite et al., 2009). For partners and others in the home, a Black woman's responsibilities may include scheduling and keeping medical appointments, providing or arranging transportation, and visiting sick and needy people in their families and communities. This role becomes exacerbated for Black women when the family member has a disability (Mendenhall, 2018). Black male privilege in families may also compound such situations. In families, although multiple people can help with the care of loved ones with a chronic and extended illness, a Black woman is tasked with primary responsibilities, with few stepping up to provide support. The Black woman herself may not request help, although the burden of health caregiving and the care of children and households is enormous.

10.3.4   Conducting Financial Oversight

Black women are often the primary wage earners in families (Landry, 2002). Some of their many responsibilities include working multiple jobs to provide for one or more households; applying for and maintaining Social Security benefits, Medicaid, or pension payments; paying bills; and providing supplemental financial support for other family members. Some situations can be complex. For instance, Black women are the most significant percentage of bail payers in the United States, with the cash bail system being a multimillion-dollar industry that primarily impacts Black women (Rabuy & Kopf, 2016). Even though Black men outnumber Black women in the carceral system, Black women financially cover bail bonds. This action can lead to women's financial detriment, including the use of their house and savings accounts as security for the bond.

10.3.5   Offering Psychosocial Support

Family members in crisis due to substance abuse and chemical dependence or intimate partner violence in relationships often reach out to their closest Black woman family member for recovery support. Attending court cases is emotionally taxing for Black women (Cavanagh & Cauffman, 2015); they usually accompany the youth or even an adult family member to the courthouse. Living in dangerous neighborhoods is also a source of stress for Black women, who traverse areas characterized by crime (Gutman et al., 2005). With lesbian, gay, bisexual, transgender, and/or queer (LGBTQ) family members, Black women take on active roles in supporting them, such as learning about their loved one's identity or providing support to a trans person in the family who is seeking gender-affirming medical care. Black women have also strived to maintain family connections when grandparents or loved ones rebuff a gender-fluid child. For example, Black women might step in to mediate when grandparents wish to cut off a nonbinary grandchild. Black women also serve as role models of acceptance for younger cousins and family members (Carruthers, 2018). As discussed earlier in this chapter, single-parent homes additionally create a large set of psychosocial support responsibilities for Black women, from taking on traditional father roles to finding safe male role models for their children in place of fathers (Taylor & Conger, 2017).

10.3.6   Providing Caregiving in the Community

The extent to which Black women internalize the caretaker role shows in Black women's caregiving at the community level locally and nationally. Black women are highly likely to participate in transformative justice and efforts to address social inequalities especially at the local level (Morgan, 2018). Many engage in efforts to provide food, shelter, and social support for those on the streets, in prison, in shelters, and in families. Many Black women's outreach activities are connected to their faith communities, their political organizations, or sororities. Many can feel urgency to become advocates for social change, and while Black women bring enormous talent in community organization and philanthropy, such work adds to their caregiving burden (Dumais, 2020). For instance, the prison abolition movement was started by Black women who were incarcerated after protecting their children and themselves from abusers.

10.4   Black Women's Caregiving: Therapy Themes

In addition to the challenges they navigate in caregiving, Black women also find much beauty, strength, and resilience emerging from these roles. Therapists should recognize and celebrate Black women's caregiver resilience. While caregivers' expectations are numerous and the lifestyle can be exhausting, there are positives to celebrate.

First is the support provided to family and kinfolk. Orienting to caregiving in this way acknowledges that Black women participate in the community's development in a positive way. If the care recipient is a senior person, this supports the value of respecting elders, which is an important principle across the Black diaspora. The second aspect of caregiving to celebrate is Black women's role in curating family traditions and history for younger generations.

This connection of past and future occurs through natural engagement between the older and younger generation or formal documentation of the family's current life and history, given the technological resources available (e.g., cell phone, tablet, laptop). Third, Black women receive affirmation and can take pride in how much their families depend on them (e.g., cooking; arranging outings or family reunions). Black women experience periods of pleasure and happiness in caregiving, which can enhance their sense of self-gratification. They feel good contributing to the physical health and psychological well-being of those they love (Boyd-Franklin, 1989).

At the same time, however, many Black women and girls are socialized to believe they have little choice in fulfilling caregiving roles. This lack of choice is fueled by a sense of disempowerment rooted in cultural and family traditions pervasive in Black communities. As mentioned earlier, Black women may also agree to caregiving requests (e.g., taking a child or adult into their homes) to reciprocate the support they received in the past. A Black woman's choice to do this may rest on the belief that "she knew one day it would be expected" and that she must "pay up." As they get older, some Black women may resent these expectations and the internalization of cultural norms and values (Beauboeuf-Lafontant, 2009; Whitley et al., 2001). Therapists should understand Black women's anger and resentment in the caregiving role performance, which can be overt or covert. Therapists should encourage their Black female clients to express their thoughts and feelings to externalize and deconstruct them. A therapy goal might be to help the client reconcile cultural loyalties with present capacities. The key to working along these lines is to help women balance family and self-needs (Nelson, 2011).

In addition, Black women may internalize cultural norms that they are responsible for family members: nuclear, extended, or non-kin. For some women, displaying loyalty through caregiving is an honor, while other women may feel obligated to care for family members who abused or neglected them (Erickson & Egeland, 2002). Women may feel pressured to ignore the painful traumas of childhood and adolescence and honor the value of looking out for family members and the community, even to the detriment of their individual needs. These dynamics may drive internal conflicts and angst in women who experience pressures to "let go of the past" or ignore unhealed wounds. Black women may be unable to reject the prescribed role of caretaker even in fractured intimate relationships or dysfunctional family dynamics.

Traumas of childhood and adolescence are discussed in Chapter 3.

10.5   Strategic Therapy Interventions

Therapists must view Black women's mothering and caregiving through a lens of cultural humility and competence. Therapists who are not of a similar race or ethnicity to their Black female clients should honor the client's racial and cultural traditions unless the client agrees to engage in questioning. Be careful about confronting clients about their story, whatever narratives are shared. Therapists can research and seek professional input from peers of their clients' same race/ethnicity for clarification or more evidence. We encourage therapists to be mindful of the tension many Black women feel between taking on the honored role of being a mother or caregiver and the burdens they experience in these roles. Therapists should guide clients to explore and articulate their thoughts and feelings about these roles and support them in making empowered choices related to giving care while also maintaining boundaries.

See Chapter 6 for more on cultural self-awareness.

Therapists should also be aware that gendered-racism and colorism in the Black community can also affect Black women and may have influenced the care they received and the care they currently give. Black women themselves may show internalized colorism by favoring lighter-skinned children over darker ones. In addition, women may experience microaggressions by having people ask if their children with skin color variations are from the same father. Intracommunity and intrafamily pressure can be just as painful and impactful. Black women's experiences of oppression from any source will touch every aspect of identity and role, including caregiving.

The therapy interventions detailed in this section are interdependent; the impact of one will strengthen others. Therapists should coach Black female caregivers in setting boundaries, developing new ways of communicating that promote their self-interests, and establishing self-care routines. The therapist can help Black women reframe these skills as critical for maintaining appropriate familial relationships and boundaries and promoting conviviality among family, especially at family gatherings (Robinson, 2014; Taylor & Conger, 2017). When Black women prioritize and address their own needs, it can shift the relationships to improve caregiving efficacy.

10.5.1   Clarify Caregiving Demands

Therapists must understand the maternal and caregiving arrangements of Black women, and constructing a multigenerational genogram can help with this understanding. Black women's caregiving roles and responsibilities increase their stress (Braithwaite et al., 2009; Fernandez Collins, 2019). Creating Black women's genograms can reveal the nature of their family structure and relationships, including caregiving roles and responsibilities that drive fatigue. Therapists can use the genogram to grasp clients' socialization and developmental experiences, such as their experience as caregivers during girlhood and the residual impacts of such burdens in their present lives. Genogram information can be helpful in illuminating mothering and caregiver identities in the present (Boyd-Franklin, 1989).

10.5.2 Show Radical Empathy

Radical empathy addresses the power dynamics in the relationship. It refers to a therapist's posture of actively striving to understand clients' feelings and experiences (Fernandez Collins, 2019). Therapists practicing radical empathy withhold assumptions, operate from an antideficit model, lean into their curiosity, and listen to what is shared as well as what is not shared (Koss-Chioino, 2006). Using radical empathy, therapists can work with Black women to expand their thinking in developing a vision for how they wish to engage in their caregiving roles moving forward and take active steps. This could look like supporting a Black woman in processing her complex mix of emotions related to the ongoing needs of an adult child with significant disabilities. She might feel a sense of love and gratitude for her child and pride related to how she has cared for the child over the years.

10.5.3 Encourage Celebration and Self-Affirmation

Black women make profound contributions to their families, and although some family members acknowledge this, some do not. Black women themselves may not be fully conscious of their sacrifices and influences in family life. Therapy can be a setting in which Black women learn to affirm their identities and capacities (Boyd-Franklin, 1989). Most Black women appreciate compliments for making positive decisions and personal or structural changes when going through a family storm. Therapists can offer praise and reinforce small gains and suggest healthy ways the client can celebrate significant changes. Many people feel entitled to the caregiver's nurturance. They do not even think to be grateful for it, much less express that gratitude. Helping Black women feel comfortable recognizing their contributions will help them reframe caregiving from something they "have to do" to something they can choose to do with love and care.

10.5.4   Employ Empowerment Feminist Therapy Techniques

Empowerment feminist therapy (EFT), highly compatible with Black feminist theory as discussed in Chapter 5, focuses on gender, social location, and power, with the aim of empowerment and social transformation (Schwarz, 2017). A technique developed by feminists and used often in feminist therapy is cultural analysis, which includes gender-role analysis and power analysis. Gender-role analysis involves working with Black women to (a) identify the messages they have internalized about gender and related roles about caregiving; (b) examine the impact of those gendered messages and beliefs on their emotions, cognitions, and behaviors; (c) help clients consciously decide which gendered internal messages about caregiving they want to keep and which messages they want to discard; and (d) make a plan for shifts and adjustments in their relationships with family members to balance self and family needs (Schwarz, 2017). EFT techniques include assertiveness training, advocacy, group work, and bibliotherapy to manage caregiving responsibilities. Often, Black women self-silence and do not challenge the status quo. In EFT, Black women can learn assertive communication skills. Assertiveness training involves psychoeducation around the differences between assertive, aggressive, and passive behaviors. In therapy, coaching Black women in functional and concrete skills to manage conflicts and set boundaries can help them to translate such skills to their situations at home (Schwarz, 2017).

10.5.5   Increase Network Support

Most Black women have natural network support systems that they may use for caregiving support. Such support can come through "sister circles," social groups in which women seek support and mutual aid. Even in families with an only child or a small number of siblings, Black communities flourish through a range of fictive kin relationships. Whether blood-folk, kinfolk, church-folk, or even next-door neighbors, in general, Black people as an ethnic group rally around each other in crisis and occasionally even for the long haul (Chatters et al., 1994; Jones & Hodges, 2002). Those in a Black woman's network support system can provide before- or after-school care, cook and deliver a meal during the day, or provide transportation to a doctor's appointment. Some neighbors might sit with a friend during cancer treatment or visit a new teenage mother. Supports can also include Meals on Wheels, Boys & Girls Clubs, free financial planning services, and more. As mentioned earlier, even colleagues in the workplace occasionally volunteer to perform caregiver tasks, thereby providing emotional and sometimes financial relief. Therefore, helping Black women to identify and utilize their network support systems is crucial, especially for those who have difficulty asking for help.

See Chapters 5 and 14 for more on sister circles as a source of support.

Some Black women argue that they do not have a network support system, but they can learn to develop them (Jones & Hodges, 2002). Studies show that individuals with a greater diversity of relationships and involvement in a wide range of social activities have healthier and longer lives than those who lack such support. Therapists can help Black women strengthen their support networks by discovering their passions, interests, and hobbies (using discussion or inventories). Once Black women identify activities or experiences that hold their interest, therapists can help them target social or community groups or activities consistent with their interests and culture.

10.5.6   Promote Caregiving Stress Management

Research shows that Black people as a group experience adverse outcomes from chronic stress, such as high cortisol levels associated with mood disorders, persistent inflammation, and a range of health problems (Sahakian et al., 2020). Additionally, from childhood, Black women face institutionalized biases, inequities in the educational system, colorism, relational ambiguity, domestic/sexual violence, low-paying jobs, and systemic racism, all of which add to the ongoing stress of caregiving. The ability to regulate emotions and self-soothe enhances decision-making skills and reduces the fight/flight/freeze/fawn response. Black women can learn numerous activities to decrease or increase stress arousal to address their individual responses to stress. They can practice these skills with feedback in therapy sessions.

Chapter 13, on physical health and wellness, further examines the negative impacts of stress, including a decline in general well-being, physical health, and decision-making skills.

One powerful resource for Black women may be their spiritual and religious foundation, which anchors their caregiving values. Many Black women believe in a higher power, often God or Jesus, and find solace and inspiration for life's difficult times in spiritual disciplines such as prayer, sacred literature, and worship (Reed & Neville, 2014). Therapists' lack of acknowledgment of Black women's spiritual identity will serve as a barrier in the therapy relationship (Tan & Johnson, 2005). Also, when making the tough decisions of life, Black women often feel comforted and reassured by the belief that their labor honors their deity and will be rewarded in this life and the next.

We encourage therapists to understand women's spiritual and religious frameworks and entertain women's spiritual and clergy support (Reid & Neville, 2014). Therapists might also support women to find inspiration to connect their caregiving values and ideals to religious and spiritual thought. Women might also seek the help of religious communities for encouragement and instrumental support.

See Chapter 15 for more on religion and spirituality in Black women's lives.

10.5.7   Focus on Acceptance and Small Changes

Black women's influence, roles, responsibilities, and tasks as mothers and caregivers are incredibly complex, and their client narratives may contain multiple themes and angles that therapists must grasp. In our practices, we have used creative strategies that women find acceptable in tweaking their caregiving burden, including taking *sabbaticals*, agreeing for a period to refrain from accepting new responsibilities. This strategy is beneficial for women doing intensive caregiving in community or religious organizations. Another approach is activating *cheerleaders*, including other family members or arrangements that might lighten a caregiving task. Women can also take *caregiving vacations*, such as giving up hosting events, doing less cooking, and letting families enjoy leftovers. Involving older children in load sharing such as meal preparation or laundry also helps. These small changes can help women reduce stress and manage their caregiving roles in ways that seem acceptable to them.

Case Example

Damita, a 40-year-old woman sought therapy on her supervisor's advice. The supervisor had supported Damita for several years and knew her family situation. The supervisor believed that Damita needed professional help to sort out feelings of being burdened. Damita was in remission from breast cancer. The supervisor was concerned about a recurrence of this condition because of stress. Damita lived in an apartment with her teenage sons and held a stable but demanding job.

In constructing a genogram with Damita, the therapist understood that her immediate family system did not live in one residence but spanned two households within a mile of each other. Apart from her household responsibilities and job,

(*cont.*)

Damita provided care for her disabled mother, whose home she visited every day before and after work. She described the relationship with her mother as respectful but not particularly close. While her mother was always present in her life, Damita was raised primarily by an older sibling. Damita was dating a man who did not live at her residence but spent time frequently at her home. This partner helped with some responsibilities, but they were on a "break" at the time of therapy.

Damita described a very dense weekday caregiving schedule, including predawn trips to her mother's house to prepare her for the day. She then traveled back home to get her sons off to school before making her way to work. Afternoons involved going back to her mother's home. She also picked up groceries, did other shopping, prepared dinner, and supervised homework. Most nights, Damita fell asleep on her couch in front of the TV. This daily routine was becoming harder to manage. Saturdays involved the same care of her mother as the weekdays. Around midmorning, she took her sons to basketball and other sporting activities. Damita also spent time with her partner at her home or his before their breakup.

Two other anxieties made her feel unrested. Her father, with whom she shared a cordial relationship, was evicted from his apartment and asked to temporarily stay with her until he was back on his feet. Also, one of her sons got into a fight at school, which the school alerted her could spill into the community. They recommended that she caution her son to tone things down. They advised her to monitor him closely in case other fighting occurred. The school incident triggered Damita's long-term anxiety about raising her teenage sons close to a neighborhood known for gang violence, and she wanted to move to a safer community. In addition to the daily grind of caregiving, Damita felt discouraged and powerless thinking of her sons' safety. She started strongly considering moving to a far suburb; her mother became panicked and anxious when Damita told her of this plan.

The therapist viewed Damita as overwhelmed by caregiving responsibilities for her children and household, parents, and other family members. The therapist also noted that Damita had trouble defining what boundaries to set. She rarely turned down a request for her help. Her days from early morning until early evening were filled with "work," but giving up anything seemed impossible. The therapist recognized that Damita could benefit from a plan to balance the need to honor her loyalties to her mother and children while also finding time to rest and refresh her own life. The therapist began the conversation by having Damita create a log of her daily routines. Damita agreed that she was overworked. Transitions between households and from home to work, in addition to navigating the commute to work, left her feeling stressed about being tardy. Morning and evening routines seemed most burdensome, and the therapist invited deeper conversations on them.

(*cont.*)

Before discussing changes, the therapist sought to understand and clarify Damita's principles and values around supporting her parents. Damita's desire to honor her parents by caring for their needs was strong, yet conflicted. Often, she said yes to their requests automatically, without considering what it meant for her own life. Her commitment to her mother was far more substantial than her sense of obligation to her father. The therapist focused first on her relationship with her father with the idea of helping Damita to balance honoring boundaries. Damita was open to following two suggestions. The first was to gather detailed information from her father about his situation before deciding to offer him a place to stay. The second was to consult her siblings about the best way to support her father before offering help. These conversations yielded a solution. Rather than sheltering her father in her household, Damita and her siblings helped her father arrange to stay temporarily in his sister's basement space. The siblings also covered the cost of storing belongings in a nearby storage facility. Her father was welcome to stop by Damita's for Sunday meals.

Damita's caregiving for her mother was where she carried the most significant burden. The therapist realized that Damita felt bound to her mother by an invisible yet unexamined loyalty. Her mother had been a substantial source of encouragement for Damita during her 3-month cancer recovery period. Although her mother could not help physically, she called Damita daily with words of encouragement and inspiration. During these conversations, her mother asked that Damita not abandon her in illness. Damita felt bound by this pledge and felt that she had no choice but to support her mother, whose disability persisted. The therapist felt this bind was untouchable, but naming it offered some solutions. The therapist worked with Damita to find a way to attend to her mother's household and her own to lower the daily stress burden. Damita investigated and helped her mother to apply for a state-supported home health aide. Damita found a cousin willing to take on the responsibility of her mother's daily routines, receiving weekly payment from the state. Once it unfolded, this arrangement freed Damita from the daily morning and evening routines. Her mother was very disappointed, and Damita validated those feelings, although they triggered her guilt. But with the therapist's encouragement, Damita did not call off the arrangement. Damita visited her mother at least twice weekly and talked with her on the phone daily. With more support for daily routines, Damita felt considerably less stressed and found evenings and weekends a bit less hectic. She also got to work early enough to leave before the daily rush hour. The anxiety she felt about her son's well-being abated slightly. She committed to examining the possibility of moving to another neighborhood but lived in the same place when therapy terminated.

10.6   Conclusion

A takeaway from Damita's case is that Black women often face complex mothering and caregiving arrangements, balancing multiple values and commitments to family members and themselves. Extricating themselves from these arrangements may not be a top priority for women. Therapists should exercise caution in offering ideas and suggestions of what women must or should do in caregiving arrangements that they insist must remain untouched. Apart from the complete abandonment of an agreement, the therapist can work for small wins. Coach and collaborate with the client to identify periods of respite, rest, and self-care. Work collaboratively with women to design adjustments that help them live according to their values while protecting their self-interests and representing their needs and desires.

A culturally informed and collaborative framework avoids a one-size-fits-all approach to helping women manage caregiving roles. Primarily, therapy experiences can help Black women feel empowered to ask for what they need and set boundaries in caregiver roles and responsibilities. Therapists can help clients focus on small changes and creative strategies to prioritize their well-being within their caregiving roles. Therapy also supports women to address the guilt of saying no while affirming their right to prioritize rest and self-compassion. Even a 25% reduction in caregiving demands and stress can leave Black women feeling less stressed. Often, for the Black woman at the center of family life in the United States, small wins in self-care is as good as it gets, and that can be enough.

Therapist Reflection Questions

1. What caregiving roles and responsibilities do you take on in your own family?
2. What caregiver burdens might Black women have in common with women of other racial and ethnic groups?
3. What aspects of Black women's caregiving as discussed in this chapter are surprising to you?
4. What are your responses to the anxieties and fears in Black mothers concerning their children's safety with regard to law enforcement and the legal system?
5. What experience do you have working with caregiving themes in Black clients?
6. What are two or three strategies you might use after reading this chapter?

Resources

Articles

Johnston, D. D., & Swanson, D. H. (2003). Invisible mothers: A content analysis of motherhood ideologies and myths in magazines. *Sex Roles, 49*(1), 21–33.

Nichols, T. R., Gringle, M. R., & Pulliam, R. M. (2015). "You have to put your children's needs first or you're really not a good mother": Black motherhood and self-care practices. *Women, Gender, and Families of Color, 3*(2), 165–189.

Organizations

Black Emotional and Mental Health Collective. (n.d.). https://www.beam.community/

Books

Dow, D. M. (2019). *Mothering while black: The boundaries and burdens of middleclass parenthood.* University of California Press.

McClain, D. (2019). *We live for the we: The political power of black motherhood.* Bold Type Books.

Podcasts

Bradford, J. H. (Executive Producer). (2020, August 5). The importance of self compassion (167) [Audio podcast episode]. In *Therapy for black girls.* iHeartRadio. https://therapyforblackgirls.com/2020/08/05/session-167-the-importance-of-self-compassion/

Films

Lewis, S. P. (Director). (2021). *In our mothers' gardens* [Film]. House of the Seven Sisters, Netflix.

Tillman, G., Jr. (Director). (1997). *Soul food* [Film]. Twentieth Century-Fox.

Media Resources

Nettles, A. & Eng, M. (Executive Producers). (2019, August 27) *Having "the talk": Expert guidance on preparing kids for police interactions* [Radio broadcast]. NPR: WBEZ Chicago. https://www.npr.org/local/309/2019/08/27/754459083/having-the-talk-expert-guidance-on-preparing-kids-for-police-interactions

Successful Black Parenting Magazine. (n.d.). https://successfulblackparenting.com/

References

Assini-Meytin, L. C., & Green, K. M. (2015). Long-term consequences of adolescent parenthood among African-American urban youth: A propensity score matching approach. *Journal of Adolescent Health, 56*(5), 529–535. https://doi.org/10.1016/j .jadohealth.2015.01.005

Ayodeji, E., Dubicka, B., Abuah, O., Odebiyi, B., Sultana, R., & Ani, C. (2021). Editorial perspective: Mental health needs of children and young people of Black ethnicity. Is it time to reconceptualise racism as a traumatic experience? *Child and Adolescent Mental Health, 26*(3), 265–266.

Barnes, S. L. (2001). Stressors and strengths: A theoretical and practical examination of nuclear, single-parent, and augmented African American families. *Families in Society, 82*(5), 449–460.

Beauboeuf-Lafontant, T. (2009). *Behind the mask of the strong Black woman: Voice and the embodiment of a costly performance*. Temple University Press.

Bezusko, A., (2013). Criminalizing Black motherhood: How the war on welfare was won. *Souls (Boulder, Colo.), 15*(1–2), 39–55. https://doi.org/10.1080/10999949 .2013.803813

Bowman, B. T., Comer, J. P., & Johns, D. J. (2018). Addressing the African American achievement gap: Three leading educators issue a call to action. *Young Children, 73*(2), 14–23.

Boyd-Franklin, N. (1989). *Black families in therapy: A multisystems approach*. Guilford Press.

Braithwaite, R. L., Taylor, S. E., & Treadwell, H. M. (Eds.). (2009). *Health issues in the Black community*. John Wiley & Sons.

Carruthers, C. (2018). *Unapologetic: A Black, queer, and feminist mandate for radical movements*. Beacon Press.

Cavanagh, C., & Cauffman, E. (2015). Viewing law and order: Mothers' and sons' justice system legitimacy attitudes and juvenile recidivism. *Psychology, Public Policy, and Law, 21*(4), 432–441.

Chatters, L. M., Taylor, R. J., & Jayakody, R. (1994). Fictive kinship relations in Black extended families. *Journal of Comparative Family Studies, 25*(3), 297–312.

Collins, P. H. (2005). The meaning of motherhood in Black culture and Black mother-daughter relationships. In M. B. Zinn, P. Hondagneu-Sotelo, & M. A. Messner (Eds.), *Gender through the prism of difference* (3rd ed., pp. 285–295). Oxford University Press.

Dilworth-Anderson, P., Brummett, B. H., Goodwin, P., Williams, S. W., Williams, R. B., & Siegler, I. C. (2005). Effect of race on cultural justifications for caregiving. *The Journals of Gerontology Series B: Psychological Sciences and Social Sciences, 60*(5), S257–S262.

Dumais, E. (2020, July 14). *How to balance activism and self-care, according to a wellness coach*. Refinery29. https://www.refinery29.com/en-us/activism-burnout-self-care

Elliott, S., Powell, R., & Brenton, J. (2015). Being a good mom: Low-income, Black single mothers negotiate intensive mothering. *Journal of Family Issues, 36*(3), 351–370. https://doi.org/10.1177/0192513X13490279

Elliott, S., & Reid, M. (2019). Low-income black mothers parenting adolescents in the mass incarceration era: The long reach of criminalization. *American Sociological Review, 84*(2), 197–219.

Erickson, M. F., & Egeland, B. (2002). Child neglect. In J. E. B. Myers, L. Berliner, J. Briere, C. T. Hendrix, C. Jenny, & T. A. Reid (Eds.), *The APSAC handbook on child maltreatment* (pp. 3–20). Sage Publications.

Farkas, G. (2003). Racial disparities and discrimination in education: What do we know, how do we know it, and what do we need to know? *Teachers College Record, 105*(6), 1119–1146.

Fernandez Collins, E. (2019, March 11). *How can we practice radical empathy and self-care?* https://elenafernandezcollins.com/2019/03/11/how-can-we-practice-radical-empathy-and-self-care

Flick, L. (1997). Boyz II Men: A Song for Mama [Review of Boyz II Men: A Song for Mama]. *Billboard, 105*(45), 76. Prometheus Global Media.

Forte, A., Agosto, D., Dickard, M., & Magee, R. (2016, November). The strength of awkward ties: Online interactions between high school students and adults. In S. Lukosch (Ed.), *Proceedings of the 19th International Conference on Supporting Group Work* (pp. 375–383). Association for Computing Machinery.

Goodman, C., & Silverstein, M. (2002). Grandmothers raising grandchildren: Family structure and wellbeing in culturally diverse families. *The Gerontologist, 42*(5), 676–689.

Gutman, L. M., McLoyd, V. C., & Tokoyawa, T. (2005). Financial strain, neighborhood stress, parenting behaviors, and adolescent adjustment in urban African American families. *Journal of Research on Adolescence, 15*(4), 425–449.

Harris-Perry, M. V. (2011). *Sister citizen: Shame, stereotypes, and Black women in America.* Yale University Press.

Hill, P. C. (1987). *The meaning of motherhood in Black culture and Black mother/daughter relationships.* Sage, 4(2), 3–10.

Johnston, D. D., & Swanson, D. H. (2003). Invisible mothers: A content analysis of motherhood ideologies and myths in magazines. *Sex Roles, 49*(1), 21–33.

Jones, L. V., & Hodges, V. G. (2002). Enhancing psychosocial competence among Black women: A psycho-educational group model approach. *Social Work with Groups, 24*(3–4), 33–52.

Kan, M. L., & Ramirez, D. D. (2020). Preventing subsequent teenage pregnancy: A multisite analysis of goal orientation and social supports. *Children & Schools, 42*(4), 225–235.

Kendall-Tackett, K. A. (2001). *The hidden feelings of motherhood: Coping with stress, depression, and burnout.* New Harbinger Publications.

Koss-Chioino, J. D. (2006). Spiritual transformation, relation and radical empathy: core components of the ritual healing process. *Transcultural Psychiatry, 43*(4), 652–670.

Landry, B. (2002). *Black working wives: Pioneers of the American family revolution.* University of California Press.

Leadbeater, B. J. R., & Way, N. (Eds.). (2007). *Urban girls revisited: Building strengths.* New York University Press.

Losada, A., Márquez-González, M., Peñacoba, C., & Romero-Moreno, R. (2010). Development and validation of the Caregiver Guilt Questionnaire. *International Psychogeriatrics, 22*(4), 650–660.

Mendenhall, R. (2018). The medicalization of poverty in the lives of low-income Black mothers and children. *The Journal of Law, Medicine & Ethics, 46*(3), 644–650.

Morgan, D. F. (2018). Visible black motherhood is a revolution. *Biography, 41*(4), 856–875. https://doi.org/10.1353/bio.2018.0082

Murray, L. (2010). Secrets of an "illegitimate mom." *Journal of the Motherhood Initiative for Research and Community Involvement, 1*(2).

Neal-Barnett, A., Stadulis, R., Murray, M., Payne, M. R., Thomas, A., & Salley, B. B. (2011). Sister circles as a culturally relevant intervention for anxious Black women. *Clinical Psychology: Science and Practice, 18*(3), 266–273.

Nelson, S. (2011). *Black woman redefined: dispelling myths and discovering fulfillment in the age of Michelle Obama.* BenBella Books.

Nichols, T. R., Gringle, M. R., & Pulliam, R. M. (2015). "You have to put your children's needs first or you're really not a good mother": Black motherhood and self-care practices. *Women, Gender, and Families of Color, 3*(2), 165–189.

O'Neal, L. (2020, May 30). *George Floyd's mother was not there, but he used her as a sacred invocation.* National Geographic. https://www.nationalgeographic.com/history/article/george-floyds-mother-not-there-he-used-her-as-sacred-invocation

Parks, S. (2010). *Fierce angels: The strong black woman in American life and culture.* One World/Ballantine Books.

Paschal, A. M., Lewis-Moss, R. K., & Hsiao, T. (2011). Perceived fatherhood roles and parenting behaviors among African American teen fathers. *Journal of Adolescent Research, 26*(1), 61–83.

Pashos, A., & McBurney, D. H. (2008). Kin relationships and the caregiving biases of grandparents, aunts, and uncles. *Human Nature, 19*(3), 311–330.

Querusio, D. (2015). From Mammy to Mommy: Michelle Obama and the reclamation of Black motherhood. *Elements, 11*(1).

Rabuy, B., & Kopf, D. (2016). *Detaining the poor: How money bail perpetuates an endless cycle of poverty and jail time.* Prison Policy Initiative.

Reed, T. D., & Neville, H. A. (2014). The influence of religiosity and spirituality on psychological wellbeing among Black women. *Journal of Black Psychology, 40* (4), 384–401.

Robinson, R. L. (2014). Seen but not recognized: Black caregivers, childhood cruelties, and social dislocations in an increasingly colored America. *West Virginia Law Review, 117*, 1273.

Rosenthal, L. & Lobel, M. (2016). Stereotypes of Black American women related to sexuality and motherhood. *Psychology of Women Quarterly, 40*(3), 414–427.

Sahakian, B. J., Langley, C., & Kaser, M. (2020, March 11). *How chronic stress changes the brain – and what you can do to reverse the damage.* The Conversation. https://theconversation.com/how-chronic-stress-changes-the-brain-and-what-you-can-do-to-reverse-the-damage-133194

Schwarz, J. (2017). *Introduction to empowerment feminist therapy: Counseling women across the life span: empowerment, advocacy, and intervention.* Springer Publishing Company.

SmithBattle, L. (2018). The past is prologue? The long arc of childhood trauma in a multigenerational study of teen mothering. *Social Science & Medicine, 216*, 1–9.

Tan, S.-Y., & Johnson, W. B. (2005). Spiritually oriented cognitive-behavioral therapy. In L. Sperry & E. P. Shafranske (Eds.), *Spiritually oriented psychotherapy* (pp. 77–103). American Psychological Association.

Taylor, Z. E., & Conger, R. D. (2017). Promoting strengths and resilience in single-mother families. *Child Development, 88*(2), 350–358.

Tillman, G., Jr. (Director). (1997). *Soul food* [Film]. Twentieth Century-Fox.

Tsuruta, D. R. (2012). The womanish roots of womanism: A culturally-derived and African-centered ideal (concept). *Western Journal of Black Studies, 36*(1), 3–10.

Vanzant, I. (1999). *Yesterday, I cried: Celebrating the lessons of living and loving.* Simon and Schuster.

Wane, N. N. (2000). Reflections on the mutuality of mothering: Women, children, and othermothering. *Journal of the Motherhood Initiative for Research and Community Involvement, 2*(2). https://jarm.journals.yorku.ca/index.php/jarm/article/view/2143

West, K. (2000). Hey Mama! [Song]. On *Late registration* [Album]. Roc-A-Fella.

Whitley, D. M., Kelley, S. J., & Sipe, T. A. (2001). Grandmothers raising grandchildren: Are they at increased risk of health problems? *Health & Social Work, 26*(2), 105–114.

Woods-Giscombé, C. L. (2010). Superwoman schema: African American women's views on stress, strength, and health. *Qualitative Health Research, 20*(5), 668–683.

11 Black Women's Romantic and Intimate Relationships

In romance and intimacy, our Black female clients tell us they want what most women want. Romance refers to longings, connectedness, and desires toward a partner. Intimacy centers on closeness, openness to disclosures and feedback, and psychological chemistry expressed verbally and physically (Acevedo & Aron, 2009; Sternberg, 1987). Our therapy experiences show that Black women want to date successfully and to have partners committed to them. They want to be loved and cherished by their significant others. Black women want to be respected and honored for their relationship contributions. Most want stable and permanent unions, that is, marriage or long-term cohabitation. Most Black women want children, ownership of their bodies and their sex lives, and influence with partners. Black women long to be a cornerstone of Black families and advance Black culture in the United States. Over many years, these are the narratives of Black women with whom we have worked in therapy, individually, or as part of a couple.

Strikingly, scholarship on Black women's normative love and intimacy longings and patterns is sparse in the literature that informs mental health practice (Burton & Tucker, 2009). Much of the literature on romantic relationships available to therapists describes White love, intimacy, and coupling quite well. However, Black women's love and intimacy are represented primarily in terms of their vulnerabilities and deficits (Barnes, 2015). We draw on several sources to provide information on core relationship matters around which Black women might seek therapeutic support. In our study of Black women's psychotherapy (described in Chapter 1), 38% of our sample of Black women sought therapy for intimate relationship matters. Thus, therapists are likely to encounter these themes for Black women alone or with their intimate others.

The chapter summarizes themes in Black women's heterosexual and lesbian unions, including gender role dynamics. We also discuss the declining marriage rates and Black women's dating interests and challenges. We examine Black women's sentiments on interracial unions, including Black men's interracial romantic interests. We offer a few perspectives on Black women's sex lives and discuss two challenges, concurrent partnerships and intimate partner violence, that threaten Black women's health and lives. Finally, we recommend strategies to work with Black women and their partners in couples therapy.

11.1   Complexities of Black Women's Unions

The humanities and, specifically, the literary and performing arts offer insights into the dynamics of intimate partnerships of cisgender, heterosexual Black women. We offer a few examples that align well with Black women's therapy narratives. Representations of Black queer women's love and intimacy are sparse in most scholarly sources. We point to some artistic sources that illuminate the dynamics of Black queer love.

In the movie *Love Jones* (Witcher, 1997), a Black woman feels an immediate attraction to a man as creative as herself. The relationship has moments of joy and struggle. The woman wants to commit, but fears and insecurities challenge the couple's love. Staying true to self while loving another often arises in relational therapy with Black women. In *Waiting to Exhale*, the book by Terry McMillan (1992) and movie by McMillan and colleagues (Whitaker, 1995), four Black women friends support each other around their longings and fantasies for love and intimacy. As in our sessions, the characters talk about the complexities of Black love. Themes are waiting and longing to find husbands, infidelity, concurrent partnerships, angst over Black men's attraction to White women, and choosing self and children over romance. Other movies capture the impact of racism and oppression on Black unions. In *Poetic Justice* (Singleton, 1993), a Black woman battles depression after her boyfriend's murder. She meets a man who has also experienced heartache and pain. Violence, loss, and trauma are aspects of the bond that draw the couple together. Black female clients experience similar dynamics in their partnerships. *If Beale Street Could Talk* (Jenkins, 2018), based on James Baldwin's book (1974) by the same name, also shows Black women's tenacity in love relationships amid matters of justice. A Black woman is pregnant with a lover's child and joins his efforts to clear his name in a biased judicial system. Themes of racism, prejudice, and oppression in the movie and book reflect real-life scenarios in therapy. Finally, Tina Turner's song "What's Love Got to Do with It" (1993) and movie by the same name (Gibson, 1993) chronicle the artist's life of success and struggle. Represented in Turner's story are Black women's experiences of childhood abuse and neglect, dominance and maltreatment. Like Turner, Black women struggle for personhood and survival in relationships. Some make relationship choices in their best self-interests, while others do not.

The stories we have mentioned so far center on romance and intimacy in heterosexual Black women's lives. Increasingly, Black gay women's love stories are also showing up in the literary arts and culture. A few sources capture the dynamics of lesbian love. Audre Lorde (1982) tells her life story through a partially autobiographical book. Strongly present in this work is Lorde's search for love and intimacy with women she encounters in different life stages and geographical locations. Lorde tells this story with the backdrop of family values and ruptures, discrimination, personal struggles, and advocacy. Another story that captures the complexities of Black lesbian love and intimacy is *Pariah* (Rees, 2011). In the movie, a college-bound Black girl navigates her lesbian identity within romance, family relationships, and professional and academic pursuits. The young woman faces several complex identity matters that we hear of in therapy.

Our main point in sharing these fictional examples of Black women's love stories is how much they match Black women's true-to-life experiences. Black women experience compounded and simultaneous experiences of inequality based on race, gender, social class, sexuality, disability and more in their pursuit of their romantic and sexual interests. Therapists must expand their understanding of the complexities of Black women's intimate joys and struggles and listen to the core themes in Black women's narratives of heterosexual and queer unions, including gender roles and expression. With examples from our clinical experiences, we provide a background that we hope other therapists will find useful.

11.1.1 Black Women in Heterosexual Marriages

11.1.1.1 Black Marriage Strengths Therapists should be aware of the strengths and resiliencies of Black marriages, which are often overlooked. We summarize these strengths of Black marriages to encourage therapists to amplify and remind Black women or couples of what they do well, to counterbalance distortions of Black coupling. While scant, the empirical literature has identified Black women's roles in the success of such unions (Marks et al., 2008). Black married couples show (a) tenacity to work through complexities that might dissolve other unions, (b) a willingness to adopt flexible roles and responsibilities in family life, (c) load sharing in household arrangements, (d) shared values in advancing Black families and Black culture, and (e) religious compatibility and values (Chaney, 2010; Marks et al., 2008). Black women are creative in managing the power dynamics in relationships and consistent in supporting their husbands to keep their couple unions afloat. Generally, Black married women have more income, fewer economic troubles, increased prestige, and status than Black unmarried women, especially when marriages are at the center of Black family life (Marks et al., 2008). Research also suggests that Black women in married unions, versus Black single women, might experience a greater sense of well-being (Phillips et al.,

2012). In general, Black women of middle or higher socioeconomic status (SES) are likely to marry at higher rates and are more likely to date success-fully than low-income Black women (Chaney, 2010; Gooden & Chambers, 2016; Marks et al., 2008). In the resource list at the end of this chapter, we suggest two excellent articles on the strengths of Black couples.

11.1.1.2 Declining Marriage Rates for Black Women In the United States, heterosexual marriage rates are declining overall, but the most dramatic declines since the 1960s have been among Black women (Chambers & Kravitz, 2011). Black women marry later and less than all other racial/ ethnic groups in the United States. For example, data from the US Census and other sources for 2008–2012 show that by age 40, 9 of 10 White and Asian/Pacific Islander women have been married at least once (Raley et al., 2015). The same is true for 8 in 10 Hispanic women and more than three quarters of American Indian/Native Alaskan women. However, around 33% of Black women were married by their early 40s, and the lower rates of marriage for Black women occur at every level of education and SES (Raley et al., 2015).

Black women experience more marital dissolutions. At any age of marriage, divorce rates were higher for Black women than for women of other racial and ethnic groups (Raley et al., 2015). Knowing these trends, therapists should discourage their Black female clients from thinking that their inability to find a marriage partner is due solely to personal qualities such as their attractiveness or desirability. Research is clear that Black women's declining rates of mar-riage are mainly connected to a combination of structural factors, many outside Black women's control (Chambers & Kravitz, 2011).

The availability of male partners to marry is a factor that partially explains the declining marriage rates of Black women. This factor is rooted in the economic, social, cultural, and familial conditions affecting Black people in the United States. For example, there are more Black women desiring marriage than available Black men to marry, and this trend has been tracked for several decades (Gooden & Chambers, 2016; Raley et al., 2015). The low availability of Black mates for Black women is associated with Black men's high mortality rates, high incarceration rates, and substance abuse (Chambers & Kravitz, 2011). Additionally, Black women tend to value employment and educational advancement in potential spouses. Black men have disproportionately lower levels of educational attainment due to racism and the school-to-prison pipeline (Banks, 2012; Raley et al., 2015). Black men are also less likely than Black women to gain a college degree. Black wives' rates of education and employment are higher than Black husbands' rates. These dynamics also create tensions and power struggles in Black married couples, leading to marital instability (Boyd et al., 2021).

Black women also believe that their low marriage rates relate to Black men's pursuit of non-Black spouses. We address this topic in relation to Black women's dating challenges later in this chapter. Therapists should also be aware of the class differences in Black women's marriage orientation and here we point to the intersection lens of being race, ethnicity, gender and social class. Middle- and upper-class Black women have opportunities to meet partners of all races and ethnic groups and are more likely to marry. Working-class Black women may have fewer options for marriage. Further, for low-income unmarried Black women, marriage may be de-incentivized by the potential loss of important social or welfare benefits by combining incomes with a partner (Banks, 2012).

We began this chapter by noting that Black women want what other women want. Many Black women want happy and stable marriages. In therapy, we hear the stories of those predominantly ages 21–60 for whom the dream of marriage feels elusive. We strongly encourage therapists to represent the low marriage rates among Black women as a continuing pattern of structural factors, gendered racism, and economic realities rather than resulting from personal attributes of women themselves. Black women's inability to find an eligible mate after dating creates a sense of loss and stress. Therapists must be ready to help Black women name the longings and loss they feel around marriage, juxtaposed against their sense of disempowerment and disadvantage.

We offer three suggestions that guide such work. First, the framework of *grieving* the loss of marriage possibilities resonates with many Black women. Black women may suffer the loss of a dream many have held since childhood; thus grief work applies. Second, Black women's sense of loss around the inability to marry is connected to another real or anticipated loss, that of motherhood. Many Black women have children outside of marriage and are happy to raise them. But many, especially religiously involved Black women, nurture a hope to raise children in marital unions. These dynamics must be named and deconstructed. Therapists might also integrate feminist and womanist viewpoints in their counsel to women. Feminism is the pursuit of women's rights based on equality of the sexes, a movement driven by the enthusiasm of White middle-class women. Womanism is a feminist framework embraced by women of color, predominantly Black women (Bowen, 2021). Both frameworks support the advancement of women's rights and freedoms, asserting that an unmarried life is not a broken or compromised life. Black women can build a meaningful and high-quality life without being a wife or spouse. Black women's lives can be marked by other symbols of status, success, and accomplishment, apart from their marital status.

11.1.1.3 Black Women and Cohabitation While rates of heterosexual marriage have declined among Black women, this does not mean they are without romantic and sexual partners. Cohabiting unions have increased among US couples, although recently rates have leveled off (Horowitz et al., 2019). In general, these unions are not well understood, especially among Black women. Black women are more likely than many other women to be in nonmarital partnerships throughout their adult lives. These unions have benefits and drawbacks (Horowitz et al., 2019; Raley & Bumpass, 2003). Cohabiting arrangements confer many of the benefits of marriage, including improved economic, emotional, familial, and social standing. Many of the strengths of Black married couples apply to cohabitating relationships (Chaney, 2014). An additional strength is a capacity to adapt to a cohabitating arrangement as a stable and abiding union, including raising well-adjusted children. Also, as Black women settle into cohabitation, their longings for marriage can subside.

Cohabitation also contains unique risks for Black women. For non-Black women, cohabitation is often related to pooling income and resources to lay a foundation for marriage. In Black women's unions, cohabitation is often not likely to lead to marriage, because of their partner's choices. For example, some Black men's decision to cohabitate rather than marry may be related to their economic marginalization (e.g., difficulties finding stable employment). Black men's cohabitation choices may also be influenced by the educational achievement of partners (e.g., the Black female partner having more formal schooling; Chaney, 2014; Chambers & Kravitz, 2011; Raley et al., 2015). Black women may be in cohabitation relationships in which they are providing the primary financial support. Black women's cohabitation often includes children. Further, given high rates of dissolution of Black couples, Black women in cohabitation relationships are more likely to parent alone (Osborne et al., 2007). Notably, three times more Black children than White children will experience parental relationship dissolution. Thus, cohabitation can become a pathway for single parenting.

Therapists should encourage Black women to be aware of the costs and benefits of cohabitation arrangements. Low marriage opportunities may pressure Black women to choose cohabitation with a partner. On the other hand, in cohabitation, the likelihood of marriage may remain low, and relationship instability may be high. Therapists can help Black women examine all angles to account for the costs of economic stability, marriage, motherhood, career, and the desire for personal freedom and autonomy (Ford, 2018).

11.1.2   Black Queer Unions

Therapists should understand the similarities and differences in personal and social meanings of Black heterosexual and Black queer marriages. Generally, Black lesbian, gay, bisexual, transgender, and/or queer (LGBTQ) couples have benefited from the legalization of LGBTQ marriage to recognize their love and intimacy and marriage vows. Like heterosexual marriage, marriage in Black queer couples symbolizes commitment, permanency in partnership, emotional and sexual fidelity, and comingling of assets in a shared life (Brooks, 2017). Black LGBTQ spouses can act on behalf of the other in health and family matters (Brooks, 2017; Chiang & Aronekar, 2019). LGBTQ spouses can also have rights to marital assets, inheritance, and survivor benefits.

In addition to its personal and legal significance, marriage for Black queer couples can mean more. Black queer couples balance fidelities to two cultural communities (LGBTQ and Black), with neither offering full acceptance. Black queer couples may reject the White LGBTQ community's focus on marriage citizenship while ignoring other oppressions of Black LGBTQ people (Brooks, 2017; Gainous & Rhodebeck, 2016). In Black queer couples, marriage might act as a symbol of respectability combating homophobia in their families and communities. By marrying, Black queer couples announce their preparedness for long-term unions, negating the idea of queer relationships as transient (Brooks, 2017).

Also, unlike White queer couples for whom religion may not be salient, Black queer couples often hope marriage increases their acceptability within the Black church. Black queer people struggle for acceptance in the Black church. Their religious faith may be silenced by their sexuality (McQueeney, 2009). Black queer women might hope that religious congregations will offer inclusion, defeating stigma, rejection, and cultural marginalization with marriage. Black queer couples may value church traditions, such as a traditional wedding with the presence of family and community witnessing an exchange of vows. Black queer women may also marry to advance gender parity and gender role equality, an image often missing in heterosexual unions and in representations of LGBTQ relationships in media and popular culture (Brooks, 2017).

Therapists serving Black women may be overly focused on cultural sensitivity around racial matters and less on gender and sexuality. This notion could impact their capacity to work with Black queer individuals and couples. We have emphasized that Black women's lives represent intersection of identities that explain their statuses in US society. The intersection of Black racial, ethnic, gender, and sexuality identities as well as social class creates a unique sets of conditions for the Black LGBTQ intimate unions that can be misunderstood in the mental health field and practice.

In Chapter 6, we discuss the development of cultural self-awareness that can facilitate a therapist's capacity to work intersectionally with Black couples of all backgrounds.

11.2   Gender Roles in Black Couples

11.2.1   Gender Roles in Black Heterosexual Couples

Studies shed light on how Black women navigate the gendered dimensions of relationships. Therapists should be alert to gender role dynamics in Black couples, especially how gender-based privilege might show up (Stanik et al., 2013). By gender role dynamics, we include *gender attitudes*, which describe ideas about the ideal degree of similarity between women's characteristics, behaviors, and activities and those of other genders. *Gender expression*, reflecting appearance, behaviors, and mannerisms, is also an aspect of gender identities.

Interestingly, Black women, as a result of their religious involvement, often believe in traditional gender roles, such as husbands as heads of household and providers. Behaviorally, though, Black women demonstrate an egalitarian posture in family life. They divide labor into household responsibilities and raising children. Black women's long history of working outside the home may explain this stance (Hill, 2005).

Unlike other racial groups in the United States, Black women have been consistently in the workforce for decades. Working in and outside the home, Black women have been primary financial supporters of homes and families (Stanik et al., 2013). This idea may explain why they gladly share household responsibilities with partners. Recent scholarship suggests that a husband's traditional values may lower marital satisfaction for both partners since husbands may desire that their wives work more at home (Hill, 2005; McClintock, 2020; Stanik et al., 2013). Additionally, Black husbands and wives who spend similar amounts of time on tasks deemed stereotypically "female" display more attachment and intimacy over time (McClintock, 2020; Stanik et al., 2013). Practicalities of managing work and family life may encourage Black couples to embrace more egalitarian gender role structures. But there are other gendered dynamics that can be painful to women in their intimate relationships.

We identify two gendered dynamics that we encounter in therapy with Black women. First, Black women can adopt the Strong Black Woman persona to manage conflicts the relationship. Second, Black women might engage in *shifting* to manage power dynamics and avoid being stereotyped. Both dynamics can lead women to overly focus on their partner's wants and needs while neglecting their own. Black women may also self-silence to manage conflict and adopt pseudo-personalities to defend against typical stereotypes of Black women.

Chapter 8 addresses the impact of the Strong Black Woman persona on Black women's mental and emotional health. See Chapter 9 for a detailed overview of shifting and Chapter 4 for discussion of stereotypes.

Black women experience internalized stereotype threat in their relationships, and this can play out in several ways. For example, a partner might describe a Black woman's legitimate irritations in an argument as angry, emasculating, or sassy. Many Black women hate these labels and feel unfairly judged by them. Black women may then choose to mask their natural reactions in arguments to manage their image or persuade partners to see them differently. Black women might embrace submissiveness, voicelessness, or subordination, which is how many manage power dynamics in couple relationships. While adopting such personas can smooth the present conflicts, over time the psychological impacts of living with a forced self can be destructive (McClintock, 2020). Finally, Black women might embrace a Strong Black Woman persona in their desire to gain their partner's admiration of them as a good wife, lover, or homemaker. Black women might expend themselves in caring for their partner and home, carrying a stress burden that affects their wellness.

11.2.2   Gender Roles in Black Queer Couples

Therapists should understand how gender role dynamics play out in Black queer couples. Briefly, in the 1940s and 1950s, the *butch-femme* queer couple was a familiar pairing. Butch-femme represented a way to organize relationships along lines of gender and sexual identity (traditionally, Butch referred to a masculinized lesbian identity, while femme referred to the feminine expression (Gainous & Rhodebeck, 2016). The butch-femme lesbian couple distinguished themselves through appearance and clothing and some behaviors (Gainous & Rhodebeck, 2016). This pairing challenged the heterosexual culture of women waiting for the advances of men to be with a partner (Kennedy & Davis, 1993). Before the 1940s, lesbians had to choose either butch or femme roles to be accepted in the LGBTQ community. Butch-butch couples were rare, as were femme-femme partners (Gainous & Rhodebeck, 2016).

The rise of feminism brought critiques of the butch-femme lesbian pairing, and around the 1980s, androgynous queer identity seemed valuable. This gender expression was a muted feminine and masculine presence, standing in defiance of the oppression in the butch-femme roles. Queer women could then celebrate being butch or femme with flexibility and claim any pairing they wished (Levitt & Hiestand, 2005). However, the shift toward androgyny in the White queer community never took hold among low-income Black women. In contrast, rather than androgyny, the fluidity of gender role expressions remained strong for many middle-class to upper-class queer Black women (Wilson, 2009).

For low-income queer Black couples, a "stud-femme" gender expression remained prominent, with culturally important symbolism. Stud (a parallel role to butch in White lesbian couples) refers to Black queer women who adopt masculine energy and take on a traditionally masculine role in relationships. As in the White LGBTQ community, Black stud-femme couples express their gender identity through masculine and feminine dress and mannerisms (Fleishman et al., 2019; Levitt & Hiestand, 2005). Middle- and upper-class lesbians are apt to forgo gender labels and gender role expectations in the relationships and to claim any gender identity or gender role expression that they wish. Rather than historical understanding of androgyny, educated and high-income Black queer women reject the notion of gaining acceptability through a defined gender role. Thus, the stud, femme, or androgyny labels will not apply well (Fleishman et al., 2019).

11.3   Black Women and Dating

Single Black women, especially those who are young, educated, and middle class, hope to date freely and successfully and eventually settle down with a partner of their choice. Many struggle to date, and some never marry. Single Black women and those hoping to partner again after dissolution have discussed their struggles about dating in therapy. Here, we summarize four themes that appear in Black women's postures and narratives about dating (Romano, 2018).

First, the dating market is not color blind. Black women experience limitations on dating that other racial and ethnic groups do not experience (Montique, 2017). Among nearly all other racial/gender groups, Black women are least likely to be pursued romantically by partners of other races. For example, a study of millions of online dating profiles examined several thousands of heterosexual White male dating profiles (Adeyinka-Skold, 2020). Content in these profiles showed that most non-Black men would not consider dating a Black woman (Mendelsohn et al., 2014). In contrast, non-Black women were 2.5 times more likely to include Black men in their interest profiles (Adeyinka-Skold, 2020). This finding indicated that non-Black men on dating websites mostly ignore Black women (Boyd et al., 2021; Mendelsohn et al., 2014).

Second, the lack of dating success makes some Black women upset about the idea that Black men, of their race, seem to reject them. Few topics in Black culture generate as much angst, even anger, as Black-White interracial dating and marriage. Most Black interracial couples are Black men partnered with White women (Boyd et al., 2021). Black women have strong views on this, with personal, cultural, and structural concerns related to their objections. In general, Black women can express feelings of being "passed over" by Black men, who desire non-Black partners, and Spike Lee's film *Jungle Fever* (1991) conveys these real-life dynamics well. *Jungle Fever* is about a married Black man who has an affair with his White female secretary. Much of the film is about how Black women respond, especially in discussing the affair's impact on the Black man's wife. Black women lament that White women seem to be throwing themselves at Black men, who are only too happy to receive them. Black women also discuss White women as "stealing" Black men, leading to Black men's insufficient availability as partners for Black women. Black women's frustrations about Black men's interracial romantic interests have nuances that therapists should grasp.

Frequently, Black women's opposition to Black men's relationships with White women may seem primarily personal, but research suggests that social and cultural factors are predominant in Black women's viewpoints (Childs, 2005). Black women's views on Black men's interracial dating habits relate to a perceived shortage of available romantic partners. Therefore, Black women's primary objections may not be about White women themselves but about a perceived *inequality of opportunities*. Black women may also feel disheartened that Black men seem to hold the same racial, gender, and class bias that they experience from non-Black people. Black women's sentiments about Black men's interracial interests also relate to their dreams of launching and supporting Black families.

Third, Black women often experience a proliferation of voices (e.g., girlfriends, family, self-help dating sources) encouraging them to date or marry interracially, which also causes frustrations. Therapists must understand the complexity of interracial dating suggestions. Black women's hesitations about interracial relations are related to the importance they place on the Black family and to the political history of Black–White relationships in general. Black women often have dreamed of themselves in Black intimate partnerships, preferably marriage, as matriarchs of strong Black families. This imagery is old and predominant in Black culture. It informs the gender scripts of Black women and their understanding of self in culture (Montique, 2017). In contrast, Black women are also encouraged by others to ignore messages about choosing a non-Black partner. Family or friends may suggest that interracial marrying betrays their families and communities (Montique, 2017). Proponents of interracial marriage also viewed such marriages as revolutionary and as a way of addressing the problems of a shortage of Black men as partners.

We strongly believe that Black women should not be shamed for their hesitations about interracial dating. Neither should Black women's singleness be attributed to a lack of interest in dating interracially (Montique, 2017). The real culprit of Black women's lack of dating success is gendered-racial oppression. The assumption that Black women can easily overcome daunting bias and stereotypes to pursue interracial relationships ignores the powerful legacies of sexual ownership and abuse between Black women and White men.

Therapists should understand the historical, sociocultural, and economic issues related to Black women's attitudes and beliefs about interracial unions (Montique, 2017). While the idea of interracial dating could be helpful to Black women, we encourage therapists to be careful in offering it without asking Black women about their thoughts on interracial dating. Therapists must resist using a solution-finding mode to help Black women strategize around dating. Instead, therapists should focus on addressing women's sadness and loss around dating opportunities. The same strategies we discuss in helping Black women deal with marriage interests also apply to dating. In both dating and remaining unmarried, Black women can experience shame, grief, and loss and we have seen our clients overcome such experiences to lead powerful and transformative lives.

11.4   Black Women and Sex

Despite the societal aspersions about their body or beauty, many Black women are confident in their sex appeal (Angelou, 1994). They also express healthy and normal libido, have high body acceptance, and celebrate their sexuality. These dynamics emerge as Black women walk, dress, and carry themselves in social spaces (Capodilupo & Kim, 2014). Alternatively, Black women face powerful social and cultural images, stereotypes that distort an understanding of their sexual selves. The destructive impacts of Black women's exploitation during slavery reverberate to the present day. The right to their bodies and sex was a weapon of oppression and maltreatment. Enslaved Black women were frequently raped and risked beatings and other abuse for refusing owners' overtures. Enslaved Black women learned to submit sexually to survive (Jackson & Greene, 2000; Wyatt, 1997). These distortions in messages about Black women's sexuality persist to this day. Some caregivers raise Black daughters to think of sex as dirty and shameful. Black girls are still warned to close their legs and not give their "milk for free to men who will not buy the cow" (Jackson & Greene, 2000; Wyatt, 1997). Black women's understanding of their sexuality is fraught with confusion, shame, and stigma.

Chapter 4 discusses several historical and present-day stereotypes of Black women. These stereotypes play out sexually in several ways. Stephens and Phillips (2005) identify eight stereotypes related to Black women and sex.

These stereotypes distort the picture of how Black women relate to their sexual partners or behave in sexual encounters. The stereotype of the Black *diva* is one of being a temptress, a toned-down Jezebel playing sexual games with sex partners. Using transactional sex to get material items from a sex partner is the Black *gold digger*'s strategy. The Black *freak* projects a saintly image but is sexually aggressive and controls partners through sex. The Black *dyke* hates men and resists their advances as partners. The Black *gangster bitch* uses emotional aggression and transient sex to please partners and to show loyalty. The Black *sister savior* holds conservative views about sex and its links to spiritual transcendence and may be asexual. The Black *earth mother* is politically and socially focused, shows sexual agency with partners, and rejects exploitation. The Black *baby mama* stereotype begins when a woman has a man's child and uses sex to maintain his attention and love and to obtain survival needs (Stephens & Phillips, 2005).

Normative aspects of Black women's sexuality continue to be understudied, with recent studies emphasizing adverse health outcomes such as sexually transmitted infections (STIs) and unwanted pregnancies (Rao et al., 2018). More recently, voices have advocated for studies of Black women's positive and healthy sexual development experiences. Suggested themes for studying Black women's sex lives include what they find pleasurable in sex and what affects their sexual health, sexual agency, and sexual expression (Hargons et al., 2018). Along these lines, a population study, the Sexual Exploration in America study (Herbenick et al., 2017), sheds light on the everyday sexual behavior of Black women. Black women 18 years and older completed online surveys about sex in various unions. The study focused on Black women's sexual variety and sexual satisfaction. *Sexual variety* refers to the intimate moments that are part of sexual encounters in person or virtually, with a partner or solo (e.g., cuddling). *Sexual satisfaction* refers to how Black women felt during sexual activity and how they felt, such as libido, relationship dynamics, or partner attraction (Heiman et al., 2011; Mark & Herbenick, 2014; Mark & Murray, 2012; Milhausen et al., 2015).

The Sexual Exploration in America study (Herbenick et al., 2017) suggested that around 66% of Black women study participants over age 30 were sexually active. Generally, Black women were sexually satisfied. Black women in midlife and older who had a partner in the home remained sexually active. Although older Black women were having sex less, sexual satisfaction increased with age. Sexually satisfied Black women were more likely to value sex in a relationship and to voice satisfaction with the relationship and with communication with a partner. In general, while the quality of a relationship with a partner is often a factor in sexual variety and satisfaction, this was not the case for Black women in the study. Menopausal and postmenopausal Black women had decreases in libido. These women reported lower sexual satisfaction, especially if they did not have a partner at home. Most Black women valued sexual variety even in self-pleasuring. This finding was more accurate for young women than for those who were middle aged and older. About 20% of Black women in the study were not sexually active, but many also indicated being sexually satisfied.

We encourage therapists working with Black women or Black couples to show competence and skills in addressing Black women's sexuality. Therapists should assess Black women's sexual scripts, partnership status, and sexual attributions. They should understand the sexual stereotypes that can shape societal views of Black women's sexuality (Herbenick et al., 2017; Wyatt, 1997). Therapists should be familiar with Black women's psychosexual histories, women's agency in sexual encounters, and how women might feel silenced and stigmatized. Another aspect to inquire about is Black women's internalized ideas and attributions about sex and religious values. Other areas of emphasis include Black women's skills and efficacy to engage in sexual behavior and their feelings about advocating for their own sexual needs and setting boundaries for their safety (Wyatt, 1997). Therapists should also ask Black women about their comfort in sexual communication and how they feel about reclaiming their sexuality.

11.5 Black Women's Relationship Risks and Threats

Therapists should be aware of two intimate relational risks that can dramatically alter Black women's health and quality of life. These two risks are nonconsensual concurrent sexual partnerships and intimate partner violence. Both can affect women's health directly and indirectly and can end their lives. Therapists should be alert to the presence of these conditions in Black women's narratives and help them to prioritize their safety and well-being.

11.5.1 Nonconsenting Concurrent Partnerships

A concurrent sexual relationship is one in which at least one partner is sexually active with more than one person at the same time. Such relationships can be *consensual, reluctantly consensual, or nonconsensual*. Some Black women may be involved in a concurrent consensual relationship with two or more partners. These types of unions are not the focus on this discussion. Polyamory or consensual nonmonogamy might be fully informed and not necessarily create a risk to Black women's health and well-being. However, some Black women may be reluctantly or nonconsensually involved with partners who are sexually involved with others. These types of partnerships are disproportionately related to Black women's elevated rates of STIs. Among women diagnosed with HIV/AIDS in the United States, 64% were Black women (Hargons et al., 2018; Ludema et al., 2015). Among those infected, almost

85% acquired HIV through heterosexual contact, suggesting that sexual networks drive STI risk. Black women may not be aware that their male partners are sexually involved with others. Overlapping sexual partnerships can increase the speed at which STIs spread (Ludema et al., 2015). Research shows that most Black women assume norms of monogamy in their sex lives. Correspondingly, women are apt not to use condoms or other STI protection, placing them at greater risk. Most frequently, a choice to forgo STI protection is driven by a request or demand from a male partner or women's fears of losing sexual influence (Ludema et al., 2015; Rao et al., 2018).

Black women may also feel pressure to accept a concurrent sexual arrangement because of limited financial resources, making low-income women particularly vulnerable to STIs (Rao et al., 2018). For example, low-income Black women in concurrent partnerships were more likely to receive practical support from their partners, such as a place to live and support for children. Those in consensual simultaneous sexual relationships were least likely to need help with finances or material resources such as food (Ludema et al., 2015; Rao et al., 2018). Therapists should listen for concurrency in Black women's relations, without their consent, to help women advocate for their safety and protect their well-being. At the very least, women should understand the strong links between concurrency and sexual risk.

11.5.2   Intimate Partner Violence

Black women experience higher rates of intimate partner violence (IPV) than women of other racial/ethnic groups. In addition, IPV survivor profiles show that young and poor Black women residing in urban areas are the more frequent targets of relationship violence (Donovan & Hester, 2014). Black women experiencing IPV are more likely than non-Black women in IPV situations to be the sole providers of their families. Typically, these women might have financial burdens, do more caretaking of children, and have no car. The necessity to stay in a violent setting becomes more prevalent for Black women who do not have the stability to separate themselves from a relationship (Taft et al., 2009).

Ongoing research shows the countless clinically significant mental health outcomes of IPV for Black women, including depression, anxiety, posttraumatic stress disorder, dissociative disorder, low-self-esteem, feelings of helplessness and hopelessness, maladaptive and cognitive distortions, as well as social isolation (Reviere et al., 2007). The experience of decreased mental health in Black women may make them less likely to leave a relationship, intensifying the cycle of violence.

A recent study also found links between IPV and suicidal tendencies in Black women (Reviere et al., 2007). Black women who attempted suicide were

2.5 times more likely to report physical partner abuse. They were also 2.8 times more likely to report emotional partner abuse within 12 months than similar women who had not attempted suicide (Reviere et al., 2007). Therapists should be alert for IPV experiences in Black female clients, who may be at higher risk. While IPV occurs in relationships of all SESs and even among educated women, people experiencing IPV also face systemic inequalities in power associated with gender roles, race, and SES. A therapist working with clients experiencing IPV must support them in advocating for themselves outside the therapy room (Donovan & Hester, 2014).

11.6   Culturally Informed Strategies for Black Couples in Therapy

Therapists might work with their Black female clients on love and intimacy in couples therapy or individual therapy. Earlier in this chapter we offer several themes that might arise in individual therapy when Black women face emotional turmoil related to intimate relationship dynamics. Here, we offer suggestions related to the treatment of Black couples. The idea is to work with a couple in the context of their cultural background and worldviews. In the absence of culturally informed therapy, the risk of dropout increases. Black women in our study gave opinions on this. One participant said: "One couples therapist we had wasn't a good fit in addressing our dynamic, but we didn't continue seeing them for long." Another wrote: "A White therapist I went to with my husband didn't seem to understand us as a Black couple." We use the following case example to illustrate how therapists can work with central themes in Black couples.

Case Example

A Black couple, Rosemarie and Jamal, in their mid-40s, engaged in two separate stints with a therapist over 24 months. The therapist first saw the couple when they planned to move in together. The couple eventually married and returned to therapy about a year after their daughter was born. In the first and second periods of therapy, similar themes surfaced. Rosemarie was a university professor with a substantially higher income than Jamal, which affected her sense of burden. She carried a heavier financial load. The fact that her income supported the home triggered generalized anxiety for her. She described herself as jittery and unrested at work and home. Rosemarie felt that Jamal was sensitive and reactive when she sought his help to manage their financial affairs. Rosemarie experienced postpartum depression a few months after the baby's birth. Still, she felt that Jamal did not seem to care.

(*cont.*)

Jamal held a job as a school janitor and was a beloved worker. In both stints of therapy, he expressed joy and satisfaction in describing his interactions with teachers and students at work. Jamal reported that those positive vibes plummeted when he got home. He viewed himself as a competent and giving partner but felt like a failure in Rosemarie's eyes. Prominent in Jamal's history was his father's suicide and being raised by his single mother, whom he loved and admired. His mother hustled and held the family together with few complaints. Other family dynamics showed up in the couple's grievances related to their children outside the marriage. Rosemarie had been a teenage mother, and her 24-year-old daughter lived close. The daughter was frequently dependent on Rosemarie for financial support, and this upset Jamal. Jamal had two children at an early stage in life with a former wife. Jamal's 13-year-old son regularly made unscheduled visits. Rosemarie did not feel especially attached to this child.

One area in which the couple bonded deeply was their antiracism advocacy. Both had grown up in poor communities and were active in local Black Lives Matter organizations. Rosemarie was also a churchgoer, and although Jamal did not regularly attend, he was a spiritual man, and she remained hopeful that one day they might do church together.

11.6.1   Acknowledge Black Couples' Strengths

Couples may be married or cohabiting, may be involved in arrangements such as parenting children that live in other homes, and may have deep connections with extended family members. Couples may have gender role patterns that may not fit traditional family life. Women are central to the complexities of Black family life work, showing a profound capacity to adapt to changing circumstances in the family. Rather than seeing pathology or dysfunction, the therapist should celebrate and support the resilience of Black couples in maximizing role flexibility and egalitarian values in the relationship.

With Jamal and Rosemarie, the therapist conducted a genogram to get a solid understanding of the couple's relationship history and family backgrounds. Both their nuclear and extended families were complex. The therapist pointed out the couple's strong work ethic, which came from their mothers. On both sides, their families had inspired their community awareness and organizing. Trauma on both sides of the family and the adverse childhood experiences of each partner were vulnerabilities and created needs and longings. In Rosemarie's case, being a teen parent and putting herself through school with loans led to her deep emotional longing to be cared for in the relationship. She sent Jamal many cues about this need that Jamal missed. Therapy offered an opportunity for her to explain her emotional needs carefully and to have him listen.

11.6.2   Manage Boundaries with Extended Families

As mentioned, Black women and partners are often in complex family arrangements. The support of large and extended families is a strength of Black unions, but, often, boundaries with extended families are needed to allow couples to catch their breaths. Black women in relationships are typically more sensitive to this need. The therapist can help Black women set boundaries sensitively but firmly to restore energy to the primary unit.

The complexity of setting boundaries in Black women's caregiving roles is discussed further in Chapter 10.

In Rosemarie's case, she was often irritated by Jamal's chaotic visitation arrangement with his son's mother. Visits occurred sporadically and unpredictably. Rosemarie wanted more predictability so the couple could plan better to integrate the child into their home. Rosemarie uncovered a feeling of resentment that she seemed to play second fiddle to a child of boundless energy. Jamal felt that Rosemarie was very lax in setting her boundaries with her adult daughter. Often, the couple's arguments involved one-upping about whose parenting skills were lacking. After several tense conversations, the couple committed to working more skillfully to manage their children to promote strong relationships with the other stepparent.

11.6.3   Maximize Untapped Areas of Intimacy in the Relationship

An overemphasis on emotional and sexual intimacy in Black couples' relationships can miss the importance of healthy intimacies in the relationship. Several types of intimacies can strengthen a love relationship, and Black couples benefit from maximizing them. For example, a Black couple's bond can deepen through friendship activities, connections about faith, and shared cultural experiences. Recreational interests such as travel, the arts, or music can draw the couple closer. Even painful experiences such as working through conflicts or experiencing shared loss, cultural pain, or joy can expand a couple's commitment to their union. We discuss the untapped and unrecognized intimacies in Jamal and Rosemarie's relationship that the therapist reminded them of.

Jamal and Rosemarie had several untapped areas to maximize their connectedness and friendship, including an untapped resource of cultural intimacy and a love of community organizing. As a professor of sociology, Rosemarie loved studying the history of Black racism, antiracism, and related topics. For Jamal, observing his father suffer from untreated depression as a war veteran inflamed his passion for working with young Black men. The couple understood that their community work offered opportunities to talk as equals, share good humor, and engage in something meaningful together. They also valued having a mentoring role in the lives of each other's children in the spirit of advancing Black families and making cultural contributions. The therapist helped them to uncover the possibilities of this dimension of their lives, using it to forge intimate conversations about their shared dreams. Other intimacies were related to their love of jazz, their interest in good food, and their desire to raise their daughter in their Baptist faith.

11.6.4 Root Out Gendered-Racial Stereotypes in the Relationship

Often in Black couples, stereotyping comes into play in the relationship. Stereotypes must be addressed through illumination and deconstruction. Black partners in heterosexual or LGBTQ relationships may view their Black female partners through the same stereotypes of Black women found in the general culture. For example, the tendency to misunderstand Black women's assertive style as "angry," demeaning, and emasculating is popular in modern performing and media arts. The stereotype of Black women as "sassy" captures this dynamic. Black women can also experience colorism, hair texture bias, and size discrimination in their intimate unions even if their partners are of their same race and gender. We discuss how Rosemarie and Jamal's union involved subtle stereotyping of each other.

See Chapter 4 for more on the stereotypes that affect Black women.

Rosemarie held an image of Black men that resulted from her teen pregnancies and poor treatment by men in her life. She held Jamal up to a stringent standard for what she wanted in a husband. She also secretly felt ashamed of his educational standing in comparison with her friends' partners, who were pre-dominantly non-Black. Rosemarie also internalized the fear of being too over-powering or too strong. Jamal internalized his mother's care for him and longed for it many days when he got home from work. When Rosemarie asked for support or gently complained that she did not receive it, he felt she was nagging, which he believed his mother never did. The therapist worked with each individual to bring stereotypes to the forefront for narrative work, showing their emotional impacts and areas for improvement.

11.6.5   Connect Black Couples to Nontherapy Resources

Black couples are unlikely to spend extensive time in therapy. Like other couples, they lead complicated lives, and accessing therapy every week can be difficult. Black couples can use enrichment resources available for a self-help approach. Resources include marriage retreats at Black churches, podcasts to listen to together, and couples' friendship groups. Black couples can also watch movies with Black characters and talk about how the themes apply to their relationships. At the end of this chapter, we offer resources that may be useful along these lines. Conversations with other Black couples over dinner or in other activities can support relationship progress. Resources also include theater and musical shows to stimulate conversation, education, and self-help.

Rosemarie was a historian and was excited at the idea of curating experiences that they might enjoy as a couple and as a family. Before their therapy ended, the therapist encouraged the couple to read an excerpt of an article on "cinematherapy" for Black couples (see the resources section of this chapter). The couple picked three movies to watch over 6 weeks. Each recorded how a character or dynamic resembled them or aspects of their relationships. The conversations about the movies the couple selected were lighthearted but also deeply evocative of the experiences they longed for in each other. Jamal and Rosemarie also began to watch the reality show "Couples Therapy" on Showtime regularly, and this seemed to increase their leisure time and also their curiosity about how they compared to the couples they viewed interacting with therapists on the show.

11.7   Conclusion

Black women's capacities to give their all in their relationships are clearly seen in real life and in fictional depictions. What is remarkable is the depth of commitment, generosity, and tenacity Black women bring to their unions. Black women try to make relationships work because they want vital romances and deep intimacies with partners. Black women are also aware that at the center of Black families are adults in intimate relationships, around which the family units form and adapt. Throughout the book, we have discussed the profound impacts of gendered racial dynamics. Black women's romantic partnerships are arenas in which structural and personal dynamics collide. Black women's intimate unions can be a source of joy, and they can also be a source of pain and struggle in unique ways. In Black women's dating, marriage, and sex lives, marginalization and oppression cannot be ignored. A multifaceted understanding of Black women's intimate unions is essential. Our work in individual and couples therapy with Black women does not produce fairy-tale endings. Black women love profoundly and often endure loss in love. We have been privileged as therapists to help them recover, thrive, and find meaning in their own lives.

Therapist Reflection Questions

1. Watch the movie or read the book *Waiting to Exhale*. What feels similar or different from the critical themes of this work in the intimate partnerships you have had? If you are a non-Black person, what feels different culturally?
2. What are your experiences in mental health practice with Black lesbian couples? What information might you still need to acquire to work competently with this segment of Black women in America?
3. This chapter presents the idea that personal dynamics of romance, love, and intimacy can be affected by structural inequalities. How do you see this in your own life? How do you see this dynamic in the lives of people of color?
4. What are your views on interracial dating and marriage? What do you believe are its pros and cons? What are your experiences with Black and non-Black interracial couples?
5. How might you counsel or advise Black women who are in concurrent relationships with and without their consent? (Recall a concurrent relationship is one which person may be involved in more than one emotional or sexual union at the same time.)

Resources for Therapists and Clients

Books

Angelou, M. (1994). *Phenomenal woman: Four poems celebrating women.* Random House.

McMillan, T. (1996). *Waiting to exhale.* Black Sawn.

Stewart, D. M. (2020). *Black women, black love: America's war on African American marriage.* Seal Press.

TV Series and Films

Despres, E. B., Kriegman, J., Steinberg, E., & Malhotra, V. (Executive Producers). (2019-present). *Couples therapy* [TV series]. Edgeline Films; Loveless; Showtime Networks.

Oliver, C. E., Oliver, T., & Mulligan, B. (Executive Producers). (2017-present). *Black love* [TV Series]. Confluential Films; OWN: The Oprah Winfrey Network.

Whitaker, F. (Director). (1995). *Waiting to exhale* [Film]. New Line Home Entertainment.

Scholarly Articles

Brooks, S. (2017). Black on black love: Black lesbian and bisexual women, marriage, and symbolic meaning. *The Black Scholar, 47*(4), 32–46.

Dunham, S. M., & Dermer, S. B. (2020). Cinematherapy with African American couples. *Journal of Clinical Psychology, 76*(8), 1472–1482.

Phillips, T. M., Wilmoth, J. D., & Marks, L. D. (2012). Challenges and conflicts. . . strengths and supports: A study of enduring African American marriages. *Journal of Black Studies, 43*(8), 936–952.

Media Resources

Black Marriage Day. (n.d.). http://www.blackmarriageday.com/

Raphael, R. (2019, March 7). What women want: Love, marriage and dating. *Ebony.* https://www.ebony.com/what-women-want-love-marriage-and-dating/

References

Acevedo, B. P., & Aron, A. (2009). Does a long-term relationship kill romantic love? *Review of General Psychology, 13*(1), 59–65.

Adeyinka-Skold, S. (2020). *Dating in the digital age: Race, gender, and inequality* [Doctoral dissertation, University of Pennsylvania]. ProQuest.

Angelou, M. (1994). *Phenomenal woman: Four poems celebrating women.* Random House.

Baldwin, J. (1974). *If Beale Street could talk.* Dial Press.

Banks, R. R. (2012). *Is marriage for white people?: How the African American marriage decline affects everyone.* Plume.

Barnes, R. J. D. (2015). *Raising the race: Black career women redefine marriage.* Rutgers University Press.

Bowen, A. (2021). Calling the question: Is womanism feminism? by Angela Bowen. *Journal of International Women's Studies, 22*(8), 179.

Boyd, B., Stephens, D. P., Eaton, A., & Bruk-Lee, V. (2021). Exploring partner scarcity: Highly educated black women and dating compromise. *Sexuality Research and Social Policy*, *18*, 702–714. https://doi.org/10.1007/s13178-020-00493-3

Brooks, S. (2017). Black on Black love: Black lesbian and bisexual women, marriage, and symbolic meaning. *The Black Scholar*, *47*(4), 32–46.

Burton, L. M., & Tucker, M. B. (2009). Romantic unions in an era of uncertainty: A post-Moynihan perspective on African American women and marriage. *Annals of the American Academy of Political and Social Science*, *621*, 131–148.

Capodilupo, C. M., & Kim, S. (2014). Gender and race matter: The importance of considering intersections in Black women's body image. *Journal of Counseling Psychology*, *61*(1), 37–49.

Chambers, A. L., & Kravitz, A. (2011). Understanding the disproportionately low marriage rate among African Americans: An amalgam of sociological and psychological constraints. *Family Relations*, *60*(5), 648–660.

Chaney, C. (2010). "Like Siamese twins": Relationship meaning among married African-American couples. *Marriage & Family Review*, *46*(8), 510–537.

Chaney, C. (2014). "No matter what, good or bad, love is still there": Motivations for romantic commitment among Black cohabiting couples. *Marriage & Family Review*, *50*(3), 216–245. https://doi.org/10.1080/01494929.2013.851056

Chiang, H., & Aronekar, A. (Eds.). (2019). *Global encyclopedia of lesbian, gay, bisexual, transgender, and queer (LGBTQ) history*. Charles Scribner's Sons.

Childs, E. C. (2005). Looking behind the stereotypes of the "angry Black woman": An exploration of Black women's responses to interracial relationships. *Gender & Society*, *19*(4), 544–561.

Donovan, C., & Hester, M. (2014). *Domestic violence and sexuality: What's love got to do with it?* Policy Press.

Fleishman, J. M., Crane, B., & Koch, P. B. (2019). Correlates and predictors of sexual satisfaction for older adults in same-sex relationships. *Journal of Homosexuality*, *67*(14), 1974–1998.

Ford, L. (2018).*That's the way love goes: An examination of the romantic partnering experiences of Black middle class women* [Doctoral dissertation, Duke University]. ProQuest.

Gainous, J., & Rhodebeck, L. (2016). Is same-sex marriage an equality issue? Framing effects among African Americans. *Journal of Black Studies*, *47*(7), 682–700. https://doi.org/10.1177/0021934716642590

Gibson, B. (Director). (1993). *What's love got to do with it* [Film]. Touchstone Home Video.

Gooden A., & Chambers A. (2016). Black men in couples and families. In J. Lebow, A. Chambers, & D. Breunlin (Eds.), *Encyclopedia of couple and family therapy* (pp. 281–285). Springer.

Hargons, C. N., Mosley, D. V., Meiller, C., Stuck, J., Kirkpatrick, B., Adams, C., & Angyal, B. (2018). "It feels so good": Pleasure in last sexual encounter narratives of Black university students. *Journal of Black Psychology*, *44*(2), 103–127.

Heiman, J. R., Rupp, H., Janssen, E., Newhouse, S. K., Brauer, M., & Laan, E. (2011). Sexual desire, sexual arousal and hormonal differences in premenopausal US and

Dutch women with and without low sexual desire. *Hormones and Behavior, 59*(5), 772–779.

Herbenick, D., Bowling, J., Fu, T. C., Dodge, B., Guerra-Reyes, L., & Sanders, S. (2017). Sexual diversity in the United States: Results from a nationally representative probability sample of adult women and men. *PLoS ONE, 12*(7), e0181198. https://journals.plos.org/plosone/article?id=10.1371/journal.pone .0181198

Hill, S. A. (2005). *Black intimacies: A gender perspective on families and relationships.* Rowman Alta Mira Press.

Horowitz, J. M., Graf, N., & Livingston, G. (2019, November 6). *Marriage and cohabitation in the US.* Pew Research Center. https://www.pewresearch.org/ social-trends/2019/11/06/marriage-and-cohabitation-in-the-u-s/

Jackson, L. C., & Greene, B. (Eds.). (2000). *Psychotherapy with African American women: Innovations in psychodynamic perspectives and practice.* Guilford Press.

Jenkins, B. (Director). (2018). *If Beale Street could talk* [Film]. Twentieth Century Fox Home Entertainment.

Kennedy, E. L., & Davis, M. D. (2019). *Boots of leather, slippers of gold: The history of a lesbian community.* Routledge.

Lee, S. (Director). (1991). *Jungle fever* [Film]. Universal Pictures.

Levitt, H. M., & Hiestand, K. R. (2005). Gender within lesbian sexuality: Butch and femme perspectives. *Journal of Constructivist Psychology, 18*(1), 39–51.

Lorde, A. (1982). *Zami: A new spelling of my name.* Crossing Press.

Ludema, C., Doherty, I. A., White, B. L., Villar-Loubet, O., McLellan-Lemal, E., O'Daniels, C. M., & Adimora, A. A. (2015). Characteristics of African American women and their partners with perceived concurrent partnerships in 4 rural counties in the southeastern U.S. *Sexually Transmitted Diseases, 42*(9), 498–504. https://doi.org/10.1097/olq.0000000000000325

Mark, K. P., & Herbenick, D. (2014). The influence of attraction to partner on heterosexual women's sexual and relationship satisfaction in long-term relationships. *Archives of Sexual Behavior, 43*(3), 563–570.

Mark, K. P., & Murray, S. H. (2012). Gender differences in desire discrepancy as a predictor of sexual and relationship satisfaction in a college sample of heterosexual romantic relationships. *Journal of Sex & Marital Therapy, 38*(2), 198–215.

Marks, L., Hopkins, K., Chaney, C., Monroe, P., Nesteruk, O., & Sasser, D. (2008). "Together, we are strong": A qualitative study of happy, enduring African American marriages. *Family Relations, 57*(2), 172–185.

McClintock, E. (2020). Occupational sex composition and marriage: The romantic cost of gender-atypical jobs. *Journal of Marriage and Family, 82*(3), 911–933. https:// doi.org/10.1111/jomf.12657

McMillan, T. (1992). *Waiting to exhale.* Viking.

McQueeney, K. (2009). "We are God's children, y'all:" Race, gender, and sexuality in lesbian- and gay-affirming congregations. *Social Problems, 56*(1), 151–173. https://doi.org/10.1525/sp.2009.56.1.151

Mendelsohn, G., Shaw Taylor, L., Fiore, A., & Cheshire, C. (2014). Black/white dating online: Interracial courtship in the 21st century. *Psychology of Popular Media Culture, 3*(1), 2–18.

Milhausen, R. R., Buchholz, A. C., Opperman, E. A., & Benson, L. E. (2015). Relationships between body image, body composition, sexual functioning, and sexual satisfaction among heterosexual young adults. *Archives of Sexual Behavior, 44*(6), 1621–1633.

Montique, C. S. (2017). *The struggle is real: the dating dilemma for educated Black women interested in educated Black men* [Doctoral dissertation, American University]. ProQuest.

Osborne, C., Manning, W. D., & Smock, P. J. (2007). Married and cohabiting parents' relationship stability: A focus on race and ethnicity. *Journal of Marriage & Family, 69*, 1345–1366.

Phillips, T. M., Wilmoth, J. D., & Marks, L. D. (2012). Challenges and conflicts. . . strengths and supports: A study of enduring African American marriages. *Journal of Black Studies, 43*(8), 936–952.

Raley, R. K., & Bumpass, L. (2003). The topography of the divorce plateau: Levels and trends in union stability in the United States after 1980. *Demographic Research, 8*, 245–260.

Raley, R., Sweeney, M., & Wondra, D. (2015). The growing racial and ethnic divide in U.S. marriage patterns. *The Future of Children, 25*(2), 89–109.

Rao, D., Andrasik, M. P., & Lipira, L. (2018). HIV stigma among Black women in the United States: Intersectionality, support, resilience. *American Journal of Public Health, 108*, 446–448.

Rees, D. (Director). (2011). *Pariah* [Film]. Focus Features.

Reviere, S. L., Farber, E. W., Twomey, H., Okun, A., Jackson, E., Zanville, H., & Kaslow, N. J. (2007). Intimate partner violence and suicidality in low-income African American women. *Violence Against Women, 13*(11), 1113–1129. https://doi.org/10.1177/1077801207307798

Romano, R. (2018). Something old, something new: Black women, interracial dating, and the Black marriage crisis. *Differences, 29*(2), 126–153. https://doi.org/10.1215/10407391-6999802

Singleton, J. (Director). (1993). *Poetic justice* [Film]. Columbia Pictures Corporation.

Stanik, C. E., McHale, S. M., & Crouter, A. C. (2013). Gender dynamics predict changes in marital love among African American couples. *Journal of Marriage and Family, 75*(4), 795–807. https://doi.org/10.1111/jomf.12037

Stephens, D. & Philips, L. (2005) Integrating Black feminist thought into conceptual frameworks of African American adolescent women's sexual scripting processes. *Sexualities, Evolution, and Gender, 7*(1), 37–55.

Sternberg, R. J. (1987). Liking versus loving: A comparative evaluation of theories. *Psychological Bulletin, 102*(3), 331–345.

Taft, C. T., Bryant-Davis, T., Woodward, H. E., Tillman, S., & Torres, S. E. (2009). Intimate partner violence against African American women: An examination of the socio-cultural context. *Aggression and Violent Behavior, 14*(1), 50–58. https://doi.org/10.1016/j.avb.2008.10.001

Turner, T. (1984). What's love got to do with it [Song]. On *Private dancer* [Album]. Capitol Records.

Whitaker, F. (Director). (1995). *Waiting to exhale* [Film]. New Line Home Entertainment.

Wilson, B. D. (2009). Black lesbian gender and sexual culture: Celebration and resistance. *Culture, Health & Sexuality, 11*(3), 297–313.

Witcher, T. (Director). (1997). *Love Jones* [Film]. New Line Cinema.

Wyatt, G. (1997). *Stolen women: Reclaiming our sexuality, taking back our lives.* Wiley.

12 Appearance Prejudice and Discrimination against Black Women

with Tonya Davis[*]

A California company hired and then fired a Black woman, Chastity Jones, before her start date because of her appearance, and she filed a lawsuit against them (Fernandez-Campbell, 2018). This incident happened in May 2010, when she applied for a customer service position with a company that provides streamlined communication for crises and disasters. Chastity got the job after an interview, but shortly after, the company told her to cut her dread locs before her start date. Chastity questioned the request, but the human resource manager indicated that this hairstyle did not adhere to the grooming policy and tended to get messy. The company policy stated that hairstyles should reflect a business/professional image. When Chastity refused the request to cut her locs, the company withdrew its job offer. A US Court of Appeals upheld the company's decision (Gutierrez-Morfin, 2016).

As a result of what Chastity and other people of color experience, California created the CROWN Act (JOY Collective, 2019) to eliminate hairstyle and hair texture discrimination in workplaces and schools. Chastity's hairstyle discrimination mirrors typical experiences Black women face every day in the United States and in many places around the world. Black women experience criticism, rejection, and exclusion, directly and indirectly, because of one or more aspects of their appearance. Black women also internalize appearance shame, which dramatically affects their self-concepts and mental and emotional dispositions (Cotter et al., 2015). Therapists working with Black women must understand the pervasiveness and complexities of the invalidation Black women receive about their appearance. Therapists must also help their clients deal with these dynamics, especially when Black women internalize this discrimination (Cotter et al., 2015). In this chapter we offer information, contextual framing, and strategies to help therapists ally with Black women to address appearance-related psychological injuries, help them love and accept themselves, and frame their body images within cultural beauty ideals.

---

[*] T. Davis, D. Baptiste, & Gooden, A. (2023). Appearance prejudice and discrimination against Black women. In D. Baptiste & A. Gooden, *Promoting Black women's mental health: What practitioners should know and do*. Cambridge University Press.

12.1   Appearance Bias or Lookism

We use *lookism* and *appearance bias* interchangeably in this chapter to describe acts of stereotyping, prejudice, or discrimination because of a person's looks or appearance and whether their appearance is pleasing to an observer's eye (Adomaitis et al., 2017). In the United States, Black women experience lookism at alarming rates, with everyday invalidations and insults that affect their self-esteem and confidence (Hall, 1995). Lookism includes biases related to body features, shape and size, skin color, hair texture and styles, personal grooming choices, and other appearance-related variables (Adomaitis et al., 2017). Black women receive messages about not meeting mainstream beauty standards, based on what is present or missing among their features or body traits (Gordon, 2008). For example, dark skin is viewed as undesirable, while fair skin is favorable. A heavy body is unattractive, while a lean or slender frame is preferred. The tight curl of Black hair is "nappy," while straight or silky hair is deemed ideal, and so on (Garrin & Marcketti, 2018).

Appearance messages can consist of explicit or subtle shaming or rejection. Chastity Jones experienced an explicit rejection of her hairstyle. Subtle rejection of Black women's appearance occurs in ways that might go unnoticed; for example, department stores may carry a range of products for White, fair- or straight-haired women (e.g., skin or hair care, makeup, clothing), but similar products may be unavailable for Black women of different hair textures. A lack of or limited availability of Black grooming products sends the message that Black women's looks are inferior based on Eurocentric characteristics (Robinson-Moore, 2008). Therapists must be alert to the clinical impacts of racialized appearance biases that make many Black women feel erased or invisible. The goal is to help clients to reject lookism and adopt body and appearance positivity to strengthen their well-being and empowerment. Therapists must ally around the idea that "there are many individuals and many cultures that do not find the narrow mainstream definition of beauty attractive" (Adichie, 2017, p. 46).

In considering the confidence and self-efficacy of Black women about their bodies, therapists should be aware that the lookism faced by Black women has two sides. Black women's appearance can be devalued while simultaneously being eroticized, and this duality can be present in the same encounter (Banks, 2000). Both aspects lead to stereotyping and discrimination. For example, one author of this chapter, a Black woman, recalls how a White man asked her out on a date. He stated his rationale: "I've never been with a beautiful Black woman." In his attempts to compliment this woman, he also exoticized, objectified, and offended her. Rather than genuine interest, his quest was to encounter a woman he considered exotic (see also Awad et al., 2015).

Invalidations of Black women's looks can unfold in multiple ways. In this chapter, we discuss everyday experiences, each with their messages of shame and rejection related to hair, skin color, and body shape and size.

12.2   Hair Bias

12.2.1   Hair Beauty Standards

Historical and generational hair biases explain Black women's anxiety and stress related to hair texture and styles. A 1980s advertisement by Procter & Gamble typifies the prejudicial standard. Procter & Gamble's Pantene hair care advertisement showcased mostly White women with long, silky hair saying the line "Don't hate me because I'm beautiful." Occasionally, the ad featured famous women of color with phenotypically White features, also saying the same line. In this advertisement, the absence of course or curly Black hair texture (e.g., an Afro) suggested it lacked beauty, and this one-sided beauty standard has been a bone of contention for many Black women. This standard alludes to what Harris-Perry (2011) refers to as Black women living in a "crooked room," having to survive privileged social and cultural dynamics that do not fit them. Rather than having women think that something is wrong with them (e.g., wrong hair texture), Harris-Perry encourages Black women to deconstruct the "crooked room" to reject an untenable standard. In a good sign of change, the Pantene line now includes the Gold Series hair care products, marketed to Black women wearing their hair in its natural state or relaxed. Procter & Gamble also supports a website and resources dedicated to uplifting Black and ethnic beauty (My Black Is Beautiful, n.d.).

12.2.2   Hair Texture

Westernized or European standards that value silky, long, and straight hair have haunted Black women for centuries (Garrin & Marcketti, 2018). Black women are 1.5 times more likely than women of other racial and ethnic groups to be sent home from the workplace because of hairstyles (JOY Collective, 2019). Black women's desire to have straight or relaxed hair does not equate to having a low body image, nor is wanting straightened hair itself a big deal (Dawson et al., 2019). The issue relates more to the assumption, including by Black women themselves, that Black hair is inferior in its natural state. Black women's hair inferiority contributes to their negative self-image and reflects the wounding aspects of lookism. A 2018 Netflix movie, *Nappily Ever After* (al-Mansour, 2018), beautifully captures this viewpoint.

In *Nappily Ever After*, a young Black girl, Violet, grew up with regular messages from her mother that a perfect look for Black women starts with straight and long natural hair. As an adult Black woman, Violet can identify the familial, societal, and corporate messaging regarding beauty standards. She grasps how straightening her natural hair and keeping it perfect is symbolic of everything she could not have growing up (e.g., loss of freedom to be a child, playing outside, swimming). Violet finds the courage and confidence to be free of the need to be "perfect," which means shaving her hair off. When Black women accept and love themselves unconditionally, wearing their chosen hairstyle can reflect personal freedom and self-acceptance. Having hair or not having hair can be uniquely symbolic and beautiful (al-Mansour, 2018).

Having "good hair" versus "bad hair" has been a painful bias and cause of shame for women within the Black community, and we have seen it first hand (Banks, 2000; Dawson & Karl, 2018). When someone says, "you have good hair," it insinuates that naturally straight, silky, or loose curl pattern hair is best. This distorts Black women's self-confidence in two ways. First, the Black woman perceived to have "good hair" has the potential to experience a sense of superiority because her hair is better (Garrin & Marcketti, 2018). Second, the Black woman perceived to have "bad hair" can experience self-doubt and internalize negative self-images (Garrin & Marcketti, 2018). Black women's social pressures to wear their hair straight or natural adds unique stress. Women experiencing alopecia or pattern baldness may be even more anxious. Common findings are that "Black women are 30% more likely to be made aware of the formal workplace appearance policy" and "Black women are 80% more likely to agree with the following statement, 'I have to change my hair from its natural state to fit in at the office'" (JOY Collective, 2019).

12.2.3   Fostering Hair Acceptance

We strongly encourage therapists to understand the historical and generational context regarding hair texture and styling and how it impacts Black female clients. Hair insecurity can be one of the most challenging subjects to raise with a White therapist because this non-Black therapist may represent the very privilege that Black women are stacked against (Holcomb-McCoy & Moore-Thomas, 2001). Black clients may not discuss hair insecurity directly, but the therapist might intuit hair-related stress and anxiety from the client's narratives (Ratts et al., 2016). Therapists should support a sense of empowerment regarding Black women's hairstyle preference. Therapists should also endorse messages of hair beauty and attractiveness in any style (Dawson et al., 2019).

Black women may prefer to alter the texture of their hair chemically. Some may wear their hair naturally or protect it by covering their natural hair (e.g., braids or headwear). Black women may choose to have hair or to wear locs, braids, wigs, relaxed styles, weaves, or other hairstyles (Wilson et al., 2018). A recent and growing trend is that Black women show hair acceptance and culturally attuned notions of beauty by returning to natural hairstyles. This is an act of self-love and self-actualization, and therapists should notice and support this trend (Banks, 2000).

Therapists might use the cultural messages about hair textures, and references in media and music can be starting points for discussion. For example, Beyoncé's lyrics to "Sorry" (2016) refer to the straight and silky hair worn by a White woman named Becky competing for a partner's interests. Its underlying message is the rejection of a kinky-haired Black woman. India Arie's song "I Am Not My Hair" (2006) describes being more than what society says about her hair or the color of her skin – a message that therapists should advance and embrace. By showing a deep understanding of hair anxiety and trauma and a willingness to talk about it, therapists build the foundation for a deep alliance with Black women and support their client's attempts to transcend hair shame.

12.3   Colorism

Colorism or shadeism, which invites bias against many racial-ethnic groups, is prejudice or discrimination against an individual because of skin color (i.e., glorifying White or lighter skin). Colorism is one of the most internalized dynamics that generate shame in Black women and begins in girlhood. Chapter 3 details a social experiment (the CNN doll studies) showing how Black girls as young as 5–7 years begin to understand that their skin color is not preferred. Black women with dark skin tone can feel ashamed and derided (Raskin et al., 2001). Through no fault of their own, *light-skinned Black women* have enjoyed preferred status denied to Black women of darker skin tones. We must also note that shaming comments have also been directed at women of lighter hues for having a skin color close to that of White women. This emphasis on "passing for white" or "white looking" has also been very painful for light skinned Black women who proudly own their Blackness. Internalized colorism can lead people to undergo skin bleaching, iris implant surgery to change one's eye color, and other procedures (Salaudeen, 2020). In the Black diaspora, around 40% of women seek skin bleaching services (Borgen Project, 2020). Colorism within Black culture is one of the more painful appearance invalidations for Black people, and therapists should know the historical underpinnings of these sentiments (Clark, 2004; Hunter, 1998; Raskin et al., 2001; Robinson-Moore, 2008).

The Future of the Race by Black icons Henry Louis Gates and Cornel West (Gates & West, 1996) documents a historical standard of colorism dating back to the sixteenth century. This standard originated in New Orleans, Louisiana. A Black person's skin was compared to the shade of a brown paper bag to approve or disapprove of the person. Skin tones lighter than the bag were desirable, and skin darker than the bag was seen as undesirable (Hunter, 1998;

Keith et al., 2010; Raskin et al., 2001; Robinson-Moore, 2008). This led to rampant acts of skin color bias and discrimination during Black enslavement that continued for decades. Compounding this dynamic is the historical preference for lighter or fairer skin, reaching back thousands of years and found in many other cultures besides Black or African. For example, in South Asia and East Asia, colorism is rampant and affects who is loved and gets married, among other questions (Dixon & Telles, 2017). In these cultures, skin bleaching to get lighter skin tones is also common. Thus, Black women with dark skin (e.g., darker than the brown paper bag) are apt to be universally rejected in African-centered and other cultural groups (Berry & Duke, 2011).

Therapists should be aware of the historical contexts of colorism in the United States, closely connected to slavery as a social system. During slavery, the amount of melanin in one's skin often determined the workload. For example, individuals with more melanin worked the property grounds or fields (i.e., hard labor). Enslaved Black people with less melanin worked inside the home performing lighter duties such as housekeeping chores and childcare (Hunter, 1998). Furthermore, this skin color distinction frequently caused dissension between Black people, particularly Black women (Hunter, 1998). Lighter-skinned enslaved women experienced favor because they were the biological children of slave owners, and so skin color came with unique privileges (Clark, 2004). Throughout the history of slavery, a well-known practice involved slave owners intentionally pitting darker-skinned against lighter-skinned enslaved people to instigate rivalry and maintain their own social control (Clark, 2004). Due to this rivalry, lighter-skinned women were made to feel superior, which caused darker-skinned women to resent them (Hunter, 1998; Raskin et al., 2001; Robinson-Moore, 2008). Many Black people internalized the idea that lighter skin was better because it came with many privileges.

Present-day skin color dynamics subtly mirror historical realities. It is not uncommon to learn of tensions between dark- and light-skinned Black people in families, schools, and other settings (Hunter, 1998). Having a darker skin tone has also affected employment opportunities, such as in the beauty industry, modeling, the media, and education (Keith et al., 2010). Dark-skinned Black women have been undervalued and invalidated for centuries, and this experience has been associated with deep-rooted traumas (Temin & Dahl, 2017). Alternatively, light-skinned Black people have also been denigrated with taunts of "passing," or pretending to be White, acting "bougie," or looking down on those with dark skin. Many light-skinned Black women recall painful teasing and ostracism in their peer groups. For example, in Spike Lee's 1988 film School Daze, two sororities play out colorism. One sorority had dark-skinned members, and the other sorority had light-skinned members. The brown paper bag test was enforced to determine membership in the light-skinned sorority, while the other sorority, which included dark-skinned Black women rejected from the privileged group, battled to prove that skin tone did not matter to all-around capability (Temin & Dahl, 2017).

The psychological trauma of colorism is captured in the Netflix documentary *Skin* (Naya, 2019). Although focused on colorism in Africa, much of what this documentary depicts is rampant in the United States. In the documentary, dark-skinned children and adolescents were taunted and bullied, and many internalized a sense of inferiority. Dark-skinned women were also less likely to be desired and pursued. Dark-skinned women became desperate to alter their skin tones through harmful practices such as skin bleaching with a product containing mercury (Tate, 2016). Naya, the documentary producer, told CNN she suffered low self-esteem when she was bullied for her dark skin color while growing up in the United Kingdom. She noted: "I had crooked teeth, and I had really bad eczema .... And even though I fixed my teeth and my skin cleared over time, the damage had already been done to my mental state and how I saw myself. So as I got older, I realized that I just didn't feel beautiful" (Salaudeen, 2020, para. 6). Naya said that in her early 20s, she began to regain her self-confidence by learning to love herself. She believes one way to minimize skin bleaching and combat colorism is to create an environment where darker-skinned women feel loved and beautiful. Therapists should adopt this posture and the message Naya recommends for Black women and especially for dark-skinned Black female clients: "From a young age, we need to start affirming the beauty of dark skin so that girls can grow up confident in being Black" (Salaudeen, 2020, para. 36).

Our personal experiences align with these recommendations. Adia's mother intentionally affirmed her dark brown skin while she was growing up and discouraged her from wearing makeup, saying that she did not need it. These efforts supported Adia in developing a positive view of her skin tone that carries through to the present day. Donna, a dark-skinned Black woman, recalls telling her son, "You are such a beautiful boy, with your dark velvety skin and white teeth. You are such a handsome child." Tonya, a coauthor on this chapter, also encouraged her son and daughter to love their caramel skin tones and to celebrate their skin color as special. As in our examples, parents can use an intentional strategy to help children fight the strangulating effects of dark-skin self-hatred.

Demonstrating an understanding of the breadth and depth of historical and contemporary colorism can lead to a profound alliance with Black female clients. The clinical impacts of colorism are deep and wide, and therapists must know what to look for and how it shows up. A Black woman is not likely to reveal skin bleaching or other skin lightening practices, which are done secretly. However, clients might more readily discuss family or peer dynamics in childhood, adolescence, or present life that suggest the presence of colorism. The therapist should be curious about the client's disclosures, probing such disclosures with gentle curiosity. Clients may represent storylines related to overlooked by Black men in favor of White women or Black women whose features are phenotypically White. Clients may also reference staying out of the sun or avoiding the beach for fear of a darkened skin tone. These narratives may hint at a Black woman's anxieties and worries about how skin color may affect her social standing or dating life. Black women may also make strides in body acceptance in several areas (e.g., hair texture) while struggling with others, such as a dark skin tone. Therapists' radical acceptance of the client and readiness to hold a sensitive conversation with compassion and cultural understanding will be the platform for building trust (Ratts et al., 2016). Strong voices in Black culture are challenging colorism, and those voices are growing louder. An important one is a dark-skinned star, Lupita Nyong'o (2019), whose children's book tells of Sulwe, the darkest child in her family, desperate to lighten her complexion until she understands the beauty of her skin. One night, Sulwe is visited by a shooting star that tells her an allegorical story of dark and light skin tones as the cycle of night and day, each as essential and valuable as the other.

12.4 Body Image Bias

For Black women, body image stress also relates to their body shape and size, complexion, and hair texture (Awad et al., 2015). Whereas hair and skin color are unique dimensions of body image struggles, Black women are also shamed for other body traits, such as weight, girth, buttocks, height, body hair, and facial features such as lips and nose. Black women's struggles with body image acceptance are connected to historical and present-day realities (Cotter et al., 2015). Black women's body consciousness is connected to broader experiences of racism and sexism. These painful oppressions in daily life make it difficult for Black women to dismantle destructive realities around how they are depicted (Gordon, 2008). Body part bias creates discomfort, rejection, and shame in Black women. The following two examples show how Black women's bodies can be devalued or exoticized, both postures being demeaning (Banks, 2000).

In the 2018 US Open title match, Serena Williams lost to rival Naomi Osaka. The match's dynamics, which included a confrontation between Williams and the match umpire, garnered worldwide scrutiny (Prasad, 2018). In days following the game, a controversial cartoon of Williams by Australian cartoonist Mark Knight in the Australian *Herald Sun* newspaper went viral globally. The furor centered on a rather unflattering cartoon depiction of Williams, with "large lips, a broad flat nose ... and ... positioned in an ape-like pose" (Davidson, 2018). Osaka, who is also considered Black, with a Black Haitian father and Japanese mother, was drawn as a blond-haired White woman. The cartoon drew widespread criticism as racist and sexist, and the National Association of Black Journalists in the United States denounced it "repugnant on many levels" (Davidson, 2018). It was one of the dozens of times that Williams' body was denigrated. Even as an elite athlete with impressive accomplishments, Williams, like Black women in everyday life, has been shamed for body features that do not fit privileged standards of beauty (British Broadcasting Service, 2019). Our point here is that both Williams and Osaka experienced caricatures about their appearance. The treatment of Williams was harsher.

The second example offers a more nuanced and culture-specific representation of Black women's bodies in Sir Mix-a-Lot's (1992) song "Baby Got Back." The song has been cited as shifting how the Black female body is celebrated. Beason (2017) suggests that "Baby Got Back" "simultaneously objectifies and subjectifies Black and Brown women, reframing an under-appreciated physical attribute as the ultimate symbol of desirability" (para. 12). Some of its lyrics celebrate physical features not typically affirmed in mainstream cultural representations. As a result, Sir Mix-a-Lot's song creates a sense of empowerment and, unapologetically, a platform for women of color to celebrate their body types, otherwise ostracized and excluded from the mainstream (Beason, 2017). While we too have danced to this song, the sexist reflections on Black women's buttocks also gives us pause.

The rejecting messages that some Black women have received in childhood and adolescence are critical to the lack of body acceptance. Women's therapy narratives often capture the pain of such experiences. In girlhood, social media plays a significant role in influencing the development of healthy self-esteem (Epstein et al., 2017). For Black girls, unhealthy self-esteem and lack of confidence develop from feeling erased in mainstream media publications (Gordon, 2008). Black magazines such as *Essence*, *Ebony*, *Jet*, and *Right On* are just a few places where young Black girls can receive positive messaging about developing bodies' beauty. The tension of loving the skin one is in can become difficult for a young mind (Gordon, 2008; Holcomb-McCoy & Moore-Thomas, 2001). Longing to "fit in" or admiring the beauty and body type of famous people rather than one's own body and self can spark unpredictable outcomes such as eating disorders, extreme exercising, adolescent plastic surgery, or other unhealthy practices (Hall, 1995; Umberson & Hughes, 1987). Young Black girls may find themselves hiding or covering up blossoming bodies because they do not know how to love and appreciate their bodies and develop body confidence (Porter et al., 2013; Raskin et al., 2001).

Chapter 3 outlines Black girls' experiences and discusses the adultification of Black girls' bodies that can begin even before puberty and sexual maturation.

Often, the challenges Black girls and women face in loving their bodies are not their own but projections of other people's biased perspectives (Adomaitis et al., 2017). Therapists must then become aware of the intensity of cultural norms, including ones they also hold, and how such norms shape perception of Black female bodies (Gordon, 2008). Black body rejection does not reside in individual actions but in societal norms and systems that define how Black women's bodies are understood (Temin & Dahl, 2017). Inept messaging, such as dress codes emphasizing modesty and conservatism, only exacerbates the problem (Temin & Dahl, 2017). A change in messaging about Black bodies can be powerful in the therapy room. One strategy is to name body bias as an "inner tyrant," a part of a Black woman that functions as an inner critic using every opportunity to shame and denigrate her appearance. Women are tortured and uncomfortable if their inner tyrants are loud and influential. Advancing the metaphor, therapists must help Black women to mute or quiet the tormenting tyrant and to supplant its loud and shaming voice with their own self-affirmations about their appearance.

A note of caution is that therapists must be crystal clear on the differences between a woman taking care of her health and having a sound body image. For example, if a Black woman is overweight, this does not mean she is unhealthy. If a Black woman is thin, it does not mean that she is not eating enough. Therapists must address the idea that Black women and girls struggle with obesity, but this issue is distinct and separate from internalized shame for not being in the "right body." The therapist must help Black women to reconcile the concepts of healthy body weight with body acceptance and self-love as a right that people have at any weight.

Specific strategies to support Black women in their physical health and wellness are shared in Chapter 13.

12.5 Clinical Strategies to Address Appearance Bias

12.5.1 Avoid Replication of Appearance Bias in Therapy

Clinical strategies to address clients' lookism distress begin with therapists' scrutiny of their own points of view. Therapists can use the reflection questions offered at the end of this chapter to begin that exploration. These questions involve exploring your own experience with lookism and privilege related to your appearance as well as biases that you may have held. White female therapists, who represent the idealized other to whom Black women are often compared, should be prepared for transference dynamics with clients. This may show up as a rejection of overtures, statements of mistrust, silence, distance, or unwillingness to go deep or to stay in the moment. The therapist's skillful ability to recognize women's transference dynamics and to show understanding and readiness to hold space for them in the therapy session will be vital to deepening the alliance.

12.5.2   Recognize Signs of Internalized Lookism

Internalized lookism distress can be explicit or subtle. In the *Bluest Eye* by Toni Morrison (1970) and *Sisters of the Yam* by bell hooks (2015; first published in 1994), these authors chronicle Black women's journey from self-hate to self-love. Through reading these stories, therapists can gain a sense of how internalized lookism dynamics might manifest in women's lives. The therapist must attend to the contextual realities faced in individual homes and communities. Often, clients' internalized lookism can be linked to negative coping attributes such as overeating, spending addictions, isolation, hyperawareness, and perfectionism in personal grooming. Clients with the most substantial internalized lookism dynamics may be more vulnerable to everyday slights, anxieties, and stress centered on their appearance. Binge eating disorders may be viewed as an accepted practice in Black households because Black women are more inclined to accept their body type than White women are (Cotter et al., 2015). While eating "comfort" food may not be labeled overeating, disordered eating may be missed or overlooked because of the misconception that Black women love good food, mostly fried, or love their curves. It is important for the therapist to take a deeper look at the need for comfort in eating (Porter et al., 2013). Black women's eating disorders linked to internalized lookism may go undiagnosed because of a lack of documentation or in-depth inquiry (Gordon et al., 2010).

12.5.3   Connect Internalized Lookism and Sexual Trauma

Lookism dynamics may be represented in women's sexual trauma narratives, and both the sexual trauma stories and internalized lookism dynamics may be problematic (Adomaitis et al., 2017). Here gendered-racial dynamics drive this lens. Personal trauma is challenging to navigate, and it becomes harder to manage when internalized lookism dynamics may be linked to a Black woman's experience of sexual assault. Lookism has also been connected to women's capitulation to consensual but abusive sexual encounters because of body anxieties (Buchanan et al., 2009, 2013; Keith et al., 2010). The bodies of Black girls and women have been hypersexualized, which in many cases can even lead to rape and assault (Decker et al., 2019). Because of these stereotypes, Black women and girls must navigate a higher standard in legal and social systems to prove that they did not entice the perpetrator through provocative dress or aspects of their appearance. While this factor has been documented in cases of rape or assault of women of all races, Black women and girls are far less likely than other women to have their stories believed or supported by law enforcement, judicial systems, or even family (Temin & Dahl, 2017). It is not acceptable that Black women and girls are blamed for being raped or assaulted. Research indicates that reports of sexual assault or rape of Black women are described or recounted differently by law enforcement. Black women are presented as less favorable than White women in stories of how the rape occurs (Decker et al., 2019; Keith et al., 2010).

Also, sexually traumatic experiences heavily steeped in appearance bias, such as being sexualized, stereotyped, exoticized, and objectified, may emerge within therapy. While Black women may not term their experiences "rape" or "assault," they may be unusually vulnerable to being groomed, inappropriately influenced, or subjected to harsh sexual encounters because of poor self-concerns and damaged body images (Buchanan et al., 2009, 2013). Even if such encounters cannot be proven in legal or judicial systems, therapy can be a setting in which Black women reclaim their bodies. They must also confirm in their own minds and hearts that they may have been preyed on when they were most vulnerable. Black women may tell these stories with shame and self-loathing. Still, therapists can help Black women forgive themselves and accept that their social standing and social dynamics played a part in their victimization. Having a good grasp of the historical and societal contexts of the sexualization of Black women's bodies will help therapists in supporting Black women who experienced consensual but shaming sex.

Specific practices for internal healing are highlighted in Chapter 14.

12.5.4 Focus on Messages That Increase Black Women's Self-Love

In general, while the media contributes to perpetuating stereotypes of Black women, some media messages have been created to help Black women love and embrace their hair, skin, and body types. Great songs are "I Am Not My Hair" (2006) and "Brown Skin" (2001) by India Arie, "Pretty Hurts" (2013) by Beyoncé, and "Anaconda" (2014) by Nicki Minaj. These are just a few songs with messages created to empower and equip women with self-love and confidence, encouraging them to reject messages referring to superficial and unrealistic standards of beauty and love themselves regardless of what society says. While Black women experience stigmas related to size shaming, hearing positive messages can help Black women understand what it means to be healthy and experience healthy well-being and happiness.

We return to an earlier discussion to showcase how things are changing, although not quickly enough. Procter & Gamble, the creators of the "Don't hate me because I'm beautiful" ad that infuriated Black women, now sponsor the website My Black Is Beautiful (www.mbib.com), designed by and for Black women. While some might view the website with suspicion because of its corporate backing, others might be impressed by its aim to "acknowledge and uplift Black community and culture through the lens of Black beauty." Resources like My Black Is Beautiful can go a long way toward Black women's improved self-esteem and confidence in their appearance. In writing this chapter, we struggled with how well we were able to present the *pervasiveness of appearance bias* against Black women, while conveying hope about change. Here we also felt sisterhood and outrage with women of other racial-ethnic groups (e.g., Asian, Latina) who also experience appearance bias, internalized and externalized. The voices of objection and dissent against lookism experienced by Black women are increasing and we encourage our colleagues in the mental health field to be numbered radically in this chorus. We show how one therapist works skillfully with a client to help her to reject lookism standards.

Case Example

Shay, a 24-year-old, cisgender, heterosexual, Black woman, sought therapy related to feelings of insecurity, unhappiness, and imperfection. She was a second-year law student at a public university and portrayed a posture of "I'm fine" while she experienced self-doubt and psychological distress. In therapy, she wanted to explore the root of her deep-seated emotional stress. Shay felt that understanding where distressing feelings came from was essential to self-understanding and better life quality.

Shay had not been in a romantic relationship since her junior year in college. She had been focused on her studies and was planning to become a sports attorney. She grew up in a home where she received negative messages related to how she should present herself at work. Shay remembered getting her hair pressed (straightened) and then relaxed while living in her parents' home – her parents firmly believed that wearing her hair straight was professional. They also thought hair grooming was a priority. Shay remembered her mother asking random Black female students with "nice hair" where they got their hair done because she wanted Shay to find a hairstylist on or near campus.

Some unfinished business was also emerging for Shay as she recounted the reason for her relationship breakup during her undergraduate years. Shay discovered that her boyfriend was secretly comparing her to a White female classmate that he found attractive. He wanted Shay to duplicate this young woman's hairstyle and clothing. Shay found out about this attraction because she saw the woman on her boyfriend's phone. The picture, her boyfriend told her, showed examples of the personal changes he wanted her to make. Shay was not sure if she wanted to alter her hair or make the adjustments her boyfriend wanted, and she was troubled by low self-esteem and self-doubt. Even though Shay was not sure about the newly requested changes, she did find the courage to break up with her boyfriend. If he could not accept her as she was, she did not want a relationship with him. At one point during therapy, when thinking about her ex-boyfriend's comparisons, Shay asked herself, "Am I not beautiful because I don't look like her?" This question came from a place of sadness, pain, and anger.

Shay also struggled to conform to the societal standards of beauty pushed by her parents. Shay often spoke of her paternal grandmother as her one place of refuge and acceptance. In talking with her grandmother, she did not feel the type of pressure regarding her looks and fitting in that she received from her parents, professors, and friends. They commented on her hair texture, eye color, skin tone, and other physical characteristics. Shay stated that she could not help but compare herself to White women working in the type of career she desired.

The therapist and Shay explored correlations between societal beauty standards and the messaging she received from her parents growing up and from her ex-boyfriend. Shay was able to identify that she felt ashamed and inferior in their eyes, but how they felt about her appearance said more about their values than about her. While she was sad that she had been compared to another person by someone she thought loved her, Shay's anger at her ex-boyfriend showed up in her laughter, dismissiveness, and invalidation of how much he had hurt her in her statements like "It wasn't that bad" or "He was only trying to help me."

The therapist empathized with Shay's sadness, pain, and anger, and the resultant climate was supportive and empowering for her. The therapy goal was to ensure that Shay experienced acceptance by her therapist and understood how to love herself with only the changes she chose to make. Shay realized how empowering it would be to honor her thoughts and feelings, and in her words, "If no one else is going to honor me, I can choose to honor myself." Shay represented Erykah Badu's song "Bag Lady" (1998) – she could not thrive because she was holding on to "stuff" that did not belong to her. Over time, Shay also began to incorporate affirmations that her grandmother shared with her to help her see herself as a beautiful woman.

12.6   Conclusion

In her book *Sisters of the Yam*, bell hooks (2015) summarized how lookism affects Black women internally:

One also cannot really talk about black female body self-esteem without talking about the politics of skin color, about the way internalized racism encourages and promotes self-hatred and/or self-obsession. A fair-skinned black female who may be able to feel that she is lovely and desirable because of her skin color may rely so much on looks to negotiate her way through daily life that she will not develop other areas of her life, like a grounded personality or her intellectual skills. She may become so obsessed with seeking constant affirmation of her "beauty" that she may learn no skills that would enable her to fully self-actualize. Concurrently, darker-skinned black females who internalize the assumption that dark is ugly and constantly assault themselves by inner negative feedback also cannot fully actualize. This is tragic. Without a doubt dark-skinned black females suffer the most abuse when black people internalize white-supremacist notions of beauty. (pp. 69–70)

This quote from bell hooks shows the depth of the effects of lookism, and therapists need to be aware of how it affects Black women. Yet we see encouraging signs of change as well. In the last two decades, there has been a robust and growing movement to encourage Black women to love themselves and their bodies. Natural hairstyles are more popular, and there is significant pushback against skin bleaching and more inclusivity of darker-skinned women and a range of body types. For example, we celebrate Rihanna's *Fenty* line of lingerie and make up targeted all sizes and skin tones. Her models of the Fenty products showcase this diversity (Barton, 2017). Black women are also embracing healthier bodies to address obesity and good nutrition without loss of body love and confidence (Porter et al., 2013). Therapists can draw on these sources in their work with Black female clients.

The rise in web resources and discussion groups about denigration of Black women's looks and bodies has created an army of observers of all races, viewing and watching posts and setting the record straight with savvy and culturally informed rebuttals. Often, these situations begin in obscurity and become viral on social media, leading to change (Papenfuss, 2021). For example, the International Swimming Federation faced swift and powerful backlash when the organization disapproved of an Olympic swim cap designed for Black women, suggesting that the cap did not fit "the natural shape of the head." Social media posts quickly pointed out the White bias embedded in the connotation of "the natural shape of the head." Black women celebrated the cap's design because it comfortably fit their Afros and braids and other uniquely Black hairstyles and allowed Black women to swim without worry in chlorinated pools. The media backlash prompted the federation to reconsider its position and review the swim cap. This is only one example of the swift and informed reactions to persistent biases around Black women's appearance. This type of advocacy can dramatically change the landscape of appearance oppressions that Black women have endured, and we celebrate it.

Therapist Reflection Questions

1. Before you read this chapter, what was your understanding of lookism and appearance bias in women of color, especially Black women?
2. What societal stereotyping, prejudice, or discrimination have you experienced because of your appearance? How has your skin color, hair, or body type made you disadvantaged or privileged?
3. When you were growing up, how was Black women's appearance characterized in your family or peer groups?
4. What are your experiences of internalized lookism in yourself and in your clients?
5. Of the strategies recommended in this chapter to address the client's experience of lookism, which ones resonate with you?
6. How comfortable would you feel talking to a Black woman about experiences of appearance shaming?
7. In what areas would you want more training or development on working with lookism in Black women?

Resources for Therapists and Clients

Books

Adichie C. N. (2017). *Dear Ijeawele, or A feminist manifesto in fifteen suggestions.* Knopf Publishers.

Bird, A. (2016). *Be unapologetically you: A self love guide for women of color.* Couronne Publishing.

Dabiri, E. (2020). *Twisted: The tangled history of black hair culture.* Harper Perennial.

Gandy, D. J. (1998). *Sacred pampering principles: An African-American woman's guide to self-care and inner renewal.* Quill.

hooks, b. (1993) *Sisters of the yam: Black women and self-recovery.* Taylor & Francis.

Jenkins, M. (2018). *This will be my undoing: Living at the intersection of Black, female, and feminist in (White) America.* Harper Perennial

McKenzie, V. M. (2002). *Journey to the well: 12 lessons on personal transformation.* Penguin Compass.

Norwood, K. J. (Ed.). (2014). *Color matters: Skin tone bias and the myth of a postracial America.* Routledge.

Stanley, J. (2017). *Every body yoga: Let go of fear, get on the mat, love your body.* Workman Publishing.

Taylor, S. R. (2018). *The body is not an apology: The power of radical self-love.* Berrett-Koehler Publishers, Inc.

TV Series

Bowser, Y. L., Lebedev, J., Moore, J., Simien, J., Allain, S., Dibai, N., Lebedev, L., & Shepard, D. (Executive Producers). (2017–present). *Dear white people* [TV series]. SisterLee Productions; Culture Machine; Code Red Productions; Homegrown Pictures; Roadside Attractions; Lionsgate Television; Netflix.

Films

Naya, B. (Writer) (2019). *Skin* [Documentary film]. Netflix.
Stilson, J. (Director). (2009). *Good hair* [Film]. Chris Rock Entertainment; HBO Films.

References

Adichie, C. N. (2017). *Dear Ijeawele, or a feminist manifesto in fifteen suggestions.* Anchor.
Adomaitis, A. D., Raskin. R., & Saiki, D. (2017). Appearance discrimination: Lookism and the cost to the American woman. *The Seneca Falls Dialogues Journal, 2*(6), 73–92.
al-Mansour, H. (Director). (2018). Nappily ever after [Film]. Netflix.
Arie, I. (2001). Brown skin [Song]. On *Acoustic Soul* [Album]. Motown Records.
    (2006). I am not my hair [Song]. On *Testimony: Vol. 1, life & relationship* [Album]. Motown.
Awad, G. H., Norwood, C., Taylor, D. S., Martinez, M., McClain, S., Jones, B., Holman, A., & Chapman-Hilliard, C. (2015). Beauty and body image concerns among African American college women. *Journal of Black Psychology, 41*(6), 540–564.
Badu, E. (1998). Bag lady [Song]. On *Mama's gun* [Album]. Motown Records.
Banks, I. (2000). *Hair matters: Beauty, power, and Black women's consciousness.* New York University Press.
Barton, G. (2017, November 14). *How beauty brands failed women of color.* Vox. https://www.vox.com/videos/2017/11/14/16649180/rihanna-fenty-beauty-makeup-inclusivity
Beason, T. (2017, May 3). We cannot lie: The cultural significance of Sir Mix-A-Lot's baby got back. *The Seattle Times.* https://www.seattletimes.com/entertainment/music/we-cannot-lie-the-cultural-significance-of-sir-mix-a-lots-baby-got-back/
Berry, D. C., & Duke, B. (Directors). (2011). *Dark girls* [Film]. Duke Media.
Beyoncé. (2013). Pretty hurts [Song]. *On* Beyoncé [Album]. Columbia.
    (2016). Sorry [Song]. *On* Lemonade [Album]. Parkwood.
Borgen Project. (2020, September 11). *Skin bleaching in Africa and public health.* https://borgenproject.org/skin-bleaching-in-africa

British Broadcasting Service. (2019, February 25). *Serena Williams: Cartoon accused of racism cleared by press watchdog*. BBC News. https://www.bbc.com/news/world-australia-47352854

Buchanan, N. T., Bergman, M. E., Bruce, T. A., Woods, K. C., & Lichty, L. F. (2009). Unique and joint effects of sexual and racial harassment on college students' well-being. *Basic and Applied Social Psychology, 31*, 267–285.

Buchanan, N. T., Bluestein, B. M., Nappa, A. C., Woods, K. C., & DePatie, M. M. (2013). Exploring gender differences in body image, eating pathology, and sexual harassment. *Body Image: An International Journal of Research, 10*, 352–360.

Clark, R. (2004). Interethnic group and intraethnic group racism: Perceptions and coping in Black university students. *Journal of Black Psychology, 30*, 506–526.

Cotter, E. W., Kelly, N. R., Mitchell, K. S., & Mazzeo, S. E. (2015). An investigation of body appreciation, ethnic identity, and eating disorder symptoms in Black women. *Journal of Black Psychology, 41*(1) 3–25. https://doi.org/10.1177/0095798413502671

Davidson, H. (2018, September 11). "Repugnant, racist": News Corp cartoon on Serena Williams condemned. *The Guardian*. https://www.theguardian.com/media/2018/sep/11/repugnant-racist-news-corp-cartoon-serena-williams-mark-knight

Dawson, G., & Karl, K. (2018). I am not my hair, or am I? Examining hair choices of Black female executives. *Journal of Business Diversity, 18*(2), 46–56.

Dawson, G. A., Karl, K. A., & Peluchette, J. V. (2019). Hair matters: Toward understanding natural Black hair bias in the workplace. *Journal of Leadership and Organizational Studies, 26*(3), 389–401. https://doi.org/10.1177/1548051819848998

Decker, M. R., Holliday, C. N., Hameeduddin, Z., Shah, R., Miller, J., Dantzler, J., & Goodmark, L. (2019). "You do not think of me as a human being": Race and gender inequities intersect to discourage police reporting of violence against women. *Journal of Urban Health, 96,* 772–783. https://doi.org/10.1007/s11524-019-00359-z

Dixon, A. R., & Telles, E. E. (2017). Skin color and colorism: Global research, concepts, and measurement. *Annual Review of Sociology, 43*(1), 405–424. https://doi.org/10.1146/annurev-soc-060116-053315

Epstein, R., Blake, J., & González, T. (2017). Girlhood interrupted: The erasure of Black girls' childhood. *SSRN Electronic Journal*. https://doi.org/10.2139/ssrn.3000695

Fernandez Campbell, A. (2018, April 18). *A Black woman lost a job offer because she wouldn't cut her dreadlocks. Now she wants to go to the Supreme Court*. Vox. https://www.vox.com/2018/4/18/17242788/chastity-jones-dreadlock-job-discrimination

Garrin, A., & Marcketti, S. B. (2018). The impact of hair on African American women's collective identity formation. *Clothing and Textiles Research Journal, 36*(2), 104–118. https://doi.org/10.1177/0887302X17745656

Gates, H. L., Jr., & West, C. (1996). *The future of the race*. Vintage Books, Random House

Gordon, K. H., Castro, Y., Sitnikov, L., & Holm-Denoma, J. M. (2010). Cultural body shape ideals and eating disorder symptoms among White, Latina, and Black college women. *Cultural Diversity and Ethnic Minority Psychology, 16*(2), 135–143. https://doi.org/10.1037/a0018671

Gordon, M. K. (2008). Media contributions to African American girls' focus on beauty and appearance: Exploring the consequences of sexual objectification. *Psychology of Women Quarterly, 32,* 245–256.

Gutierrez-Morfin, N. (2016, September 21). *U.S. court rules dreadlock ban during hiring process is legal.* NBC News. https://www.nbcnews.com/news/nbcblk/u-s-court-rules-dreadlock-ban-during-hiring-process-legal-n652211

Hall, C. C. (1995). Beauty is in the soul of the beholder: Psychological implications of beauty and African American women. *Cultural Diversity and Mental Health, 1*(2), 125–137.

Harris-Perry, M. V. (2011). *Sister citizen: Shame, stereotypes, and Black women in America.* Yale University Press.

Holcomb-McCoy, C., & Moore-Thomas, C. (2001). Empowering African American adolescent females. *Professional School Counseling, 5*(1), 19–27.

hooks, b. (2015). *Sisters of the yam.* Routledge.

Hunter, M. L. (1998). Colorstruck: Skin color stratification in the lives of African American women. *Sociological Inquiry, 68*(4), 517–535.

JOY Collective. (2019). *CROWN Research Study.* https://static1.squarespace.com/static/5edc69fd622c36173f56651f/t/5edeaaa09a3c4b1e68d153af/1591650978262/DOVE_2019HAIR_reseach.pdf

Keith, V. M., Lincoln, K. D., Taylor, J. R., & Jackson, J. S. (2010). Discriminatory experiences and depressive symptoms among African American women: Do skin tone and mastery matter? *Sex Roles, 62*(1-2), 48–59.

Lee, S. (Director). (1988). *School daze* [Film]. Columbia Pictures.

Minaj, N. (2014). Anaconda [Song]. On *The pinkprint* [Album]. Young Money.

Morrison, T. (1970). *The bluest eye.* Holt McDougal.

My Black Is Beautiful. (n.d.). http://www.myblackisbeautiful.com

Naya, B. (Writer). (2019). *Skin* [Documentary film]. Netflix.

Nyong'o, L. (2019). *Sulwe.* Simon & Schuster Books for Young Readers.

Papenfuss, M. (2021, July 5). *Swim caps for Black hair banned at Olympics because they don't fit "natural" head shape.* HuffPost. https://www.huffpost.com/entry/soul-cap-olympics-fina-ban_n_60e22c34e4b08f6f784bf0e7

Porter, J. S., Stern, M., Mazzeo, S. E., Evans, R. K., & Laver, J. (2013). Relations among teasing, body satisfaction, self-esteem, and depression in treatment-seeking obese African American adolescents. *Journal of Black Psychology, 39*(4), 375–395.

Prasad, R. (2018, September 11). *Serena Williams and the trope of the "angry Black woman."* BBC News. https://www.bbc.com/news/world-us-canada-45476500

Raskin, P., Coard, S. I., & Breland, A. M. (2001). Perceptions of and preferences for skin color, Black racial identity, and self-esteem among African Americans. *Journal of Applied Social Psychology, 31*(11), 2256–2274.

Ratts, M. J., Singh, A. A., Nassar-McMillan, S., Butler, S. K., & McCullough, J. R. (2016). Multicultural and social justice counseling competencies: Guidelines for the counseling profession. *Journal of Multicultural Counseling and Development, 44,* 28–48.

Robinson-Moore, C. L. (2008). Beauty standards reflect Eurocentric paradigms-So what? Skin color, identity, and Black female beauty. *Journal of Race & Policy, 4* (1), 66–85.

Salaudeen, A. (2020, July 3). *British-Nigerian actress shines a light on colorism in Netflix documentary.* CNN. https://www.cnn.com/2020/07/03/africa/colorism-documentary-africa/index.html

Sir Mix-a-Lot. (1992). Baby got back [Song]. On *Mack daddy* [Album]. Def American.

Tate, S. A. (2016). A brief Black/White/light history of skin bleaching/lightening/toning. In *Skin bleaching in Black Atlantic zones: Shade shifters* (pp. 5–36). Palgrave Pivot. https://doi.org/10.1007/978-1-137-49846-5_2

Temin, D. M., & Dahl, A. (2017). Narrating historical injustice: Political responsibility and the politics of memory. *Political Research Quarterly, 70*(4), 905–917.

Umberson, D., & Hughes, M. (1987). The impact of physical attractiveness on achievement and psychological wellbeing. *Social Psychological Quarterly, 50*(3), 227–236.

Wilson, I. P., Mbilishaka, A. M., & Lewis, M. L. (2018). White folks ain't got hair like us: African American mother-daughter stories and racial socialization. *Women, Gender & Families of Color, 6*(2) 226–248.

Part IV

Helping Black Women Recover and Thrive

13   Improving Black Women's Physical Health and Wellness

with Kimlin Tam Ashing[*]

> Get to know your client and be sincerely interested in their physical and mental health.
>
> Study participant

The US medical system has a history of mistreating Black women (Washington, 2006), and Henrietta Lacks is a classic example. Henrietta was a 31-year-old Black woman who died from cervical cancer in 1951 (Skloot, 2017). After experiencing vaginal bleeding, she sought medical treatment at Johns Hopkins Hospital, where her doctor discovered a tumor on her cervix. In addition to treating Henrietta's cancer, the doctor also took a sample of her tissue without asking permission and sent it to a researcher. Henrietta's cells proved invaluable to biomedical science. These cells multiplied rapidly, making them useful to researchers who have continued to use them in biomedical science to understand illnesses and develop medications. Specifically, cells from Henrietta (HeLa cells) have been used in research on cancer, HIV, and COVID; there have been more than 100,000 scientific articles published about research using HeLa cells; and three Nobel Prizes have been given for the discoveries scientists made using HeLa cells (Jackson & Utter, 2020; National Institutes of Health, 2020). However, none of the money earned through this research came to Henrietta's family ("Henrietta Lacks," 2020). Henrietta died shortly after being diagnosed with cervical cancer because the treatment administered was not effective. Though her cells advanced biomedical research, she received no credit or compensation. Too often, Black women have been used and abused by the medical system and denied life-saving treatment. This reality is important for therapists to recognize and care about.

Henrietta's medical treatment symbolizes how Black women may be treated in health care institutions in the United States. Too often, Black women are underserved and mistreated by medical systems (Washington, 2006). Further,

[*] A. Gooden & K. Ashing. (2023). Improving Black women's physical health and wellness. In D. Baptiste & A. Gooden, *Promoting Black women's mental health: What practitioners should know and do.* Cambridge University Press.

311

Black women's contributions are often overlooked or diminished, and they rarely benefit from optimal treatments that may reflect biomedical advancements. Such treatment is not only experienced by poor and uneducated Black women, who tend to get the worst of it. Even privileged Black women and girls can be marginalized by health and mental health providers.

In addition to the mental and emotional challenges of racism, sexism, and other traumas, Black women experience more health concerns than women of other racial groups. Specifically, compared with White women, Black women suffer from more illnesses and experience higher mortality rates from infectious diseases (e.g., COVID-19, HIV, and hepatitis) and chronic diseases (e.g., heart disease, cancer, and diabetes) (Sengupta & Honey, 2020). Research connects the health issues Black women experience to societal injustices and weathering (Braveman et al., 2010; Geronimus et al., 2010). Weathering is the biological aging Black women experience as a result of stress due to racism, sexism, poverty, and other stressors (Geronimus et al., 2010).

> Chapter 2 discusses the social determinants of health and mental health for Black women and highlights the role of policies and structural factors that influence Black women's health.

We know that physical and mental health are intimately connected. We encourage therapists working with Black women to support them to radically care for their physical health as they work on their mental health. Black women are more likely than White women to experience somatic symptoms in response to depression and anxiety (Bagayogo et al., 2013; Robins & Regier, 1991). Many Black women neglect their physical health as they prioritize care for their loved ones. Further, in both historical and contemporary contexts, many Black women have not had the time or resources for optimal care of their bodies.

Black women receive messages that their bodies are not beautiful and prized or worthy of protection and care in the United States. The body devaluation and disrespect that we discuss in Chapter 12 on appearance bias and lookism also play out in medical systems where Black women are denied care. Medical professionals often provide inferior care that may include not listening to patients, withholding pain medication, and failing to treat patients with dignity and compassion. They also fail to communicate, educate, and bond with their Black patients to create an effective clinician–patient health partnership.

The devaluation of Black women's bodies and the discrimination Black women experience in health systems have significant consequences. The stress Black women experience from gendered racism and the poor medical treatment they receive drive disparities in Black women's disease risks, quality of life, and life expectancy. Concerns about receiving discriminatory treatment leads many Black women to put off routine exams or life-saving interventions until it is too late (Lannin et al., 2002). The late Dr. Martin Luther King Jr. stated that "of all the forms of inequality, injustice in health is the most shocking and the most inhuman."

Although therapists do not directly address the physical health of Black women, it is important for therapists to acknowledge the connection between mental and physical health. Psychotherapists are apt to underemphasize mind–body connections, which is a critical omission, especially for Black women. We encourage therapists to prioritize the relationship between the mental and the physical to help women understand and address the connection between their physical and psychological health and wellness (Evans et al., 2017). In this chapter, we provide an overview of the common physical health challenges Black women experience. We also discuss the connection between mental and physical health. We recommend how Black female clients can advocate for better health care to take care of their physical health proactively. We provide strategies for stress management to improve physical and mental wellness.

13.1   Black Women's Health Challenges

13.1.1   Aging

A common saying in the Black community is "Black don't crack." This saying refers to the fact that Black women tend to look significantly younger than non-Black women. Black women's skin can glow and remain wrinkle free as they age. Despite looking physically younger than White women, research demonstrates that Black women are biologically "older" than White women in middle age. Accelerated biological aging results from the experience of stress from racism, sexism, and poverty (Geronimus et al., 2010). Health statistics show numerous bodily/internal premature signs of aging among Black women. For example, Black women often experience an earlier onset of chronic disease, including diabetes, heart disease, stroke, arthritis, and even cancer (Beckie et al., 2011; Warren-Findlow, 2006). Overall, Black people have higher mortality rates of stroke and cardiovascular disease and are diagnosed with these diseases at younger ages than White people (Havranek et al., 2015). Specifically, Black women are diagnosed with and die from these illnesses at least 5–10 years younger, depending on the disease, than White women (Havranek et al., 2015). Additionally, Black women have higher mortality rates of all cancers (Ashing et al., 2022), including endometrial and cervical cancer (American Cancer Society, 2021; Collins et al., 2014). Further, despite younger age at diagnosis and more aggressive cancers, Black women are typically not referred to genetic counseling and testing to best inform their treatment (George et al., 2021). High stress, minoritization, elevated environmental exposures due to the legacy of deliberate Black community redlining and targeted deprivation (Ribeiro et al., 2018), inadequate health care, and limited engagement in health-promoting practices explain Black women's disease outcomes including being burdened with multiple chronic illnesses. Unhealthy coping patterns that increase Black women's risks for disease and mortality include unhealthful eating and insufficient physical activity.

13.1.2   Sexual and Reproductive Health

Black women have been stereotyped as hypersexual and are bombarded with negative societal messages about sexual health and sexuality. Black women can be disconnected from their sexuality and sexual pleasure, and may have difficulty exercising boundaries to maintain sexual health. For example, Black women and girls age 13 and older are significantly more likely to have HIV than their White counterparts (Centers for Disease Control and Prevention [CDC], 2022). Black women also have higher rates of other sexually transmitted infections (STIs), such as gonorrhea, syphilis, and chlamydia (CDC, 2022). Studies have found that self-reported condom use does not differ significantly between Black and White women, but Black women may have less and limited control in requiring male partners to use condoms and insufficient access to health centers where STI tests, preventive education, and treatment are available accounts for differences in STI rates (Ware et al., 2019).

In Chapter 11, we discuss how research has neglected Black women's normative sexual practices to support positive sexuality.

Black women also have high rates of maternal mortality and morbidity. These disparities are caused by a combination of factors, including inequitable prenatal care and weathering due to implicit bias, discrimination, and racism (Villarosa, 2018). Black women are three times more likely to die during pregnancy or childbirth than White women (Chidi & Cahill, 2020). The discrimination Black women navigate in their daily lives increases the stress they experience before and during their pregnancies, resulting in adverse pregnancy outcomes. Additionally, Black women experience discrimination during prenatal care and when seeking medical treatment, resulting in their concerns and complications being ignored by medical professionals during and after childbirth (Petersen et al., 2019). For example, when Serena Williams gave birth to her daughter, she was in critical condition and almost died due to a lack of attention or medical care. Serena Williams is a world-renowned tennis player who is in incredible physical shape. She has financial resources and access to the best medical care globally, yet she still had complications during childbirth and struggled to get the attention and treatment needed during the delivery and postpartum period. Thankfully, Serena survived her childbirth crisis, but there are countless heartbreaking stories of Black women or their babies dying when they did not receive adequate medical care (Villarosa, 2018).

13.2   Connections between Physical and Mental Health in Black Women

Recent decades have brought advances connecting mental and physical health. These insights apply to the experiences of Black women. Mental stress can start in the brain and manifest both emotionally and physically. Therapists may be apt to focus on emotional dimensions of stress, but physical dimensions matter as well. Research has demonstrated that one's current mental health is related to past physical health. Current physical fitness also relates to past mental health, particularly for older adults (Ohrnberger et al., 2017). Psychologist John B. Arden, an expert on the connections between the brain, body, and mental health, highlights the importance of social connection, exercise, education, diet, and sleep on our mental, emotional, and cognitive well-being (Arden, 2014). Specifically for Black women, in a qualitative study with Black women between the ages of 50 and 75, Warren-Findlow (2006) found that Black women described chronic stress as contributing to heart disease. Specifically, traumatic stress relates to physical health problems such as obesity and cardiovascular disease (McFarlane, 2010). As discussed in Chapter 5, Black women experience chronic and acute traumas and thus may be more likely to experience physical health issues as a result of trauma.

Black women are more likely to be obese than White women. Research shows that obese Black women are more likely to report experiencing anxiety and interpersonal challenges with their families while growing up (Davis et al., 2005). Evidence also shows that Black people display more somatic symptoms than non-Black people in mental health conditions such as depression and anxiety (Bagayogo et al., 2013). Specifically, in a research study of Black women and depression, McKnight-Eily and colleagues (2009) found that reports of physical health concerns were associated with current and lifetime depressive symptoms.

Black women's experience of racism and sexism increases their stress, which intensifies mental and physical health concerns (Lewis et al., 2017). Stress can be driven by significant life experiences that impact body awareness and health. Daily hassles or everyday smaller stressors such as racially based insults or invalidations can be just as devastating to physical health (Lamis & Kaslow, 2014). Further, racism and sexism may prevent Black women from taking care of their physical health. Black and Woods-Giscombé (2012) found that stress and adopting the Strong Black Woman persona may deter women from getting breast cancer screenings. Black women commonly feel that they must spend all their time and energy caring for their loved ones. It is not uncommon for them to neglect taking care of themselves in the process.

The Strong Black Woman persona is explored further in Chapter 8.

Further, if a Black woman internalizes negative stereotypes about being a Black woman, she may have difficulty valuing a physical body that society denigrates. We encourage therapists to track whether their Black female clients may have internalized stereotypes and do not value their bodies. Internalized stereotypes may cause Black women to neglect caring for their bodies. One of us has worked with a Black female client who had internalized negative views of her body related to her size. The client responded by not engaging in regular self-care practices. This in turn caused her to feel worse about herself. In addition to supporting this client in caring for her body and emotions, the therapist also helped the client to dismantle the negative stereotypes she had internalized.

Common stereotypes of Black women are discussed in Chapter 4.

13.3   Supporting Black Women's Self-Advocacy in Health Care Systems

As discussed in Chapter 2 on social determinants of health, there is a history of mistreatment of Black people in health systems in the United States. An Institute of Medicine report (Nelson, 2002) concluded that people of color receive a substandard level of care compared with White people even after controlling for socioeconomic and health insurance status. Lawmakers have made efforts to address these health disparities by passing laws to increase health care research, improve the quality of care provided to ethnic minority populations, and increase education regarding these disparities (Healthcare Research and Quality Act of 1999; U.S. PL 106-129; and the Minority Health and Health Disparities Research and Education Act of 2000; U.S. PL 106-525). These pieces of legislation have decreased the health disparities Black women experience. Additionally, in 2020, the Black Maternal Health Omnibus Act was proposed in the US Congress to address the Black maternal health crisis (Black Maternal Health Caucus, 2020). As of the writing of this book in 2022, this Act has not yet become law. But substantial health disparities persist. Therapists need to understand the policies and systemic factors that support Black women's health and also the factors that make it more difficult for them to get quality care.

Black women are aware of the legacy of their mistreatment in US medical systems. Many can recall personal negative experiences with medical professionals (Sacks, 2018). Past negative experiences and anticipation of inadequate treatment can cause Black women to delay or avoid seeking crucial medical treatment. When Black women interact with medical systems, they may even expect that they may not be taken seriously or receive high-quality care (Rao, 2020). Empirical evidence shows that medical professionals underestimate the pain that Black people experience and underprescribe pain medications to Black patients (Lee et al., 2021; Trawalter et al., 2012). For example, one participant in our study of Black women's perspectives on psychotherapy made this point about mental health and medical care, "In most cases . . . doctors do not take our issues seriously or [they think] we are being bitter Black women or too much to handle." Therapists need to acknowledge the authentic challenges that Black women experience when navigating the medical system.

> In our concluding chapter, we present the experience of one of our clients, who sought therapy partly to address shaming she received from several medical providers while dealing with a chronic illness.

We offer a recent powerful example of disparities in the medical system. In December 2020, during the COVID-19 pandemic, Dr. Susan Moore, a Black female physician, was denied life-saving care. Though she was an experienced medical professional and proactively sought treatment, she was continually ignored, denied pain medication, and sent home despite reporting life-threatening symptoms. The physician who treated her was a White man and may have held implicit biases about Black people and may have assumed that she was overstating her pain to acquire drugs illicitly. The physician's denial of pain medication caused Dr. Moore to suffer further with untreated pain. Dr. Moore spoke out about the challenges she experienced before her death. She used an example of how she was treated to emphasize what Black people face when seeking medical treatment. Dr. Moore chronicled her experience in a 7.5-minute Facebook video before she passed away. In her video, she stated, "If I were White, I wouldn't have to go through this" (Mack & Hays, 2020).

While our medical systems have a long way to go before they provide equitable care to Black women, it can still be helpful for Black women to be their own health advocates. We encourage therapists to talk with their Black female clients about how to advocate for themselves as they navigate medical systems to make it more likely that Black women will receive the care they need and deserve. Therapists can begin this conversation by acknowledging the anxiety Black women may experience when dealing with medical systems. By discussing the anxiety and apprehension Black women have related to attending medical appointments, therapists can proactively support their clients in identifying strategies to manage this anxiety and develop a plan to advocate for themselves and pursue necessary medical care even when it is uncomfortable. Black women who actively participate in their care and their family's care may see the benefits, including greater trust in their health care providers, satisfaction with care, better health, and enhanced quality of life.

In supporting a Black female client to be her own health advocate, we recommend that the therapist help the client understand that advocating for her health involves proactive planning and engaging in behaviors that nurture her health. Taking care of and advocating for her health can seem daunting, but Black women need to know that thoughtful, informed action can send a powerful message. When a Black woman communicates clearly and assertively with her health care providers, she telegraphs that she takes her health seriously. When a Black woman serves as her medical advocate, her doctors will begin to see her as a vital partner in making medical decisions. Here, we offer five recommendations for ways therapists can support Black women in being their own health advocates.

1. **Encourage Black women to interview their doctors and health care team and make sure that they have specializations related to Black women's concerns.** Therapists should let Black women know that they should never feel unsafe with their health care team. If they can choose, they should select providers who listen to their concerns and show them respect.

2. **Encourage Black women to investigate their diagnoses and symptoms before appointments.** Women should write down any concerns and questions about diagnoses and be ready to share them with providers. Because medical appointments are often rushed, preparation will help women clarify what they need to know about their conditions, treatment options, best practices, and other concerns to ensure they receive competent care.

3. **Encourage Black female clients to speak up in conversations with their medical providers.** Black culture and communities often value deferring to and respecting elders and experts. Black women may feel intimidated about questioning their physicians about health recommendations. Women may worry that questions show disrespect. Therapists

should encourage women to give up a deferential posture and press past any discomfort to get the answers they need.

4. **Encourage Black women to take notes or record information during their appointments to review later.** Health care providers often give a lot of information in a short period during medical appointments and having notes will help Black women be able to go back and research information after their appointments.

5. **Recommend that Black women bring someone to their medical appointments to provide emotional support around self-advocacy.** Medical appointments can be overwhelming, and having someone present to offer emotional support and note medical information can help women consider their medical decisions thoroughly.

In addition to these strategies, Table 13.1 provides detailed steps Black women can use when advocating for themselves and talking with medical professionals. For Black women who are pregnant, we recommend the resource "Protecting Your Birth: A Guide for Black Mothers," written by two Black women, one a gynecologist and one an expert in women's wellness and reproductive health (Chidi & Cahill, 2020). This resource was published in the *New York Times* in 2020.

Many Black women do not have health insurance or adequate health insurance, which may limit their access to their preferred medical providers. Therapists should keep the health insurance and financial flexibility of their Black female clients in mind to ensure that they provide recommendations that are accessible to them. We offer several tips in the following sections to integrate physical health themes into therapy conversations.

13.4   Coach Black Women to Care for and Honor Their Bodies

Black women's bodies are often subject to violence, trauma, and neglect. Trauma, which we discuss extensively in Chapter 5, can result in health issues and may cause Black women to experience shame related to their bodies. Supporting women to honor and care for their bodies is an essential aspect of their healing and recovery. We encourage therapists to support Black women in approaching their bodies from a place of self-compassion.

We begin with a foundation of self-acceptance and then encourage Black women to connect their physical health to their mental health and wellness. Our recommendations for how therapists can support Black women in establishing healthy routines related to sleeping, eating, physical activity, and managing stress are based on the brain health strategies outlined by Arden (2014). Having healthy routines that support physical health can help alleviate mental health symptoms and promote mental wellness.

Table 13.1 *Strategies to support Black women in being their own health advocates*

Area of Care	Strategies
Medical records	Keep up-to-date records of your general medical information, specifically details about your medical diagnoses and types of treatment.
Risks and side effects	Ask your health care team about treatment risk and factors related to possible side effects, including whether the drug was tested on Black people, potential side effects (both long term and short term), and how to manage them.
Follow-up and specialty care	Ask your health care team to help you understand which doctors you should see for routine follow-up visits or if you need specialty care (e.g., cardiologist or endocrinologist), including vision and dental care clinicians. If you are having oral surgery, ask for referral to an oral surgeon, and if you have significant gum issues, ask to see an endodontist.
Whole-person care plan	Work with your health care providers to create a whole-person care plan that addresses the symptoms and provides a cure, if possible, along with a plan to protect and promote your health. Your care team ought to educate you on what illness or medicine side effects to look for, how to reduce the risk for certain side effects (like abdominal pain due to antibiotics and constipation due to pain medication), and the risk of other illnesses due to your diagnosis and/or medications. Your whole-person care plan must consider your family or living contexts (e.g., caring for older parents and/or children) as well as your health wishes and quality of life.
Health concerns	Keep a record of health concerns (e.g., significant, unexplained weight gain or loss) and medication symptoms as they develop, and follow up with your doctor.
Treatment plans	Follow any treatment plans for medical care. Talk with your doctors if you have concerns about the recommended plans. You should contact your doctors if you feel any symptoms or need guidance on managing symptoms.
Side effects	Read up on the specific side effects or any later aftereffects that you have experienced so that you can bring questions to your health care team.
Research	Seek information and the support of other credible sources to give you the confidence to be active in your medical care. Credible sources include www.cdc.gov, www.nih.gov, www.cancer.gov, and cancer.org.

13.4.1 Honoring the Body

Therapists can help Black women be grateful for their bodies and treat them with care. Many women are socialized to criticize their bodies and to focus on what they believe are negative aspects of their appearance. Further, Black women receive constant messages that their bodies are sexual objects or are too big, unattractive, unhealthy, unworthy, or other negative qualities. Some Black women push back against negative messages and embrace their curves and other Afrocentric features. But many Black women internalize negative messages about Black female bodies and regard their bodies through a biased lens. Therapists can help Black women embrace their bodies through body love and acceptance. We include a guided body gratitude meditation (Table 13.2) that therapists may find helpful. This meditation guides clients to focus on

Table 13.2 *Body gratitude meditation script*

- Get in a comfortable position; you can either sit or lie down. Begin by taking a few deep breaths, and really notice the breath flowing in and out of your body. Notice how your body is feeling right now, and see if you can let your mind and body rest in the present moment. Notice the feeling of your body supported by the chair, couch, or bed; notice that your body is supported in this moment.
- Now, place your attention on your head. Notice any physical sensations that are present in your head. *(Pause.)* Reflect on your brain that allows you to live and think, your eyes that allow you to see, your nose that allows you to smell and breathe, and your mouth that allows you to speak and eat. Take a moment to offer all of the parts of your head gratitude for the ways that they support you in your daily activities. Now, place one of your hands gently on your head, and send some love and kindness to your head. *(Pause.)* Take a deep breath and place your hand back in your lap when you are ready.
- Now, moving your attention to your chest, reflect on your lungs and how they help you to breathe, your heart and how it keeps you alive, your ribs and chest cavity and how they protect you. Offer gratitude to these parts of your body for how they serve you. Place one or both of your hands gently over your chest and send some love to your heart and lungs. *(Pause.)* Take a deep breath.
- Move your attention back down to your stomach. Reflect on your digestive system, your stomach, your small and large intestine. Connect with gratitude for your digestive system helping you to process food and turn it into energy and fuel for your body. Place one or both of your hands over your stomach, and send some love and appreciation to this part of your body. *(Pause.)* Take a deep breath and release any unhelpful or critical thoughts that may have arisen.
- Now move your attention to your legs and feet. Reflect on how they carry you through the world, allowing you to walk, run, sit, and dance. Place your hands on your thighs and send them love and gratitude for carrying you through the world. *(Pause.)*
- As we wrap up this exercise, send love and gratitude to your entire body for keeping you alive. Take a few more deep breaths and connect to the feeling of aliveness in your body. Notice again how your body feels sitting in the chair. Bring your attention back to the room and notice any sounds that you hear, and when you are ready, you can open your eyes.

various body parts and show appreciation for how these body parts serve them. The body gratitude meditation helps women shift away from critiquing and toward appreciating their bodies. Supporting Black women in cultivating supportive, loving relationships with their bodies provides a foundation for Black women to care for their health consistently and intentionally.

In Chapter 12 we discuss appearance bias and lookism in more detail.

The Body Is Not an Apology by Sonya Renee Taylor, a Black woman, is an excellent resource for Black women struggling to love and accept their bodies. Taylor's (2018) book provides a beautiful guide on practices to engage in radical self-love and dismantle societal norms that cause us to feel bad about our bodies. Helping Black women to love and accept their bodies will enable them to have a healthy relationship with their bodies. This foundation of self-acceptance supports Black women in taking care of their physical and mental health.

Chapter 12 highlights biases and stereotypes about their bodies that Black women must reject.

13.4.2   Encourage Good Sleep Hygiene

Sleep is an essential pillar of both physical and mental health. Black people are more likely to sleep less than 5 hours or more than 9 hours compared with White people, and this tendency to sleep too little or too much can lead to health issues (Nunes et al., 2008). Research has connected the experience of discrimination to poor sleep (Slopen et al., 2016). Further, getting less than 8 hours of sleep has been associated with a higher risk of certain types of cancer for Black women (Xiao et al., 2016). We recommend therapists talk with their Black female clients about their sleeping habits. If needed, identify ways to help Black women improve their sleep hygiene and the amount of sleep they get. These discussions may start by focusing on logistical factors related to setting bedtimes; turning off cell phones, computers, and television; and doing something relaxing before bed.

If sleep issues persist, therapists might explore how their Black female clients feel about allowing themselves to rest. Many Black women have trouble allowing themselves to sleep and rest due to their responsibility to take care of others. Resting involves relaxing and not doing anything "productive" or active.

Both rest and sleep are restorative, and while sleep is largely unconscious, rest provides Black women with the space to reflect and be, without doing something. As mentioned earlier, many Black women adopt the Strong Black Woman persona (see Chapter 8), which can cause them to think their worth depends on working and caring for others at all times. Black women may feel that they always need to be doing something productive and have trouble resting their minds and relaxing their bodies. If this dynamic is present for Black female clients, the therapist should help them explore where their beliefs around always working have come from and challenge the idea that their self-worth is related to productivity. It can be helpful to encourage Black women to take steps to intentionally relax as they prepare to go to bed and to think about the reasons they deserve rest. The Nap Ministry is an initiative started by Tricia Hersey, a Black woman, to challenge capitalistic ideas that we should always be working. The Nap Ministry used the framework "Rest is resistance" to explore the "liberating power of naps" through public art installations and community organizing (Nap Ministry, n.d.). Therapists can encourage Black female clients to check out The Nap Ministry's blog (www.thenapministry.wordpress.com) or follow the initiative on Instagram (@thenapministry) for reminders about the importance of rest. If Black female clients continue to have difficulty calming their minds before bed, therapists can recommend guided meditations to help them fall asleep; see the list of resources at the end of this chapter for free guided meditation apps.

13.4.3   Support and Encourage Good Nutrition

Black communal culture involves gatherings over food. The foods (e.g., fried chicken, candied yams, macaroni and cheese, chitlins) that have been passed down through generations of Black people in the United States were once celebratory foods eaten occasionally or highly caloric foods needed to fuel long days of slave labor or sharecropping. However, these foods have now become daily or weekly traditions in many Black families. They may contribute to chronic and deadly diseases such as diabetes, high cholesterol, cancer, and heart disease. Additionally, emerging research connects eating and nutrition to mental and emotional health. Due to stress from everyday hassles, Black women are also prone to emotional eating, which has a well-documented link to obesity (Rucklidge & Kaplan, 2013).

Further, Black people in the United States are more likely to live in neighborhoods that have been classified as food deserts, with no grocery stores within 0.5 miles of their homes, or food swamps, with a plethora of fast food. These geographic factors, coupled with the food insecurity that many Black families living in poverty experience, contribute to the likelihood of having only access to food that is high in calories and low in nourishment. Research has demonstrated that African Americans living in food deserts have high rates of obesity (Ghosh-Dastidar et al., 2014). Therapists need to understand the cultural and structural factors that can inhibit Black women from engaging in healthy eating while also supporting them in finding creative ways to nourish their bodies with healthy food.

Therapists can support Black women in making choices related to their eating, drug use, and alcohol consumption with the intention of making choices that are beneficial for their bodies and well-being. We recommend that therapists guide their Black female clients in making mindful eating choices by listening to what their bodies need and paying attention to the foods that feel nourishing and the foods that make them feel sick or malnourished. Mindful eating can be a useful practice to support this awareness. Therapists can encourage clients to slow down when they are eating to really notice the smells, tastes, and textures of the food and pay attention to the physical sensations they experience after eating. Conversations about food choices can be sensitive. We encourage therapists to be cautious not to tell Black female clients what they should and should not eat.

Research has demonstrated that Black, White, and Latinx people have similar rates of eating disorders, with Black and Latinx people being more likely to have disorders that involve binge eating (Marques et al., 2011). What is troubling is that clinicians may be less likely to recognize disordered eating in their Black female clients (Gordon et al., 2006). It is important for therapists to do a thorough assessment of their clients' food consumption and any restricting, binging, and purging behaviors and to address these eating disorder symptoms appropriately. The overarching goal of supporting Black women with regard to their eating is helping them to develop a healthy relationship with food so that they can make choices about what foods to consume and ensure that their diets include enough nourishing food. The Food Heaven podcast is hosted by two Afro Latina dietitians who share culturally grounded recommendations about intuitive eating and support women of color in developing healthy relationships with food and their bodies. This podcast may be a helpful resource for Black female clients who would like support with healthy eating.

13.4.4   Exercise and Physical Activity

The systemic issues of racism, sexism, and socioeconomic disparities can make it difficult for Black women to practice physical self-care (Jean, 2020). While 70% of Black women report being physically active during their teenage years, only 45% engage in regular exercise in their 20s (Watson, 2018). Evidence shows that Black women are interested and motivated to engage in physical activity when they have adequate social support (Collins et al., 2020). Therapists should support their Black female clients in developing healthy routines around physical activity. The emphasis should not necessarily relate to changing their bodies but should be about supporting health, strength, and well-being. A qualitative research study of African American women found that they believe there is a connection between physical activity and mental wellness (Wilcox et al., 2002). We encourage therapists to discuss physical activity and body movement with their Black female clients (Craft & Perna, 2004; Jayakody et al., 2014). Regular exercise (150 minutes/week), even if very low intensity, reduces the risk of chronic illnesses (e.g., mental deterioration, heart disease, diabetes, even cancer) and improves health and well-being (e.g., better cognitive function, memory, alertness, mood, sleep, appetite, energy, and joy).

Therapists should be aware of the cultural and contextual barriers Black women may experience related to regular, intentional physical activity. For example, many Black women avoid exercise because sweat can ruin their hairstyles. As discussed in Chapter 9 on shifting and Chapter 12 on lookism, caring about hair and appearance is more than just vanity for Black women; their physical appearance can impact how people treat them. Additionally, Black women who reside in low-income neighborhoods with high levels of community violence may not feel comfortable exercising outside and in parks near their homes.

We recommend therapists open the conversation by exploring their Black female clients' relationship to exercise and physical activity. An excellent place to start is by discussing the ways that she enjoys being physically active. We encourage therapists to move conversations about exercise beyond going to the gym and running if those activities are not enjoyable for the client. The goal is to help the client identify sustainable ways to engage in regular physical activity that she enjoys. For clients who are apprehensive about exercising, it can be helpful for therapists to inform clients that people often enjoy exercising more than they anticipate (Ruby et al., 2011).

Additionally, engaging in physical exercise can be lonely and feel isolating for Black women. It can be helpful to encourage them to find group workout classes, programs, or clubs led by other women or Black people. In one study, Black people reported that they were twice as likely to avoid outdoor recreation areas if they did not have another person to go with them (Dorwart et al., 2019). This underscores the importance of social connections around exercise. Black Girls Run is a national movement aimed at inspiring Black women to participate in outdoor running activities with other Black women. With running companions, women hold one another accountable for their outdoor physical activity (Dorwart et al., 2019).

As with any behavioral change, therapists should guide Black women who want to increase their physical activity to begin by taking small steps such as taking a 15-minute walk three times per week or dancing in their living room to their favorite music for 10 minutes. Setting small goals will help the physical activity feel achievable, and small amounts of exercise can provide significant benefit. We also recommend exploring any barriers to taking these steps. Are clients concerned about messing up their hair if they sweat while working out? Have they previously tried intense exercise or weight-loss programs that felt punishing and discouraging? Are they just having trouble getting started? Exploring questions like these with clients will help to address any barriers that might arise.

13.4.5   Stress Management

We know that stress is a crucial contributor to weathering, hypertension, and other health issues for Black women. Thus, helping Black women to manage stress and practice strategies that support them in calming their minds and bodies will be beneficial. Black women can engage in meditation, yoga, dance, baths, massages, and other activities to calm their nervous systems and help themselves feel safe. Meditation can help to reduce stress, anxiety, and depression and supports people managing chronic pain. We encourage therapists to introduce meditation to their Black female clients if they do not already incorporate meditation into their wellness routines. When introducing meditation, first explore whether clients have a religious or spiritual view of its practice. Black clients, especially those of devout Protestant backgrounds, might consider meditation a new-age practice they are encouraged to avoid. We encourage therapists to talk with clients who are religious about how meditation or contemplative practices can be integrated into their existing practices of prayer and devotionals. Guided meditations aligned with various faiths, including Christian meditations, are available (see the resource list at the end of this chapter). If clients are interested in secular meditation practices, many free resources can help them get started. It can be helpful to start by guiding clients through brief meditations in therapy sessions to show them what meditation feels like. If clients are open to practicing meditation in their daily lives, suggesting apps or free meditation recordings can help them begin a regular meditation practice (see the resource list at the end of this chapter for suggested meditation apps).

We recommend that therapists support Black women in identifying culturally specific practices that they find calming, such as praying, doing religious devotionals, spending time with girlfriends, listening to music, dancing, and cooking. Therapists can guide Black women to identify self-care practices that feel good to them and determine ways to incorporate these practices into their schedules regularly. A self-care worksheet (Table 13.3) can help guide clients through creating a personal self-care plan that includes sleep, physical activity, eating, personal time, and time for fun. Overall, we

Table 13.3 *Self-care plan for Black women*

Self-Care Activity	Personalization
Sleep • How many hours do you need? • What time do you need to go to bed to get enough sleep?	
Eating • How and where will you eat? • What would you like to eat? • Do you need to bring snacks to eat during the day?	
Exercise • What exercise do you like to do (e.g., walk, run, go to the gym, dance, yoga, play sports, bike)? • How many times a week can you realistically exercise?	
Personal Time • What would you like to do during personal time (e.g., read for pleasure, meditate, listen to music, journal)?	
Time for Fun and Time with Loved Ones • What do you like to do with your loved ones? • What do you like to do for fun? • How often would you like to try to do these things?	

hope therapists consider and integrate physical health into their work with Black female clients. Our physical and mental health are intertwined, and self-care practices can support overall health and well-being.

> Further resources are shared in Chapter 14 to support Black women's thriving.

Case Example

Joan is a 51-year-old, Black, cisgender, straight woman who is single, never married, and does not have children. Joan is a working professional and attended both college and graduate school. Joan is overweight, in remission from colon cancer, and currently has diabetes and high blood pressure. Joan began therapy to address concerns related to the stress and interpersonal challenges she was experiencing at her job. Though health concerns were not her primary concern, they came up frequently during therapy. Joan acknowledged a connection between the stress that she experienced at work and her tendency to engage in stress eating to soothe herself. Overall, Joan struggled to prioritize taking care of herself and her physical health. Joan reported wanting to address her difficulty sleeping through therapy. Additionally, Joan wanted to make changes to her eating and to increase her physical activity after she had a doctor's appointment and learned that one of her diabetes medications would need to be increased. In addition to these health issues, Joan also experienced ongoing symptoms of depression and anxiety.

During sessions, Joan and the therapist explored the connection between Joan's experience of stress and her tendency to eat food that she knew would exacerbate her health conditions. The therapist guided Joan to reflect on what she was thinking and how she felt before eating certain foods to help her increase her awareness about her choices. The therapist also helped Joan reflect on how she feels after eating these foods. They discussed the steps Joan was taking to make healthy eating choices in her attempt to lose weight, which was a goal that she set for herself based on her doctor's recommendation. The therapist encouraged Joan to consider how to increase her physical activity in ways that felt good to her. Joan shared that she used to visit the gym regularly but had not exercised consistently in several years. Joan and the therapist discussed what it could look like for Joan to begin taking walks outside, which she enjoyed doing. They identified small, manageable goals for Joan related to engaging in physical activity.

Sleep was a primary concern that Joan wanted to address during sessions. Joan reported having trouble falling asleep and needing to have the TV on to fall asleep. Joan shared a pattern of staying up until around 2 a.m. or 3 a.m. and struggling to get up and get to work on time in the morning. Joan reported that her eating also affected her sleep because if she ate a heavy and greasy meal late at night, she had more trouble sleeping. The therapist reviewed sleep hygiene strategies with Joan, helping her identify what time she would like to get up in the morning and the time she would need to go to bed to get enough sleep. They discussed ways for Joan to gradually move her bedtime earlier and get enough sleep. When Joan struggled to implement these strategies, Joan and the therapist identified an underlying issue related to her sleep: she felt she always needed to be alert and aware of what was going on around her. The therapist guided Joan to explore and process her feelings of always wanting to be alert. Joan acknowledged having a traumatic experience at night while growing up but did not yet feel ready to process this trauma in therapy. The therapist helped Joan see the connection between the trauma that she experienced at night and her difficulty sleeping now. The therapist also mentioned that this trauma was also likely to be connected to Joan's health concerns; people who have adverse childhood experiences are more likely to experience physical and mental health issues. The therapist respected Joan's decision not to process the trauma in therapy at that time and provided some psychoeducation on what this would involve when she is ready.

This case highlights the connection between physical and mental health and what it looks like to support a client in taking better care of her physical health through identifying challenges, setting small goals, and processing barriers to following through on those goals. The therapist worked thoughtfully and patiently with Joan to help her shift her relationship with her body and eating. Instead of directing Joan's changes, the therapist allowed Joan to guide the discussions about body and eating to ensure that she was setting her own goals for her health and wellness. Additionally, while the therapist made suggestions for changes and strategies, she left it up to Joan to decide which strategies to implement. The therapist also guided discussions about barriers Joan experienced, particularly related to changing her sleep and eating habits. Overall, the changes Joan made were slow and intermittent, and the therapist affirmed all the progress Joan made to help encourage her in this process.

13.5   Conclusion

Health and wellness can be a personal and sensitive topic for all of us. To effectively support Black female clients in cultivating physical and mental wellness, therapists need to be aware of their own relationships with their bodies and eating. The reflection questions at the end of this chapter are intended to help therapists consider their feelings about physical wellness and identify any unhealthy aspects of their relationships with their body or food so they can address these concerns without unintentionally passing them on to their clients. We encourage therapists to take time to reflect on the questions and journal their responses.

Supporting Black women in their physical health and wellness is an ongoing process, and we encourage therapists to keep the topics discussed in this chapter in mind when working with Black female clients. For some clients, health and wellness may be established and not a topic they want to discuss in therapy. For other Black women, therapy may be most helpful if it is focused on physical health and wellness. It is not uncommon for Black women to be referred to therapy by a primary care physician who has identified both physical and mental health concerns. We encourage therapists to be thoughtful about their interventions with Black women related to health and to be mindful of countertransference that may arise.

Therapist Reflection Questions

1. What have been your personal experiences with accessing and receiving physical health care?
2. What ideas in this chapter may apply to your attitudes and actions in caring for your physical health?
3. How have you emphasized physical health in your work with Black female clients?
4. What strategies from this chapter might help you broach physical health topics with Black female clients?
5. What suggestions might you use most in helping your Black female clients to see the connections between physical and mental health and wellness?

Resources

Organizations

Black Girls Run! (n.d.). https://www.blackgirlsrun.com
Black Women's Health Imperative. (n.d.). https://bwhi.org/
Fertility for Colored Girls. (n.d.). https://www.fertilityforcoloredgirls.org/
GirlTrek. (n.d.). https://www.girltrek.org/
Nap Ministry. (n.d.). https://thenapministry.wordpress.com/

Books

Oparah, J. C., & Bonaparte, A. D. (Eds.). (2016). *Birthing justice: Black women, pregnancy, and childbirth.* Routledge.
Taylor, S. R. (2018). *The body is not an apology: The power of radical self-love.* Berrett-Koehler Publishers, Inc.

Podcasts

Lopez, W., & Jones, J. (Hosts). (2016–present). *Food heaven* [Audio podcast]. https://foodheavenmadeeasy.com/podcast/

Articles

Chidi, E. & E. P. Cahill. (2020, October, 22). Protecting your birth: A guide for Black mothers. *The New York Times.* https://www.nytimes.com/article/black-mothers-birth.html

Media Resources

10 powerful Christian meditations to use daily. (2018. April 9). Crosswalk. https://
www.crosswalk.com/faith/spiritual-life/10-powerful-christian-meditations-to-
use-daily.html
Calm.com, Inc. (2014). *Calm – meditate, sleep, relax* (Version 5.22) [Mobile app].
https://www.calm.com/
Headspace for Meditation, Mindfulness and Sleep. (2012). *Headspace: Meditation &*
sleep (Version 4.56.0) [Mobile app]. https://www.headspace.com/
Insight Network Inc. (2010). *Insight timer: Meditation, sleep, music* (Version 15.15.0)
[Mobile app]. https://insighttimer.com/
Liberate. (2019). *Liberate* (Version 1.1.28) [Mobile app]. https://liberatemeditation.com/

Instagram handles that support exercise for Black women:

- @wecoloroutside
- @melaninbasecamp
- @blackpeoplewhohike
- @blackwomendoworkout
- @officialblackgirlsrun
- @girltrek

References

American Cancer Society. (2021). *Cancer facts & figures for African Americans*
2019–2021. https://www.cancer.org/research/cancer-facts-statistics/cancer-
facts-figures-for-african-americans.html
Arden, J. (2014). *The brain bible: How to stay vital, productive, and happy for a*
lifetime. McGraw Hill Professional.
Ashing, K. T., Jones, V., Bedell, F., Phillips, T., & Erhunmwunsee, L. (2022). Calling
attention to the role of race-driven societal determinants of health on aggressive
tumor biology: A focus on Black Americans. *JCO Oncology Practice*, *18*(1),
15–22.
Bagayogo, I. P., Interian, A., & Escobar, J. I. (2013). Transcultural aspects of somatic
symptoms in the context of depressive disorders. *Cultural Psychiatry*, *33*,
64–74.
Beckie, T. M., Groër, M. W., & Beckstead, J. W. (2011). The relationship between
polymorphisms on chromosome 9p21 and age of onset of coronary heart disease
in black and white women. *Genetic Testing and Molecular Biomarkers*, *15*(6),
435–442. https://doi.org/10.1089/gtmb.2010.0222
Black, A. R., & Woods-Giscombé, C. (2012). Applying the stress and 'strength'
hypothesis to Black women's breast cancer screening delays. *Stress and Health*,
28(5), 389–396. https://doi.org/10.1002/smi.2464
Black Maternal Health Caucus. (2020). *Black maternal health momnibus.* https://
blackmaternalhealthcaucus-underwood.house.gov/Momnibus

Braveman, P. A., Cubbin, C., Egerter, S., Williams, D. R., & Pamuk, E. (2010). Socioeconomic disparities in health in the United States: What the patterns tell us. *American Journal of Public Health, 100*(S1), S186–S196.

Centers for Disease Control and Prevention. (2022). *HIV and women.* https://www.cdc.gov/hiv/pdf/group/gender/women/cdc-hiv-women.pdf

Chidi, E., & Cahill, E. P. (2020, October, 22). Protecting your birth: A guide for Black mothers. *The New York Times.* https://www.nytimes.com/article/black-mothers-birth.html

Collins, S. E., Buchholz, S. W., Cranford, J., & McCrory, M. A. (2020). A church-based culturally sensitive physical activity intervention in African American women. *Western Journal of Nursing Research, 43,* 1–9. https://doi.org/10.1177/0193945920961405

Collins, Y., Holcomb, K., Chapman-Davis, E., Khabele, D., & Farley, J. H. (2014). Gynecologic cancer disparities: A report from the Health Disparities Taskforce of the Society of Gynecologic Oncology. *Gynecologic Oncology, 133*(2), 353–361. https://doi.org/10.1016/j.ygyno.2013.12.039

Craft, L. L., & Perna, F. M. (2004). The benefits of exercise for the clinically depressed. *Primary Care Companion to the Journal of Clinical Psychiatry, 6*(3), 104–111. https://doi.org/10.4088/pcc.v06n0301

Davis, E. M., Rovi, S., & Johnson, M. S. (2005). Mental health, family function and obesity in African-American women. *Journal of the National Medical Association, 97*(4), 478–482.

Dorwart, C. E., Smith, S., & Patterson, A. F. (2019). Just more comfortable in the gym: An exploration of the constraints that contribute to adult African American females' lack of participation in outdoor recreation activities. *Journal of Outdoor Recreation, Education, and Leadership, 11*(3), 171–190. https://doi.org/10.18666/JOREL-2019-V11-I3-8878

Evans, M. B., Allan, V., Erickson, K., Martin, L. J., Budziszewski, R., & Côté, J. (2017). Are all sport activities equal? A systematic review of how youth psychosocial experiences vary across differing sport activities. *British Journal of Sports Medicine, 51*(3), 169–176.

George, S., Ragin, C., & Ashing, K. T. (2021). Black is diverse: The untapped beauty and benefit of cancer genomics and precision medicine. *JCO Oncology Practice, 17*(5), 279–283.

Geronimus, A. T., Hicken, M. T., Pearson, J. A., Seashols, S. J., Brown, K. L., & Cruz, T. D. (2010). Do U.S. Black women experience stress-related accelerated biological aging? *Human Nature, 21*(1), 19–38. https://doi.org/10.1007/s12110-010-9078-0

Ghosh-Dastidar, B., Cohen, D., Hunter, G., Zenk, S. N., Huang, C., Beckman, R., & Dubowitz, T. (2014). Distance to store, food prices, and obesity in urban food deserts. *American Journal of Preventive Medicine, 47*(5), 587–595. https://doi.org/10.1016/j.amepre.2014.07.005

Gordon, K. H., Brattole, M. M., Wingate, L. R., & Joiner, T. E., Jr. (2006). The impact of client race on clinician detection of eating disorders. *Behavior Therapy, 37*(4), 319–325. https://doi.org/10.1016/j.beth.2005.12.002

Havranek, E. P., Mujahid, M. S., Barr, D. A., Blair, I. V., Cohen, M. S., Cruz-Flores, S., Davey-Smith, G., Dennison-Himmelfarb, C. R., Lauer, M. S., Lockwood, D. W.,

Rosal, M., American Heart Association Council on Quality of Care and Outcomes Research, Council on Epidemiology and Prevention, Council on Cardiovascular and Stroke Nursing, Council on Lifestyle and Cardiometabolic Health, & Stroke Council. (2015). Social determinants of risk and outcomes for cardiovascular disease: a scientific statement from the American Heart Association. *Circulation, 132*(9), 873–898. https://doi.org/10.1161/CIR.0000000000000228

Health Research and Quality Act, Publ. L. No. 106–129, 113 Stat. 1653 (1999). https://www.govinfo.gov/content/pkg/PLAW-106publ129/pdf/PLAW-106publ129.pdf

Henrietta Lacks: Science must right a historical wrong. (2020, September 3). *Nature, 585,* 7. https://doi.org/10.1038/d41586-020-02494-z

Jackson, N., & Utter, D. (2020, September 4). *Vessels for collective progress: The use of Hela cells in COVID-19 research.* Science in the News. https://sitn.hms.harvard.edu/flash/2020/vessels-for-collective-progress-the-use-of-hela-cells-in-covid-19-research/

Jayakody, K., Gunadasa, S., & Hosker, C. (2014). Exercise for anxiety disorders: Systematic review. *British Journal of Sports Medicine, 48*(3), 187–196. https://doi.org/10.1136/bjsports-2012-091287

Jean, Y. (2020, March 10). *How Black women have historically used yoga as a tool for healing.* Well and Good. https://www.wellandgood.com/black-women-and-yoga-history

Lamis, D. A., & Kaslow, N. J. (2014). Mediators of the daily hassles–suicidal ideation link in African American women. *Suicide and Life-Threatening Behavior, 44*(3), 233–245.

Lannin, D. R., Mathews, H. F., Mitchell, J., & Swanson, M. S. (2002). Impacting cultural attitudes in African-American women to decrease breast cancer mortality. *The American Journal of Surgery, 184*(5), 418–423. https://doi.org/10.1016/S0002–9610(02)01009-7

Lee, K. T., George, M., Lowry, S., & Ashing, K. T. (2021). A review and considerations on palliative care improvements for African Americans with cancer. *American Journal of Hospice and Palliative Medicine, 38*(6), 671–677. https://doi.org/10.1177/1049909120930205

Lewis, J. A., Williams, M. G., Peppers, E. J., & Gadson, C. A. (2017). Applying intersectionality to explore the relations between gendered racism and health among Black women. *Journal of Counseling Psychology, 64*(5), 475–486.

Mack, J. L., & Hays, H. V. (2020, December 24). Black doctor dies of COVID-19 after reporting racist treatment at Indiana Hospital. *USA Today.* https://www.usatoday.com/story/news/nation/2020/12/24/susan-moore-black-doctor-covid-victim-alleges-racism-carmel-hospital/4041257001/

Marques, L., Alegria, M., Becker, A. E., Chen, C. N., Fang, A., Chosak, A., & Diniz, J. B. (2011). Comparative prevalence, correlates of impairment, and service utilization for eating disorders across US ethnic groups: Implications for reducing ethnic disparities in health care access for eating disorders. *International Journal of Eating Disorders, 44*(5), 412–420. https://doi.org/10.1002/eat.20787

McFarlane, A. C. (2010). The long-term costs of traumatic stress: Intertwined physical and psychological consequences. *World Psychiatry, 9*(1), 3. https://doi.org/10.1002/j.2051-5545.2010.tb00254.x

McKnight-Eily, L. R., Presley-Cantrell, L., Elam-Evans, L. D., Chapman, D. P., Kaslow, N. J., & Perry, G. S. (2009). Prevalence and correlates of current depressive symptomatology and lifetime diagnosis of depression in Black women. *Women's Health Issues, 19*(4), 243–252. https://doi.org/10.1016/j.whi.2009.04 .003

Minority Health and Health Disparities Research and Education Act, Publ. L. No. 106–525, 114 Stat. 2495 (2000). https://www.govinfo.gov/content/pkg/PLAW-106publ525/pdf/PLAW-106publ525.pdf

Nap Ministry. (n.d.). *About.* https://thenapministry.wordpress.com/about

National Institutes of Health. (2020, December 3). *Significant research advances enabled by Hela Cells.* Office of Science Policy. https://osp.od.nih.gov/scientific-sharing/hela-cells-timeline

Nelson, A. (2002). Unequal treatment: Confronting racial and ethnic disparities in health care. *Journal of the National Medical Association, 94*(8), 666–668.

Nunes, J., Jean-Louis, G., Zizi, F., Casimir, G. J., von Gizycki, H., Brown, C. D., & McFarlane, S. I. (2008). Sleep duration among Black and white Americans: Results of the National Health Interview Survey. *Journal of the National Medical Association, 100*(3), 317–322.

Ohrnberger, J., Fichera, E., & Sutton, M. (2017). The relationship between physical and mental health: A mediation analysis. *Social Science & Medicine, 195*, 42–49. https://doi.org/10.1016/j.socscimed.2017.11.008

Petersen, E. E., Davis, N. L., Goodman, D., Cox, S., Syverson, C., Seed, K., Shapiro-Mendoza, C., Callaghan, W. M., & Barfield, W. (2019). Racial/ethnic disparities in pregnancy-related deaths – United States, 2007–2016. *Morbidity and Mortality Weekly Report, 68*(35), 762–765. https://doi.org/10.15585/mmwr .mm6835a3

Rao, V. (2020, August, 13). *What is implicit bias? The invisible racism that makes Black women dread the doctor's office.* Today. https://www.today.com/health/what-implicit-bias-invisible-racism-hurts-black-women-doctor-s-t189105

Ribeiro, A. I., Amaro, J., Lisi, C., & Fraga, S. (2018). Neighborhood socioeconomic deprivation and allostatic load: A scoping review. *International Journal of Environmental Research and Public Health, 15*(6), 1092.

Robins, L., & Regier, D. A. (1991). *Psychiatric disorders in America: The Epidemiologic Catchment Area Study.* The Free Press.

Ruby, M. B., Dunn, E. W., Perrino, A., Gillis, R., & Viel, S. (2011). The invisible benefits of exercise. *Health Psychology, 30*(1), 67. https://doi.org/10.1037/a0021859

Rucklidge, J. J., & Kaplan, B. J. (2013). Broad-spectrum micronutrient formulas for the treatment of psychiatric symptoms: A systematic review. *Expert Review of Neurotherapeutics, 13*(1), 49–73.

Sacks, T. K. (2018). *Invisible visits: Black middle-class women in the American healthcare system.* Oxford University Press.

Sengupta, R., & Honey, K. (2020). AACR Cancer Disparities Progress Report 2020: Achieving the bold vision of health equity for racial and ethnic minorities and other underserved populations. *Cancer Epidemiology and Prevention Biomarkers, 29*(10), 1843–1843.

Skloot, R. (2017). *The immortal life of Henrietta Lacks.* Broadway Paperbacks.

Slopen, N., Lewis, T. T., & Williams, D. R. (2016). Discrimination and sleep: A systematic review. *Sleep medicine, 18*, 88–95. https://doi.org/10.1016/j.sleep.2015.01.012

Taylor, S. R. (2018). *The body is not an apology: The power of radical self-love.* Berrett-Koehler Publishers.

Trawalter, S., Hoffman, K. M., & Waytz, A. (2012). Racial bias in perceptions of others' pain. *PLoS ONE, 7*(11), e48546. https://doi.org/10.1371/journal.pone.0048546

Villarosa, L. (2018, April 11). Why America's Black mothers and babies are in a life-or-death crisis. *The New York Times Magazine.* https://www.nytimes.com/2018/04/11/magazine/black-mothers-babies-death-maternal-mortality.html?action=click&module=RelatedLinks&pgtype=Article

Ware, S., Thorpe, S., & Tanner, A. E. (2019) Sexual health interventions for Black women in the United States: A systematic review of literature. *International Journal of Sexual Health, 31*(2), 196–215. https://doi.org10.1080/19317611.2019.161327

Warren-Findlow, J. (2006). Weathering: Stress and heart disease in African American women living in Chicago. *Qualitative Health Research, 16*(2), 221–237. https://doi.org/10.1177/1049732305278651

Washington, H. A. (2006). *Medical apartheid: The dark history of medical experimentation on Black Americans from colonial times to the present.* Doubleday Books.

Watson, S. K. (2018, June 18). *After high school, young women's exercise rates plunge.* National Public Radio. https://www.npr.org/sections/health-shots/2018/06/11/618878274/after-high-school-young-womens-exercise-rates-plunge

Wilcox, S., Richter, D. L., Henderson, K. A., Greaney, M. L., & Ainsworth, B. E. (2002). Perceptions of physical activity and personal barriers and enablers in African-American women. *Ethnicity and Disease, 12*(3), 353–362.

Xiao, Q., Signorello, L. B., Brinton, L. A., Cohen, S. S., Blot, W. J., & Matthews, C. E. (2016). Sleep duration and breast cancer risk among Black and White women. *Sleep Medicine, 20*, 25–29. https://doi.org/10.1016/j.sleep.2015.11.010

14   Black Women's Inner Healing and Resources for Thriving

with Fangzhou Yu-Lewis[*]

> The therapist helped me gain insights on areas of my life that needed deeper healing. . . . I was able to have someone to talk to who affirmed my experiences . . . [and] have a safe space for healing.
>
> Study participant

For Black women, meaningful moments in the present often hold the shadows of painful and traumatic histories. A recent example is the exhilaration and even liberation many Black women felt when witnessing Kamala Harris being inaugurated as the first Black and Indian American woman to serve as vice president. In the shadow of this beautiful moment was a long legacy of Black women navigating sexism, racism, oppression, and other forms of discrimination, fighting to hold their heads high and to assert that Black lives matter in the midst of a world that says they don't. While Black women have a long history of pushing back against negative stereotypes and using their power and resilience to support themselves, their families, and their communities, many Black women carry the wounds of unhealed trauma or internalized racism and sexism. As Black women work to heal their communities, internal healing is also needed.

Inner healing involves tending to and caring for inner wounds that have negatively shaped how Black women feel about themselves and see themselves. Through the practices of self-forgiveness and self-compassion, Black women can connect to their unconditional self-worth and reclaim themselves as worthy and whole just as they are. Additionally, specifically in relation to the sexual trauma and wounds a Black woman may have experienced, guiding her to reclaim her sexuality and sensuality can be a powerful tool for inner healing.

Further, beyond inner healing, Black women deserve to thrive in this world. Many Black women approach life from a place of survival because they have had no other choice. Supporting Black women in not only healing but also

---

[*] A. Gooden & F. Yu-Lewis. (2023). Black women's inner healing and resources for thriving. In D. Baptiste & A. Gooden, *Promoting Black women's mental health: What practitioners should know and do*. Cambridge University Press.

thriving can lead to a powerful shift that enables them to be the hero in their own life and the author of their own story. In this chapter, we discuss how Black women can explore inner healing in therapy. We also share resources Black women commonly use to support their thriving and provide recommendations for ways therapists can incorporate these resources into therapy.

14.1   Inner Healing through Self-Compassion

Many Black women learned to survive trauma and hardship by being harsh with themselves. This began in past generations when the whipping from slave masters continued in the form of whoopings (spanking or other corporal punishment) from Black parents who were scared that if their children did not obey orders, they would receive much worse punishment from White people. This fear of what will happen if Black people do not obey the orders of White people continues today as parents try to prepare their children to survive encounters with police. This anxiety and fear can manifest as harshness instead of as a communication of the deep love that family members have for their children. Many Black women have internalized the harshness they received from their parents and from the world and turned it on themselves. Further, Black women in America receive constant messages that they do not deserve to be treated well or with compassion. The school-to-prison pipeline, trauma-to-prison pipeline, mass incarceration, stereotypes, and blame placed on Black women for the plight of Black families are just some examples of the lack of compassion shown toward Black people in America.

One consequence of surviving terror and trauma is learning to be tough all the time. The hope is that if a woman is tough and avoids being vulnerable, she will protect herself from emotional pain. As Black women learn to be tough, they tend to cut themselves off from intimacy with other people; maybe it wouldn't have hurt so much when a family member was killed if she hadn't expressed how attached she was to them. Black women may also cut themselves off from intimacy with themselves; maybe she could better handle abuse and mistreatment if she just suppressed her emotions and did not feel them. Black women's lack of safe spaces in which to honor their pain and to be vulnerable has left them without life-giving self-compassion.

A common objection clients may give in response to the suggestion to practice self-compassion is that if they are kind and compassionate to themselves, they will never improve and will be stagnant. Many Black women have confused criticism, internalized stereotypes, and feeling like they are never good enough with healthy striving for growth and development. It can be helpful to explain to a Black female client that being compassionate to herself does not mean giving herself a pass or letting herself off the hook for mistakes. In fact, self-compassion helps us to face and take responsibility for our wrongdoings. Research has demonstrated that self-compassion meditations helped to reduce self-criticism and depression among African American participants (Johnson et al., 2018).

Black female clients might also argue that Black people do not have time for self-compassion, that they need to be fighting police brutality, mass incarceration, and infringement on voting rights, among other issues facing the Black community. Clients might assert that these issues are more pressing than learning to be compassionate with themselves and others. It can be helpful to remind clients of a powerful quote from Audre Lorde, a Black lesbian feminist: "Caring for myself is not self-indulgence, it is self-preservation, and that is an act of political warfare" (Lorde, 2017, p. 130). Reminding Black women that taking good care of themselves is radical in the context of society can help to quiet their concerns that this is selfish. Black self-compassion challenges the stereotypes that Black people are just hard and tough, not deserving of or in need of compassion. Black women's self-compassion pushes back against any racism they may have internalized and supports their inner healing. Four core components of Black self-compassion bring together the established components of self-compassion (mindfulness, self-kindness, and common humanity) and a fourth component: contextualizing pain. A final component of Black self-compassion, honoring the body, is reviewed in depth in Chapter 13 and is not repeated here.

14.1.1   Mindfulness

Mindfulness involves being aware, curious, and nonjudgmental in the present moment. A qualitative study with African American women found that mindfulness-based interventions helped to improve coping with depressive symptoms (Burnett-Zeigler et al., 2019). Therapists can support Black female clients in practicing mindfulness by encouraging them to notice what is happening without judgment or attempting to struggle against what they are experiencing in the moment. Mindfulness supports inner healing by helping a Black female client to be present with herself in times of pain and sorrow and to fully embrace times of joy and excitement. To help clients practice mindfulness as part of self-compassion, therapists can guide their clients to explore with curiosity when they experience difficult emotions in a therapy session (e.g., sadness, anger, disappointment, shame). The therapist can guide the client to focus her attention on the physical sensations associated with the emotion and notice all the elements that make up these feelings. Therapists should encourage their clients to let go of negative or judgmental thoughts, return their attention to the emotions and physical sensations, and try to allow the feelings to exist.

14.1.2   Self-Kindness

Self-kindness is the second core component of self-compassion. For Black women, learning to be kind to themselves can be one of the hardest parts of engaging in self-compassion. Many Black women, particularly those who adopt the Strong Black Woman persona, often push themselves to be selfless and to prioritize everyone else in their lives and may be harsh and self-critical when they do not meet the needs or demands of others in their lives. Supporting Black women in transforming their relationship with themselves to be kind and encouraging instead of harsh and critical can be powerful and healing. Therapists can help a Black female client connect to her capacity for self-kindness by guiding her to reflect on how she would respond to a friend or loved one in distress. Would she give them a hug? Sit with them? Tell them that she sees how hard the situation is for them? Say something comforting? Remind them that they are not alone? Once she has identified how she would be kind and comforting to someone else, the therapist can encourage her to be kind to herself in those same ways.

14.1.3   Common Humanity

Common humanity is the third component of traditional conceptualizations of self-compassion. Common humanity involves remembering all the other people who are experiencing similar pain and difficulty. Often when people are having a hard time and experiencing difficult emotions, they feel alone in their pain. A Black woman may feel that the hardship reflects something wrong with her; she may feel shame and think that if she were different or better, she would not be suffering in this way. When therapists help Black female clients connect to their common humanity, they can begin to let go of these unhelpful thoughts and self-judgments. Common humanity reminds a Black female client that her pain is a normal part of being human and that experiencing difficult emotions means that we are human and care about things.

14.1.4   Contextualizing Pain

The final component of Black self-compassion involves helping Black female clients to contextualize their pain. Although this is connected to common humanity, it moves beyond simply recognizing that all people experience pain to acknowledging the societal and systemic causes of the pain Black women experience. Helping a Black female client understand her emotions and reactions in the context of racial microaggressions, racial trauma, and other types of trauma can help her to be more understanding and gracious with herself. Layering self-blame on top of pain and trauma only serves to exacerbate the pain that we experience. In contrast, helping Black women to remember the context of her pain will help her to heal and acknowledge that much of what she has gone through is not her fault. Creating space for discussions about the social and political challenges and discrimination Black women experience is an important component of providing culturally responsive treatment and supports the therapeutic alliance (Greene, 1997; Williams, 2005).

We discuss the therapeutic alliance in Chapter 7.

14.2   Inner Healing through Self-Forgiveness

In addition to cultivating self-compassion, self-forgiveness can be a powerful process to support internal healing for Black women. Many people who go through trauma experience shame as a result, and women are more likely than men to experience shame in response to trauma (Aakvaag et al., 2016). While guilt can be a healthy response to a mistake, a failure, or an action that causes harm to self or others, shame causes people to feel that they are bad or wrong and can overwhelm them, disconnecting them from their sense of worthiness. Shame can also cause people to feel that it is impossible to make amends or to learn and grow from a painful situation. The process of self-forgiveness can help to free clients from shame.

We encourage therapists to explore with their Black female clients whether they are experiencing shame related to past traumas or other difficult experiences. Helping Black women to release a belief that there is something wrong with them is a powerful healing intervention that self-compassion (Au et al., 2017) and self-forgiveness can facilitate. It is helpful to begin with the self-compassion practices outlined earlier in this chapter because clients will need to have a foundation of self-compassion before engaging in the process of self-forgiveness. Self-forgiveness involves accepting what happened in the past, acknowledging how it was harmful to self and others, identifying the wisdom that can be drawn from the experience, and allowing yourself to move forward. Next, we offer step-by-step guidance for therapists who want to support their clients in the process of self-forgiveness.

14.2.1   Explore

We encourage therapists to begin facilitating the process of self-forgiveness by exploring clients' thoughts and feelings about forgiving themselves. People often worry that forgiveness involves saying that what happened to them was okay, so it is important to differentiate between acknowledging the reality and endorsing what happened. Clients will also benefit from understanding the consequences of not forgiving themselves. When we do not forgive ourselves, we carry the burdens of the past into the future. We hold on to them and weigh ourselves down with the pain, guilt, and shame; this keeps us from moving freely in our lives. In contrast, when we offer ourselves forgiveness, we are able to identify the lessons, growth, and wisdom we gained from the experience and move forward with that instead of with the burdens from the past. We encourage therapists to talk with their Black female clients about both their fears and hopes related to forgiving themselves.

14.2.2   Accept

A major aspect of forgiveness involves accepting what happened in the past. Often, clients withhold forgiveness from themselves because they do not want to fully acknowledge and accept what happened. It can feel easier to think about all the ways the situation should have or could have turned out differently than to accept that the past cannot be changed. We encourage clinicians to explore with their Black female client any fears she might have about accepting what happened. As noted earlier, many people believe that acceptance is the same as saying that something was good or acceptable. Therapists can clarify that in this context, acceptance means that a client acknowledges the truth of what happened and stops believing that they can change the past. This acceptance may bring up grief for clients as they allow the reality to sink in. We encourage therapists to give clients the space to process their grief or other emotions that arise.

14.2.3   Acknowledge the Pain

The next step in the process of self-forgiveness is to guide the client to acknowledge the hurt and pain they experienced because of what happened. People often focus on feeling angry at themselves and others because of what happened to them and fail to attend to their own emotional wounds. Guiding a Black female client to acknowledge the hurt she experienced helps her to offer herself compassion for what she went through. There are countless images of Black women being stoic in the face of great tragedy and trauma, standing strong to support their families and communities during these times. Supporting Black female clients in acknowledging their emotional wounds may go against their image of themselves as a Strong Black Woman, but this is an essential aspect of inner healing. We encourage therapists to be gentle and patient when guiding Black women through this process because it may take time for them to be willing to be vulnerable with themselves and with the therapist.

See Chapter 8 for more on working with clients who exhibit the Strong Black Woman persona.

14.2.4   Identify the Lessons

Once a client has attended to her emotional pain and offered herself compassion and comfort, she can be guided to identify what she learned from the experience. Therapists can guide clients to connect to a compassionate part of themselves as they explore how the challenging experience helped them to learn, grow, and increase their wisdom. When clients are caught up in wishing that a negative experience did not happen, they often overlook how the experience shaped them in positive ways. This exploration is not intended to diminish the pain caused by the experience or say that it was positive but to identify the growth and progress that came from the experience. For example, did the client learn to set better boundaries for herself? Did she learn to trust her intuition? Did she learn to better advocate for herself? Guiding clients to acknowledge the lessons they have taken from the difficult experience will support them in releasing the experience and allowing the burden to stay in the past while carrying the wisdom forward.

14.2.5   Offer Self-Forgiveness

The last step in the self-forgiveness process is to guide the client to forgive herself and allow herself to move forward. This involves taking a compassionate look at the whole picture, including what led to the situation, the pain it caused, and the lessons she learned, and offering herself forgiveness. It can be helpful for clients to write a letter of self-forgiveness to themselves, incorporating these things into the letter. Therapists should encourage clients to include the phrase "I forgive you" in the letter or to say this out loud to themselves as many times as would be helpful. We encourage therapists to guide clients through the self-forgiveness process gradually and go at a pace that helps the client feel safe and supported.

14.3   Inner Healing through Self-Love and Acceptance

Many Black women grew up feeling they were not smart enough, not pretty enough, and not good enough. They may have received messages from their family members, community, or society at large, and over time, they may have begun to believe this about themselves. Sonya Renee Taylor, a feminist author who identifies as Black, fat, and queer, writes powerfully about radical self-love in her book *The Body Is Not an Apology: The Power of Radical Self-Love.* In this book, Taylor (2018) highlights the ways that society marginalizes the bodies of people who are BIPOC (Black, Indigenous, and people of color), people with disabilities, and people who are lesbian, gay, bisexual, transgender, and/or queer (LGBTQ) and can cause people who live in these bodies to apologize for themselves and their bodies. Taylor advocates for radical self-love through making peace with difference and making peace with our bodies.

Part of self-love involves Black women connecting to and reclaiming their sexuality. For Black women who have experienced sexual trauma or for those who have been hypersexualized or seen as not sexual at all, it can be powerful and healing to connect to their personal sexuality and sexual expression that feels safe and empowering for them. As discussed in Chapter 4 on stereotypes, the Mammy image of Black women is strongly associated with nonsexual traits (Amoloku, 2019). In contrast, the Jezebel was seen as a hypersexual woman who used her sexuality to manipulate men. Many Black women have found themselves caught between these stereotypes, potentially internalizing them and losing touch with themselves and their true sexuality in the process. Awakening the sexual side of the body is one way for Black women to heal from trauma and stereotypes (Amoloku, 2019; Griffin, 1996; Muncie, 2010).

In *Pleasure Activism* by adrienne maree brown (2019), people who identify as BIPOC and LGBTQ are called to embrace their physical and sexual pleasure as a means of healing and activism. She encourages her readers to engage in individual sexual pleasure and to explore what makes them feel good. So often, Black women are encouraged to focus on the wants and needs of other people and connecting to themselves through sexual or other pleasure is a powerful pathway to inner healing. Inspired by Marvin Gaye's song "Sexual Healing," Griffin (1996) discusses how sensual touch helps Black women to reclaim their bodies and resist internalized oppression. Black women's sexual healing is not dependent on a partner and can happen through sensual self-exploration. Historically, Black women have not had ownership of their sexuality, leading to ambivalence or embarrassment about their sexuality and pleasuring (Shulman & Horne, 2003). We encourage therapists to talk with clients about their feelings about themselves, their bodies, and their sexuality. We recommend that therapists assess any sexual issues or concerns their Black female client might have during the assessment phase of treatment. However, it is important for therapists to wait until a strong therapeutic relationship has been established before bringing up issues of sexuality and sexual pleasure unless the client brings up the topic. It is essential for the therapist to have a nonjudgmental stance when exploring these topics and to support their Black female clients in identifying what feels good to them.

14.4   Inner Healing through Spirituality and Religion

Spirituality and religion have long offered a source of emotional and spiritual healing strategies. Black women's faith has soothed their spirits and offers hope and inspiration. In a study on Black Christian youth, Gooden and McMahon (2016) found that belief in God or a higher power and feeling supported by people in a religious community was connected to higher levels of thriving. Hayman et al. (2007) found a positive relationship between self-esteem and spirituality, meaning that the more spiritual a person is, the higher levels of self-esteem they report. They researched college students and found that spirituality influenced the relationship between stress and self-esteem. They also found that if an individual is more spiritual, their stress will have a lower impact on their self-esteem. Religion also increases life satisfaction and happiness. Religious disciplines, such as prayer, worship, and study, have been found to promote a healthy lifestyle (Levin, 2010). Specifically, with Black women, Bacchus and Holley (2004) found that spirituality serves as a mechanism for coping with life stressors by acting as a protective factor, driving personal strength, providing general guidance in decision-making, and helping women to process stressful experiences by reframing them.

> Chapter 15 provides an extensive discussion of Black women's spirituality and religiosity, especially connected to the Christian faith.

Religious services, particularly Black Protestant church services, can be powerfully healing and uplifting. These church services commonly include music that is soothing, joyous, and uplifting; testimonies that are encouraging; and a sermon that is inspiring and instills hope. Many Black women attend church services for a regular dose of encouragement and inspiration as they navigate the stressors of life. Historically, religious worship has provided a space of joy within the Black community (Thomas, 2016), and the Christian church community has served as a safe, supportive, and comfortable space for Black women. Note, however, that the patriarchal frameworks that exist within many Black churches can inflict wounds (Wiggins, 2004). Black women reported that while they appreciate the Black church's historical and social aspects and religious experience, they connect most strongly with the individual spiritual transformation (Wiggins, 2004). This need for spiritual connection and a desire for progress has driven some Black women to reconnect with ancestral religions.

Many Black women reconnect with traditional spiritual disciplines to liberate themselves from the negative stereotypes and racism. In an interview with

Vice magazine, Nakia Brown (2017) explained that she left the Black church after her father passed away. Nakia had a hard time praying and "talking to a God who has caused so much pain." She found the answers she needed within the Yoruba faith. It is one of the few traditional religions of African descent in the United States to have survived the trans-Atlantic slave trade (Brown, 2017). As a Black woman, Nakia found it difficult to pray to a pale and blue-eyed Jesus primarily depicted within western societies. The Yoruba religion celebrates Blackness, gender norms, and sexuality without White society's influence.

The movement of Black women away from the traditional Protestant Christian church is not limited to following the Yoruba faith. For example, womanist theology has recently gained traction with theologians but has flourished within the lives of Black women of the Christian faith for decades. Womanism originated around Black women's kitchen tables, on front porches, in beauty shops, in women's clubs, and even within women's spaces within the Black Church (Turman, 2019). The following quote from Alice Walker illustrates that Black women don't necessarily expect to find God in church and are able to access God anywhere.

Have you ever found God in Church? I never did. I just found a bunch of folks hoping for him to show. Any God I ever felt in Church I brought in with me. And I think the other folks did too. They come to Church to share God, not find God. (Walker, 1982, p. 193)

The womanist spiritual movement not only values God and other religious realms of the Christianity, but it also highlights Black women's experiences and difficulties. Womanism moves away from God's depiction as a White patriarch and instead allows Black women to envision themselves within the religious text. It also moves away from the sexist and patriarchal structure of the typical Christian church. Womanism's core is self-love in a world that has historically despised Black women (Turman, 2019).

In addition to Christianity, many Black women are Muslim and actively involved in those religious communities. Other Black women are engaged in Buddhism. Further, Black women may engage in a range of spiritual practices such as tarot cards, reiki healing, astrology, and witchcraft.

We encourage therapists to be thoughtful about exploring their Black female clients' religious and spiritual beliefs and practices and incorporating them into therapy as appropriate to support their healing. For example, therapists can ask Black female clients how their religious or spiritual beliefs affect their view of the challenges they are experiencing and if they can draw any coping strategies or other healing practices from their religious or spiritual practices. If a Black female client finds it helpful to pray, meditate, or read a devotional, the therapist can encourage her to incorporate this activity into her daily or weekly routine to reduce stress and increase her sense of grounding and connection to herself and her beliefs. Therapists must be cautious not to project their own religious beliefs (or lack of religious beliefs) onto their client and to remember that even if the therapist and client practice the same religion, the intricacies of their faith and beliefs may be different.

Finally, it is important for therapists not to make assumptions about their Black female clients' religious beliefs but to ask directly. While many Black women do identify as Christian, not all Black women are Christian, and making an assumption about a client's faith can cause a rupture in the relationship. In our study of Black women's experiences in and views on therapy, at least one respondent expressed her frustration that a therapist assumed she was Christian.

> We provide guidance on how to ask about a client's religious beliefs and practices in Chapter 15.

14.5   Resources for Inner Healing and Thriving

In addition to providing guidance on how therapists can support their Black female clients in the process of inner healing, here we highlight some powerful resources that can support Black women's efforts to thrive. These culturally specific resources address the fact that many Black women end up operating in survival mode as they navigate racism, sexism, and other stressors. Therapy can be an opportunity for Black women not only to heal but to thrive and live the lives they desire. These resources will not all be a good fit for each client, and we encourage therapists to be thoughtful about introducing these resources to clients or discussing them. Also, Black female clients may already be engaging in many of these practices, and then the therapist can support the client in being more intentional about utilizing these resources rather than teaching them about the resources.

14.5.1   The Arts and Creative Expression

Throughout history, creative expression has been linked to mental health and wellness. Inner healing and recovery, such as recovery from trauma, has been long associated with the arts (Stephenson & Rosen, 2015). In Jensen and Bonde's (2018) study, participation in the arts, such as poetry, literature, music, and community art projects, promoted physical and mental health benefits. Artistic creativity is holistic and includes writing, dancing, drawing, painting, making music, acting, photography, and other forms of creative expression. Creative expression can help Black women manage the stress, sadness, and anxiety caused by oppression (Kilgore et al., 2020) and can also support them in thriving. In particular, writing personal narratives and creative stories that reflect personal experiences can be therapeutic and support internal healing and thriving (Kilgore et al., 2020).

14.5.2   Writing

Black women have long used creative and autobiographical writing to heal themselves and support the growth and healing of other Black women. Maya Angelou's (1969) autobiography *I Know Why the Caged Bird Sings* is a powerful story of resilience, overcoming trauma, and claiming her power. Ntozake Shange's (1974) play *For Colored Girls Who Considered Suicide/ When the Rainbow Is Enuf* is a powerful representation of the life experiences of seven Black women navigating heartache, abandonment, and trauma. Shange weaves their stories together beautifully and highlights the healing power of sisterhood, bearing witness and collective support. The play premiered in 1976, was made into a movie in 2009, and continues to be performed today; the message of resilience and thriving despite challenges is inspiring and uplifting for Black women. Written works like these offer Black women guidance, wisdom, and strength, which are functional pathways to healing oneself (Phifer, 2017, p. 17). Other examples of writings that promote healing and thriving are *The Bluest Eye* by Toni Morrison (1970), *Hunger: A Memoir of (My) Body* by Roxane Gay (2017), and *Their Eyes Were Watching God* by Zora Neale Hurston (1973). As Phifer (2017) emphasizes, literary self-expression provides Black women space to minimize feelings of invalidation, conflict, or misunderstanding, and this assists their internal healing.

Many Black women use writing to confront oppression, advocate for themselves and their communities, and assert their full humanity. Self-affirming writing increases joy and helps to alleviate mental distress (Kilgore et al., 2020). Blogger Mariam I. Williams (2020) describes using writing and other art forms as

powerful tools for exploring how the political, historical, and cultural affect the personal. My work strives to do for others what centuries of black women writing, choreographing, and performing literature and dances of the African diaspora have done for me: reveal black humanity, give dimensionality to Black womanhood, and provide new ways of thinking, healing, and being for all people. (para. 1)

We encourage therapists to explore with their clients whether texts by Black female authors might help them feel less alone in the challenges they experience. We have included at the end of this chapter a list of texts by Black women, which therapists can recommend. If clients are interested in writing and find it enjoyable, therapists might encourage them to use writing as a form of self-expression and validation of their own experiences and life journeys. This writing can include journaling, writing fiction and nonfiction, and writing poetry. Hythia Phifer, a Black woman, scholar, writer, and therapist, shared that writing poetry helped her to heal and validate her own experience:

[Writing poetry] did validate my suffering in unique and profound ways. The creative process lateralized my grief as a real and also traumatic event. I no longer had to prove to myself or anyone else that I struggle for a reason. It was extremely gratifying to know I was not insane or weak. It empowered me to allow myself the space to be broken and devastated and Black and woman in a society that does not allow this. (Phifer, 2017, p. 23)

Writing poetry helped Phifer to heal after the grief and trauma she experienced by helping her validate her experience and empowering her to offer herself compassion.

14.5.3   Dancing

Dancing is another major form of creative expression for Black women. Whether engaging in line dancing (e.g., the Electric Slide) at a party, doing the latest dance moves with friends, or engaging in a formal dance class or performance, dancing can be a powerful form of self-expression and stress relief. Camille A. Brown, an award-winning choreographer, defines social dance as a community coming together expressing a language in a shared art form of dance (Benton, 2017; Brown, 2016). Dancing enables Black women to express joy, excitement, and even sorrow and provides a space of connection beyond words. In her TED Talk, Brown (2016) asserts that Black communities dance together "to heal, to remember, and to say: 'We speak a common language. We exist and we are free.'"

We encourage therapists to explore with their Black female clients whether dancing, either formally or informally, could be a useful resource to support their thriving. Dancing can relieve stress, serves as a form of physical exercise, and involves creative expression. Black women who are interested in doing more dancing but are unsure of how or where to do this might be encouraged to turn on their favorite songs and dance in their homes or to join an African dance class or another dance class that centers the movement of Black people.

14.5.4   Music

Music is another powerful art form that supports both healing and thriving. Music serves as a salve to heal emotional pain and is the backdrop for many celebrations in the Black community. The music Black people create is listened to around the world because of its widespread recognition of the pain and oppression Black people have endured along with its resonance of the joy, confidence, and celebration Black people engage in. In Black Christian churches, music enables congregations to mourn and celebrate, and Black women make up the majority of singers and choir members in most churches. In his book *My Grandmother's Hands*, Resmaa Menakem (2017) highlights the power of humming, a type of musical expression, as a form of healing from trauma. Deep, spiritual humming is commonly heard in the Black church when words are inadequate to express the mix of emotions congregants are experiencing. Black women may engage in creative expression through music by playing instruments, composing songs, singing or listening to music that moves them. Therapists can explore with their Black female clients whether singing, making music, or listening to music can serve as a resource for them. Clients might consider creating a playlist of soothing and uplifting songs that they can use at various times of the day and to enrich their life overall.

14.5.5   Art Therapy

Lindsey Vance (2020), a board-certified art therapist, illustrates the importance of art as an intervention for Black women struggling with their mental health. In her blog post titled "Creative Healing Spaces: Healing from Racial Wounds," she addresses racial trauma by offering Black people, including many women, space to express themselves creatively through visual and symbolic expression (Vance, 2020). Adanna Dill (2020), a Black woman, digital content creator, podcast cohost, and blogger, shared her experience of engaging in art therapy. She describes how the creative nature of engaging in art has been therapeutic and how it allowed her to begin dealing with her trauma in a way that felt comfortable to her. It has helped her gain a deeper understanding of herself, subsequently helping her gain perspective on how she can heal. Art therapy and artistic expression can take many forms, including painting, drawing, photography, and acting. If clients have difficulty expressing themselves verbally, art therapy may be a helpful medium for them to process and express their emotions.

14.5.6   Supportive and Educational Social Media and Podcasts

While social media has many challenges, artists, writers, and activists have also used their social media platforms to support the healing and thriving of Black women. Social media can support Black women in thriving through self-presentation and identity construction. Bailey et al. (2020) postulated that using social media to express oneself and communicate with like-minded people strengthens well-being. Stanton et al. (2017) noted that social media could help members of racial or ethnic minorities develop positive racial identity formation, self-presentation, and even social activism. The Instagram page for The Body, a Home for Love (Ivory, 2019), which is run by Deun Ivory, demonstrates this (King, 2020). This organization seeks to amplify how Black women can heal from sexual trauma. The page displays quotations, infographics, pictures, and discussions with Black women about self-care, healing, and coping methods.

Therapists can encourage their Black female clients to be thoughtful about how they express themselves online in a way that is not a reaction to societal expectations but reflects what they truly wish to share about themselves. Further, it can be helpful for clients to curate the profiles they follow on social media to ensure they are following people who share images and messages that affirm who they are as Black women.

In addition to social media, many podcasts are aimed at supporting the healing and thriving of Black women. Podcasts can be an accessible way for Black women to listen to and connect with the stories and experiences of other Black women and learn about strategies for healing, self-care, and thriving. At the end of this chapter is a list of podcasts created by Black women that can be a resource for healing and thriving. We encourage therapists to recommend the podcasts that would be helpful and appropriate for the client.

14.5.7   Sister Circles

Sister circles are both formal and informal groups of Black women who come together for mutual support, encouragement, and celebration. Black women commonly adopt the Afrocentric values of communalism, which involves valuing interdependence and a focus on relationships. Therefore, sister circles can be a powerful source of healing and thriving for Black women. A sister circle could be a sorority chapter (Black female sororities have a long history in the United States, and many Black women engage in these groups with high levels of pride), a women's group at church, or a group of girlfriends who get together frequently. Sister circles provide space for Black women to share their challenges and their wins, to support and encourage each other through life's ups and down. Many Black women cite the support they have received from other Black women in their life as helping them on their journey.

We encourage therapists to explore with their clients the places and spaces where they can find support from other Black women. If the client does not believe she has access to a supportive community currently, group therapy might be a helpful resource. Group therapy can also tap into the power of Black female relationships to support healing and thriving. For example, one of us ran a therapy group for women of color at a university counseling center;

the majority of the group members identified as Black, and at least one cohort of the group was all Black women. The 9-week program guided group members to explore their relationships with themselves through the processes of self-forgiveness and self-compassion, explore what it looks like to engage in self-acceptance and self-love, and cultivate joy in their lives. Each week, the group began with a mindfulness meditation or other grounding exercise and an opportunity for each group member to check in. Group members shared with authenticity and vulnerability about their experiences navigating racism and sexism, we explored the inner criticism that held many members back, and group members were guided in practicing self-compassion. Group members engaged thoughtfully in the group sessions and connected deeply with each other, offering support and encouragement. What the group members experienced could not have been facilitated solely in the context of individual therapy. Tapping into the resource of sister circles enabled the group members to go beyond learning coping strategies. The relationships they developed enabled the group to support healing and thriving.

To further tap into the power of sister circles, the facilitators maintained more relaxed boundaries with the group than in a typical therapist–client relationship and supported group members' desire to connect outside of the group after the nine weeks were over. Group members expressed feeling seen, heard, and uplifted through this group. The theme of empowerment ran through the course of the group with the facilitators sharing wisdom, offering encouragement, and empowering group members to tap into their internal wisdom to guide themselves and other group members. We encourage therapists who offer or are thinking about offering group therapy to consider integrating some of the resources mentioned in this chapter for healing and thriving in their group therapy offerings for Black women.

Case Example

Shola was in her early 70s and attended therapy in bright and colorful clothing. In her first session she wore a red beret and a long, colorful dustcoat paired with black leather boots. Her confidence was palpable. She shared stories about her multiple lovers, especially the last one. Her face lit up every time she described their strong connection and how much her lover admired her natural beauty and youth. Those affirmative sexual relationships were evident in her strong sense of identity and high self-esteem. Yet as the therapist got to know Shola better, she learned there was not just a rosy story. Shola had struggled with her marital relationship almost all her life, battling depression and the inner conflict she experienced growing up as a Black woman in this society. After years of struggling on her own, Shola finally decided to seek therapy when she turned 70. While

(cont.)

she was hoping for a Black therapist, Shola was happy to work with an Asian woman therapist. During the therapy, she shared how she sought strength through art and nature. She recounted a memory of a field of daffodils in front of her parents' home. She described how it was such a powerful and soothing experience for her then, and she kept coming back to that scene in the therapy sessions. Every spring she would soak herself in the sea of yellow daffodils. "If someone brings me a daffodil, she can be my best friend," Shola said.

Shola introduced the therapist to Etta James's classic song "At Last" and Nina Simone's "Ain't Got No, I Got Life." The therapist and Shola laughed together when her sense of humor came into play. They cried together when Shola recalled the heartbreaking memory of Dr. King's death. Time and time again, in the therapy office, the history and Shola's individual life were interwoven with each other.

The therapist appreciated how Shola opened the door and allowed her to see the pain and joys of her life, which the therapist told Shola she could write a book about. The therapist discovered that Shola's colorful and stylish clothing were her "daffodils" – an artistic representation of the parts of her life that she celebrated and that soothed her spirit daily. The therapist understood the power of this metaphor and expanded the conversation about daffodils to help Shola embrace a strategy for self-love and personal renewal. Buying daffodils, visiting botanic gardens to see daffodils, and displaying pictures of daffodils were incorporated into the strategies the therapist suggested to help Shola expand her inner resources for healing.

14.6   Conclusion

In many settings, Black women attend to the physical and emotional needs of others, and they also need attention, healing, and recovery themselves. Our recommendation is that Black women begin to prioritize themselves. The importance of inner healing as a continuous process through Black women's lives cannot be overemphasized. Griffin (1996) argues the internal healing process is not permanent. It requires constant effort and attention, and therapy can be an arena that supports Black women to keep up with their emotional lives and find renewal in postures and activities that soothe, increase joyful abandonment, and restore laughter and flow. In inner healing work, Black women learn to love their bodies, souls, and spirit, which may be battle scarred from their life experiences.

Therapist Reflection Questions

1. How do self-love, loving-kindness to self, and self-compassion play out in your own life?
2. For what reasons have you needed inner healing and how have you found it?
3. What are your thoughts and feelings about using the strategies discussed in this chapter with Black female clients?
4. What connections do you make between Black women's inner healing and their resilience against oppression?
5. What specific benefits do you see in Black women's use of art, media, and literature in inner healing work?
6. How can spiritual resources help Black women cope with painful memories?

Resources for Clients

Books

Angelou, M. (1993). *Wouldn't take nothing for my journey now.* Random House.
brown, a. m. (2019). *Pleasure activism: The politics of feeling good.* AK Press.
Elle, A. (2022). *How we heal.* Chronicle Books.
hooks, b. (1993). *Sisters of the yam: Black women and self-recovery.* South End Press.
    (2000). *All about love.* Morrow.
    (2002). *Communion: The female search for love.* Morrow.
Hunt, K. (2020). *Girl, gurl, grrl: On womanhood and belonging in the age of black girl magic.* Amistad.
Taylor, S. L. (1994). *In the spirit.* HarperPerennial.
Taylor, S. R. (2018). *The body is not an apology: The power of radical self-love.* Berrett-Koehler Publishers.

Podcasts

Alfred, L. (Host). (2018–present). *Balanced black girl* [Audio podcast]. https://www.balancedblackgirl.com/podcast/
Ash, L. (Host). (2016–present). *Black girl in Om* [Audio podcast]. https://www.blackgirlinom.com/podcast
Bradford, J. H. (Host). (2019–present). *Therapy for black girls* [Audio podcast]. https://therapyforblackgirls.com/podcast/
Gooden, A. (Host). (2021–present). *Unconditionally worthy* [Audio podcast]. https://dradiagooden.com/podcast
Tubbs, S. (Host). (2019–present). *Black girls heal* [Audio podcast]. https://www.blackgirlsheal.org/podcast/

References

Aakvaag, H. F., Thoresen, S., Wentzel-Larsen, T., Dyb, G., Røysamb, E., & Olff, M. (2016). Broken and guilty since it happened: A population study of trauma-related shame and guilt after violence and sexual abuse. *Journal of Affective Disorders*, *204*, 16–23. https://doi.org/10.1016/j.jad.2016.06.004

Amoloku, O. M. (2019). *The mammy, the breeder and the race woman: Storytelling as subversion in selected novels by contemporary Black women writers.* (Publication No. 13859120) [Master's thesis, Middle Tennessee State University]. ProQuest Publishing.

Angelou, M. (1969). *I know why the caged bird sings.* Random House.

Au, T. M., Sauer-Zavala, S., King, M. W., Petrocchi, N., Barlow, D. H., & Litz, B. T. (2017). Compassion-based therapy for trauma-related shame and posttraumatic stress: Initial evaluation using a multiple baseline design. *Behavior Therapy*, *48*(2), 207–221. https://doi.org/10.1016/j.beth.2016.11.012

Bacchus, D. N., & Holley, L. C. (2005). Spirituality as a coping resource: The experiences of professional Black women. *Journal of Ethnic and Cultural Diversity in Social Work*, *13*(4), 65–84.

Bailey, E. R., Matz, S. C., Youyou, W., & Iyengar, S. S. (2020). Authentic self-expression on social media is associated with greater subjective wellbeing. *Nature Communications*, *11*(1), 4889. https://doi.org/10.1038/s41467–020-18539-w

Benton, H. (2017, February 2). Black history, culture told through dance. *Citizen Times*. https://www.citizen-times.com/story/news/local/2017/02/02/black-history-culture-told-through-dance/97103982

brown, a. m. (2019). *Pleasure activism: The politics of feeling good.* AK Press.

Brown, C. A. (2016, June). *A visual history of social dance in 25 moves* [Video]. TED Conferences. https://www.ted.com/talks/camille_a_brown_a_visual_history_of_social_dance_in_25_moves?language=en

Brown, N. (2017, July 30). I left Christianity for an ancient African faith. Vice. https://www.vice.com/en/article/ywg9w5/i-left-christianity-for-an-ancient-african-faith

Burnett-Zeigler, I., Satyshur, M. D., Hong, S., Wisner, K. L., & Moskowitz, J. (2019). Acceptability of a mindfulness intervention for depressive symptoms among African-American women in a community health center: A qualitative study. *Complementary Therapies in Medicine*, *45*, 19–24. https://doi.org/10.1016/j.ctim.2019.05.012

Dill, A. (2020). *I'm a Black woman in art therapy for 8 months! Here's my experience.* https://adannadill.com/im-a-black-woman-in-art-therapy-for-8-months-heres-my-experience

Gay, R. (2017). *Hunger: A memoir of (my) body.* HarperCollins.

Gooden, A. S., & McMahon, S. D. (2016). Thriving among African-American adolescents: Religiosity, religious support, and communalism. *American Journal of Community Psychology*, *57*(1–2), 118–128. https://doi.org/10.1002/ajcp.12026

Greene, B. (1997) Psychotherapy with African American women: Integrating feminist and psychodynamic models. *Smith College Studies in Social Work*, *67*(3), 299–322. https://doi.org/10.1080/00377319709517495

Griffin, F. J. (1996). Textual healing: Claiming Black women's bodies, the erotic and resistance in contemporary novels of slavery. *Callaloo*, *19*(2), 519–536.

Hayman, J. W., Kurpius, S. R., Befort, C., Nicpon, M. F., Hull-Blanks, E., Sollenberger, S., & Huser, L. (2007). Spirituality among college freshmen: Relationships to self-esteem, body image, and stress. *Counseling and Values*, 52(1), 55–70.

Hurston, Z. N. (1937). *Their eyes were watching God*. J. B. Lippincott & Co.

Ivory, D. [@thebodyahomeforlove]. (2019). Posts. [Instagram profile]. Retrieved November 2020 from https://www.instagram.com/thebodyahomeforlove

Jensen, A., & Bonde, L. O. (2018). The use of arts interventions for mental health and wellbeing in health settings. *Perspectives in Public Health*, 138(4), 209–214. https://doi.org/10.1177/1757913918772602

Johnson, S. B., Goodnight, B. L., Zhang, H., Daboin, I., Patterson, B., & Kaslow, N. J. (2018). Compassion-based meditation in African Americans: Self-criticism mediates changes in depression. *Suicide and Life-Threatening Behavior*, 48(2), 160–168. https://doi.org/10.1111/sltb.12347

Kilgore, A. M., Kraus, R., & Littleford, L. N. (2020). "But I'm not allowed to be mad": How Black women cope with gendered racial microaggressions through writing. *Translational Issues in Psychological Science*, 6(4), 372–382. https://doi.org/10 .1037/tps0000259

King, A. (2020, January 19). How this organization is making space for Black women to heal from sexual trauma. *Vogue*. https://www.vogue.com/article/how-this-organization-is-making-space-for-black-women-to-heal-from-sexual-trauma

Levin, J. (2010). Religion and mental health: Theory and research. *International Journal of Applied Psychoanalytic Studies*, 7(2), 102–115.

Lorde, A. (1988). *A burst of light and other essays*. Firebrand Books.

Menakem, R. (2017). *My grandmother's hands: Racialized trauma and the pathway to mending our hearts and bodies*. Central Recovery Press.

Morrison, T. (1970). *The bluest eye*. Holt McDougal.

Muncie, I. (2010). *Black mothers and the nation: Claiming space and crafting signification for the black maternal body in American women's narratives of slavery, reconstruction, and segregation, 1852–2001* (Publication No. 3403252) [Doctoral dissertation, Ball State University]. ProQuest Publishing.

Phifer, H. (2017). *Black, woman and alive: Black women's practices of nontraditional healing and freedom* (Publication No. 1) [Master's thesis, Lesley University]. Digital Commons. https://digitalcommons.lesley.edu/expressive_ theses/1

Shange, N. (1974). *For colored girls who have considered suicide/when the rainbow is enuf*. Simon and Schuster.

Shulman, J. L., & Horne, S. G. (2003). The use of self-pleasure: Masturbation and body image among African American and European American women. *Psychology of Women Quarterly*, 27(3), 262–269.

Stanton, A. G., Jerald, M. C., Ward, L. M., & Avery, L. R. (2017). Social media contributions to Strong Black Woman ideal endorsement and Black women's mental health. *Psychology of Women Quarterly*, 41(4), 465–478. https://doi.org/10 .1177/0361684317732330

Stephenson, K., & Rosen, D. H. (2015). Haiku and healing: An empirical study of poetry writing as therapeutic and creative intervention. *Empirical Studies of the Arts*, 33(1), 36–60. https://doi.org/10.1177/0276237415569981

Taylor, S. R. (2018). *The body is not an apology: The power of radical self-love.* Berrett-Koehler Publishers.

Thomas, T. (2016, February 11). *The legacy of women in the Black Church.* Christianity Today: Women Leaders. https://www.christianitytoday.com/women-leaders/2016/february/legacy-of-women-in-black-church.html

Turman, E. M. (2019, February 28). Black women's faith, Black women's flourishing. *The Christian Century.* https://www.christiancentury.org/article/critical-essay/black-women-s-faith-black-women-s-flourishing

Vance, L. (2020, February 24). *Creative healing spaces: Healing from racial wounds.* American Art Therapy Association. https://arttherapy.org/blog-creative-healing-spaces-healing-from-racial-wounds

Walker, A. (1982). *The color purple.* Pocket.

Wiggins, D. C. (2004). *Righteous content: Black women's perspectives of church and faith.* New York University Press.

Williams, C. B. (2005). Counseling African American women: Multiple identities – Multiple constraints. *Journal of Counseling & Development, 83*(3), 278–283.

Williams, M. I. (2020, February 19). *Mariam I. Williams on Black woman writing for self-knowledge.* Nick Virgilio Haiku Association. https://www.nickvirgiliohaiku.org/blog/2020/mariam-i-williams-on-black-women-writing-for-self-knowledge

15   Black Women's Spiritual and Religious Coping

with Taheera Blount[*]

> Thinking that the Lord can solve all . . . problems . . . is true, but the Lord also put therapists in this world to help.
>
> Study participant

For many Black women, their *religious* and *spiritual* values and associated practices are tremendous sources of joy, celebration, community, and sanctuary as they navigate life. In this chapter, we discuss religion and spirituality together, but the distinction between these terms reflects how they might operate differently in people's lives. For example, we (the authors of this book) were all raised in the Christian religion. Two authors continue to identify as spiritual and also religious in their embrace of Christianity. The other author maintains a belief in a higher power but considers herself more spiritual than religious and has no affiliation to any religious organization. Black female clients in our practices fall along the same lines.

The term *spirituality* comes from the Latin word *spiritus*, or spirit (Belgrave & Allison, 2010). Mattis (2002) refers to spirituality as "an individual's belief in the sacred and transcendent nature of life, and the manifestation of these beliefs in the sense of connectedness with others (e.g., human, spirits, and God), and in quest of goodness" (p. 310). African-centered belief systems have shaped expressions of Black spirituality in the United States. For example, in West African spiritual thought, the psyche and the spirit are one (Mbiti, 1990; Nobles, 2004). Many Black women express psychological pain or distress in spiritual terms (Boyd-Franklin, 2010; Constantine et al., 2000; McGoldrick et al., 2005; Wimberly, 1997). We should note that such expressions are common even when Black women do not subscribe to specific religious traditions. Black women may not practice spiritual disciplines but may still believe in God and have a spiritual understanding of the world.

---

[*] T. Blount, D. Baptiste, & A. Gooden. (2023). Black women's spiritual and religious coping. In D. Baptiste & A. Gooden, *Promoting Black women's mental health: What practitioners should know and do*. Cambridge University Press.

The word *religion* comes from the Latin word *religio*, meaning good faith (Belgrave & Allison, 2010). Boyd-Franklin (2010) describes religion as "a core set of beliefs and the formal practice of those beliefs through membership in a church or other faith-based institution" (p. 978). Mattis and Jagers (2001) defined religion as "a shared system of beliefs, mythology, and rituals associated with god or gods, whereas religiosity refers to one's adherence to the prescribed beliefs, doctrines, and practices of a religion" (p. 522). In spite of these nuanced definitions, in Black women, religious and spiritual identities and practices coalesce in a manner that would be difficult to categorize and disentangle. Therefore, from this point onward as it relates to Black women, we use both terms to talk about their faith, distinguishing one or the other where relevant.

In this chapter we indicate how mental health practice, in general, has ignored the salience of spirituality and religion in clients' lives. We remind therapists of the centrality of Black women's spiritual and religious orientation, including how Black women might connect stress, suffering, and psychological distress to religious and spiritual narratives. We discuss Black women's use of spirituality and religiosity to cope with life's difficulties. We examine how spiritual and religious involvement can also contribute to Black women's experiences of oppression, self-loathing, and self-silencing. For therapists, we offer a framework for integrating religious and spiritual issues in order to work with Black female clients from a culturally skilled perspective. This framework includes supporting women to use religious and spiritual support and resources for recovery and wellness. We begin by discussing two aspects of Black women's religiosity and spirituality that therapists should be aware of: Black women's dedication to their faith organizations and the centrality of spiritual and religious beliefs in daily coping.

15.1   Black Women's Labor of Love in Faith Organizations

Black women express their spirituality and religion through worship, prayer, reading religious or viewing religious media, attending conferences, meditation and service (Marroquin, 2011; Mattis & Jagers, 2001). Black women's expression of these disciplines have been connected to the Black church, where many find sanctuary and community to build a life of purpose and service (Cheadle et al., 2014).

As used here, the "Black church" is not a singular or monolithic entity. Instead, the Black church refers to religious organizations whose memberships are primarily Black people with Protestant values and affiliations. Black churches have been the nucleus for education, political activism, community leadership, and socialization (Belin et al., 2006; Bourjolly, 1998; Levin et al., 1995; Mattis & Watson, 2008; Wilmoth & Sanders, 2001). Notably, Black faith traditions helped to fuel the civil rights movement, most prominently in the 1960s and 1970s. The Black church has provided forums for discussing critical political issues and has offered vital community resources such as social organizing, access to valuable networks, and leadership training (Mattis & Watson, 2008; Taylor & Chatters, 1991). Black religious leaders, primarily men, wield political power in advancing social, cultural, and economic conditions for Black people.

Black women are a cornerstone of most Black congregations. Although rarely in official or high leadership, Black women have fully given themselves to serving their God through affiliation with a local body. Some women have grown up in Christian churches and denominations, which they have never left (Marroquin, 2011).

Black Americans are the most religious cultural group in the United States (Mohamed, 2021) and therapists should be aware that many Black women love their work in churches and other religious organizations. Most Black Americans are Christians, and approximately 74% believe in God, with 43% reporting that they attend religious services every week or once or twice a month. Close to 69% of Black women in our study (see Chapter 1) described themselves as very religious/spiritual. Around 28% were somewhat religious/ spiritual, and only 3% described themselves as not at all religious/spiritual. Black Americans' religious and spiritual traditions convey a vibrancy that shows the integration of West African cultural heritage, worldviews, distinctive beliefs, and worship patterns. This style of worship in and of itself can be a balm to weary souls. It is not uncommon to see religious gatherings with intense and expressive worship, communication with the Holy Spirit, dancing, clapping, flag-waving, and other spontaneous and joyful actions (Chatters et al., 2008; Maynard-Reid, 2000). A view from the pulpit of many Black congregations will be Black women singing, dancing, and sometimes lost in the joy of music. Black women are foundational to most Black Christian congregations, making up 70%–90% of most Black churches (Reed & Neville, 2014).

Historically, Black women's labor has been influential in building and expanding the Black church. Church work mainly involves women (Jacobs, 2014). However, many are in traditional areas of church work rather than the top leadership positions. For example, Black women run various ministries and staff outreach agencies connected to missions and education (Grant, 1989). Many women do not mind church work. They are committed to it because it strengthens their spiritual and religious identities, status, and influence. Women's church work and fellowship provide outlets for friendships and activities (Reed & Neville, 2014). Women's engagement in important ministries also confers status and belonging. For example, women might be a part of outreach ministries (e.g., in prisons or food pantries). They may be part of political activism or women's social clubs in the church. Women also hone leadership skills in subsidiary ministries, such as intercessory prayer, singles and marriage ministries, hospitality committees, or pastor's aid, to name a few (Reed & Neville, 2014. As a result, Black women experience deep meaning and high reward for their accomplishments in their labor over multiple years, giving generously of their time in many roles.

Although protestant Christianity is the preferred faith background of most Black people, some Black women are among the 3% of Black Americans who follow other religious traditions. These traditions include Judaism, Islam, Buddhism and Hinduism (Masci, 2018). In addition, 8% of Black Americans self-identify as Jehovah's Witnesses, Mormons (Masci, 2018). In small but increasing numbers, Black women are also adherents to African religions such as the Yoruba faith (Reed & Neville, 2014). Religious practices may be expressed differently among various faiths, and women may hold different statuses and roles in their religious groups. It would also be true to say that Black women of other faiths may feel similarly about the centrality of faith and give of themselves.

For example, similar to Christian religious organizations, many urban mosques embrace the mission of combating poverty, crime, drugs, and violence in communities around them. They also facilitate urban youth development through sponsored programs and outreach. Mosques also commit to urban redevelopment and revitalization through Islamic community life (Akom, 2007). Women give back to their faith organizations in many ways.

15.2   Black Women's Spiritual and Religious Coping

Historically, spirituality and religion served as sources of comfort, strength, and sustaining power as African Americans endured years of slavery, discrimination, and oppression (Taylor et al., 2004). Religion and spirituality offer Black women an internalized compass and meaning system to understand hardships and seek self-encouragement. This system of meaning relates primarily to the sense that suffering contains both anguish and beauty (Greer, 2011; Shorter-Gooden, 2004). Religious Black women who experience hardship or suffering pray, read sacred literature for inspiration, and look to religion for inspirational perspectives on life. These disciplines help some women to maintain a positive sense of self, seek social support, and bond over a shared experience of troubles, which helps them to counteract the negative impact of a racist society (Greer, 2011; Shorter-Gooden, 2004).

The Black church provides Black women with opportunities for activism; spiritual, emotional, and social support; and platforms to speak out against oppressive social, political, and economic conditions (Taylor et al., 2004). For Black women, religious institutions provide a place to discuss life stressors, engage in community activities, and have meaningful conversations with like-minded individuals. Being a member of the Black church offers Black women the space to improve the Black community (Lincoln & Mamiya, 1990). This sense of empowerment, connectedness, and advocacy in an extended family provides a great deal of meaning in Black women's lives.

In navigating times of trauma and loss, spirituality is a significant vehicle for healing and recovery for Black women (Boyd-Franklin, 2010; Dass-Brailsford, 2010). Moreover, religion and spirituality is a survival mechanism that has contributed to the resilience of Black people in coping with the psychological pain of racism, substance use, discrimination, trauma, and oppression (Bowen-Reid & Harrell, 2002). For example, Cheney et al. (2014) conducted a mixed-method study that compared and contrasted the religious and spiritual dimensions of cutting down and stopping cocaine. The study included 28 African Americans in rural and urban areas in the South. Results revealed that participants drew on diverse religious and spiritual beliefs and practices that consisted of (a) participation in organized religion, (b) reliance on a personal relationship with God, (c) use of religious symbols and idiomatic expression, and (d) use of biblical scriptures to interpret and make sense of their substance-use experiences to reduce and abstain from cocaine use. Religious faith and spirituality can serve as a resource for overcoming addiction and trauma and thriving for Black people.

In addition, Black women cope with stress by seeking social support, finding diversions, avoiding problems, and seeking spiritual help. Prayer is one form of religious coping that many Black women utilize and can serve as a source of comfort, support, and hope (Greer & Abel, 2017). Additionally, prayer and religious engagement assist with personal problems, including cancer, recovery from substance use, pregnancy or infant loss (Bourjolly, 1998), agoraphobia, bipolar disorder, racism, and depression (Brome et al., 2000; Neighbors et al., 1998; Smith et al., 1999; Van, 2001). Dessio and colleagues (2004) examined how Black women use religion and spirituality to cope with health issues. The study found that 43% of participants utilized religion and spirituality to manage serious health problems such as cancer, heart disease, and depression (Dessio et al., 2004). Given this knowledge, it can be helpful to integrate religious coping strategies into therapy as is appropriate and relevant to Black female clients. We provide specific recommendations on how to do this later in the chapter.

Pastoral support has been related to thriving in Black youth for African American adolescents (Gooden & McMahon, 2016). The same is likely valid for Black women. Many people consider their fellow congregants extended family and refer to them as their church family (Mattis & Jagers, 2001). Black women involved in Black churches can find space to express both joys and sorrows within their church community. Many sister circles that Black women participate in originated in the Black church through various ministries, such as the choir, the deacon board, or the dance ministry. These networks provide social and emotional support, and given their grounding in religious faith, Black women in these groups can make prayer requests, which serves as an opportunity to share personal struggles and challenges. These groups are also spaces where Black women give and receive encouragement when difficulties arise. Although these groups often develop through Black women's church involvement, another recommendation would be for licensed, trained clinicians to host group therapy sessions within the Black church (Avent-Harris et al., 2019). Therapists can explore their clients' use of religious coping strategies by asking them to identify positive aspects of the Black church and the instrumental role they serve within the community.

> We give an example of sister circles as a form of group therapy in Chapter 14.

While Black women benefit significantly from religious and spiritual involvement, engaging with religious institutions can also be a source of burden, shame, and even trauma for Black women. In this section, we detail some negative experiences that our Black female clients have sought our help on in navigating their faith beliefs and affiliations. As we have helped women to explore and manage these religious and spiritual stressors we have not denigrated clergy or congregations in a bid to ally with women's suffering. We encourage our colleagues who work with Black women around their faith journey to adopt our posture. It is possible to ally with a client and validate their wounds and sense of injustice, while maintaining respect for the multiple angles, contexts, and complexities of faith groups and practices.

15.3   Religious and Spiritual Stressors in Black Women's Therapy Narratives

15.3.1   Overwork

The flip side of Black women's love of the Black Church and institutions of other faiths is how *overworked* women can feel at times. While Black women are clear that their labor are acts of love for their congregations, and an expression of their faith, Black women may be the only source of labor to keep faith institutions running (Day, 2012). Women may be expended in saying yes to multiple and layered requests, making it difficult to set healthy boundaries around their own energy and need for rest. Because Black women are extremely dependable, loyal, and dedicated and put the needs of others first, they may neglect their own wellness and self-care. We encourage therapists to probe women on the reality that they may be saying "yes" when their hearts are saying "no." One strategy to balance selflessness in faith with self-care is to carefully analyze and help Black women to set careful boundaries.

> See Chapter 10 for more on Black women's caregiving work and Chapter 13 for more on physical health and wellness strategies.

15.3.2   Religious and Spiritual Hurts and Ruptures

Conflicts are inevitable within any organization, and this is equally true for the Black churches and other religious organizations (Cashwell & Swindle, 2018). When a person has a conflict with a faith institution related to communication problems, organizational structures, social networks, or identity negotiation, this can result in ruptures and disengagement not unlike those that occur in families (Cooper & Mitra, 2018). Kramer (2011) conducted a study that examined the assimilation process of volunteer members of a community choir in a Black church. The results revealed that some members left the choir with or without plans to return, or without notifying leaders.

When a therapist is working with a Black female client who has exited a religious organization because of feelings of being hurt or misunderstanding, the therapist should ask the client about her decisions to exit, listening for the history and dynamics of the rupture or cutoff. Did the disengagement occur because of spiritual or religious rejection or neglect? If so, a therapist can process how the rupture happened, how it impacted the client, ways to soothe pain and vulnerability, and if possible, to repair it with the organization's leadership. At stake is that Black women's hurts in one congregation may lead to their disenchantment and distance from others (De Wit, 2011). In cutting themselves off from a faith community, Black women may lose far more than a place to worship. A rupture with a congregation may mean an end of social gatherings, friendships, meaningful service, a sense of purpose, leadership training and education, and more. The loss of these opportunities can leave deep holes in women's lives. The therapist can help the client develop strategies for overcoming the church hurt and envisioning how they can move forward, perhaps to another church.

15.3.3   Sexist Bias in Leadership

While the Black church can serve as a source of support and acceptance, it can also be a space where Black women experience sexism and judgment, especially around matters of sexuality. Many Black churches continue to uphold patriarchal views of gender and power and promote the idea that women should submit to men (Wiggins, 2004). While Black women often serve as the backbone of Black churches, they are commonly restricted to the shadows and to helping behind the scenes. Although more Black women are now serving in pastoral roles, there are still many denominations that do not ordain women or have no Black women leaders. One way for the therapist to broach this subject would be to discuss the hierarchy of leadership in a Black woman's congregation or denomination and how to express their faith under this hierarchy (Williams & Wiggins, 2010). If the client has expressed a desire to hold a leadership role in their religious community, the therapist can help the client to process any reservations they may have about the leadership ranks or the process of becoming a leader within the church.

15.3.4 Sexual Abuse

Troublingly, sexual abuse and molestation within the Black church can cause harm and trauma for Black women. There have been instances of pastors sexually abusing parishioners. Further, as in many areas of our society, there may be Black ministers who have affairs with parishioners. As when working with clients who have experienced sexual abuse by a family member, therapists must be aware of the complicated relationship that a survivor might have with the person who abused them (Abcarian, 2018). When a woman or girl is abused by a leader seen as a "righteous" person in the church, they may be more likely to blame themselves for the abuse they experience. Further, if a Black woman chooses to leave her church due to mistreatment, she may experience significant grief and loss.

15.3.5 Sexuality Rejection

Black churches are becoming more accepting. There are open and affirming Black churches that actively support and accept church members who identify as lesbian, gay, bisexual, transgender, and/or queer (LGBTQ; Chaney, 2011). However, homophobia is still present in many Black churches. In a 2006 Black Pride Survey, 54% of respondents reported that homosexuality was taught to be a sin in their church (Chaney, 2011). Black women who identify as LGBTQ may experience homophobia and/or transphobia and may have been encouraged to stay in the closet by church members. Feeling judged and outcast could lead to abandonment and relational trauma for LGBTQ Black women. Many have had to leave their churches to live confidently in their identities. Further, sex in general is often discussed as something shameful for women in particular, leading many Black Christian women to develop a conflicted relationship with their sexuality. Therapists must gently explore possible experiences of trauma and pain associated with the Black church to have a nuanced understanding of their Black female client's experiences and perspectives.

See Chapter 14 for more on Black women's internal healing from trauma.

15.3.6 Stigmatization of Mental Health Treatment

Recently, Black ministers have been encouraging their parishioners to seek therapy. Some are even sharing that they have therapists themselves, and such disclosures are helpful. Despite these promising signs of change, it is not uncommon for Black women to feel discouraged from seeking mental health treatment due to messages they receive in church. These messages may be that you can "pray your pain away" or that if a person's faith were strong enough, they would not need therapy. Additionally, statements by Black Christian women such as "I'm too blessed to be stressed," while self-affirming in its own way, could imply that acknowledging stressors or challenges invalidates blessings (Williams & Wiggins, 2010). Pastoral counseling can serve as a significant source of support for Black women who are going through challenging time (Carelock, 2009). Black women seeking therapy may worry that receiving this kind of support indicates that their faith is not strong. We encourage therapists to be thoughtful when exploring these dynamics with their Black female clients.

15.3.7 Confusion between Sickness and Sin

Therapists may sometimes have to gently guide their clients to deconstruct the lens through which they view their mental health symptoms. The symptom as "sin or sickness" often comes up in the context of behavior that religious groups regard as sinful or deviant. A therapist looking at the same conduct might see connections to a behavioral, medical, or neurological disorder. In the case example later in this chapter, we discuss a client's sexual addiction that was a direct result of child sexual abuse spanning several years. The sexual addiction symptoms had many troubling features that the client's family members or minister might label a "sin" condition. Compassionately, the therapist chose to encourage the client to see the addiction as the impact of a childhood injury to the sexual self. This injury grew as the child grew, and in adulthood it felt overpowering. Many Black women may be dealing with mental illness, addictions, or other conditions that explain some of their choices. Our hope in therapy is to remove their self-hatred and shame so that their recovery can be unhampered.

We offer several strategies that therapists might use to integrate and use a religious and spiritual emphasis with Black women in therapy.

15.4   Broaching Religious and Spiritual Conversations with Black Women

Therapists should explore their clients' interest or willingness to incorporate religious and spiritual beliefs into treatment. While some clients may find this integration incredibly helpful and supportive of their healing, other clients may want their therapy to be free from religious themes. Further, some Black female clients no longer identify as religious even as they continue to adhere to some of the cultural traditions of their faith community. Therapists who follow the same faith as their clients can consider this a shared culture and foster connection and rapport related to this shared culture (Wolf & Stevens, 2001). Given that beliefs can vary widely within religions, it is essential for therapists not to assume that their ideas about religion are the same as their client's.

Earlier in this chapter, we offered suggestions related to Black women's understanding of their faith identities. Here we discuss specific strategies therapists can use to integrate religious and spiritual perspectives into therapy with Black women. First, therapists should ask about their Black female clients' religious and spiritual beliefs and avoid making assumptions about their client's religiosity and spirituality. Helpful questions include these: (a) Are you religious or spiritual at all? (b) Tell me about your religious and spiritual beliefs. (c) What has been helpful about your religious and spiritual involvement? (d) What, if anything, has been a difficulty about your religious and spiritual involvement? (e) Are you engaged in a religious or spiritual community? and (f) What benefits and challenges have you experienced through your engagement in a religious or spiritual community?

The therapist can also ask the client about how their religious and spiritual beliefs may influence their coping mechanisms. These questions may include the following: (a) How do your religious or spiritual beliefs influence how you make sense of your experience? (b) Are there religious or spiritual practices that help you to cope when you feel stressed? If yes, what practices help? and (c) Are there religious texts that offer you support and encouragement? If yes, what materials do you find helpful? Asking these questions during therapy can prompt a Black female client to share how she uses her faith to cope with challenges and gently remind her of the coping strategies she can use to align with her beliefs.

15.5 Exploring Your Own Religious and Spiritual Beliefs and Values

Therapists should seek to understand the religious and spiritual beliefs and practices of their Black female clients and incorporate them into therapy as appropriate. Before integrating religious and spiritual coping into therapy, however, therapists should be aware of their own religious/spiritual belief practices or bias against religious and spiritual beliefs and practices. Post and Wade (2009) maintain that being aware of one's spiritual beliefs and practices will help prevent the therapist from imposing their values and beliefs on their clients. Additionally, Wiggins (2008) suggests that therapists conduct a spiritual autobiography as a method to explore and examine their own religious and spiritual views and values. Almost no one is entirely neutral in their thoughts and feelings about religious and spiritual beliefs. Some therapists may view their religious and spiritual beliefs as a resource in their own lives. Others may have had negative or even traumatic experiences with religion that have caused them to see religious involvement in a negative light. Religion and spirituality can be sensitive topics. We encourage therapists to seek supervision or consultation to address countertransference related to your client's religious or spiritual beliefs or engagement. We have included a few therapist reflection questions at the end of this chapter.

15.6 Amplifying Black Women's Spiritual and Religious Coping Strategies

There is evidence that integrating religion into psychotherapy can benefit religious clients (Wolf & Stevens, 2001). One way to incorporate religion and spirituality into therapy is to utilize faith as a resource for a client's mental health (Wolf & Stevens, 2001). Therapists do not need to have the same religious or spiritual views as their Black female client to integrate religion and spirituality in this way. Richards and Bergin (2005) identified the following religious and spiritual interventions that can be incorporated into psychotherapy with clients: (a) therapist prayer or client and therapist prayer, (b) teaching scriptural concepts or making reference to scriptures, (c) religious or spiritual self-disclosure, (d) spiritual assessments, (e) religious relaxation or imagery, (f) encouragement of forgiveness, (g) encouragement of confession, (h) spiritual journaling, (i) spiritual meditation or relaxation, (j) religious bibliotherapy, and (k) scripture memorization. Therapists must be thoughtful and intentional about using these interventions with clients. We caution therapists not to utilize interventions such as praying with clients or teaching spiritual concepts without specific training on integrating religion and spirituality into psychotherapy. However, we do encourage therapists to encourage forgiveness, spiritual journaling, meditation, religious bibliotherapy, and scripture meditation. It can be helpful for therapists to guide clients to identify their favorite practices and scriptures to utilize. We also encourage therapists to remember that there are many sects within the same faith. Therefore, as noted earlier in this chapter, it is important not to assume that a client and therapist following the same religion have the same religious beliefs.

Further, therapists should access spiritual interventions appropriate to the client's individual needs. We recommend the therapist ask the client what religious and spiritual practices they find helpful and support them in integrating these practices into their daily lives. For example, praying can be psychologically beneficial for people who believe that God is loving (Burnett-Zeigler, 2021). For therapists who plan to incorporate religion and spirituality actively into their work with clients, it can be helpful to establish partnerships with clergy and religious/spiritual leaders within the community. Therapists can work collaboratively with clergy to identify the mental health needs within their church, increase access to treatment, and provide education on coping with mental illness (Mengesha & Ward, 2012). Partnerships between mental health professionals and religious leaders can help to reduce the stigma associated with mental illness in the Black community.

It can also be helpful to support Black women in connecting to aspects of God within themselves. For example, many Black Christian churches highlight the fact that people are made in the image of God and that God, or the Holy Spirit, resides within them. Therapists can ask their Black female clients if they believe this to be true and guide them to connect to God or the spirit within as a source of strength and power. Additionally, spiritual and gospel music can serve as a source of comfort and healing for Black women. Therapists can encourage Black women to access this comfort through listening to or making their music that reflects their experiences and hope for the future.

> See Chapter 14 for more on how Black women can use artistic and creative expression, which may include religious themes, for inner healing and thriving.

15.7   Responding to Religious and Spiritual Vulnerabilities

Therapists should respect and honor Black women's fidelity to their faith beliefs and their congregations. They may observe contradictions in their clients' narratives related to women's status in the church. However, they must bracket their personal views or values and honor what their Black female clients find important to their well-being. Therapists might help Black women to understand that while religious beliefs and practices can be tremendously helpful at times, they can also be harmful.

One participant in our study mentioned a bit of advice from her grandmother about spurning mental health support. The participant said: "I remember when I told my grandma that I was going to pursue finding a therapist and she told me that 'Jesus is your therapist, girl.' Family pressure to take it to the lord in prayer without any acknowledgement on how hard it is to be a Black woman in America." Although the grandmother's advice may have been well intentioned to stoke the client's faith, such advice can also work against Black women's mental health and wellness. While taking care not to denigrate any religious institution or belief system, therapists might gently note where beliefs collide. For example, therapists might point out how views related to ignoring mental health difficulties and stress can harm Black women's wellness. For example, Walker-Barnes (2014) describes how some religious beliefs can intensify the Strong Black Woman persona, increasing Black women's stoicism around suffering, self-silencing, and denial of mental health support. Some sectarian religious and spiritual sentiments can also intensify the shame and self-loathing that some women internalize, defeating their sense of joy and empowerment. Patriarchy and gender oppression can also exist in the church. Black women may also be disadvantaged by religious values upholding marriage as a symbol of true womanhood, discouraging them from pursuing exciting careers and influencing beliefs related to financial management.

Some Black women may also be encouraged or supported to stay in relationships that present a clear and present danger to them or their children. When religious and spiritual beliefs present harm to women's mental health and wellness, we encourage therapists, especially those whose faith beliefs are dissimilar, to proactively name the risks they perceive and advocate for their clients, carefully considering the totality of the circumstances at hand. Consulting with clergy and others of like faith or connecting women to religious and spiritual advocacy groups are also strategies that can be in women's best interests.

The case demonstrates how engaging clients on these topics can open up constructive conversations. We also showcase how the therapist must listen for cues to understand precisely how a client's religious values may be influencing their current behaviors or mental health symptoms.

Case Example

Kendra sought therapy for matters she described as relationship issues. In the first few sessions, the therapist broached some questions to ascertain Kendra's religious and spiritual orientation. This led to a series of pleasant conversations about similarities in the therapist's and Kendra's faith backgrounds. Kendra discussed several matters she wanted to explore in therapy, but topics seemed safe. She discussed relationships with coworkers, the potential to switch careers, and challenges with dating. The therapist sensed that Kendra was holding back some critical disclosures and asked gently about this. The therapist said she wondered if their conversations about faith beliefs were preventing Kendra from opening up and talking about her concerns. This specific probe made Kendra sob for several minutes. The therapist reassured Kendra of her nonjudgmental stance toward client stories. She emphasized listening and working with clients, not as their minister or Christian sister, but as an ally and advocate. This helped Kendra open up fully.

From ages 6–10 years, Kendra was regularly sexually abused by an older brother. She hid the secret from her mother and grandmother, with whom she lived. She felt guilty that she came to look forward to the sexual activity, although she felt confused and guilty. A painful experience of pelvic cramps at school and a hospital visit revealed a sexually transmitted infection. This revelation brought on a flurry of school changes, mental health interventions, and legal activities. Kendra was sent to live with her father. The family dynamics became extremely difficult, and many days Kendra experienced anxiety and discouragement. In her father's home, she also experienced sexual violations by her older half-sister that lasted until the sister went away to college.

At age 34, Kendra was a well-educated woman in an exciting career, and she wanted to be married. She was a highly regarded leader in her Lutheran congregation and a committed Christian who counseled youth in her church. She was encouraged to become a minister and was seriously considering seminary study. Kendra then revealed to the therapist the stress of having a sexual addiction that she could not control. She slept with strangers randomly and enjoyed it, always taking care to use condoms. She hated this aspect of her life but did not feel that she could talk about it with her church leaders. On several occasions, she tried to tell her pastor but felt physically ill. She confessed that on first meeting the therapist, the connection around matters of faith made her feel ashamed and embarrassed to say what had made her seek therapy in the first place. This conversation led to identifying the powerful feelings of shame and self-loathing that Kendra felt in almost every setting. She had previously managed such feelings through overachievement and perfection in academics, sports, and church leadership. The therapist normalized the transference experience that Kendra felt, and she discussed the childhood sexual abuse as trauma that robbed Kendra of agency and choice as a child. The therapist also explained the normalcy of arousal in the presence of sexual stimulation. The therapist then worked with Kendra on viewing herself as the adult survivor of childhood sexual abuse, naming the sexual addiction as the result of a traumatic injury.

(*cont.*)

> The therapist distinguished the therapy environment from church settings, indicating that the client's healing, recovery, and wellness were goals. While honoring the client's deep connection to a religious community, the therapist also helped Kendra understand that her sexual addiction had been the result of her psychological vulnerability, not an intentional choice, something that Kendra had not recognized, something that Kendra had not done to this point. In offering a compassionate and nonjudgmental stance toward sexual addiction, the therapist helped Kendra identify her persistent feelings of unworthiness and sinfulness as originating in her religious community. The therapist also helped the client make connections between the trauma and sexual triggers. Kendra began to enact 12-step recovery principles based on the Sex Addicts Anonymous program. After 18 months of regular therapy, the addiction behaviors subsided, and she felt that she had more control. Of her own choice, she disclosed her treatment to her pastor and her highly supportive mother.

15.8   Conclusion

The case example showcases how faith beliefs and practices helped but also hindered this Black female client's efforts to address a psychological injury. This client experienced a traumatic and long-term injury, yet her religious and spiritual disciplines, which began in adolescence, helped her to anchor her life, decrease self-pity and bitterness, and also practice forgiveness. Forgiveness in this case meant that she was never in close quarters or alone with her childhood abusers but was superficially respectful when she attended family gatherings. This was, she says, a way to honor and join in family traditions that she dearly loved.

Intentionally, this client had internalized some values of her faith community that amplified her experiences of trauma as sin and shame, and at the time she sought therapy, her self-loathing was deep and added to her suffering. The case showcases how religiously based transference experiences can show up in a therapy session. In this case, the therapist and clients were of the same faith and religious background. These similarities were assets in building a comfortable relationship, but for this client, such synergy could have become a barrier to necessary disclosures that were key to her psychological recovery. Making a careful distinction between the religious context and the therapy context enabled the therapist and client to make progress on the treatment goals. We recommend this strategy to therapists who will likely navigate similar terrain, especially with highly religious Black female clients.

Therapist Reflection Questions

1. How would you describe your spiritual and religious identities?
2. How have you navigated your spiritual and religious identities with clients of similar and dissimilar backgrounds?
3. What, if any, positive or negative experiences have you had with religion or spirituality?
4. What, if any, religious beliefs and values might bring up unpleasant emotions or memories for you?
5. How do you feel about people who are not religious, atheist, or agnostic?
6. How do you navigate sex, sexual orientation, marriage, sin, and related topics in therapy with clients?
7. What experiences do you draw on to forge a strong alliance with religiously involved clients?
8. How do you feel about integrating religion and spirituality into therapy if appropriate for the client?

Resources

Books

hooks, b. (1994). *Sisters of the yam: Black women and self-recovery*. South End Press.

Paloutzian, R. F., & Ellison, C. W. (1982). Loneliness, spiritual wellbeing, and quality of life. In L. A. Peplau & D. Pearlman (Eds.), *Loneliness: A sourcebook for practice* (pp. 358–364). Wiley Interscience.

Pierce, Y. (2021). *In my grandmother's house: Black women, faith, and the stories we inherit*. Broadleaf Books.

Press, S. L. (Ed.). (2021). *Spiritual self care for black women: A spiritual journal for self discovery*. Stress Less Press.

Walker-Barnes, C. (2014). *Too heavy a yoke: Black women and the burden of strength*. Wipf and Stock Publishers.

Scholarly Article

Avent Harris, J. R. (2021). The Black Superwoman in spiritual bypass: Black women's use of religious coping and implications for mental health professionals. *Journal of Spirituality in Mental Health*, *23*(2), 180–196.

References

Abcarian, R. (2018, September 18). Column: In black churches, pastors recognize a #MeToo moment among their clergy. *The Los Angeles Times*. https://www.latimes.com/local/abcarian/la-me-abcarian-women-pastors-20180918-story.html

Akom, A. A. (2007). Cities as battlefields: Understanding how the Nation of Islam impacts civic engagement, environmental racism, and community development in a low income neighborhood. *International Journal of Qualitative Studies in Education, 20*(6), 711–730.

Avent-Harris, J. R. Garland-McKinney, J. L., & Fripp, J. (2019). "God is a keeper": A phenomenological investigation of Christian African American women's experiences with religious coping. *The Professional Counselor, 9*(3), 157–170. https://doi.org/10.15241/jrah.9.3.157

Belgrave, F. Z., & Allison, K. W. (2010). *African American psychology from Africa to America*. Sage Publications.

Belin, P., Washington, T., & Greene, Y. (2006). Saving grace: A breast cancer prevention program in the African American community. *Health and Social Work, 31*(1), 73–76. https://doi.org/10.1093/hsw/31.1.73

Bourjolly, J. (1998). Differences in religiousness among Black and white women with breast cancer. *Social Work in Health Care, 28*(1), 21–39. https://doi.org/10.1300/J010v28n01_02

Bowen-Reid, T. L., & Harrell, J. P. (2002). Racist experiences and health outcomes: An examination of spirituality as a buffer. *Journal of Black Psychology, 28*, 18–36. https://doi.org/10.1177/0095798402028001002

Boyd-Franklin, N. (2010). Incorporating spirituality and religion into the treatment of African American clients. *The Counseling Psychologist, 38*(7), 976–1000. https://doi.org/10.1177/0011000010374881

Brome, D. R., Owens, M. D., Allen, K., & Vevaina, T. (2000). An examination of spirituality among African American women in recovery from substance abuse. *Journal of Black Psychology, 26*(4), 470–486. https://doi.org/10.1177/0095798400026004008

Burnett-Zeigler, I. (2021). *Nobody knows the trouble I've seen: The emotional lives of Black women*. Amistad.

Carelock, J. L. (2009). *Church hurt can make you bitter or better: You choose*. Xulon.

Cashwell, C. S., & Swindle, P. J. (2018). When religion hurts: Supervising cases of religious abuse. *The Clinical Supervisor, 37*(1), 182–203. https://doi.org/10.1080/07325223.2018.1443305

Chaney, C. (2011). The invisibility of LGBT individuals in Black mega churches: Political and social implications. *Journal of African American Studies, 15*(2), 199–217.

Chatters, L. M., Taylor, R. J., Bullard, K. M., & Jackson, J. S. (2008). Spirituality and subjective religiosity among African Americans, Caribbean Blacks, and Non-Hispanic Whites. *Journal for the Scientific Study of Religion, 47*(4), 725–737. https://doi.org/10.1111/j.1468-5906.2008.00437.x

Cheadle, A. C. D., Dunkel Schetter, C., Gaines Lanzi, R., Reed Vance, M., Sahadeo, L. S., & Shalowitz, M. U. (2014). Spiritual and religious resources in African American women: Protection from depressive symptoms after childbirth. *Clinical Psychological Science, 3*(2), 283–291. https://doi.org/10.1177/2167702614531581

Cheney, A. M, Curran, G. M., Booth, B. M., Sullivan, S. D., Stewart, K. E., & Borders, T. F. (2014). The religious and spiritual dimensions of cutting down and stopping cocaine use: A qualitative exploration among African Americans in the South.

Journal of Drug Issues, 44(1), 94–113. https://doi.org/10.1177/0022042613491108

Constantine, M. G., Lewis, E. L., Conner, L. C., & Sanchez, D. (2000). Addressing spiritual and religious issues in counseling African Americans: Implications for counselor training and practice. *Counseling and Values, 45,* 28–39. https://doi.org/10.1002/j.2161-007X.2000.tb00180.x

Cooper, W. P., & Mitra, R. (2018). Religious disengagement and stigma management by African-American young adults. *Journal of Applied Communication Research, 46*(4), 509–533. https://doi.org/10.1080/00909882.2018.1502462

Day. K. (2012). *Unfinished business: Black women, the Black church, and the struggle to thrive in America.* Orbis Books.

Dass-Brailsford, P. (2010). *Crisis and disaster counseling: Lessons learned from Hurricane Katrina and other disasters.* Sage.

Dessio, W., Wade, C., Chao, M., Kronenberg, F., Cushman, L.E., & Kalmuss, D. (2004). Religion, spirituality, and healthcare choices of African-American women: Results of a national survey. *Ethnicity & Disease, 14*(2), 189–197.

De Wit, J. R. (2011). *Forgiving the church – How to release the confusion and hurt when the church abuses.* IUniverse.

Gooden, A. S., & McMahon, S. D. (2016). Thriving among African-American adolescents: Religiosity, religious support, and communalism. *American Journal of Community Psychology, 57*(1–2), 118–128.

Grant, J. (1989). *White women's Christ and Black women's Jesus.* Scholars Press.

Greer, T. W. (2011). Coping strategies as moderators of the relation between individual race-related stress and mental health symptoms for African American women. *Psychology of Women Quarterly, 35*(2), 215–226. https://doi.org/10.1177/0361684311399388

Greer, B. D., & Abel, M. W. (2017). Religious/spiritual coping in older African American women. *The Qualitative Report, 22*(1), 237–260. https://doi.org/10.1016/j.cpr.2-11.09.005

Jacobs, T. D. (2014). African-American women elders in Adventist congregations. *Journal of Applied Christian Leadership, 8*(1), 38–54.

Kramer, M. W. (2011). A study of voluntary organizational membership: The assimilation process in a community choir. *Western Journal of Communication, 75,* 52–74. https://doi.org/10.1080/10570314.2010.536962

Levin, J., Taylor, R., & Chatters, L. (1995). A multidimensional measure of religious involvement for African Americans. *Sociological Quarterly, 36*(1), 157–173. https://doi.org/10.1111/j.1533-8525.1995.tb02325.x

Lincoln, C. E., & Mamiya, L. H. (1990). *The Black church in the African American experience.* Duke University Press.

Marroquin, B. (2011). Interpersonal emotion regulation as a mechanism of social support in depression. *Clinical Psychological Review, 31*(8), 1276–1290. https://doi.org/10.1016/j.cpr.2011.09.005

Masci, D. (2018, February 7). *5 facts about the religious lives of African Americans.* Pew Research Center. https://www.pewresearch.org/fact-tank/2018/02/07/5-facts-about-the-religious-lives-of-african-americans/

Mattis, J. S. (2002). Religion and spirituality in the meaning-making and coping experiences of African American women: A qualitative analysis. *Psychology of Women Quarterly, 26,* 309–321.

Mattis, J. S., & Jagers, R. J. (2001). A relational framework for the study of religiosity and spirituality in the lives of African Americans. *Journal of Community Psychology, 29*(5), 519–539. https://doi.org/10.1002/jcop.1034

Mattis, J. S., & Watson, C. R. (2008). Religiosity and spirituality. In B. M. Tynes, H. A. Neville, & S. O. Utsey (Eds.), *Handbook of African American psychology* (pp. 91–102). Sage Publications.

Maynard-Reid, P. U. (2000). *Diverse worship: African-American, Caribbean and Hispanic perspectives.* InterVarsity Press.

Mbiti, J. S. (1990). *African religions & philosophy* (2nd ed.). Heinemann Publishing.

McGoldrick, M., Giordano, J., & Garcia-Preto, N. (2005). *Ethnicity and family therapy* (3rd ed.). Guilford Press.

Mengesha, M., & Ward, E. C. (2012). Psychotherapy with African-American women with depression: Is it okay to talk about their religious/spiritual beliefs? *Religions, 3*(1), 19–36. https://doi.org//10.3390/rel3010019

Mohamed, B. (2021, May 14). *10 new findings about faith among Black Americans.* Pew Research Center. https://www.pewresearch.org/fact-tank/2021/02/16/10-new-findings-about-faith-among-black-americans/

Neighbors, H. W., Musick, M.A., & Williams, D. R. (1998). The African American minister as a source of help for serious personal crises: Bridge or barrier to mental health care? *Health Education Behavior, 25*(6), 759–777. https://doi.org/10.1177/109019819802500606

Nobles, W. (2004). African philosophy: Foundation of Black psychology. In R. Jones (Ed.), *Black psychology* (4th ed.). Cobb & Henry Press.

Post, B. C., & Wade, N. G. (2009). Religion and spirituality in psychotherapy: A practice-friendly review of research. *Journal of Clinical Psychology, 65*(2), 131–146. https://doi.org/10.1002/jclp.20563

Reed, T. D., & Neville, H. A. (2014). The influence of religiosity and spirituality on psychological well-being among African American women. *Journal of Black Psychology, 40*(4), 384–401. https://doi.org/10.1177/00957984134909

Richards, I. S., & Bergin, A. E. (2005). *A spiritual strategy for counseling and psychotherapy.* American Psychological Association.

Shorter-Gooden, K. (2004). Multiple resistance strategies: How African American women cope with racism and sexism. *Journal of Black Psychology, 30*(3), 406–425. https://doi.org/10.1177/00957984042660500

Smith, L. C., Friedman, S., & Nevid, J. (1999). Clinical and sociocultural differences in African American and European American patients with panic disorder and agoraphobia. *Journal of Nervous and Mental Disease, 187*(9), 549–560. https://doi.org/10.1097/00005053-199909000-00004

Taylor, R. J., & Chatters, L. M. (1991). Extended family networks of older Black adults. *Journal of Gerontology, 46*(4), S210–S217.

Taylor, R. J., Chatters, L. M., & Levin, J. (2004). *Religion in the lives of African Americans: Social, psychological, and health perspectives.* Sage Publications.

Van, P. (2001). Breaking the silence of African-American women: Healing after pregnancy loss. *Health Care Women Internationally, 22*(3), 229–243. https://doi.org/10.1080/07399330120995

Walker-Barnes, C. (2014). *Too heavy a yoke: Black women and the burden of strength.* Wipf and Stock Publishers.

Wiggins, D. C. (2004). *Righteous content: Black women's perspectives of church and faith*. New York University Press.

Wiggins, M. I. (2008). Therapist self-awareness of spirituality. In J. D. Aten, & M. M. Leach (Eds.), *Spirituality and the therapeutic process* (pp. 53–74). American Psychological Association.

Williams, C. B., & Wiggins, M. I. (2010) Womanist spirituality as a response to the racism-sexism double bind in African American women. *Counseling and Values, 54*(2), 175–186.

Wilmoth, M., & Sanders, D. (2001). Accept me for myself: African American women's issues after breast cancer. *Oncology Nursing Forum, 28*(5), 875–879.

Wimberly, E. P. (1997). *Counseling African American marriages and families.* Westminster John Knox Press.

Wolf, C. T., & Stevens, P. (2001). Integrating religion and spirituality in marriage and family counseling. *Counseling and Values, 46*(1), 66–75.

Conclusion

How Psychotherapy Helps Black Women

---

with Susan Branco[*]

> It was the best decision I made for myself and my life. Understanding myself
> better, and how to navigate discrimination as a Black female.
>
> Study participant

In the Introduction to this book, we discuss the awesomeness of Black women, whose leadership and societal contributions are essential to the well-being of the United States and the world. Any resource, in any sphere of life, that helps Black women to maximize their quality of life and extend their life span is well worth the investment. Mental health care is one such resource. Black women's behavioral, mental, and emotional health and well-being can dramatically improve with skillful, culturally informed, professional counseling and psychotherapy. In our clinical practices, we have had the privilege of witnessing such transformations. We want our mental health care colleagues of all backgrounds and identities to believe that their work with Black women can be similarly transformative. Our invitation is to share this concluding chapter with new or potential clients to demonstrate the value of therapy. We hope this chapter starts the exploration of a Black female client's goals for therapy, an open and transparent discussion of cultural fit, and readiness to construct a solid therapy relationship.

The Black women in our study of Black women's psychotherapy perspectives and experiences (described in Chapter 1) had a lot to say about why therapy has been helpful to them. One participant appreciated "being allowed to talk and feeling listened to without judgment. . . . [having] someone who will push back on my perspectives without making me feel pressured. . . . Someone who is knowledgeable about multiple frameworks, so they can apply different techniques unique to my needs at the time." Another participant said, "Being heard and affirmed. Identifying what is and had caused my discontent. Resources to help me cope and improve circumstances."

---

[*] S. Branco, D. Baptiste, & A. Gooden. (2023). Conclusion: How psychotherapy helps Black women. In D. Baptiste & A. Gooden, *Promoting Black women's mental health: What practitioners should know and do*. Cambridge University Press.

C.1   How Therapy Helped: Black Women in Our Practices

In our combined 55 years as providers (Donna, Adia, and Susan) we have been privileged to help Black women recover from painful life experiences and transitions. We have also helped Black women cope with experiences of marginalization of many types, including in their own families. We describe some of this work in the case studies in this book. We have seen therapy strengthen Black women's capacity for resilience, authenticity, and lightheartededness in relationships with themselves and others. In addition, therapy has increased Black women's self-understanding, self-love, and self-compassion. These self-qualities anchor Black women amid a hostile and restless society and communities, building their confidence to navigate life experiences. Therapy has also helped Black women give themselves joyfully to their significant others, children, family members, friends, and others. Yet, in these relationships, Black women have also learned to prioritize their own needs. They learn to set appropriate boundaries, reject stereotypes, and ask for what they need from others to live well.

Therapy has encouraged Black women to make peace with painful personal and social legacies, including emotional trauma and marginalization. Black women's growth from suffering has expanded their agency and voice in advocacy and outreach for marginalized people. Therapy also buttresses Black women's embrace of their deity and other transcendent values. These uplifts improved their religious and spiritual coping and clarified their life's purpose. Therapy has supported Black women to accept their Black womanhood proudly. It has encouraged them to be comfortable in their identities in the United States, where the predominant images of Black women are broken and distorted.

Some of these benefits of therapy for Black women in our practices have not occurred in a singular experience or in brief encounters. These benefits have also not happened for all Black women. Some encounters might have even left Black women disappointed and discouraged. Although our clients have significantly benefited from our work, some have not, and we say so quite honestly. Not every client-therapist relationship is a good fit, and a few of our clients have benefit from working with other therapists and not us. In those cases we have been glad to help with referrals.

C.2   How Therapy Helps: Our Own Experiences as Clients

We have also experienced the usefulness of therapy as clients ourselves. Each of us has found therapy helpful in coping or recovering from difficult life experiences. For example, one of us sought therapy during the anxiety and stress of a search for a birth family and subsequent reunion. Therapy was a place to imagine several occasions in the birth family search, to plan for the emotional upheaval of discovery and analysis, and to heal a primal wound of adoption. Another one of us sought therapy after a relational dissolution, traumatic losses of family members, and, most recently, to cope with the impacts of COVID-19. Therapy was a meeting place for self and to remain accountable to self-care. The practitioner was a sounding board and guide to dealing with painful emotions and parenting effectiveness considering family changes. Another one of us used therapy for better self-understanding to cope with stress, anxiety, and perfectionism. Our understanding of the usefulness of therapy to Black women derives from our roles as clients and mental health practitioners. We have cared for Black female clients, many of whom were of different backgrounds and worldviews than ours.

Beyond our own experiences, in the rest of this chapter, we offer additional reflections on psychotherapy as a resource to Black women. Specifically, we share two stories of our therapy clients. Finally, we discuss how benefits of doing psychotherapy with Black women have transcended the therapy room.

C.3   How Therapy Helps: Our Client in Her Own Words

This story from one of our long-time clients, shared with her permission, shows some of the reasons Black women may seek therapy and some of its many benefits:

I am a 56-year-old Black woman with graduate-level education and professional background in marketing, graphic design, and project management. I have been a client in psychotherapy for about 26 years. Without mental health support, I am not sure I would be around today. My life story is complicated, and parts are incredible even for me to tell. I marvel at how much better I am doing now than 2 to 3 years ago, but this has been a journey to get here.

I grew up in a good home with a mother and father who raised my sibling and me to be good people and good citizens. My parents were loving but not perfect. Over the years of therapy, I have discovered aspects of my relationship with them that affected my life. These things are difficult to share because I do not hold grudges of any kind towards my deceased father and my mother. My mother is alive and in decent health, and I adore her.

My childhood and adolescent years were ones of verbal and sexual abuse and bullying from my sibling. My sibling may have been someone with a mental health condition. My mother probably knew of this, and there are ways in which she did not protect me. My first stint in any counseling was as an older teen, when I sought the help of my minister, an older African American woman who led my church. I was dealing then with the effects of childhood physical and sexual abuse and was very depressed. My minister's counseling helped me, and I was grateful for her support. Despite these difficulties, I achieved well in school and college and fought to live with joy and ease.

In my late 20s, my boyfriend died tragically. That loss left me so grief-stricken that I sought the help of a professional counselor. My therapist was White, and while I did not feel an intense connection with her, I found therapy comforting and it helped me feel that my life can go on. As a result, I started advancing in my job and career, and life for me returned to normal.

In my 30s, I started getting very sick with conditions that medical people did not understand. Most symptoms were excruciating. Others were debilitating, and seemingly no part of my body was untouched. These conditions have persisted over the past 26 years. I have had over 25 hospitalizations, 24 surgeries, still not knowing the cause. Twenty-one surgeries occurred after my 40th birthday. My physicians treated each bout of illness or disease, and I fought to get better. Finally, my illness has turned out to be an unnamed autoimmune condition. As a result, I have been unable to work in my profession. My quality of life has been dramatically affected.

My current therapist was the one that identified how medical traumas had affected my mental and emotional help. I had grown hardy toward my illness and have learned to fight to manage my symptoms. What has been extremely difficult for me is the racism and sexism that I have experienced in medical systems as a sick Black woman. I have been insulted by physicians and stereotyped. A few dismissed my physical and mental distresses. Some medical providers have thought of me as "pretending to be sick." Yet, at the same time, others have been kind, competent, and restful. I have also experienced similar conditions in housing. I must be honest to say that along with being sick, at times, my fight to live with dignity has been so heavy that I have thought of taking my own life.

A current therapist has been alongside me and has seen some of the worst of these experiences as I fight to keep myself going every day. I try to wake up, find something meaningful to do. I try to keep up with my emotions and to know when I am in trouble. My therapist helped me understand and address some of the racist experiences and, most recently, an experience of sexual harassment on the part of a medical provider when I was most vulnerable. There are still days when I am in pain, when my life's suffering seems like it is not worth it, but my therapist helps me to talk these feelings out, to use my strengths to make each day a better one than I have had previously. I also try to maintain my self-love and self-compassion, although my body is scarred. I recall the day I got a name for my condition, and when I told my therapist, she was so delighted. She was there through my stints of breast cancer and reconstructive surgeries. She has always believed me and respected my experiences. Even if she does not agree with my choices or sentiments, she has tried to encourage me when I need it most.

My therapist has had the idea that I wake up and fight to make that day a good one and plan for the next week, tomorrow, and the following week. She has also helped me to know when I need to ask for help. Overall, I have found that therapy is not shaming but affirming. With the right therapist, it can be awakening, healing, comforting, and empowering. Therapy is not the only thing that has helped me. But I reached for it when I needed it, and it has been a resource.

C.4 How Therapy Helps: A Non-Black Colleague's Lens

Dr. Susan Branco, an Indigenous/Latinx therapist and our coauthor on this chapter', describes her experiences working with a Black female client, highlighting the importance of cultural awareness:

Non-Black therapists, like me, should consider it a joy to have Black women as clients in their practices. As a clinician for over 20 years, I am glad this has been my experience. I work with my Black female clients from a deep and compassionate understanding of their social and cultural histories. Black and Latinx women share experiences of marginalization. However, I am aware that I hold privileges that Black women do not have. Here, I discuss the importance of being a culturally responsive therapist, who begins with my cultural self-awareness.

As an Indigenous and Latinx therapist, I was privileged to work with Tara, aged 26, who identified as a biracial, Black and White, cisgender woman. Tara sought counseling with me because of my clinical specialties in transracial adoptions. Tara as a Black woman and I, as a Latina, were transracially adopted and raised by White parents and grew up in primarily White communities. Tara needed support to integrate her multiple and intersecting identities. In addition, Tara was seeking therapy to prepare for a potential reunion with her birth family, whom she recently found on social media. Although we shared the background of transracial adoption, I knew that our experiences would differ. Therefore, I wanted to engage Tara from a place of "not knowing" rather than from an "expert" stance to enter her world as a transracial adoptee.

On meeting Tara, I revealed the curiosity I felt about Tara using myriad cultural opportunities to see her through the lens of her cultural background and identities. For example, I asked Tara how she self-identified rather than assume her status. Tara shared that her childhood was spent in primarily White spaces, where she developed a longing to be in the presence of and around others identified as Black. Tara described her racial and ethnic identity as fluid and evolving. She learned more about her place as a Black woman within her community. When I met Tara, she had graduated from a Historically Black College and University, which further grounded her identity.

Additionally, she described her social support networks and romantic partnerships predominantly within the Black community. Each aspect of her narrative presented rich cultural opportunities that allowed me to be curious, welcoming, and, above all, nonjudgmental. I included my knowledge about how transracially adopted persons reclaim, or "reculturate," including the cultural heritages removed from them upon permanent adoption. This framework both normalized and validated Tara's lived experience.

As a transracial adoptee also engaged in a significant inquiry into my own racial and ethnic identity development for my work, I developed a close working alliance with Tara. Part of my life experience felt familiar to her. She seemed at ease discussing her trepidation, anxieties, and ambiguities with me. Yet, as a lighter-skinned Indigenous and Latinx woman, I had not experienced the world as a Black woman. Therefore, I could not presume to know experientially how structural racism and oppression shaped and continued to impact Tara. I tried to be culturally humble with Tara about this reality and leaned into it, rather than avoiding it, in building the relationship. In so doing, together, Tara and I delved into the racism and microaggressions she experienced as a child both within and outside of her adoptive family. This allowed us to build intimacy and a shared understanding of the racial trauma Tara experienced. While these conversations were painful and uncomfortable to Tara, they were crucial to our work together, particularly as Tara prepared to explore connections with her birth family.

I broached the subject of Tara's salient identities in their first session by asking, "How do you self-identify racially and ethnically?" This fundamental question allowed Tara to share her narrative of being raised in an ethnically European, Irish American home while outwardly appearing brown skinned. This conversation set the tone for ongoing discussions related to our work together from differing identities and how these dissimilarities influenced the counseling relationship. For example, when Tara described celebrations and romantic relationship struggles, I felt challenged to bracket my internal responses to choices and decisions she made. They clashed with my value system. There were small ruptures in our relationship that we repaired. For example, once, Tara shared she felt judged by my reaction, not verbally but through an eyebrow raise. Of importance, the strength of our therapeutic relationship allowed Tara to feel able to share her transparent response with me. I was also willing and able to respond quickly to admit my mistake. I used a multicultural orientation in that moment of repair of the rupture, and we were able to move forward. Cultural humility guided me on what Tara needed from us during our sessions.

I worked with Tara for about 12 months. During this time, Tara reunited with her first family while balancing her loyalties to her adoptive family. The reunion offered more cultural opportunities to address the racial, ethnic, and class differences within Tara's first and adoptive families. When termination neared, both Tara and I felt a sense of accomplishing much ground while also feeling sad that the relationship ended. Tara shared that our work together enabled her to fully integrate her adoptive and racial identity into a more coherent whole.

C.5   How Therapy Helps: Voices of Black Influential Women

Increasingly, prominent Black people are serving as mental health ambassadors. We celebrate their influence in helping the Black community seek professional mental health support. The voices of these ambassadors are making a difference, and we showcase a few in the United States who routinely champion mental health counseling as a resource. For example, Taraji P. Henson, an award-winning actor, launched the Boris Lawrence Henson Foundation (BLHF) in honor of her father, Boris. Henson witnessed her father struggle with untreated posttraumatic stress disorder from his service in the Vietnam War. As a child, she also saw her mother's violent mugging outside of their apartment (Butler, 2020). What Henson describes in managing her mental health parallels the experiences of many Black women: "As Black people, we're conditioned to push through and be strong and pray our problems away. And after a while, that . . . wasn't working" (Butler, 2020). As an adult, Henson sought psychotherapy for herself and her son. In the process, she experienced how challenging it was to find a culturally sensitive clinician equipped to understand and support the unique concerns of Black people. Henson's impetus for creating the BLHF spotlights the stigma surrounding mental conditions and seeking mental health care. The BLHF promotes culturally sensitive mental health practitioners and resources. Henson also does a twice-weekly Facebook Live program, "Peace of Mind with Taraji," which examines many topics related to Black women's mental health (Butler, 2020).

Athletes Serena Williams and Simone Biles have publicly discussed how they draw on therapy to manage the demands of their sport and cope with life experiences (Grant, 2020). Williams sought treatment to overcome postpartum emotions when she became a new mother (Gillespie, 2018). Biles, a decorated US gymnast, sought therapy to manage the psychological toll of Olympic training. Mental health support also helped Biles to organize the effects of sexual victimization by a trusted medical provider. Biles' international exposure to what she and other gymnasts experienced was also stressful. She leaned on therapy as she spoke out about the abuse. Biles stated, "I go to therapy because at times I did not want to set foot in the gym" (Brockes, 2019). In July 2021, she took a major step for mental health when she prominently withdrew from the Olympic team competition. During the "Tokyo 2020 Olympics" (held in 2021), Biles and Naomi Osaka became exceptionally powerful messengers for prioritizing mental health and wellness, even in the face of pressures. The messages of Black women as sports ambassadors have started significant conversations nationally and internationally. These messages are sure to resonate widely with ordinary Black women.

Actors Issa Rae, Kerry Washington, and Halle Berry also extol the benefits of therapy. In a situation familiar to many Black women, Rae described how the Strong Black Woman lifestyle (described in Chapter 8 of this book) initially interfered with her ability to seek help. Rae thought her mother and grandmother lived such lifestyles. Rae stated: "I watched my mom do it. I watched my grandmother do it. It's just, you take it on, and you're just like, that's life, and you don't want to burden other people with your emotions" (Wells, 2019). Therapy helped Rae seek collaboration and support and avoid self-silencing and isolation in dealing with challenging circumstances. Kerry Washington views having a therapist for mental health care like having a dentist to care for oral health. For Washington regular therapy decreased anxiety and stress and increased self-love (Rolling, 2020). She stated: "Learning how to love myself and my body is a lifelong process. But I definitely don't struggle the way I used to. Therapy helped me realize that maybe it's OK for me to communicate my feelings. Instead of literally stuffing them down with food, maybe it's OK for me to express myself" (Rolling,

2020). Similarly, Halle Berry described being in therapy since age 10 for a difficult family situation and finding consistent value in discussing her struggles with professional mental health support (Ong, 2021).

Former first lady Michelle Obama (2018) is one of the most influential mental health ambassadors and publicly discussed how therapy enhanced her marriage to the 44th president. Obama commented on her initial misconceptions about marriage counseling and her discovery of its benefits: "You go because you think the counselor is going to help you make your case against the other person. . . . And lo and behold, counseling wasn't that at all. It was about me exploring my sense of happiness and my voice" (Oprah Winfrey Network, 2018). The personal endorsements of these prominent Black women in entertainment, sports, and politics are powerful testimonies to the benefits of psychotherapy as a resource in healing and recovery. In addition, Black men such as President Obama (Jacoby, 2021), Jay-Z (King, 2018), and LeBron James (Daniels, 2019) have also been mental health advocates.

C.6   How Therapy Helps: How Our Work with Black Women Clients Changed Us

Black women can benefit from working with a therapist of any background, and as therapists enter the world of a Black female client with cultural humility, their world can also change and improve. We use this idea of therapist personal and professional transformation to discuss how our work with Black female clients has impacted us in ways that transcend the therapy room. We hope that by sharing our experiences, we will encourage therapists to reflect on the deep value of their work with Black women clients and encourage Black women to seek the benefits of therapy.

Donna Baptiste shares how her work as a therapist has enriched her own life and passions:

I am humbled when Black women find my encouragement and support helpful. When it feels relevant, I also let my Black female clients know how my work with them changes me. A beautiful gift of doing therapy with Black women is listening to myself ask questions about a range of matters in life, including relationship to self, partners, children, etc. I challenge clients on their self-care and wellness strategies and around existential themes such as finding their life's purpose. When I probe these matters in my Black female clients, I also probe them in myself. Frequently after therapy, my question to myself is: Are you doing these things you suggested to your clients?

Through my Black clients' lives, I feel the pressures of racism, gender biases, and other marginalization. I grieve with the Black mothers that have lost children to gun violence. I am enraged that Black women feel powerless against microaggressions in the workplace, and Black women long to find love, partnership, and family. I think of the tender pain of Black girls whose youthful joy is interrupted by body shaming. These encounters are painful to me, and yet it has given me clarity about my purpose, calling and voice. My passion for equality and justice has crystallized and matured, and that passion permeates all aspects of my life and extends my sphere of influence. Working with clients of all racial/ethnic and gender backgrounds also presses me to fight for a value of compassion and kindness, about love for flawed humanity, which includes all of us. Being a therapist has transformed and enriched me, and it has been good for my soul.

Adia Gooden reflects on the honor of being able to offer a healing space and guide Black women through therapy:

I am honored to hold space for the Black female clients. I believe therapy provides a refuge for these women, a safe space to tend to their wounds and reclaim their power and vision for their lives. The process of bearing witness and creating space has increased my patience and calm with my clients and myself. My capacity to be a compassionate presence has improved for my Black female clients and my own life. Often, I celebrate my expanded understanding of the healing power of therapy. I see myself as a guide and a facilitator but not the ultimate expert or authority on what my clients need. That keeps me very humble and grateful. I cherish the therapeutic relationships I have cultivated with Black women initially hesitant about being vulnerable and sharing themselves so authentically. It has also encouraged me to look at how I show up in places when I seek help and support. And I am grateful for my clients' trust in me and willingness to engage in the process. Finally, my work as a therapist with Black women has required me to live authentically. Black women tend to spot inauthenticity quickly, which has required me to show up as my whole self because I encourage them to do the same.

Susan Branco shares how her Black female clients have inspired her to advocate for societal change:

I am always honored to journey with clients and feel particularly privileged when working with Black women to bear witness to their triumphs, resilience, and pain. I am especially attuned to the cultural misalignment that many transracially adopted persons experience in my area of specialization. This is the sense of disorientation, grief, loss, and overall disconnection clients experience when removed from their birth families, and cultures can be acute. Working alongside my clients, most of whom are Black, Indigenous, and people of color, I have helped them facilitate their identity development and engage in the often arduous work of reculturation. My work with Black female clients fuels my longstanding interest in social advocacy. I have expanded my platform and voice in seeking adoption reforms. My work has made a difference in many settings, even outside the United States.

Black women's curiosity about using therapy to advance their mental health and wellness is growing. Present conditions in the United States and abroad will generate new and profound mental health needs in Black people, particularly women. We encourage therapists, of all identities, to be ready for a groundswell of new clients. We suggest a few questions therapists may invite clients to reflect on as they begin the therapy experience. Positive signs suggest that the multiple and varied nudges of Black women to seek therapy are bearing fruit. Numerous Black therapist-specific social media platforms have arisen. A notable one is Therapy for Black Girls (n.d.). This site also includes a list of Black female therapists to help potential clients find a therapist to work with in their area. These are examples of Black mental health professionals answering the call to serve and support their communities. Unfortunately, an underserved market remains, as poor and less educated Black women are less likely to afford therapy. Mental Health America (n.d.) describes the urgent need for mental health care for underserved and marginalized Black women and underscores the importance of persistent advocacy.

C.7   Beyond Therapy: Black Women's Resources

Psychotherapy can be a source of wellness and self-care for Black women. However, it is not the only resource for Black women's mental health and wellness. Flanigan (2020) offers several recommended practices that can support and supplement overall wellness for Black women. Such guidelines include wellness-focused exercise and good nutrition. Therapists need to support Black women in seeking any resource to support their wellness efforts. Black women are also empowered with self-help mental health resources. Web searches yield many self-help resources, including blogs, podcasts, videos, news pieces, radio commentary, and the like. Black women can find help on common and uncommon life experiences, including postpartum depression, trauma, coping with the loss of a child, and surviving the foster care and child welfare system. Family, couple, and friendship relationship concerns and workplace struggles are all topics that therapists address. Black women can also take advantage of groups that discuss therapy hesitance. Faith communities are championing mental health support, and we welcome their voices in the mix.

Many influences are expected to drive Black women to seek mental health support over the next decade and more. We, and our colleagues in the mental health profession are waiting to serve our Black female clients and we are eager to help them to maximize the benefits of therapy in their lives.

Client Reflection Questions

1. What messages have you received from people in your life (e.g., family, friends, religious entities, coworkers) about getting mental health treatment?
2. What are your values and beliefs now about protecting your mental health and wellness?
3. What is important to you in working with a therapist of the same or different race and gender?

4. What would a therapist need to do to gain your confidence and trust?
5. How do you think a Black woman seeking therapy might respond to the ideas in this chapter?

Therapist Reflection Questions

1. How do you measure your own success in counseling Black women?
2. What benefits have you received from working with Black women as clients?
3. What are your areas for growth or improvement in counseling Black women and where can you find support?
4. Outside of therapy with you, what other resources do you channel to your Black female clients?
5. How do you use your own therapy for increased self-awareness and growth?
6. How might you use this concluding chapter with your new Black female clients?

Resources for Therapists and Clients

Organizations

Black Girls in Om, a wellness site. (n.d.). https://www.blackgirlinom.com
Healing Black Women. (n.d.). https://www.healingblackwomen.com/
The Boris Lawrence Henson Foundation: Break the Silence, Break the Cycle. (n.d.). https://borislhensonfoundation.org
Therapy for Black Girls. (n.d.). https://therapyforblackgirls.com

Books

Harris, T. W. (2021). *Dear black girl: Letters from your sisters on stepping into your power.* Berrett-Koehler Publishers.
Taylor, K. Y. (2017). *How we get free: Black feminism and the Combahee River Collective.* Haymarket Books.

Podcasts

Shani, T. (Executive Producer). (2020–present). *The Shani Project* [Audio podcast]. https://www.audible.com/pd/The-Shani-Project-Podcast/B08JJP5LHN or https://open.spotify.com/show/5GvieDmKNmcUWXH7VVdz3E

Media Resources

Barnes, Z. (2020, June 2). 44 mental health resources for black people trying to survive in this country. *Self.* https://www.self.com/story/black-mental-health-resources

Oprah Winfrey Network. (2019, September 15). *Black women discuss therapy: Black women OWN the conversation* [Video]. YouTube. https://youtu.be/1blnmyfTeZY (2020). Why seeking therapy is seen as "a sign of weakness" in the Black community. *Dark girls 2* [Video]. https://www.oprah.com/own-darkgirls2/the-stigma-of-seeking-therapy-in-the-black-community

References

Brockes, E. (2019, March 16). Simone Biles: "I go to therapy, because at times I didn't want to set foot in the gym." *The Guardian*. https://www.theguardian.com/sport/2019/mar/16/simone-biles-therapy-times-didnt-want-set-foot-gym

Butler, B. (2020, December 14). Taraji P. Henson wants Black people to talk more openly about mental health. Her new show does just that. *The Washington Post*. https://www.washingtonpost.com/arts-entertainment/2020/12/14/taraji-p-henson-peace-of-mind-q-and-a/

Daniels, T. (2019, December 10). *LeBron James talks mental health, says he lost "love for the game" in 2011*. Bleacher Report. https://bleacherreport.com/articles/2866319-lebron-james-talks-mental-health-says-he-lost-love-for-the-game-in-2011

Flanigan, A. (2020, December 14). *Mental health alternatives to therapy*. Therapy for Black Girls. https://therapyforblackgirls.com/2020/12/14/mental-health-alternatives-to-therapy/

Gillespie, C. (2018, October 3). Serena Williams explains why she doesn't use the term "postpartum depression." *Self*. https://www.self.com/story/serena-williams-doesnt-use-the-term-postpartum-depression

Grant, J. (2020, December 6). We applaud these Black celebs for helping to erase mental health stigmas with their testimonies: There's no shame in seeking help to get back to happy and these celebrities are living proof of that. *Essence*. https://www.essence.com/lifestyle/health-wellness/black-celebs-help-erase-mental-health-stigmas-encourage-therapy/

Jacoby, S. (2021, March 11). Former president Obama on how he managed his mental health while in office. *Self*. https://www.self.com/story/barack-obama-mental-health

King, A. (2018, January 27). *Jay-Z says therapists should be in schools*. CNN. https://www.cnn.com/2018/01/27/us/jay-z-on-therapists-cnntv/index.html

Mental Health America. (n.d.). *Black and African American communities and mental health*. Retrieved September 27, 2022, from https://www.mhanational.org/issues/black-and-african-american-communities-and-mental-health

Obama, M. (2018). *Becoming*. Crown Publishing Group.

Ong, J. (2021, December 25). *The real reason why Halle Berry still sees a therapist*. TheThings.com. https://www.thethings.com/halle-berry-sees-therapist/

Oprah Winfrey Network. (2018, November 12). *The pivotal lesson Michelle Obama learned from marriage counseling* [Video segment]. YouTube. https://www.youtube.com/watch?v=WPFa23sZ7AY

Rolling (2020, October 7). *Kerry Washington struggling with "a lot of anxiety and stress."* Rollingout.com. https://rollingout.com/2020/10/07/kerry-washington-struggling-with-a-lot-of-anxiety-and-stress/

Therapy for Black Girls. (n.d.). *Find a great therapist for Black girls in your area.* Retrieved September 27, 2022, from https://providers.therapyforblackgirls.com

Wells, V. (2019, December 18). *Nobody gives a f*ck about you." Issa Rae talks the importance of going to therapy when you work in Hollywood.* Madame Noire.com. https://madamenoire.com/1120911/nobody-gives-a-fck-about-you-issa-rae-talks-the-importance-of-going-to-therapy-when-you-work-in-hollywood/

Appendix
Black Women and Psychotherapy Study Methods

This appendix details the methodology of the study presented in Chapter 1, which informed our ideas and approach throughout the book. The survey targeted Black women who had never been therapy clients as well as those currently or previously in therapy. The Qualtrics survey, available on request from the authors, ran from July to September 2020. The research was approved by Northwestern University's Institutional Review Board (IRB).

A.1 Participant Recruitment

We posted IRB-approved flyers or announcements to personal and institutions' social media platforms (e.g., Facebook). Professional colleagues also distributed our recruitment announcements to their clients and personal networks. We also posted on the websites of religious groups, Black sororities, community agencies, and others. To participate in the study, women had to meet the following criteria: (a) be age 20 years or older, living in the United States; (b) self-identify as racially Black or African American; and (c) self-identify as a woman.

A.2 The Survey

Our experiences conducting the Psychotherapy with Black Women workshop shaped the questions in the survey. We worked with a research assistant (RA) team to develop and pilot the survey. Over several meetings with these RAs, we brainstormed topics and themes. Three factors determined questions in the pilot survey. First, we included items with specific gaps in the existing literature (e.g., how Black women searched for therapists). We also asked about topics specific to our goals and interests for the book (e.g., why Black women might avoid therapy). Finally, we wanted practical recommendations from Black women to pass on to therapists. We piloted the survey with 10 Black women to ensure that the questions were understandable, meaningful, and appropriate. The survey completion time was reasonable. The pilot helped us to make several additional refinements.

A.3 Informed Consent and Risks

The survey was entirely anonymous, collecting no identifying personal information (such as IP addresses or device details). On the introductory pages, people read the consent information and clicked "I consent to participate" or "I do NOT consent to participate." Clicking "I consent to participate" activated the rest of the survey. Clicking "I do not consent" led to the ending page. Section 1 of the survey included consent information and a statement of risks and benefits of the research.

People who started the survey but did not meet the inclusion criteria were screened out. For example, if an individual indicated that they were not Black or female, they received the ending page. People who started the survey but did not wish to continue could also close the survey browser. Sixty-six participants consented and began the study but did not complete it. Since the survey was anonymous, we did not follow up with those who started and withdrew. Participating did not incur costs, and participants did not receive any compensation.

A.4 Data Analysis

The study data remained in a secure system at Northwestern University until we ended data collection. We then downloaded the data to a secure site for data analysis. Data were checked and cleaned (e.g., coded, recoded, labeled) in Excel before analysis in SPSS (version 17.0). We used all data that met inclusion criteria and were complete. Quantitative analyses helped us to summarize participants' responses to specific questions. In addition, qualitative analyses enabled us to collate information from open-ended questions.

A.5 Coding of Open-Ended Responses

To analyze and summarize the open-ended responses, we worked with a qualitative data consultant and three RAs to assist with coding and thematic analyses of these data. All statements from participants were downloaded and provided to the RAs to conduct the coding. For question one, there were 220 individual statements; for question two, 224 statements; for question three, 175 statements; and for question four, 173 statements. Two RAs separately read each statement and picked out the themes that fit the categories we provided. See Table A.1 for the categories our RAs used to code each question. We designed these coding categories based on our experience working with Black women clients and the literature on Black women's therapy and help-seeking. We expected that parts of each statement might fit more than one category. The RAs coded each question independently, looking at words and

Table A.1 *Initial coding for four open-ended questions*

Why might some Black women avoid therapy?

Code for mention of:
Something personal
Something about the therapist
Some fear worries or anxiety
Something that seems like a barrier
Some prior experience
Something about being Black or female

What are your recommendations for therapists who work with Black women as clients?
Code for mention of:
Therapist attitude or disposition
Therapist action
What therapist should avoid
Therapist disclosure
Therapist relationship skill
Therapy quality

Overall, in therapy, what have you liked? Overall, in therapy, what has been helpful?
Code for
Helpful atmosphere
Helpful experience
Helpful therapist quality
Helpful context
Helpful relationship quality

Overall, in therapy, what have you not liked? Overall, in therapy, what has been helpful?
Unhelpful atmosphere
Unhelpful experience
Unhelpful therapist quality
Unhelpful context

phrases to determine where to categorize them. Following the initial coding, the RAs discussed the coding to review their degree of consensus, and then the qualitative analyst reviewed the coding and identified themes in the data, as detailed in Chapter 1.

A.6 Limitations of the Study

While information from the study is essential and valuable, we were disappointed in our sample's low diversity concerning education and income, despite our additional recruitment efforts to address this gap. In addition, this cross-sectional study provides a snapshot of Black women's points of view at the time of data collection. From these data, we can make no causal inferences. Further, an anonymous and brief survey like ours, which collected no identifying information on participants, limits our capacity to collect follow-up data. For example, constructs of interest in our study, such as the most endorsed stressor for Black women, "Being a Black woman in America," could be further explored in focus groups or in-depth interviews with subsamples of women. A survey of this type, especially designed for personal mobile devices, meant omitting several follow-up questions that would have required more complex survey structures. In close to 800 unique written statements, women provided complex opinions about their therapy perspectives and ideas, but these statements were brief. The capacity for more extensive conversations about participants' views would have enriched the understanding of help-seeking.

Finally, while some questions in our survey captured Black women's views about their personal experiences and perspectives, we also asked why Black women may or may not seek therapy in general. Women may have answered some questions about Black women other than themselves. Participants may have overstated the prevalence of some experiences. Alternatively, Black women may have responded to questions globally while speaking of their own experiences.

Index

Numbers in **bold** = table, *italics* = figure

Printed in the United States
by Baker & Taylor Publisher Services